ISOLATE OR ENGAG

ISOLATE OR ENGAGE

Adversarial States, US Foreign Policy, and Public Diplomacy

Edited by Geoffrey Wiseman

Stanford University Press
Stanford, California

Stanford University Press
Stanford, California

© 2015 by the Board of Trustees of the Leland Stanford Junior University.
All rights reserved.

Printed on acid-free, archival-quality paper

Printed and bound in Great Britain by
Marston Book Services Ltd, Oxfordshire

Library of Congress Cataloging-in-Publication Data

Isolate or engage : adversarial states, US foreign policy, and public diplomacy / edited
by Geoffrey Wiseman.
    pages   cm
  Includes bibliographical references and index.
  ISBN 978-0-8047-9388-9 (cloth : alk. paper)
  ISBN 978-0-8047-9552-4 (pbk. : alk. paper)
    1. United States—Foreign relations—1945–1989—Case studies. 2. United States—
Foreign relations—1989—Case studies. I. Wiseman, Geoffrey, editor.
E744.I693 2015
327.73009'04—dc23   2014044179

ISBN 978-0-8047-9555-5 (electronic)

For Donna, Brady, and Dylan

Contents

Acknowledgments

THIS BOOK IS THE RESULT OF A PROJECT SUPPORTED by a National Science Foundation (NSF) grant under the Minerva Research Initiative. The basic idea motivating the project, which I first broached in a 2008 conference paper, was that while there had been a substantial interest in public diplomacy—generated mainly by the September 11, 2001, terrorist attacks and the US wars in Iraq and Afghanistan—years later no comparative multicountry study had been written on the role of public diplomacy with key adversarial states where the US maintains no, or less than full, diplomatic relations.

The project and this book benefited from the contributions of many individuals. I wish to acknowledge the contribution to the original project proposal made by Sherine Badawi Walton, USC Center on Public Diplomacy at the Annenberg School, and Shawn Powers, then a doctoral student working at the center. At the USC Center for International Studies (CIS), the project received superb support from Professor Patrick James and also from Erin Barber, Marisela Schaffer, and Indira Persad. Furthermore, CIS provided supplementary funding support for the project at a critical moment. At the USC School of International Relations, Robert English, Linda Cole, Karen Tang, and Ashley Bonanno helped enormously. I also acknowledge the splendid organizational and editing contributions of Christina Gray as project coordinator, and the assistance of students Landry Doyle, Katherine Hill, and Anna Phillips. For his research, editing, and advice, I warmly thank Scot

Macdonald. I also gratefully thank Jeri O'Donnell for her wisdom and assistance, and Dan Caldwell and Stan Rosen for their advice. At NSF, Jacqueline Meszaros oversaw the grant with energy and professionalism. I am extremely grateful for the time and energy that the reviewers devoted to their comments on the manuscript. They were not simply reviewing a manuscript but also engaging in field development. My final and very deep thanks go to Geoffrey Burn, James Holt, Tim Roberts, Kay Kodner and all at Stanford University Press.

—GRW

Contributor Biographies

Mark Philip Bradley is the Bernadotte E. Schmitt Professor of History at the University of Chicago. He is the author of *Imagining Vietnam and America: The Making of Postcolonial Vietnam*, which won the Harry J. Benda Prize from the Association for Asian Studies; *Vietnam at War*; and is the coeditor of *Making Sense of the Vietnam Wars* and *Truth Claims: Representation and Human Rights*.

Robert D. English is director and associate professor in the School of International Relations at the University of Southern California. His publications include *Russia and the Idea of the West: Gorbachev, Intellectuals, and the End of the Cold War* and *Rebirth: A Political History of Europe since World War II* (coauthored with Cyril Black and Jonathan Helmreich). He formerly worked as a policy analyst for the US Department of Defense and the Committee for National Security.

William LeoGrande is a professor in the Department of Government at American University and a former dean of the School of Public Affairs. He is a specialist in Latin American politics and US foreign policy toward Cuba and Central America. He is coauthor with Peter Kornbluh of *Back Channel to Cuba: The Hidden History of Negotiations between Washington and Havana* and coeditor of *A Contemporary Cuba Reader: The Revolution under Raul Castro*. LeoGrande has served on the staffs of the Democratic Policy Committee of the US Senate, and the Democratic Caucus Task Force on Central America of the US House of Representatives.

Suzanne Maloney is a Senior Fellow at the Brookings Institution's Saban Center for Middle East Policy. In 2003–2004, Maloney was Project Director for the Council on Foreign Relations' Task Force on US-Iran Relations, where she oversaw activities of a task force cochaired by Zbigniew Brzezinski and Robert Gates. She has testified in Congress on US policy toward Iran. Maloney is the author of *Iran's Long Reach: Iran as a Pivotal State in the Muslim World*. In 2007, Maloney received a Meritorious Honor Award from the US Department of State.

Viet Thanh Nguyen is associate professor of English and American Studies and Ethnicity at the University of Southern California. Nguyen is the author of *Race and Resistance: Literature and Politics in Asian America* and the novel *The Sympathizer*. He is also the coeditor of *Transpacific Studies: Framing an Emerging Field*.

Robert S. Ross is a professor of Political Science at Boston College and associate at the John King Fairbank Center for East Asian Research, Harvard University. His publications include *Normalization of US-China Relations: An International History*; *Re-Examining the Cold War: US-China Diplomacy, 1954–1973*; and *Negotiating Cooperation: The United States and China, 1969–1989*. Ross is a member of the US-China Working Group, established by the US Congress, the Council on Foreign Relations, and the National Committee for US-China Relations.

William Rugh is the Edward R. Murrow Visiting Professor of Public Diplomacy at the Fletcher School of Law and Diplomacy, Tufts University. He holds a PhD in international relations from Columbia. His publications include *Front Line Public Diplomacy; The Practice of Public Diplomacy; Engaging the Arab and Islamic Worlds through Public Diplomacy;* and *American Encounters with Arabs: The "Soft Power" of U.S. Public Diplomacy in the Arab World*. Ambassador Rugh was a career US Foreign Service officer, serving among other diplomatic postings as Deputy Chief of Mission in Damascus and as US ambassador to Yemen and to the United Arab Emirates. He received the Murrow Award for Excellence in Public Diplomacy in 1991.

Michael Shifter is president of the Inter-American Dialogue and an adjunct professor of Latin American Studies at Georgetown University's School of Foreign Service. He is coeditor of *Constructing Democratic Governance in Latin America* and author of "In Search of Hugo Chávez" (*Foreign Affairs*,

May/June 2006). Shifter has regularly testified before Congress about US policy toward Latin America. Before joining the Inter-American Dialogue, he directed the Latin American and Caribbean program at the National Endowment for Democracy and, before that, the Ford Foundation's Governance and Human Rights Program in the Andean Region and Southern Cone.

Scott Snyder is senior fellow for Korea Studies and director of the Program on US-Korea Policy at the Council on Foreign Relations. Snyder lived in Seoul, South Korea as Korea Representative of the Asia Foundation (2000–2004). His publications include *North Korea in Transition: Politics, Economy, and Society* coedited with Kyung-Ae Park, *China's Rise and the Two Koreas: Shifting Security Dynamics*, and *Negotiating on the Edge: North Korean Negotiating Behavior.*

Dirk J. Vandewalle is associate professor of Government at Dartmouth College. Vandewalle is a Libyan specialist and has published many works on the country including *Libya since 1969: Qadhafi's Revolution Revisited* and *A History of Modern Libya.* He served as political advisor to UN Special Advisor Ian Martin, coordinator for the UN's postconflict planning for Libya. He is currently also the Carter Center field office director in Tripoli, Libya.

Geoffrey Wiseman is Professor of the Practice of International Relations and university fellow at the Center on Public Diplomacy, University of Southern California. He has worked in the Strategic Planning Unit of the Executive Office of the UN Secretary-General, and in the International Affairs Program at the Ford Foundation. He is a former Australian foreign service officer, serving in three diplomatic postings (Stockholm, Hanoi, and Brussels) and as private secretary to the Australian Foreign Minister, Gareth Evans. His publications include *Concepts of Non-Provocative Defence: Ideas and Practices in International Security*; *The Diplomatic Corps as an Institution of International Society* (coedited with Paul Sharp); *American Diplomacy* (also coedited with Paul Sharp); and *Diplomacy in a Globalizing World: Theories and Practices* (coedited with Pauline Kerr).

Introduction

Geoffrey Wiseman

SINCE THE FOUNDING OF THE STATE SYSTEM, GOVERN-ments have had to decide whether to isolate or engage adversarial states. And with the rise of democracy and the belief—sometimes supported, sometimes not—that a state's citizens can influence government policy, the question of whether techniques to influence foreign public opinion should play a role in dealing with isolated adversarial states has grown in importance.

The United States has been far from immune to these issues. Over the past century it has faced a list of adversarial states, including some that for extended periods and in different ways have frustrated US foreign policy interests: the Soviet Union (USSR)/Russia, the People's Republic of China (PRC)/China, North Korea, Cuba, and Vietnam; and, most recently and notably, Iran, Libya, Syria, and Venezuela.

Against the backdrop of changes in the international context and wider US strategies and policies—such as isolationism, containment, co-option, and deterrence—this book explores one key element of these ongoing issues for the United States: When the United States pursues strategies that seek to isolate an adversarial state—manifested by the absence or limited presence of official diplomatic relations with that state—how (and how effectively) does the United States attempt to influence that state's public so that it, in turn, can influence its government to adopt less hostile and more favorable views of US foreign policies and of American society in general?[1] Furthermore, are US policies that seek to isolate an adversarial state by limiting or cutting diplomatic relations counterproductive in that they limit Washington's ability to influence the views and perceptions of that state's public that could ameliorate the government's hostility? In light of these questions, the book examines the challenges and opportunities associated with engaging the *peoples* of adversarial states when their *governments* are the subjects of official US isolationist policies. It looks at whether the United States has wisely or imprudently pursued *isolation-inducing* rather than *engagement-inducing* policies against states it considers adversarial, thereby limiting Washington's potential to influence those states' governments through their publics.

The key criterion (some may prefer to call it "the independent variable") used to highlight "adversarialness" in this book is the level of formal bilateral diplomatic relations between the United States and the state deemed adversarial. Generally speaking, mutual tension is high but the situation is short of conventional war, and the United States has decided to have limited or no formal diplomatic relations with the state. Arguably, policy literature on US relations with adversarial states typically focuses on variables such as historical enmity, hostile public statements by leaders of both sides, the existence of trade or other economic sanctions, or ideological and military tension. Recently, the key criteria for adversarial status have tended to be weapons of mass destruction (WMD) possession or ambitions, support for international terrorism against the United States, and extensive human rights abuses. This book focuses on adversarial states with which the United States has limited or no formal diplomatic relations.

In the field of diplomatic studies, and in general diplomatic practice, a key norm of diplomacy is *continuous dialogue*: a belief in the utility of diplomatic representation and communication even between states that have reached a hostile relationship short of war. This norm was a key element in what Harold Nicolson called the "French method" of diplomacy, "originated by Richelieu, analysed by Callières, and adopted by all European countries during the three centuries" up to the end of World War I (Nicolson 1954, 99; also see Hamilton and Langhorne 2011). The norm carries with it the idea of not isolating adversarial states, the underlying assumption being that new, revolutionary, enemy, and/or recalcitrant states will at some point become socialized through contact with the community of sovereign states. In this view, war between states is thought to be less likely if diplomatic dialogue and communication are conducted continuously through the bilateral exchange of diplomatic missions in the respective capitals. This bilateral normative system was complemented in the twentieth century by more formalized multilateral diplomacy, designed after World War I to have the same war-avoiding effects at the international level. Within this system, a declaration of war represents a sharp rupture, delineating where dialogue stops and fighting starts. This rupture takes the form of abruptly closed embassies, withdrawal of diplomats, cessation of trade and other ties, and, ultimately, a breaking off of all diplomatic relations (Berridge 1994).

Historically, European countries have tended to seek to change the behavior of adversarial states by engaging them and socializing them to the norms of international society through diplomatic relations.[2] The US approach stands in sharp contrast. Since its rise to global preeminence approximately a hundred years ago, the United States has often declined for long periods to establish formal diplomatic relations with adversarial states. The United States also requires that adversarial states meet specified conditions before it will engage them diplomatically. This approach is evident in all nine of the historical and contemporary cases in this book (Armstrong 1993; Wiseman 2010a).

But while the United States has traditionally either refrained from establishing or has cut formal diplomatic ties with adversarial states, it has often simultaneously employed public diplomacy to communicate with and influence those countries' publics. This influence is sought in hopes that "public opinion" will constrain the adversarial government or move it to adopt a more accommodating stance toward the United States. Different public diplomacy instruments are used. The best-known example of what may be called *offshore public diplomacy* is international broadcasting, which for the United States has traditionally taken the form of Voice of America and Radio Free Europe (Metzgar 2013). Other instruments in this category include *track two diplomacy*—informal diplomacy involving nonofficials or officials acting in a personal capacity—and *cultural and exchange programs*, such as sports exchanges, the Fulbright Program, and traveling art and music shows (Snow 2008).

The pattern here is that the United States believes in the effectiveness of isolating adversarial states' governments and yet appears to also believe in the effectiveness of engaging their publics, perhaps reflecting an optimistic view about the wisdom of the people and a pessimistic view about governments (its own included). Most of the authors in this book have come to a rough consensus of skepticism as to whether an isolationist approach has worked historically and whether it works today. The important question now is: Can it work in the future, in a hyperconnected world that appears at times to be increasingly driven by popular trends and movements rather than by what governments do?

This book is not intended as a practical guide for US administrations on how best to conduct public diplomacy with adversarial states, although policy implications arise and are addressed. Its purpose is to raise fundamental questions about the wisdom of carrying out official, state-based public diplomacy while refusing to have formal diplomatic ties with such states.

Primarily, this book seeks to add to our knowledge about how best to deal with adversarial states in several ways. First, it adds case study evidence and empirical data to contemporary policy assessments and public debates about the merits of engaging versus isolating adversarial states, notably in relation to US strategic policy choices. Second, it casts new analytical light on a special group of adversarial states that for extended periods and in different ways have proven challenging for international security in general and for US foreign policy in particular. Such countries have variously been referred to as revolutionary, pariah, rogue, or outlier states (Litwak 2000; Litwak 2013). Third, this book's examination of the strategic potential and limitations of US efforts to influence publics in nine adversarial states—under conditions of restrictive diplomatic relations—represents a set of particularly hard cases for (and hopefully therefore adds heft to the cumulative knowledge of) three fields of study: international security studies, diplomatic studies, and public diplomacy. This last point warrants elaboration.

International security studies, the largest and most epistemically developed of the three fields, has tended to focus on the larger question of whether to engage adversarial states. Interest in this question has historical roots that reached their high point in the appeasement debates of the 1930s. Appeasement has not lost its rhetorical and ideological uses and misuses, especially in US foreign policy debates (Rock 2000). Recent scholarship has sought to answer the isolation-engagement question in more analytical terms (Nincic 2006; Nincic 2012; Henrikson 2012; Crawford 2013). This book's cases cast a stronger light—via diplomatic representation and the role of publics—on the isolation-engagement question.

The field of *diplomatic studies* arose following the Cold War in reaction to diplomatic history's narrative and nontheoretical tendencies (Jönsson and Hall 2005, 9–12). While this field has quietly emerged internationally, its influence in the United States is notably weak (Murray et al. 2011). Almost all scholars who would self-identify as belonging to diplomatic studies emphasize (in ways not understood by most International Relations scholars) the importance of such concepts as diplomatic recognition, which implies official diplomatic relations and the exchange of ambassadors and diplomatic missions. There are excellent international legal texts on recognition (Franck 1990; Jönsson and Hall 2005). G. R. Berridge's *Talking to the Enemy*, a major study, examines a range of devices that allow states not maintaining diplomatic relations to communicate, such as special envoys and the working funeral, although it does not deal specifically with public diplomacy challenges and opportunities in such circumstances (Berridge 1994; Berridge 2010a). Moreover, Berridge has argued that public diplomacy remains a form of "white" propaganda, meaning that, in contrast to "black" propaganda, the information source is admitted. Berridge also suggests that nothing is particularly new in the "new public diplomacy," discussed further below (Berridge 2010a; Berridge 2010b). Generally, diplomatic studies scholars tend to see the state of diplomatic relations as an important variable in international relations in general and between certain states within the international system, including the Great Powers. These scholars also stress how often the extent and level of diplomatic relations are used to convey policy, send signals, and protest or reward. The present volume contributes to this field by analyzing the role of means of communication between states that are less direct and more public than traditional diplomatic channels.

The *public diplomacy field* grew in importance following the September 11, 2001, terrorist attacks on New York and Washington, DC. Since that time, interest in the study and practice of public diplomacy has grown dramatically, a trend well documented by, among others, Jan Melissen (2005; 2013a), Kathy R. Fitzpatrick (2007), Geoffrey Cowan and Nicholas J. Cull (2008), Nicholas J. Cull (2008), Nancy Snow and Philip M. Taylor (2008), Philip Seib (2009), Bruce Gregory (2012) and R.S. Zaharna, Amelia Arsenault, and Ali Fisher (2013). Public diplomacy is a multidisciplinary field of academic study. The fields of communication and diplomacy studies, both of which deal with soft power, have produced considerable literature on public diplomacy, as have such fields as media studies, public relations, and place branding. Contributions—some highly important—have also come from International Relations scholars, regional specialists, and historians of US foreign policy, but the overall contribution from these groups to the study of public diplomacy has been less.[3] Our case studies address this imbalance and demonstrate what can be gained by doing so. New authorial collaborations and a mix of scholars from a range of disciplines produced the cases. One sign of these new collaborations is that I have not worked with any of the book's authors before. With one or two exceptions, these authors would likely not be card-carrying members of any of the three fields of study just described—international security studies, diplomatic studies, and public diplomacy. And only one is a former public diplomacy practitioner. In this sense, the book may offer unique perspectives on the theoretical and policy issues discussed above.

In the early stages of our project, we hoped to increase its multidisciplinary nature by including a chapter on the media's role in engaging adversarial states where diplomatic relations were either absent or limited. This did not prove possible, but it is nonetheless crucial to point out that the media can play two important roles in the isolation-engagement process. One is *external*: Media can be essential communication conduits with foreign governments and citizens. The televised ultimatum that President John F. Kennedy sent to the USSR during the 1962 Cuban Missile Crisis and the media's extensive coverage of President Richard M. Nixon's groundbreaking 1972 visit to China provide two powerful examples of what has been referred to as "media diplomacy" (Gilboa 1998). Most of the chapters in this book refer to the traditional media's role in the isolation-engagement process. Moreover, new media technologies provide governments with unprecedented opportunities to engage foreign publics, primarily through the Internet. For example, the US State Department has established a team of researchers who engage with the Arab blogosphere (Price, Haas, and Margolin 2008; Ross 2011; Youmans and Powers 2012).[4]

The second role media can play is *internal*: Diplomatic isolation creates a lack of access for journalists in adversarial states, which, in turn, causes these countries to be misunderstood by the US public. This loss of immediate and consistent exposure to the adversarial state's narratives, as reported by journalists, seriously weakens the information base required for policy making. Does Iran's burgeoning blogosphere present an opportunity for constructive dialogue between US and Iranian citizens? Or are these connections a potential Trojan horse for extremist groups? One caution: While it is important to understand both how diplomatic isolation impacts the media's ability to accurately cover events in isolated countries and what role the new media technologies play in this process of learning about and engaging adversarial countries, the media are not true public diplomacy actors and would not want to be so characterized. Thorny conceptual questions, such as who is a public diplomacy actor and what are public diplomacy's boundaries, are discussed below.

While the reasons for the multidisciplinary approach to our book's subject were many, there was one common denominator underlying all of the contributors' participation: the desire to advance the debate about (public) diplomacy's role in US foreign policy in general and in dealing with adversarial states in particular. The case for making public diplomacy more central to US foreign policy considerations today has been forcefully stated in the 2002 US National Security Strategy, in the 9/11 Commission report, and in the Defense Department's 2008 National Defense Strategy. As Bruce Gregory has argued in his writings over many years, public diplomacy is crucial to national security and must be improved (e.g., Gregory 2008). Thus, a consensus emerged that understanding the successes and failures in the practice of public diplomacy is significant for US foreign policy. A key reason for this emerging consensus was recognition within the US military establishment itself—most notably by President Barack Obama's first secretary of defense, Robert Gates—that public diplomacy should be integrated with other tools into wider foreign policy goals, and implemented not only at the strategic level but also at operational and tactical levels.

Some Method Issues

In choosing the research devices for this project, we were mindful of the multidisciplinary background of the case study writers. In the context of debates about US global security interests, we identified nine cases that together offer a comparative, cross-regional set of perspectives from which to answer the book's key question and the subquestions that arise from that question.

We drew heavily on the case study method, notably the well-known structured, focused comparison approach devised and developed by Alexander L. George and others (George and Bennett 2005). The book systematically examines nine countries with which the United States has had extended adversarial relations: the USSR/Russia, China, North Korea, Cuba, Vietnam, Iran, Libya, Syria, and Venezuela. In each chapter the authors were asked to address specific research questions.

Two criteria were used in choosing the nine cases: (1) US relations with the country must have been manifestly hostile for an extended period, and (2) the

United States must have either refused to recognize or had less than full diplomatic relations with the country for an extended time. Venezuela is the only
case that does not properly meet the second criterion. However, Venezuela's
expulsion of the US ambassador in September 2008 against the background of
incendiary comments by President Hugo Chavez about the United States and
President George W. Bush justifies Venezuela's inclusion. Moreover, because
Venezuela provides a "short-term" problem case from Latin America, it is a
useful point of regional comparison with Cuba, a "long-term" problem case
covering more than half a century. Some of the case studies also discuss the
vexing question of whether the adversarial state has a program to develop
weapons of mass destruction, but from the outset we did not think WMD
ambitions were necessary for the status of adversarial state.

There are, of course, other adversarial states that might have been included,
beginning historically with the founding of the republic and strained relations
with Britain, then conflicts over Cuba with the declining Spanish empire, and
moving forward to the question of isolating or engaging Nazi Germany, Mus-
solini's Italy, and Imperial Japan. In more recent times, Washington struggled
with relations with Afghanistan under the Taliban, Somalia because of its
piracy issues, and Lebanon because of its role as a base of attacks on Israel
during the 1980s; or, in terms of short-term cases, with South Africa during
the later stages of apartheid and with Panama under Manuel Noriega near
the end of his rule. And the United States downgraded its level of diplomatic
representation in Burma from ambassador to chargé d'affaires following the
1988 military coup and the regime's subsequent failure to respect the 1990
parliamentary election results. Moreover, there have been even smaller adversaries, such as Grenada in the 1980s. However, our goal was not to pronounce
on the conduct of US engagement with the foreign publics of all hostile adversaries throughout history, but, rather, to employ a wide selection of historical
and contemporary cases to show how US engagement with such states can be
analyzed.

By its nature, this book involves a relatively high degree of historical counterfactual argument—for example, what if the United States had retained an
embassy in Moscow from 1917, after the Russian Revolution, to 1933, when
relations were resumed? What if Washington had recognized Vietnam's revolutionary government under Ho Chi Minh in the 1950s rather than siding
with the French? What if the United States had recognized Mao Zedong's
China in 1949 rather than 1979? While such questions are extremely difficult

to answer, many of the authors here have used this device as an important analytical tool, one that can help guide future decisions.

Case Study Sequencing

In deciding how the cases should be presented, we considered grouping those in which diplomatic relations were severed as a result of "revolutionary action" (the USSR, China, Cuba, Vietnam); those in which diplomatic relations were severed or restricted as a direct result of war (North Korea, Vietnam) or because the adversary took actions that the United States deemed "unacceptable" (Iran, Libya, Syria); and those in which diplomatic relations ended through "self-isolation" (North Korea) (Turku 2008). Other possibilities were to present the cases regionally or to present them chronologically according to when a state became adversarial.

Our final decision was to group the cases according to region and "chronological adversarial tipping point." The regional basis underscores Barry Buzan's idea of *regional security complexes*, in which diverse regional patterns of security have become more prominent since decolonization (Buzan and Waever 2003). Thus, in the Cold War context, in which the USSR was a central player, the China, North Korea, and Vietnam cases were linked in important ways in an Asian regional security complex where the actions of one state impacted the others. Because of the USSR's distinction as the "first," most important, and most persistent US adversary of the twentieth century, including during the Cold War, it is discussed first. Serendipitously, China appears as the second case study, underlining the intriguing likelihood that China will be the most important and persistent US adversary in the twenty-first century. The order we settled on then is: the USSR/Russia; the Asian cases—China, North Korea, Vietnam; the Middle East cases—Libya, Iran, Syria; and the Latin American cases—Cuba, Venezuela.

Initial Framing Questions

Our method for structuring the project was for each author to initially address five questions:

1. How would you characterize the overall bilateral diplomatic context or relationship between the United States and "your" country? What main issues have been divisive?

2. Do US diplomatic isolation and/or lower levels of diplomatic representation affect the behavior of an adversarial state? Under what conditions does

the existence of a US embassy or some other form of diplomatic representation significantly increase (or decrease) the capacity for the United States to make informed judgments on or influence government policy and public opinion in the adversarial state?

3. (a) How do American diplomats, especially the ambassador and those with a public diplomacy role, manage or mediate public opinion pressures at home (including those from Congress and the media)? (b) At the operational level on the ground, how do diplomats deal with cultural differences and host government actions (e.g., censorship, travel restrictions) of the adversarial state?

4. When there is no or limited diplomatic representation in the adversarial state, how does diplomacy directed at the adversarial state's public operate? How well does such public diplomacy work when conducted "offshore" (e.g., international broadcasting) from the United States or from another country? Do modern communications technologies mitigate the disadvantages of conducting offshore public diplomacy?

5. Which public diplomacy strategies seem to work well, and which should be ruled out as ineffectual in furthering the interests of US and international security?

Then, based on common themes and questions that arose in an authors' workshop and email discussions, we enhanced the project's consistency across cases by having each author explicitly address three additional questions:

6. What were "pre-adversarial relations" like (and, if appropriate, post-adversarial relations)?

7. Who was/is primarily responsible for the adversarial relationship?

8. What kind of causal/explanatory claims or conclusions can you reach about the various questions we are addressing? In your case, is the absence of diplomatic relations a significant causal and explanatory factor in the public diplomacy battle of ideas?

In asking that these eight questions be addressed in each case, we were seeking to achieve a measure of consistent (structured/focused) treatment while acknowledging the authors' significant variations in disciplinary style and conventions, especially on the causation question.

The book's findings are summarized in terms of four major subquestions of overall interest (see the Conclusion for full details):

1. When diplomatic relations are limited, how does the United States try to *influence* publics in adversarial states?

2. Do US strategies that invoke specific policies to isolate and punish an adversarial state, such as by limiting or severing diplomatic relations, constrain Washington's ability to influence the views and perceptions of the state's public with an eye toward ameliorating the adversary government's hostility toward the United States? In short, does cutting or limiting diplomatic ties *damage* US interests?

3. When diplomatic relations are limited, what are the *challenges* for public diplomacy in adversarial states?

4. When diplomatic relations are limited, what are the *opportunities* for public diplomacy in adversarial states?

Ultimately, although the findings in this book are *mainly* about the United States, they may also be relevant for, and applied to, *other* countries with adversaries. Furthermore, they tell us much about the nine adversarial states studied here.

Definitional Issues

Several definitional issues need to be aired at this point, as they impinge on the cases and arguments that follow. First, the book introduces and develops the concept of a *special case of adversarial state*—that is, a sovereign state with which the United States maintains limited or no formal diplomatic relations because of mutual hostility in a situation short of conventional war, and that has frustrated US foreign policy for extended periods and in different ways.

Second, the book makes the analytical distinction between foreign policy and diplomacy. In essence, *foreign policy* is taken to mean the formulation of a state's grand strategy or worldview, while *diplomacy* is the implementation of that grand strategy or worldview. Traditional diplomacy is typically conducted in two forms: bilateral and multilateral. *Bilateral diplomacy* most often is carried out through embassies and diplomats in each of two states' capitals. *Multilateral diplomacy* is usually conducted at ad hoc or permanent meetings of three or more states, such as at the United Nations (UN) or the World Bank. A third, more recent form, what I call *polylateral diplomacy*, is the conduct of systematic relations between sovereign state and nonstate entities.[5]

Third, it is crucial to distinguish, again for analytical purposes, traditional diplomacy from public diplomacy, while being mindful that some scholars are increasingly challenging this distinction. *Traditional diplomacy* is used here to mean the practical implementation of a country's foreign policy. The general idea is that states should ideally use peaceful means rather than military force in dealing with each other. The customary foundation for traditional diplomacy is continuous dialogue or negotiation through mutual recognition and representation, typically via foreign ministries, embassies, and diplomats, generally operating confidentially or at least out of the public limelight. In contrast to this type of "closed," or "club," diplomacy, *public diplomacy* has customarily meant the ways in which country A's government communicates with country B's citizens or publics through both official and private institutions and individuals in order to influence B's views of and policies toward A. The issue of relevance to us, as already noted, is that when the United States has limited or no official relations with a state, it has nonetheless generally persisted with public diplomacy activities, conducting them largely offshore, without the benefits of (full) on-the-ground diplomatic resources. This idea of offshore public diplomacy is central to understanding whether in circumstances of limited or no diplomatic representation between two states, public diplomacy makes any difference, positive or negative, in shaping the public context within which the adversarial government makes decisions affecting US interests.

A fourth, related definitional issue concerns what constitutes public diplomacy. As already noted, public diplomacy is a relatively new academic field of study, and there is considerable debate about defining it. To illustrate, a study by Kathy Fitzpatrick (2010, 89) noted 150 definitional statements of public diplomacy. Moreover, the official US usage has been to distinguish between *public affairs* (informing/engaging with one's own citizens about foreign policy) and *public diplomacy* (informing/engaging with the citizens of a foreign country). Against this background of definitional contestation, it is important to emphasize that our authors were selected because of their regional-country expertise, not their previous work on public diplomacy. In fact, as noted above, only one of the authors had worked on public diplomacy issues before this project. Under these circumstances, we did not want to impose a single definition on authors new to the field, choosing instead to give them general guidance and some space to explore their own area of specialized knowledge through what was a different set of lenses—public diplomacy—and to see what these explorations might lead to inductively.

Thus, in addition to asking the authors to use the eight framing questions to guide their chapters, we asked them to note or discuss which, if any, of three definitions of public diplomacy was the most apparent in their case.

They could also choose to go beyond the book's organizing parameters and develop their own. These are the three definitions:

(1) *Traditional government to foreign public approach.* Public diplomacy is conducted and organized almost exclusively by the US State Department or, in the case of other countries, by the Ministry of Foreign Affairs (MFA) and is conducted largely via embassies and consulates abroad.

(2) *Wider whole of government to foreign public approach.* Public diplomacy is conducted by any branch of the government but is coordinated by a department or ministry, usually but by no means necessarily the State Department or MFA.

(3) *Broad, nontraditional or new public diplomacy approach.* Public diplomacy is conducted by many disparate actors, including governments, international governmental organizations, nongovernmental organizations, corporations, industries, media, and other legitimate international actors. This approach is said to be taking place in the context of global and regional networks of communication, rather than just through traditional diplomatic networks (Gregory 2012; Melissen 2013b; Zaharna, Arsenault, and Fisher 2013).

This three-part framework was intended not only to guide the authors but also to bring some definitional and conceptual order to the public diplomacy field as a whole—in view of the large number of competing definitions in the field. Interestingly, most but not all of the authors leaned toward the third (largely nongovernmental) approach, which leaves unanswered the question of who exactly is a public diplomacy actor and where public diplomacy conceptually crosses over into other areas and should be relabeled. The definitional trilogy described above is an attempt to advance the debate about field-challenging questions. Are nongovernmental efforts really public diplomacy, or even diplomacy? Can we distinguish between public diplomacy and other forms of cross-cultural communications? Where does one stop and the other begin? This is especially pertinent given that, as just noted, several contributors conclude that public diplomacy should be left to nongovernmental actors, and that the more these efforts are seen as being distanced from governments, the more successful they will be. Under this approach, nongovernmental efforts would not be public diplomacy, but the way in which governments seek to tap into these efforts would be. Bruce Gregory (2014) has suggested that one way through the definitional impasse is to drop the term "public diplomacy" in favor of "diplomacy and its public dimension," an important and field-challenging conceptual insight.

A further conceptual clarification is to note that, sometimes, country A will use public diplomacy and media tools to communicate with country B's *government* (as distinct from its *citizenry*), an aspect of public diplomacy that is particularly relevant when diplomatic relations are absent or limited between governments and adversarial states. There is considerable evidence in the cases to support this view, as is often seen in US relations with Iran, North Korea, and Qadhafi's Libya. Still, some may see these activities as "diplomatic signaling" and not public diplomacy.

Finally, does public diplomacy work? At a more general level, it might be fair to assume that flawed policies or failed policy outcomes are reasonable and sufficient criteria for determining whether public diplomacy is successful or not. However, this argument does not adequately take into account public diplomacy's *instrumental* nature—a point that reinforces the analytical distinction above between *foreign policy* and *diplomacy*. Public diplomacy is a means to a variety of ends, and it is or should be taken into account in the formulation of policies. It is used to support both good and bad strategies and policy goals, to persuade and mobilize on their behalf, to ameliorate their negative effects (without, of course, crossing over into propaganda), and to support other instruments of statecraft. One of the key consensus insights arising from the recent public diplomacy literature is that good public diplomacy (instruments) can never compensate for bad policy or strategy. To what extent does public diplomacy advance a good policy? Can it reduce misunderstandings and soften the edges of a flawed policy? And, importantly, can it achieve medium- and long-term goals even though its efforts to advance policies are unproductive in the short term?

Brief Description of the Nine Cases

In the context of US global security interests, the nine cases offer a wide comparative, cross-regional set of perspectives from which to approach the questions listed above. Brief descriptions of each case and justifications for their inclusion follow.

USSR/Russia. This chapter, written by Robert D. English, covers a longer historical time frame than the other cases, ranging from the 1917 Bolshevik Revolution through the rise of the Soviet Union, World War II, the Cold War, détente, and the post–Cold War US relationship with Russia. The time frame involved varying degrees of "adversarialness" and varying degrees of opportunities for public diplomacy as the relationship waxed and waned from Cold War crises, such as over Cuba, to cooperation during the first Gulf War (1990–1991). The case highlights the emerging US policy of requiring that new states behave appropriately or meet preconditions to gain US recognition, which was in contrast to the European approach of accepting that the Bolsheviks controlled the new Soviet state and typically continuing diplomatic relations.

China. Similar to the USSR case, the China case also involves the US policy of nonrecognition, which began with the victory of the Chinese Communists in 1949. The refusal to recognize a communist China kept China off the UN Security Council until October 1971. Relations were strained for decades until President Nixon's historic visit to Beijing in 1972. After the Nixon visit, the United States opened a liaison office in Beijing, in 1973, headed most famously by George H. W. Bush (1974–1975). President Carter completed the normalization process in 1979. The China case, written by Robert S. Ross, shows how the United States conducted public diplomacy toward China in three distinct phases: (1) 1949–1973 (marked by enmity); (2) 1973–1989 (improved relations and cooperation); and (3) post-1989 (characterized by traditional Great Power competition).

North Korea. Scott Snyder shows in his chapter that, just as it did with the USSR and China, Washington set rigorous standards of behavior as conditions for establishing normalized relations with Pyongyang, the end result of which is that the United States has never had diplomatic relations with North Korea. In the 1990s, however, the Clinton administration negotiated with North Korea, leading to the controversial 1994 Agreed Framework and, later, Secretary of State Madeleine Albright's visit to Pyongyang. In contrast, the George W. Bush administration rejected direct talks with North Korea until the Six Party Talks resumed in 2006 during Bush's second term. Then, in a public diplomacy gesture, the United States permitted the New York Philharmonic to visit Pyongyang in 2008. Bush then removed North Korea from the Trading with the Enemy Act, and the State Department removed North Korea from the US list of state sponsors of terrorism. This engagement with the unpalatable North Korean regime reflected the seriousness of the nuclear issue.

Vietnam. The US decision not to normalize diplomatic relations with Vietnam after the war there ended in 1975 was similar to its decisions on the USSR and China in that a communist government also ruled Vietnam. The big difference was that the Vietnam War was even longer and bloodier for the United States than the Korean War, and the United States lost in Vietnam and obtained a draw in Korea. From 1975 to the early 1990s, as Mark Philip Bradley and Viet Thanh Nguyen show in their chapter, Washington had no in-country public diplomacy programs that could gauge and influence the Vietnamese people's attitudes and opinions. In contrast, other Western countries maintained embassies in Hanoi and were thus able to conduct modest student and visitor exchange programs, as well as English-language training. It was not until 1991 that the United States and Vietnam agreed to establish an office in Hanoi to help find the remains of Americans Missing in Action (MIAs). During President Clinton's first administration (1993–1997), relations with Vietnam were normalized and the degree of adversarialness continued to decline.

The Vietnam case illustrates again how few options exist for engaging the publics of adversarial states directly in the absence of normal diplomatic relations. While some diplomatic contacts took place in the 1980s, such as informal visits by delegations representing families of American MIAs, these were generally episodic and low profile from the US perspective (though not from that of the Vietnamese authorities, who gave them extensive coverage). With the exchange of embassies in 1995, US diplomats were finally able to speak directly to the Vietnamese people. This chapter discusses US and Vietnamese efforts (by both the United States' adversary in the North and its ally in the South) to influence each other's publics up to the war's end in 1975, as well as postwar efforts by both the United States and united Vietnam up to 2010.

Libya. This case, written by Dirk J. Vandewalle, serves as another example of the US policy pattern of not engaging adversarial states until they meet certain conditions. In this case, the argument is that this policy made it more difficult to conduct public diplomacy in Libya and thereby possibly enhance US national security. After 1969, Colonel Qadhafi renounced agreements with the West and condemned the United States in vitriolic, or "undiplomatic," terms, leading to the withdrawal of the US ambassador in 1972. When the US embassy was sacked and burned in 1979, Washington closed the embassy and, in 1981, expelled all Libyan embassy personnel from Washington, thus severing direct diplomatic relations. All of this was exacerbated by the Lockerbie Pan Am bombing in 1988 and Libya's suspected WMD programs, both of which reinforced the US policy of isolating and punishing Libya for what Washington deemed bad behavior. Yet while the United States was carrying out this policy, several Western countries were maintaining diplomatic relations with Tripoli, raising an important question for all of the project's cases: Do countries with diplomatic representation in an adversarial state have a significant public diplomacy advantage over the United States? In an extraordinary reversal of behavior, Libya reached a number of agreements with the West around 2003. The United States resumed diplomatic relations with Libya in 2004, upgrading a liaison office to an embassy in 2006. The long period of isolation ended in September 2008, when Secretary of State Condoleezza Rice made an official visit to Tripoli to meet Qadhafi. The reasons for the Libyan reversal remain subject to scholarly debate (Judson 2005).

This history was turned upside down in 2011–2012, when an uprising against Qadhafi drew support from a UN-authorized NATO air campaign that led to Qadhafi's death and the overthrow of his regime. The September 2012 killing of the US ambassador to Libya during a mob attack on a US "diplomatic facility" in Benghazi then made the tragic point that the US public diplomacy challenges in Libya, and in the Muslim world more generally, are daunting, even with the presence of a diplomatic mission. This was further illustrated by the July 2014 US embassy evacuation from Tripoli. Indeed, this attack is not the first to highlight a major disadvantage of diplomatic representation for countries such as the United States: embassies and consulates are inviting targets for popular and terrorist attack.

Iran. The United States has had no embassy in Iran since the 1979 Iranian Revolution, which included the sacking of the US embassy in Tehran and the holding of US diplomats as hostages for 444 days. In contrast, many Western countries and others have maintained a diplomatic mission in Tehran since the revolution. Throughout the period of ruptured US-Iran diplomatic relations, US interests in Iran have been represented by the Swiss embassy in Tehran. Iran currently has an interests section—the practice whereby a state conducts limited diplomatic activity "under the flag of a second on the territory of a third" (Berridge and Lloyd 2012, 200)—in Washington, housed formally in the Pakistani embassy, which can reach American citizens through its website despite no Iranian diplomat being present. Reinforcing this asymmetrical representation (in Iran's favor) is the presence of an Iranian permanent mission to the UN in New York City, which is used for a wide range of public diplomacy purposes, a particular advantage when the mission is skillfully led, as was the case with US-educated Ambassador Mohammad Javad Zarif, now Iran's foreign minister. This case, written by Suzanne Maloney, examines whether public diplomacy is up to the task of substituting for formal diplomatic engagement between governments. Additionally, it asks whether other Western countries have gained in public diplomacy terms by having resident missions in Tehran, and it considers the interplay of the Iranian diaspora with US public diplomacy toward Iran.

Syria. US-Syrian diplomatic relations were severed following the 1967 Middle East War and resumed in 1974, but they have waxed and waned ever since. On one hand, Washington withdrew its ambassador for a year in 1986–1987 as a result of evidence of Syrian involvement in terrorist acts. On the other hand, there were several presidential summits, the last one between President Clinton and President Hafiz al-Assad in Geneva in 2000. And there was some limited cooperation following the September 11, 2001, terrorist attacks in the United States. However, following the assassination of former Lebanese Prime Minister Rafik Hariri in February 2005, relations deteriorated over Iraq and Syria's human rights record and Syria's alleged pursuit of WMDs. Shortly afterward, the United States recalled its ambassador, and the embassy was led by a chargé d'affaires for five years until President Obama sent Ambassador Robert Ford in 2010. The Syria case, written by William Rugh, underscores the controversial issue—one that was raised in the 2008 presidential campaign—about the wisdom (from both policy and public diplomacy perspectives) of US presidents having face-to-face summits with leaders of states intensely hostile toward the United States. Security in Syria deteriorated badly in 2011 as the country disintegrated into civil war, presenting even greater policy dilemmas for American diplomacy in general and public diplomacy in particular (Hill 2013).

Cuba. Of the nine countries included in the study, Cuba is the only one still subject to the 1917 US Trading with the Enemy Act. The United States broke off diplomatic relations with Cuba in 1961, two years after the success of Fidel Castro's revolution. The break was sparked by Cuba's demand that the US embassy's personnel be reduced drastically within forty-eight hours since, Castro claimed, the embassy was a "nest of spies." The rupture led to a complete absence of diplomatic relations until 1977, when President Carter initiated talks with Cuba that led to the two countries exchanging interests sections. Since this exchange, US diplomats have lived and worked in Havana, accredited to a large interests section that is formally within the Swiss embassy in the Cuban capital. At the same time, Cuba has maintained a reciprocal interests section formally within the Swiss embassy in Washington. This nonexchange of formal embassies and ambassadors from 1961 to the present is an excellent situation for studying how the United States conducted public diplomacy toward Cuba, first without any formal diplomatic relations, and then with severely limited relations. The author of this case, William Leo-Grande, also discusses how US public diplomacy was conducted from the United States, including via the Cuban diaspora, and also from within the confines of the Havana US Interests Section.

Venezuela. Venezuela under President Hugo Chávez (1999 until his death in early 2013) provides an interesting, final test case for the argument that opening (or maintaining) diplomatic ties with countries governed by a hostile leadership (such as, currently, Iran and North Korea) would serve US foreign policy interests by mitigating the hostile actions of the adversarial government or leader. Despite serious tensions in US-Venezuelan relations, Washington maintained a large embassy in Caracas at the ambassadorial level for many years. In September 2008, however, the US ambassador was declared *persona non grata* and expelled. It was not only Chávez's inflammatory remarks about the US president and US foreign policy that soured the relationship but also his cleverly cultivated ties with countries such as Iran—ties viewed as having possibly serious implications for access to foreign oil and therefore for US national security. There are strong trade-interest grounds for a continued US embassy, which Michael Shifter, author of this case, describes. Moreover, the consular demands are substantial—some 23,000 US citizens live in Venezuela, and 12,000 American tourists visit the country each year. Against these arguments, Shifter considers the possibility that given the late Chávez's mercurial leadership style, the presence of the US embassy in Caracas may, on occasion, have harmed rather than helped US public diplomacy.

Conclusion

The nine cases show a pattern of disrupted diplomatic relations between the United States and adversarial states that have frustrated US foreign policy interests for extended periods and in different ways.

The comparative approach adopted for this book aims to uncover the broader patterns that exist in and the strategic policy lessons that can be learned from several contemporary US foreign policy challenges related to adversarial states, as well as the role that public diplomacy can play in meeting these challenges. This comparative and cross-regional project—to the best of our knowledge, the first of its kind—seeks to explore these generally neglected issues, thereby contributing to a better understanding of public diplomacy's role in the theory and practice of US foreign policy toward adversarial states in particular and international security in general. All the authors tackle, directly or indirectly, the wisdom of policies pursued by the United States. The book's concluding chapter seeks to synthesize overall patterns and policy lessons from all nine cases, lessons that we hope US policymakers can apply in dealing with adversaries not considered in this book, such as the Taliban in Afghanistan, Hezbollah in Lebanon, the Muslim Brotherhood in Egypt, Hamas in Gaza, and Boko Haram in Nigeria. These patterns and lessons are evaluated in terms of four criteria: influence, damage, challenges, and opportunities.

The conclusion also considers theoretical lessons that can be drawn from the cases. An important one is that public diplomacy must be conceived of as much more than a one-way street of "us" influencing "them." Building on an emerging consensus in the literature that public diplomacy should be seen less in *monologic* (one-sided) terms and more in *dialogic* (two- or multi-sided) terms, the cases suggest a large and controversial idea: that the United States defines its own identity (the national "self")—and indeed that of the international order it has constructed in the twentieth century—more in relation to the adversarial, stigmatized "other" than to its international friends and allies (Adler-Nissen 2014). This self-other identity formation was most dramatically on display throughout the Cold War and can still be detected today in the China, Iran, Syria, Cuba, and North Korea cases. In short, official US diplomats and public diplomacy programs do not simply represent fixed national interests and a fixed American national identity to the rest of the world. They also reproduce and in some cases reconstitute American identity and culture: an adversarial relationship with the "other" has an effect on the "self." Thus, every act of diplomacy in general and in public diplomacy specifically is not simply an act of representation. It is also an act of identity formation and order formation in international society.

Notes

1. For a persuasive argument that US public diplomacy efforts are best viewed as accessory or adjunct to five larger government strategies or policies that the United States has pursued—(1) consolidation, (2) containment, (3) penetration, (4) enlargement, and (5) transformation—see Alan K. Henrikson, 2006, *What Can Public*

Diplomacy Achieve? Discussion Papers in Diplomacy. The Hague: Netherlands Institute of International Relations 'Clingendael' (Clingendael Discussion Papers in Diplomacy, No. 104). Accessed January 10, 2015 at http://www.clingendael.nl/sites/default/files/ What-can-public-diplomacy-achieve.pdf.

2. An important exception was the Hallstein Doctrine, under which the Federal Republic of Germany (FRG) after 1955 refused to have diplomatic relations with any state that recognized the German Democratic Republic (GDR). In practice, the doctrine was gradually abandoned in the 1960s in favor of engagement as the FRG established formal diplomatic links with countries that maintained diplomatic relations with the GDR.

3. I owe these disciplinary insights to a reviewer.

4. I am grateful to Shawn Powers, Michael Parks, and Lyn Boyd Judson for these ideas.

5. My full definition of polylateralism is: The conduct of relations between official entities (such as a state, several states acting together, or a state-based international organization) and at least one unofficial, nonstate entity in which there is a reasonable expectation of systematic relationships, involving some form of reporting, communication, negotiation, and representation, but not involving mutual recognition as sovereign, equivalent entities (Wiseman 2010b, 24).

References

Adler-Nissen, R. 2014. "Stigma Management in International Relations: Transgressive Identities, Norms, and Order in International Society." *International Organization* 68 (Winter): 143–176.

Armstrong, J. D. 1993. *Revolution and World Order: The Revolutionary State in International Society.* Oxford: Oxford University Press.

Berridge, G. R. 1994. *Talking to the Enemy.* New York: Macmillan.

———. 2010a. *Diplomacy: Theory and Practice.* 4th ed. Basingstoke, UK: Palgrave Macmillan.

———. 2010b. *The Counter-Revolution in Diplomacy and Other Essays.* Basingstoke, UK: Palgrave Macmillan.

Berridge, G. R., and Lorna Lloyd, eds. 2012. *The Palgrave Macmillan Dictionary of Diplomacy.* Basingstoke, UK: Palgrave Macmillan.

Buzan, Barry, and Ole Waever. 2003. *Regions and Powers: The Structure of International Security.* Cambridge: Cambridge University Press.

Cowan, Geoffrey, and Nicholas J. Cull. 2008. "Public Diplomacy in a Changing World." *ANNALS of the American Academy of Political and Social Science* 616 (March): 6–8.

Crawford, Timothy W. 2013. "The Strategy of Coercive Isolation in US Security Policy." Working Paper No. 260. Singapore: S. Rajaratnam School of International Studies, 1–30.

Cull, Nicholas J. 2008. *The Cold War and the United States Information Agency.* Cambridge: Cambridge University Press.

Fitzpatrick, Kathy R. 2007. "Advancing the New Public Diplomacy: A Public Relations Perspective." *The Hague Journal of Diplomacy* 2, no. 3: 187–211.

———. 2010. *The Future of US Public Diplomacy: An Uncertain Fate.* Leiden: Martinus Nijhoff.

Franck, Thomas M. 1990. *The Power of Legitimacy among Nations.* Oxford: Oxford University Press.

George, Alexander L., and Andrew Bennett. 2005. *Case Studies and Theory Development in the Social Sciences.* Boston: MIT Press.

Gilboa, Eytan. 1998. "Media Diplomacy: Conceptual Divergence and Applications." *Harvard Journal of Press/Politics* 3, no. 3: 56–75.

Gregory, Bruce. 2008. "Public Diplomacy: Sunrise of an Academic Field." *ANNALS of the American Academy of Political and Social Science,* 616 (March): 274–290.

———. 2012. "American Public Diplomacy: Enduring Characteristics, Elusive Transformation." *The Hague Journal of Diplomacy,* 6, nos. 3–4 (December): 351–372.

———. 2014. *The Paradox of US Public Diplomacy: Its Rise and "Demise."* IPDGC Special Report #1. Washington, DC: George Washington University, 1–26. Accessed February 11, 2015 at http://ipdgc.gwu.edu/ipdgc-special-reports.

Hamilton, Keith, and Richard Langhorne. 2011. *The Practice of Diplomacy: Its Evolution, Theory and Administration.* 2nd ed. London: Routledge.

Henrikson, Thomas H. 2012. *America and the Rogue States.* Basingstoke, UK: Palgrave Macmillan.

Hill, Chrisopher R. 2013. "When to Talk to Monsters." *New York Times,* May 16.

Jönsson, Christer, and Martin Hall. 2005. *Essence of Diplomacy.* Basingstoke, UK: Palgrave Macmillan.

Judson, Lyn Boyd. 2005. "Strategic Moral Diplomacy: Mandela, Qaddafi, and the Lockerbie Negotiations." *Foreign Policy Analysis* 1: 73–98.

Litwak, Robert S. 2000. *Rogue States and U.S. Foreign Policy: Containment after the Cold War.* Baltimore: Johns Hopkins University Press.

———. 2013. *Outlier States: American Strategies to Change, Contain, or Engage Regimes.* Washington, DC: Woodrow Wilson Center Press.

Melissen, Jan, ed. 2005. *The New Public Diplomacy: Soft Power in International Relations.* Basingstoke, UK: Palgrave Macmillan.

———. 2013a. "Public Diplomacy." In *The Oxford Handbook of Modern Diplomacy,* ed. Andrew F. Cooper, Jorge Heine, and Ramesh Thakur, 436–452. Oxford: Oxford University Press.

———. 2013b. "Public Diplomacy." In *Diplomacy in a Globalizing World: Theories and Practices,* ed. Pauline Kerr and Geoffrey Wiseman, 192–208. New York: Oxford University Press.

Metzgar, Emily T. 2013. *Considering the "Illogical Patchwork": The Broadcasting Board of Governors and US International Broadcasting.* CPD Perspectives on Public Diplomacy, Paper 1, 1–42. Los Angeles: Figueroa Press.

Murray, Stuart, Paul Sharp, David Criekmans, Geoffrey Wiseman, and Jan Melissen, eds. 2011. "Forum on 'The Present and Future of Diplomacy and Diplomatic Studies.'" *International Studies Review* 13 (December): 709–728.

Nicolson, Harold. [1954] 1966. *The Evolution of Diplomacy.* New York: Collier Press.

Nincic, Miroslav. 2006. "The Logic of Positive Engagement: Dealing with Renegade Regimes." *International Studies Perspectives* 7: 321–341.

———. 2012. "Getting What You Want: Positive Inducements in International Relations." *International Security* 35, no. 1 (Summer): 138–183.

Price, Monroe E., Susan Haas, and Drew Margolin. 2008. "New Technologies and International Broadcasting: Reflections on Adaptations and Transformations." *ANNALS of the American Academy of Political and Social Science* 616 (March): 150–172.

Rock, Stephen. 2000. *Appeasement in International Politics.* Lexington: University Press of Kentucky.

Ross, Alec. 2011."Digital Diplomacy and US Foreign Policy." *The Hague Journal of Diplomacy* 6, nos. 3–4: 451–455.

Seib, Philip, ed. 2009. *Toward a New Public Diplomacy: Redirecting US Foreign Policy.* Basingstoke, UK: Palgrave Macmillan.

Snow, Nancy. 2008. "International Exchanges and the US Image." *ANNALS of the American Academy of Political and Social Science* 616 (March): 198–222.

———, and Philip M. Taylor, eds. 2008. *Routledge Handbook of Public Diplomacy.* Abingdon, UK: Routledge.

Turku, Helga. 2008. *Isolationist States in an Interdependent World.* Farnham, UK: Ashgate.

Wiseman, Geoffrey. 2010a. "Engaging the Enemy: An Essential Norm for Sustainable US Diplomacy." In *Sustainable Diplomacies,* ed. Costas M. Constantinou and James Der Derian, 213–234. Basingstoke, UK: Palgrave Macmillan.

———. 2010b. "Polylateralism: Diplomacy's Third Dimension." *Public Diplomacy Magazine* 4 (Summer): 24–39.

Youmans, William Lafi, and Shawn Powers. 2012. "Remote Negotiations: International Broadcasting as Bargaining in the Information Age." *International Journal of Communication,* August 30,

Zaharna, R. S., Amelia Arsenault, and Ali Fisher, eds. 2013. *Relational, Networked, and Collaborative Approaches to Public Diplomacy: The Connective Mindshift.* New York: Routledge.

1   SOVIET UNION/RUSSIA

US Diplomacy with the Russian "Adversary"

Robert D. English

THE ISSUES THAT THIS CHAPTER ADDRESSES—THE
historical lessons of US diplomacy with Russia—are surely more
complex than those of other adversarial states. This is because there is no self-
evident single *adversary* in these relations, nor are we even dealing with a single *state*. Russia is not North Korea, a unitary, uniform regime that for some
six decades has maintained a deeply hostile posture toward the West and its
political norms. The revolutionary-era Leninist state differed significantly
from that of the 1920s, including in opportunities for diplomatic engagement
with the West, just as the possibilities of such interchange varied considerably
from the Stalinist 1930s through the years of the World War II alliance and
up to the early Cold War. Arguably even more significant were political and
social changes—and improved diplomatic prospects—from the "thaw" era
through the late Cold War, and from the epoch of *perestroika* through communism's collapse and aftermath. We are dealing with at least three qualita-
tively different political regimes, and sweeping socioeconomic transformation
over nearly a century of tumultuous international change in which any pre-
sumption of consistent US probity or diplomatic "correctness—and Russian
hostility or adversariness—simply does not hold.

This chapter will examine the practice and prospects of US diplomacy
with Russia, beginning with the period before and during the 1917 Revolution;
through several distinct phases of relations with the Union of Soviet Socialist Republics (USSR) from the revolution until 1991; and subsequent relations

with Russia after the demise of the USSR. One key lesson can be stressed at the outset, which is to endorse the general proposition or "norm" that this book advances: the importance of active, multifaceted diplomatic engagement even in periods, and with regimes, of greatest hostility. A lack of such engagement has led to stereotypes and ignorance—and consequent lost opportunities—while its presence contributed much to the most momentous diplomatic breakthrough of the twentieth century, namely the Cold War's end. One underappreciated facet of that engagement has been public diplomacy, which I see as outreach—partly though not exclusively orchestrated during the Cold War by the US State Department, and implemented by the US embassy in Moscow—to elites and citizens beyond the rarified diplomatic corps in Moscow. This view is essentially but by no means exclusively consistent with the traditional "State Department" approach to public diplomacy outlined in the book's Introduction. As will be seen, such outreach even in times of hostility has borne vital fruit in subsequent periods of relative openness. Sadly, at a time of greatest receptivity at the outset of relations with post–Soviet Russia, it fared poorly, in part due to clumsy "salesmanship," but even more because the "product" proved disappointing.

I will use a "Princeton lens" to analyze the various phases of Soviet-Russian diplomatic history by focusing on the epoch-spanning experience of three distinguished Princeton scholar-diplomats: the venerable George Kennan, longtime dean of American Russian experts, who died in 2005; his onetime diplomatic protégé and later renowned Sovietologist Robert Tucker, who passed away in 2010; and Jack Matlock, the "US ambassador to *perestroika*," who is still active as a scholar and analyst of Russian affairs. Kennan specialized in Russia from the outset of his diplomatic career in the 1920s. He was posted to Moscow when relations were established with the USSR in 1933, serving through World War II and the early Cold War years, then returning as ambassador in 1952. He was also a member of the Princeton Institute for Advanced Study for nearly fifty years. Tucker, who served in Moscow from 1942 to 1953, was later a professor at Princeton University for more than forty years. Matlock, who retired from the Foreign Service after his remarkable 1987–1991 Moscow ambassadorship, was from 1996 to 2001 the Kennan Professor of Diplomatic History at the Institute for Advanced Study as well as a visiting professor at Princeton University. Given the rare experience of these three individuals—and the necessity of employing some narrowing lens if this is not to be a multivolume chronicle—the insights of these three Princetonians offers a splendid perspective for our limited purposes.

US-Russian Relations during the Bolshevik Revolution

Historians have long debated whether the Bolsheviks triumphed as the result of popular revolution or merely a well-executed putsch, and whether their victory reflected the will of a majority of Russians or the opportunism and ruthlessness of a determined minority. They agree, however, on the crucial point that it was Russia's disastrous involvement in World War I that strained the old order beyond its breaking point and thus was a proximate cause of both the February and October 1917 revolutions (the first ended tsarist rule; the second brought the Bolsheviks to power). And it was, in turn, the World War I allies' single-minded and shortsighted insistence on Russia's continued involvement in the disastrous war against Germany that contributed mightily to the revolutions in the first place. Here we turn to Kennan, highly singular as a US diplomat for both the broad historical context of his views and his intimate understanding of Russian and German societies:

> Had they [Western statesmen] looked carefully at the Russian scene at that moment, they could have discerned in it the dilemma that was to be basic to their problem of policy toward Russia throughout the following two years . . . that not only had Russia become involved in a great internal political crisis, but she had lost in the process her real ability to make war. The internal crisis was of such gravity that there was no chance for a healthy and constructive solution to it unless the war effort could be terminated at once and the attention and resources of the country concentrated on domestic issues. The army was tired. The country was tired. People had no further stomach for war. To try to drive them to it was to provide grist to the mill of the agitator and the fanatic: the last people one would have wished to encourage at such a dangerous moment. (Kennan 1961, 14)

Germany itself was not far from collapse—the United States was soon to enter the war on the Triple Entente side—and even basic knowledge of Russia's domestic crisis in 1917 revealed the mortal danger of continued involvement in a ruinous war. Yet two key failings blinded the Western allies. One was the failure of their statesmen and foreign ministries to heed the warnings of their own well-informed ambassadors to Russia, such as France's Maurice Paleologue and Britain's George Buchanan, about the imminence of domestic collapse. This followed from a more fundamental problem, namely the allies' unshakable commitment to Germany's unconditional surrender, a fanatical anti-Germanness that Kennan saw as largely the result of the extreme demonization of enemies that democracies fall prey to in mobilizing domestic support for war.

> To the extent they took note of the disturbing signs of disintegration in Russia's capacity to make war and of the growing crisis of the dynasty, they tended to attribute these phenomena primarily to German influence. The Germans, as they saw it, had to be the source of all evil; nothing bad could happen that was not attributable to the German hand. From this fixation flowed the stubborn conviction in Paris and London that the troubles in Petrograd . . . were merely the result of German influence and intrigue at the Russian court. Allied statesmen were unable to understand that it was not German intrigue, but precisely the strain of war against Germany, which had brought Russia to this deplorable state. (Kennan 1961, 13)

All this ostensibly concerns prerevolutionary Russia, not the early Bolshevik years that are the main focus of this section. Yet the lessons of late prerevolutionary relations with Russia are crucial in several respects: the twin diplomatic pathologies of ignorance born of limited engagement and demonization of adversaries would continue in the Soviet era; and, more immediately, Western actions on the eve of revolution would strongly influence still-malleable Bolshevik attitudes toward the West.

But were Bolshevik attitudes, steeped as they were in a Marxist ideology that saw the West as inherently hostile toward socialism (due to the nature of the capitalist system), really malleable even at the outset of the new era? Kennan himself seems of two minds on this question. In some reflective analyses of Russia's relations with the West he emphasized the new Soviet leaders' cynicism, duplicity, and consequent unsuitability as partners in any "normal" sort of enduring cooperation. But elsewhere, especially in chronicling the particulars of these early relations, Kennan seemed to emphasize instead the mistakes and lost opportunities for a better initial relationship between Soviet Russia and the West. The key to this apparent contradiction (paralleling the misunderstanding that still dogs Kennan's post–World War II call for "containment" of the USSR) is that he sought a middle ground between the extremes of liberal illusions about the USSR and reactionary demonization-militarization of the "Soviet threat."

> [J]ust because the leaders of another regime were hostile and provocative and insulting . . . did not mean that one could afford the luxury of having no dealings

whatsoever with them or that there was nothing to be gained by meeting them face to face and talking about this question or that. . . . We cannot divide our external environment neatly and completely into friends and enemies . . . there must be a certain relativism about enmity, as I suppose there must be about friendship—we must learn to recognize a certain duality in our relationship to all the rest of mankind, even those who hate us most. (Kennan 1961, 63)

The problem was that, after the first 1917 revolution, Western policy continued to focus on keeping Russia in the war with Germany and, even after the Bolshevik triumph, on supporting those groups in Russia who promised to renew the war effort while spurning those forces (i.e., the new Soviet government) that wanted to bow to the inevitable and seek a separate peace. Ambassadors' warnings were ignored, while special emissaries, such as the elderly former Secretary of State Elihu Root, "returned to the United States breathing sweetness and light, confidence and reassurance, about the situation in Russia" (Kennan 1961, 26). When the Bolsheviks made good on their promise in the *Decree on Peace* and subsequent Brest-Litovsk Treaty with Germany, they were simply ignored.[1] At the allies' conference in Paris in late November 1917, British ambassador (to Petrograd) Buchanan argued:

> The Allied governments, instead of protesting the Bolshevik action, should release Russia from her formal bond and accept the inevitable with some semblance of good grace. But this was wholly unacceptable to [French Premier] Clemenceau, who declared that "if . . . all the celestial powers asked him to give Russia back her word, he would refuse." (Kennan 1961, 44)

The French were especially incensed over a new issue: the Bolsheviks' repudiation of tsarist debts, which struck French bondholders particularly hard. Nonrecognition of the new Soviet government was soon compounded by a secret Anglo-French agreement for financing prowar (and anti-Bolshevik) forces in the Caucasus and Ukraine. Thus was sown "the seed of subsequent Allied intervention" in the coming Russian Civil War (Kennan 1961, 47).

Before full-fledged military intervention was launched, however, 1918 saw a last-ditch effort to establish relations with the new Bolshevik regime on a positive footing. As experienced and clear-headed prerevolutionary Western ambassadors were recalled or resigned, exhausted and discouraged, day-to-day contacts with the new government fell to various ad hoc arrangements with lower-level officials: Jacques Sadoul, attaché to the French Military Mission in Petrograd; Bruce Lockhart, British consul general in Moscow; and

Raymond Robins, head of the US Wartime Red Cross Commission in Russia. Perhaps owing to their personal experience and insight, as well as to a certain freedom from the shackles (and anti-German blinders) of their respective governments' policies, these three "unofficial" ambassadors independently came to a similar position toward the new Soviet regime. They each endorsed proposals for Western support of the Bolsheviks, partly as the only hope of restoring a Russian effort against Germany, but chiefly as a realistic policy for engaging the country's new leaders. Kennan was deeply skeptical about the former (Germany in any event was soon to collapse in its own revolution) and impatient with the "mythology" of a lost chance for good relations with the Soviet regime. But he was simultaneously admiring of these attachés' experience and knowledge of Russia; their frequent meetings with Lenin, Trotsky, and other top Bolshevik officials; and their open-minded and clear-eyed assessment of the country's domestic prospects.

> They saw the Soviet leaders not as ogres or monsters of sorts, but as human beings, and in many ways impressive human beings at that. It was a startling experience for these men—after long immersion in the Western society of that day, where the accent was so extensively on individualism, on personal vanity, on social rivalry and snobbishness—to encounter men who had a burning social faith, and were relentless and incorruptible in the pursuit of it. . . . These [envoys] were not socialists, but were pressed by what they had seen into taking a larger view of Soviet power than was taken by a great many of their compatriots. Their firsthand knowledge could not fail to make them impatient of the stupid and prejudiced views about Russian Communism that were beginning to find currency in Western officialdom and respectable Western opinion. It fell largely to them to combat such silly and ineradicable legends as the belief that the Bolsheviki were paid German agents or that they had nationalized women. In their effort to combat these impressions, Robins and Lockhart ran the risk of sounding like Communist apologists. (Kennan 1961,: 61–62; see also Mayers 1995, 75–89)

Indeed, in an atmosphere redolent of the McCarthyism with which Kennan would later contend, Robins sought in congressional hearings to make the senators understand the difference between a partiality to the Soviet ideology and a desire to learn the truth about it. He said, "I would like to tell the truth about men and about movements, without passion and without resentment . . . I believe that when we understand what [the Russian Revolution] is, when we know the facts behind it, when we do not libel it nor slander it or do not lose our heads and become its advocates and defenders, and really know what the thing is, and then move forward to it, then we will serve our country and our time" (Kennan 1961, 62–63). But such efforts were largely in vain. Far from extending recognition to the Soviet government, the United States was drawn into the fiasco of French- and British-led efforts to mount a major military intervention in Russia.

This tragic episode is too well known to require detailed recounting here. With Kennan again as our guide, it suffices to summarize the essentials. The Allied intervention of 1918–1920 was driven by the dual chimeras of restoring an anti-German offensive in Russia (or at least saving stocks of allied-supplied munitions from falling into German hands) and restoring Russia's commitment to honor its extensive debts; a later goal was rescuing the Czech corps stranded in Siberia. These missions were crucially encouraged by the Americans' lack of accurate and timely information on the real prospects in Russia (which stemmed in large measure from Washington's, like Paris and London's, diplomatic short-sightedness) and by US President Woodrow Wilson's greater concern for the Paris Peace Conference (and need of allied support for his projected League of Nations). The intervention failed to achieve any of its goals. Instead, it served ultimately to galvanize ordinary Russians' support for the Bolsheviks, providing the Soviet leaders with a propaganda coup and apparent proof of the capitalist world's abiding hostility to socialism, and thus poisoned Soviet-Western relations at this critical early juncture.[2]

Kennan, again, had no patience with Soviet (and some Western) views that exaggerated the military impact of the intervention, or attributed it more to a grand antisocialist design than to mistakes, misjudgments, and misinformation. But one byproduct of the intervention was to compound the self-inflicted blindness of the allies:

The result was that by the end of 1918 there was no longer any official representation of any of the major Western governments in Moscow . . . this was one of the prices paid for the dubious advantages of the intervention. How high a price this really was is something about which, of course, we can only speculate. . . . It is possible, of course, that the results would have been no better even had the Allied governments contrived to retain some sort of representation there in 1918. But it is my own belief . . . that the Soviet leaders were at that time more impressionable, more accessible to outside stimuli, than they were later; that their attitude toward the United States in particular had not yet fully solidified; and that there were at that time certain slender possibilities for influencing them through personal contact, which obviously disappeared at a later date. (Kennan 1961, 84)

Space again does not permit us to detail the evolution of these relations over the postintervention/post–Civil War years. Nonrecognition of the Soviet government (which ended for most Western countries in the 1920s, but for the United States only in 1933) certainly contributed to the "terrifying naiveté as to what the Russia of that hour was really like . . . they were drawing their information exclusively from the side which they wanted to see win. The Allies had no observers, at this point, on the Bolshevik side . . . and were now paying the penalty for this sacrifice, in the form of very poor and unreliable information about Russian conditions. It was a heavy price" (Kennan 1961, 143). It contributed to such unpleasant surprises as the German-Soviet Rapallo Treaty, as well as a succession of misunderstandings and mutually provocative steps that dogged even the improved political and commercial relations of the mid-1920s.

Yet it was at precisely this time that Kennan and a small corps of other American "Russia hands" were trained in ad hoc circumstances that, perhaps paradoxically, contributed to the breadth and depth of their later insights. Kennan entered the US Foreign Service (after roughly a year of exam preparations) in 1926. After another year in the new Foreign Service School and postings in Geneva and Hamburg, he began specialized training on Russia that encompassed graduate study in Berlin and service in Russia's Baltic neighbors (in the Estonian capital Tallinn and Latvia's capital Riga). The rigor of those classical studies (language, literature, history) and richness of these early postings (especially in the old Russian imperial outpost of Riga, "in many respects a minor edition of Petersburg . . . to live in Riga was in many respects to live in Tsarist Russia") provided a preparation for diplomatic service in Russia that is impossible to imagine in any later era (Kennan 1967, 29–30; see also Mayers 1995, 96–101). At a minimum, it afforded Kennan insights into the enduring culture of Russia (and of Russian diplomacy) that inoculated him against the Cold War pathology of viewing the Soviet Union as a sui generis, exclusively ideologically driven state—a rare trait for the time that he shared with his later Moscow colleague and fellow diplomat-cum-scholar, Robert Tucker (Tucker 1972).

It is also highly revealing to read Kennan's memoirs of Berlin, Hamburg, Riga, and, when US-Soviet diplomatic relations were finally established, Moscow; to see, in contrast to his later image as distant, elitist, and supremely intellectual, a young man continually traveling to provincial museums and churches, attending plays and concerts, or riding streetcars and strolling public parks to mingle with ordinary people. His "people-to-people" contacts ranged from artists and intellectuals to humble, and thus less inhibited, workers and hitchhikers (Mayers 1995, 134). In his memoirs, Kennan devotes four detailed pages to his wide-ranging conversation with a prostitute whom he treated to a drink at a café while dismissing, in one paragraph, the growing official obsession with espionage:

> We had no secret agents, and wanted none. Experience had convinced us that far more could be learned by careful, scholarly analysis of information legitimately available concerning any great nation than by the fanciest arrangements of clandestine intelligence ... [and] nothing gave us greater pleasure than to puncture, on the basis of demonstrable fact, the absurdities of the lurid reports about conditions in Russia received by various Western governments from secret intelligence sources and sent to us for comment. (Kennan 1967, 48)

Diplomacy in Stalin's Russia

When US-Soviet diplomatic ties were finally established in 1933, much had changed. Stalin was now leader, but he had not yet launched the mass terror of 1937–1939 that Kennan (and Tucker) argued reflected his murderous will to power and his readiness to sacrifice the lives of millions—indeed, the security of his people—for his own paranoid, personal security (Tucker 1990). In 1933 the atmosphere was still relatively open, "far more friendly, pleasant and relaxed than anything Russia was to know for another two decades" (Kennan 1967, 64).

> Of no smaller importance for me, personally, than this study of the political scene was the opportunity, now for the first time extensively available, to drink in impressions of Russia itself: of its life, its culture, its aspect, its smell. ... It could well be asked how one could gain impressions at all, as a foreign diplomat in the Russia of the purges, in view of the fantastic measures taken by the regime to isolate all foreigners, and particularly diplomats, from the population at large. Actually, these measures were effective only to a degree. Some contacts and friendships with Soviet citizens continued to be cultivated, simply out of mutual liking and interest, though they naturally required ingenuity and discretion. Then there were the theater, sporting events, and public

occasions of every sort where one could rub elbows with ordinary Russians and where, particularly if one knew Russian, one could absorb a great deal of what was in the air. Finally, there was travel. There were trips to Leningrad, to the south, to the Caucasus, trips on Moscow river steamers [and] into the countryside to find out what had become of some of the beautiful medieval churches. . . . I would have undertaken the expeditions even had they yielded no side impressions. But side impressions they did yield, unfailingly and abundantly. When I look back on those years in Moscow in the mid-Thirties, I believe that what I most gained from them was a feeling for the country—for the new Russia, as it had emerged from the ordeals of collectivization and the first Five-Year Plan and as it was then entering the new ordeal of the purges. (Kennan 1967, 67–68)

Together with such outstanding colleagues as Chip Bohlen, Loy Henderson, and Charlie Thayer, and journalistic titans including Walter Duranty, William Henry Chamberlin, and Linton Wells, the American community in Moscow was generally optimistic about the new relations. The US ambassador, William C. Bullitt, encouraged his staff to pursue a "people-to-people" campaign (Bohlen 1973, 20–24). Another lengthy excerpt from Kennan is telling:

Bullitt . . . was charming, brilliant, well-educated, imaginative, a man of the world capable of holding his own intellectually with anyone, including such great intellects of the Communist movement as Radek and Bukharin, both of whom were still around then and had no objection to coming to the embassy to talk with him. . . . His greatest weakness as a diplomatist (and it was the natural counterpart of his virtues) was impatience. He came to Russia with high hopes and he wanted to see them realized at once. These high hopes were not the result of any ideological sympathy for the Soviet regime [but rather] a certain over-optimism concerning the impressionableness of the Soviet leaders. Here Bullitt was no doubt betrayed by his earlier experience with Lenin. He had gone to Russia in February 1919, during the Paris Peace Conference, with the blessing of Colonel House and at least the tacit consent of President Wilson and Prime Minister Lloyd George. He had dealt there with Lenin and other Soviet leaders of the day. He had returned with Soviet proposals which were not ideal but which did offer the most favorable opportunity yet extended, or ever to be extended, to the Western powers for . . . the creation of an acceptable relationship to the Soviet regime. He had been shabbily treated—disowned, in fact—on his return by Wilson and Lloyd

George. . . . Bullitt had then resigned in protest from the American delegation to the conference.

All this had occurred at a time when the attitude of the Soviet regime toward the United States had not yet congealed—when there was still considerable vacillation among the Soviet leadership. . . . Such pro-American tendencies in Moscow naturally received a severe rebuff in the treatment accorded Bullitt by the Western leaders. Bullitt had never forgotten this. On returning to Russia as ambassador in 1933 he had hoped, I suspect, that the approach of the Roosevelt administration, free of the prejudices of 1919, free of the rigidities of the Republican regimes that had intervened over the preceding twelve years, and prepared to correct insofar as it could the errors of that earlier day, would evoke a favorable response on the Soviet side. These hopes were quickly disappointed. This was, after all, the day of Stalin, not of Lenin. (Kennan 1967, 79–80)

Under Stalin, as the Great Terror gathered force, the Western diplomatic community grew increasingly harassed, isolated, and demonized. And even as there remained opportunities for insightful reporting to their respective capitals, those for public diplomacy—cultivating acquaintances with Russian political and cultural figures, disseminating information about the United States, and fostering contacts with ordinary Russians—dwindled. So too did any hopes of US diplomats' influence on Soviet officialdom. Soviet diplomacy and foreign policy were now exclusively Stalin's, and the long-delayed American interest in genuinely improving relations now collided with Stalin's particular view of Soviet interests and the larger movement of international forces—particularly, the rise of European fascism and growing Nazi threat. Again, this is not the place to recount in detail the collapse of "collective security" and the mutual suspicions and miscalculations that led to failure of joint efforts to prevent another world war. Kennan and Tucker persuasively argued that while shabby Western treatment of the Bolsheviks in the 1920s played its part, Stalin's pathological suspicions—his drive for absolute political control of the USSR and domination of foreign socialist-communist forces—both abetted Hitler's rise and helped scuttle common cause to contain him (Kennan 1961; Tucker 1990). The 1938 Munich agreement set the stage for the 1939 Nazi-Soviet pact that in turn unleashed World War II. But Stalin's earlier actions—from his Comintern policies and expansionist ambitions to the domestic terror that suicidally shattered the Red Army while shocking

Western public opinion with its savagery—had already made common cause with the West extremely difficult.

So when in 1941 the United States and USSR found themselves allies in a life-or-death struggle against Nazism, the demonization of "US imperialism" was seriously complicated. Some easing of ideological orthodoxy could not be avoided, as Stalin addressed his Soviet comrades as "brothers and sisters" while enlisting the Russian Orthodox Church in the national-patriotic cause. And the sheer scale of initiatives, from Lend Lease (US military and humanitarian aid) to the expansion of allied embassy staffs (particularly the Americans, to coordinate many joint activities), greatly multiplied the range of US-Soviet contacts—political, military, economic, and, inevitably, social. An example of the latter was junior attaché Robert Tucker's courtship of a young Russian woman, which culminated in one of many such "inter-allied" marriages of those years (Tucker 1982). Stalin's secret police tried to enforce ideological "vigilance." But whether they were simply overwhelmed by the vast number of new Soviet-Western associations, or whether many simply ceased to fear the police in an atmosphere of "The devil may care" and "Who knows what tomorrow may bring," the period of wartime alliance saw the popularity of Americans soar among ordinary Russians.[3] Many were deeply appreciative of lifesaving food aid, which helped undermine propaganda on America's irremediable hostility, while others admired the dynamic and prosperous society that showed through such nominally pro-Stalin initiatives as public screening of the US film *Mission to Moscow*.[4] Wartime ambassador Averell Harriman was greatly admired in Moscow and, on the whole, the desperation, dislocation, and higher common purpose of defeating fascism went far in countering nearly a decade of anti-American propaganda (Kennan 1967, 234).

The controls had hardly vanished, as the saga of Alexander Solzhenitsyn—a young Red Army officer arrested for an anti-Stalin remark—attests. But for every new Gulag inmate such as Solzhenitsyn, there were many more soldiers and administrators whom the war had brought into intimate contact with life beyond the Iron Curtain. Mindful of the seditious ideas that tsarist officers had brought back to Russia after the defeat of Napoleon and occupation of Paris, Stalin had millions of returning veterans interrogated or jailed to stanch the "contagion." Still, on the whole, the experience of war inevitably meant loss of the near-absolute control Stalin had previously exerted over knowledge and opinion about the West. Diplomats' accounts vividly convey the popular Soviet yearning for a new life—a more humane society at home, and greater openness to societies abroad—that had grown widespread by the terrible war's end. A spontaneous, joyous demonstration gathered at the US embassy upon news of Germany's surrender. Kennan—acting ambassador at that moment—received a seemingly endless ovation while junior staffers such as Tucker were saluted, cheered, embraced, and swept up in the delirious mob that for hours defied orders to disperse (Kennan 1967, 242–245; Tucker 1982).

The onset of the Cold War quickly squelched such open pro-Americanism, and the renewal of arrests and persecutions choked off the "person-to-person" diplomacy that had burgeoned during the war (in addition to heightened surveillance and secret police harassment, Soviet citizens were soon legally barred from marrying foreigners). But even among those Russians later convinced of President Truman's perfidy or various Western threats against the USSR, many maintained a lingering, sometimes powerful, admiration for America. And the knowledge and insights on Russia gained by a select group of American diplomats would last a lifetime.

American Diplomacy in the Thaw Era and Late Cold War

Viewed from afar, post–World War II issues in US-Soviet relations bear little resemblance to those that followed World War I. Instead of a shattered decrepit empire, the USSR stood astride a mighty new one; in place of a besieged Bolshevik Party confronted by civil war, the country was ruled by a powerful communist party led by the mighty Stalin. And instead of an isolationist America inclined to ignore Europe, the United States stood ready to take up the mantle of world leadership and challenge the "communist threat."

But when we turn to the challenges of diplomacy, the similarities between these two epochs impress as much as the differences. As before, the Western, particularly American, tendency to see absolutes and demonize enemies gained the upper hand. As earlier, reaction to the hostility or provocation of the adversary was tempered neither by understanding of that adversary's legitimate interests and concerns nor by moderation in the policies that resulted. As in 1918–1920, in 1948–1950 extreme "ideologization" of the conflict produced hysteria and overreaction. And as after World War I, America's Russia policy after World War II often ignored the counsel of its most experienced and insightful diplomats.

Kennan's warnings toward the end of the war against too-concessionary policies toward the USSR in Eastern Europe and too-optimistic expectations for postwar cooperation with Stalin fell on deaf ears; now the inevitable disappointment of those expectations caused the predictable swing in Washington to excessive pessimism and militarization—against which Kennan argued with equal futility (Kennan 1967, passim). Kennan's understanding of historic continuities in Russian policy and the enduring attractions of the West (and, now, America in particular) convinced him that American firmness in defending clear but limited national interests should be tempered by moderation and patience for a time during which the Soviet regime could be expected to "mellow" or reform in a liberal direction. Alas, he could not convince official Washington of the need for such moderation, and the famous "long telegram" that later became his famous "X-article" on *Sources of Soviet Conduct*—drafted with research assistance on Russian historical context by his then–embassy aide Robert Tucker—was incorrectly received as a call for purely *military* containment (Kennan and Lukacs 1997).

Tucker, for his part, joined to this appreciation of Russian history a growing fascination with personality and leadership in analyzing the "Soviet political mind" (Tucker 1972). At a time when US academic and policy-making opinion was increasingly dominated by an *ideological* interpretation of Soviet behavior and so foresaw no chance for significant change in the Marxist-Leninist system, Tucker began his lifelong study of Russia of the late 1920s through the early 1950s, which he viewed as an epoch in which policy was increasingly decided instead by the aberrant *personality* of one individual: Stalin. From Stalin's pathological drive for "vindictive triumph" over rivals at home to his perceived need for absolute security and control abroad, this approach led Tucker to hypothesize that the exit of said personality could bring radical changes in Soviet politics. These might include the end of domestic terror and a less confrontational stance in foreign affairs, possibilities that were dismissed as "crackpot" by officials in the State Department and also at the RAND Corporation, where Tucker later worked (Tucker 1982).

Quite apart from the ways in which the ideological, "totalitarian" analysis of Soviet politics exacerbated the Cold War while Stalin lived, its greater harm probably came in the missed opportunities for major improvement in US-Soviet ties when the changes that Kennan and Tucker hypothesized came to pass. Stalin died in March 1953 and was succeeded by Nikita Khrushchev, now widely understood to have brought major reform in all areas of Soviet politics.

But at the time, Khrushchev's initiatives were met with deepest skepticism by the dominant "totalitarian" school of Sovietology. De-Stalinization merely reflected a leadership struggle, it argued, and calls for "peaceful coexistence" were but a ruse to cause the West to let down its guard. Economic reforms only followed Western pressure—which should therefore be increased, not relaxed—rather than any genuine desire to decentralize or liberalize the system. The Sino-Soviet split was another trick and could not possibly reflect real disagreement between Moscow's supposed moderation and Beijing's strident Stalinism. Therefore, the apparent "thaw" could only be temporary given the imperatives of the totalitarian system, which necessitated a population kept in thrall by the terror of a "permanent purge" (Friedrich and Brzezinski 1956; Leites 1953).

There is no need to recount all the events, and lost opportunities, of the decade of Khrushchev's rule (such as policy toward a divided Germany or initiatives for disarmament). Nor is it necessary to detail Khrushchev's own mistakes and misdeeds (from Hungary to Cuba), except to note that Stalin's legacy and the continuing strength of Soviet Stalinists were impossible to overcome in a few short years, especially since, in many ways, the policies of US hardliners effectively abetted those of Soviet hardliners who opposed Khrushchev. One who understood this dangerous dynamic and sought to counter the prevailing pessimism on post-Stalin prospects was another seasoned "Russia hand," Ambassador Llewellyn Thompson. Bucking Eisenhower-era fears of a communist monolith, Thompson correctly analyzed Soviet weakness—and consequent venues for cooperation—on issues from Germany and China to nuclear arms control (Mayers 1995, 202–209). Alas, not only the dominant "totalitarian" school of analysis, but also the continuing McCarthyite legacy in politics, fueled the secrecy, suspicion, and mutual recrimination of such incidents as the U-2 spy plane scandal of 1960 that derailed major progress toward "peaceful coexistence." Surveying Washington's blinders, Kennan lamented that when the United States finally got the Soviet leader it had been waiting for, it proceeded to do much to undermine him:

[I]n the late 1940s, numbers of worthy people in this country suddenly and belatedly discovered . . . the evil of Communist subversion . . . which had actually reached its highest point several years earlier and was by that time definitely on the wane. Today [in 1960] there are many equally worthy people who appear to be discovering for the first time that there was such a thing as the Stalin era, and who evidently have much difficulty distinguishing it from what we have known since 1953. I could even name professional "Sovietolo-gists," private and governmental, who seem afraid to admit to themselves or to others that Stalin is really dead. (Kennan 1961, 397)

If Khrushchev, ousted by a conservative Politburo cabal in 1964, ultimately was unable to build enduring positive relations with the United States and also failed in efforts to reform the Stalinist economy (though the end of Stalinist terror must count as a singular positive achievement), he nevertheless suc-ceeded in laying the foundation for a more thoroughgoing Soviet-Western rapprochement a generation later. This he accomplished through policies that began a significant opening of the USSR to the outside world and a far-reach-ing revival of independent critical, liberal-reformist, and even pro-Western opinion in Russia.

Those changes began in a sense with de-Stalinization itself. If the show trials actually had been staged and the purges based on fabricated plots, forged evidence, and forced confessions, then what of the ceaseless capitalist scheming upon which the nonexistent plots had supposedly been based? If the millions imprisoned or executed were really innocent of counterrevolu-tionary activity, what actually had been—and was—the West's stance toward Soviet Russia? These questions hung in the air like a whispered indictment of the entire Leninist-Stalinist international ideology. Soon enough, by the late 1950s, the "thaw" in literary-cultural life began to supply an answer. Media images of the West, long relentlessly hostile, began to be more subtle and mul-tifaceted. Long-banned foreign authors began to be published, new or newly revived journals tentatively reappraised Western culture and philosophy, while pre-Bolshevik and early Soviet-era works that offered a very different view of the West, especially of Russia's European or Western-liberal heritage, circulated in ever-greater numbers. Reformist voices from new-generation poets to prerevolutionary vintage professors were heard everywhere from public squares to university podiums. The new official line of peaceful coex-istence, which so contrasted with Stalin's view of inevitable apocalyptic war, was but the least of this incipient "new thinking" about Russia's place in world history and politics (English 2000).

Even more numerous changes began in the early 1960s. The beginning of large-scale cultural and academic exchanges with the West opened the floodgates to long-denied information and images of life in Western societies. Foreign students began appearing at Soviet universities. For Soviet special-ists on international affairs—economists and historians, scientists and policy analysts—the "thaw" was still greater. Regular access to Western media and scholarly literature, new institutions of academic freedom to debate (albeit still behind closed doors) once-heretical ideas, and even the opportunity to travel abroad and learn about the West firsthand, all emerged seemingly overnight.

The powerful impact of these developments on a younger generation of Soviet intellectuals and, in turn, their role in the *perestroika*-era policies that ended the Cold War, have been examined in a diverse new literature on Soviet intellectual-political change (Evangelista 1999; English 2000). From the Pugwash and Dartmouth disarmament conferences to the Helsinki process, and including a vast range of lesser-known cultural and academic exchanges, such programs would wax, wane, and wax again through the post-Khrushchev, Brezhnev-détente, and post-détente eras (mid-1960s through early 1980s) with an influence largely unseen from abroad but strongly supporting the steady growth of liberal-reformist thought at home (Richmond 1987, 2000; Thomas 2001; Rotblat and Alfren 1972).[5]

What, then, of people-to-people diplomacy over these years? Key insight is offered in the career of our third Princetonian, Jack Matlock, who like Kennan and Tucker is another remarkable scholar-cum-diplomat whose experience spans these critical decades. Educated in Russian studies, after initially teaching Russian language and literature at Dartmouth in the mid-1950s, Matlock entered the Foreign Service in the Kennan mold—as a young analyst better schooled in Russian affairs than most of his superiors—and gained his first posting to Moscow in 1961 (Matlock 1995, 8–9). Some recall Matlock as the junior analyst who, in the midst of the 1962 Cuban Missile Crisis, correctly divined Khrushchev's unwillingness to escalate and so highlighted the opportunity for a crisis-ending deal with President Kennedy. Fewer are aware of Matlock's distinction in another pursuit, that of a most active "personal" diplomacy:

The Khrushchev "thaw" was just beginning, and some small cracks in the wall isolating Soviet citizens from foreign diplomats had appeared. [My wife] Rebecca and I were determined to get outside the diplomatic ghetto and mix with Soviet citizens, at least to the degree we could without endangering them. We tried every approach we could think of to meet Russians, but usually after an encounter on a train or in a restaurant, say, the contact would terminate, sometimes with apologies that another meeting was just not convenient . . . obviously the KGB had warned our acquaintances not to see us. Only two things worked. First, we began inviting American and other foreign students from Soviet universities (exchanges were just beginning) to come to our apartment for informal evenings, and as we got to know them we encouraged them to bring their Soviet friends. . . . We also learned that Soviet cultural figures eligible to visit the United States would be allowed to meet us before and after the visit and prominent Americans who came to Moscow as part of an exchange would be allowed to meet their Soviet counterparts. Thus, we were able to meet and entertain writers and scholars, particularly during Robert Frost's visit in 1962. By the time we left Moscow after a two-year tour, we had gotten to know several dozen people, including writers, artists, and theater directors, many of whom became friends for life. I had traveled to fourteen of the fifteen Soviet republics, and our family had grown from three children to five, one born in a Moscow hospital. (Matlock 1995, 9)

This unique initiative laid a vital foundation for subsequent people-to-people diplomacy in the détente-era 1970s, when Matlock was again posted to Moscow as Deputy Chief of Mission. Many others—some diplomats, but more often scientists, scholars, and journalists—played a similar role whose *cumulative* liberalizing impact probably rivaled that of other factors as diverse as foreign radio broadcasts (the influence of the BBC, Voice of America, and Radio Liberty was considerable), international summit meetings, and a Western-backed human rights movement (Alexeyeva 1986). But, as with post-Stalin cultural and scientific exchanges more generally, the "payoff" in encouraging a small but influential cadre of strongly reformist, pro-Western intellectuals and policy experts would only be realized in the 1980s when a new leader sought their counsel in a radical overhaul of the entire Soviet system.

Diplomacy during *Perestroika* and the Cold War's End

The dominant interpretation of Mikhail Gorbachev's sweeping domestic and foreign policy reforms has been the "Realist" school's power-based explanation: Gorbachev withdrew from superpower competition abroad and liberalized at home because he had no choice. The USSR was broke, with the arms race stretching the economy beyond its limits. Efforts to ground *perestroika* in liberal-humanist philosophy or to credit the Cold War's end to the discarding of Leninist ideology and the embrace of interdependence are misleading. These were just fig leaves, an effort to make a virtue of necessity. Gorbachev did what any other leader in his place would have done—he had no choice.[6] In this view, the only leader who really deserves special credit for the Cold

War's rapid and peaceful end is US President Ronald Reagan, for his first-term military buildup that supposedly pushed the USSR over the edge (Schweizer 1996).

An alternative, "leadership" interpretation of the Cold War's end instead focuses on *perestroika* author Gorbachev, arguing that he was a singular statesman for the dramatic reforms he launched, particularly given the rigid Leninist, anti-Western communist party milieu from which he emerged. Wholly unexpected in the West (at least by Realists, until after the fact when Gorbachev's reforms were seen to be inevitable), sweeping democratization of the single-party domestic system and a dramatic turn to antimilitarist, cooperative multilateralism in foreign policy were in fact rooted in Gorbachev's own liberal-humanist philosophy of politics (Brown 1996). A third, ideas-based explanation of *perestroika* at home and "new thinking" abroad emphasizes just that—*thinking*, belief systems, or ideology—as the main motive for reform. *Perestroika* came through a sweeping change of worldview that had slowly but steadily grown over the preceding decades to capture a significant portion of the post-Stalin intellectual and even policymaking elite (English 2000).

There is something to each of these explanations: economic crisis clearly encouraged Gorbachev to try increasingly bold reforms once in office and probably were responsible for the ruling Politburo's gamble on the innovative Gorbachev in the first place; but the biggest gambles were Gorbachev's. No other leadership candidate of the time possessed anything near his reformist instincts, much less his unique combination of risk-taking impulse and liberal-humanist core beliefs. These were self-evidently critical in his philosophical attraction to more sweeping domestic and foreign policy change once his initial, timid, Politburo-backed reforms failed to bear fruit. Ideas too played a partly independent role, in that neither the broader philosophy of humanism and international cooperation, nor the specific policy reforms (and reformist advisers) they supported, would have been "ready and waiting" for Gorbachev to tap were it not for their previous development and powerful ideational hold over a key cohort of Soviet intellectuals.

This third point brings us back to public and people-to-people diplomacy once again. And not just in emphasizing again the importance of such initiatives during the decades of thaw and détente in the 1960s and 1970s, but also in the period of reformist implementation during the mid- to late 1980s. On the crucial questions of when and why Gorbachev moved from moderate to radical reforms, and how he came to embrace a liberal-integrationist world-view, we know that some high-level diplomacy was vital. This refers not to the formalities of summit meetings and negotiations with US officials, but to his personal ties with mostly European figures. Some, such as those with British Prime Minister Margaret Thatcher, grew out of official state business but soon came to include wide-ranging private political-philosophical debate. Others, such as with French President François Mitterrand, were crucial in convincing Gorbachev of the prospects for common ground with the then-seemingly intractable Americans. Perhaps Gorbachev's closest European confidant was Spanish Prime Minister Felipe González, for whom Gorbachev not only developed great personal regard but whose talks with the Soviet leader about the problems of democratizing a one-party system were particularly important given that Spain was but a decade removed from Franco's dictatorship (English 2000, chaps. 5–6). A special regard eventually developed with the US Secretary of State George Shultz, who after negotiations often replaced his diplomatic hat with his professor's cap—his specialty being economics and business—to encourage Gorbachev and his allies on necessary steps along the path to a market economy.

A unique place is held by the peripatetic Matlock who—owing to his broad Soviet experience, excellent Russian, and energetic outreach to numerous individuals on all issues connected with *perestroika*—was both a superb diplomat and prominent fixture of glasnost. Of course he represented the United States, the key foreign country insofar as the international (and domestic) goals of Gorbachev's reform agenda were concerned; the US ambassador would have been a central figure in any case. But from his early advocacy to Reagan of "doing business" with Gorbachev, through his insightful analytical and crucial intermediary roles as ambassador, Matlock broke down barriers, prejudices, and stereotypes on both sides of the US-Soviet relationship. He was in close contact throughout with Soviet reformers and Gorbachev advisers, and the trust he had built was reflected in the fact that he was one of a few Moscow ambassadors—maybe the only one—who could request and get an immediate audience with the Soviet leader.

But all this is not quite public diplomacy, an area where Matlock was equally outstanding. It is impossible in just a few lines to do justice to the tremendous public outreach that occurred during his tenure in Moscow. Matlock, it seemed, met with all and sundry in the USSR—writers, reformers, dissidents, non-Russian nationalists, soldiers, and students. He traveled everywhere, always taking the trouble to deliver part (if not all) of his speech or remarks in the local language. His wife Rebecca was an equal partner in this outreach, keeping a full schedule of her own meetings with artists and teachers, presiding over exhibitions of her excellent photography, and also researching a history of Spaso House, the US ambassador's residence in Moscow. Spaso House, indeed, became at times as important as the Soviet Palace of Congresses or the Writers' Union as a vital political venue. No *perestroika*-era figure of any importance, it seemed, did not speak at or attend at least one of Spaso House's continual round of receptions, concerts, readings, and gatherings (Mayer 1995; Matlock 1995, passim). Matlock was soon as sought-after as an interview subject by the burgeoning *glasnost*-era national and local media as he was by the Kremlin as a conduit to the White House. In all these activities, no better "goodwill ambassador" and no more effective diplomatic advocate of US-Soviet rapprochement could be imagined.

If the preceding evokes some of the vital atmosphere of public intercourse in the time of *perestroika*, two additional aspects of that heady time—the mid- to late 1980s—should also be noted. One is that, by shedding taboos and injecting all manner of long-suppressed issues into the public debate, public intercourse played a crucial role in advancing Gorbachev's "new thinking" or Cold War–ending agenda. Things that Gorbachev believed, but that were still too radical for him to argue before conservative Communist Party bodies, were thus "legitimized." The second is that not only Matlock but also several other Princetonians played important parts in that ever-bolder public discourse. One was Tucker, whose publications on Stalin now appeared in Russian translation and whose public appearances and media interviews evoked enormous interest. While the story of his wartime marriage to a Russian girl and their long mistreatment by Stalin-era officials was the subject of several interviews, Tucker's insights into Stalin played a major role in *glasnost*-era reconsiderations of the Soviet past. Another was Tucker's erstwhile graduate student and Princeton faculty colleague Stephen Cohen, whose parallel work on the Soviet 1920s–1930s (and his tenure as a commentator for *The Nation* on US-Soviet issues) attracted even greater interest. Indeed, Cohen's biography of Nikolai Bukharin, and the "lost alternative" of a moderate, non-Stalinist path to socialism that he represented, attracted broad interest.[7] As inspiration for the possibility of a more social-democratic USSR, and with the author's high media profile and advocacy of bold steps to improve US-Soviet relations, Cohen became one of the most visible and influential foreign participants in *perestroika*.

A final note on Kennan, Tucker's mentor, is appropriate. Already in his mid-eighties at the outset of Gorbachev's reforms, his consequently limited stamina precluded the sort of involvement in *perestroika* that Tucker and especially Cohen engaged in. Still, his stature as the dean of US "Russia hands" lent his occasional comments much gravity. Kennan's early *perestroika*-era writings—eschewing self-congratulation at the rise of the reformism he had foreseen, to frequent scorn, decades earlier—understood the world-changing implications of Gorbachev's undertaking even as most Sovietologists remained skeptical (Kennan 1988). Long critical of the "nuclear delusion," Kennan heartily endorsed the progress on arms control that Gorbachev facilitated (even as US hardliners continued to delay and obstruct). And, again in character with long-held perspectives on US-Russia relations, he cautioned about the difficulties and opposition Gorbachev faced, and subsequently argued for restraint in the resultant turmoil of communism's collapse and the change and confusion that followed (Ullman 1999).

Cold War Diplomacy after the Cold War

This, at last, brings us to the post–Cold War period and some final observations on diplomacy—traditional, public, and people-to-people—over two decades of relations with post-Soviet Russia. Why did these ties, so strong at the beginning of the 1990s, turn so sour? And why, since 2000, have they returned to a state that so frequently recalls the Cold War past? This is not the place to recapitulate in detail all the problems at issue (e.g., NATO expansion, the Chechen and Kosovo Wars, policy toward Iran and Iraq, Georgia and Ukraine) or to analyze in depth the respective sides' missteps. Suffice it to say—indeed, I will simply stipulate, since it is a perspective broadly shared by experts—that the United States erred badly in its "triumphalist" and frequently dismissive approach to Russia in the 1990s. Our narrower concern is the diplomatic aspects of that troubled new relationship from which some key lessons are clear. First, the historian's perspective evokes the tragedy of yet another repetition of the mistake first made in 1918–1921, then again in 1945–1948: namely the high-handed or punitive treatment of a rival great power. The precise circumstances were different in each case: isolation and intervention after World War I, exaggerated fears and militarization after World War II. This time—paradoxically, given the very positive beginning and enormous goodwill fostered by public diplomacy in the *perestroika* era—a most friendly Russia was nevertheless greeted by condescension and neglect, and soon enough by a wholly unnecessary and provocative military challenge. We can do no better than to recall Kennan's warning at the time of NATO's creation, and the establishment of airfields and missile bases, around the USSR in the 1950s:

> But here again *le mieux est l'ennemi du bien*. Surely as one moves one's bases and military facilities towards the Soviet frontiers there comes a point where they tend to create the very thing they were designed to avoid. It is not for us to assume that there are no limits to Soviet patience in the face of encirclement by American bases. Quite aside from political considerations, no great country, peaceful or aggressive, rational or irrational, could sit by and witness with indifference the progressive studding of its own frontiers with the military installations of a great-power competitor. Here again, a compromise must be struck. With a view to the peculiarities of the Russian mentality and tradition . . . [let us] not operate to reduce the Soviet leaders to a state of mind in which for them the only question is not "whether" but "when." (Kennan 1967, 141–142)

Replace "Soviet" with "Russian" and this warning is as appropriate to the 1990s as the 1950s. Indeed, it could have been repeated verbatim as it was, but to an opposite purpose, in the Clinton administration's pro-NATO expansion slogan, "Not whether, but when!" As before, Kennan spoke out—joined by Cohen, Matlock, and a large group of other scholars and diplomatic veterans—to argue against what he foresaw as "the strategic blunder of the century." Yet these warnings, as before, had no corrective impact, raising yet another parallel with earlier foolish or shortsighted treatment of Russia at key historical junctures. This time—much more than the "still-malleable" Bolshevik view of America in the early 1920s or the alliance-bred, popular pro-Americanism of the mid-1940s—early post-Soviet elite *and* mass opinion included an extreme, even romanticized, admiration of America that is unlikely to be repeated anywhere again. Yet, thanks to a 1990s policy of broadly dismissing Russia's legitimate international interests, a misguided missionary or "crusading" attempt to remake Russia overnight into America's political-economic image, and a general lack of regard for the justified yet deeply wounded pride of a recent superpower fast fallen low, such "Weimar Germany" treatment almost inevitably contributed much to a "Weimar Russia" result (Cohen 2001; see also Yanov 1995).

But unlike 1920s–1930s Germany, 1990s–2000s Russia possessed vast and valuable natural resources that fueled a revival of Russian power and pride under the inevitably more authoritarian leadership of Vladimir Putin. Yet when the initially pro-Western Putin extended a hand in the aftermath of the 9/11 terrorist attacks (Nichols 2002), this "second chance" for a better post–Cold War US-Russia relationship was broadly spurned. Instead came the extreme unilateralism of the Bush administration, the scornful rejection of dialogue and disrespect for international law, and for Russia the simultaneous imposition of trade sanctions, rejection of serious nuclear arms control, and yet another round of NATO expansion—this time, right up to Russia's borders. It seemed, at its worst, a marriage of the most cavalier liberal-internationalism with conservative-ideological anti-Russianism (the same combination seen in the policy of Woodrow Wilson, with which Kennan began his historical critique).

Public Diplomacy in Post-Soviet Russia

This brings us, finally, to an evaluation of US public diplomacy. How has it fared in post-Soviet Russia? The preceding chronicle was necessary to set the context for our answer: It has fared poorly, and not chiefly because the opportunities for "selling" the United States have been lacking, but rather because both the "product" and the "sales technique" have been defective. Far from restricted, for much of the post-Soviet period the tools of public diplomacy have enjoyed broad freedom of operation. This includes a largely open country, including its borders and airwaves. Western and especially US culture enjoy virtually free access to interested Russian consumers. Private travel has ballooned. An expanded diplomatic staff can organize and meet almost wherever and with whomever they choose. Federally sponsored as well as private exchange programs are numerous. Funding for these activities, as well as for United States Agency for International Development (USAID) and US government–supported private projects, has been lavish, to the tune of billions of dollars. Nongovernmental organizations (NGOs) have operated relatively freely in areas from the environment and elections to human rights and other prodemocracy or civil society–building initiatives. It is true that, following Putin's authoritarian turn, recent years have seen restrictions on NGOs, the independent media, and foreign religious groups. However, the 1990s—a decade of nearly unfettered freedom for both traditional and public

diplomacy—was also a time when such activities failed more often than succeeded and anti-American, anti-Western attitudes grew exponentially (Shiraev and Zubok 2000). What went wrong?

Joseph Stiglitz, Nobel laureate and former senior World Bank economist,
answers unequivocally: it was the United States and leading Western states,
through ill-conceived marketization and privatization programs that they
essentially forced upon Moscow, who "lost Russia" (Stiglitz 2003). Russia had
no choice but to adopt one-size-fits-all "Washington Consensus" restructuring priorities in exchange for aid, investment, and any chance at integration
into the developed world market. This pushed a crumbling economy into
destruction of an already-weakened public sector (healthcare, education,
social services) for the false promise of a soon-to-be-thriving private sector.
Instead, rampant asset-stripping and rent-seeking destroyed numerous enterprises that a more cautious, context-sensitive restructuring program could
have revived, and the most valuable state properties—chiefly, natural resource
firms—wound up in a few corrupt hands as poverty soared (Reddaway and
Glinsky 2001). Perversely, rapid privatization was actually hailed in the early
to mid-1990s as a signal success by US officials and various government-sup-
ported private contractors and consultants. It is this network of consultants
and contractors, many generously funded by USAID in that agency's marketization, democratization, and civil society–building programs, that has been
the subject of withering critique since the mid-1990s (Stavrakis 1996; see also
Goldman 1997; Wedel 2001). As such, it is key to understanding "what went
wrong" in post-Soviet public diplomacy as well.

The charges are several: *bureaucracy and micromanagement*, which not
only wasted much time and money but also tilted aid toward a limited pool
of well-connected, "US-friendly" Russian organizations at the expense of
many smaller, local, "traditionalist" Russian activists and their often better-
grounded initiatives; *corruption*, ranging from contract-padding and petty
theft to major fraud and insider trading involving US as well as Russian officials "feeding at the USAID trough"; and *ideology*, not only that which explicitly hailed an unfettered market but also that which implicitly continued a
Cold War–tinged "neoliberal Western model—good, socially focused Russian tradition—bad" type of condescension that frequently backfired when
imposed in post-Soviet conditions. Most obvious in programs targeting
the economy, a similar mentality pervaded many private as well as USAID
democracy-promotion efforts, from civil service and public health reform to

women's rights (Stavrakis 1996; see also Funk 1993; Tucker 1996; Heitlinger 1996; Goldman 1997; Henderson 2002; McIntosh-Sundstrom 2002; Richter 2002).

Insofar as democracy-promotion is concerned, these tendencies contributed to two interrelated problems: *donor-driven demand for rapid and quantifiable results,* which led to such pathologies as "concentrating on a very narrow set of . . . professionalized NGOs" (Ottaway and Carothers 2000, 11) and "the false impression that proliferating NGOs and a blossoming civil society are one and the same thing" (Noakes 2008); and *political and cultural ignorance,* reflected in reliance on "practitioners with little knowledge of the region . . . to implement strategies for building democratic institutions that were developed in Western capitals" (Mendelson and Glenn, 2002, 3). Together these encouraged a "professionalization" of Western-savvy NGOs, with an agenda driven by Western priorities "at the expense of closer linkages with communities" (Fagan 2005, 535–536) and "local activists" who better understood the problems of democratization (Mendelson and Glenn 2002, 3). "In other words, foreign funding can sometimes cause organizations to fall out of touch with the needs of civil society at large" (Noakes 2008), while "Western normative approaches to civil society straightjacket the concept's ability, and those who wield it, to identify and address critical political and economic realities as perceived and experienced in locally distinct contexts" (Chaplowe and Engo-Tjega 2007, 263).

Millions were spent—often wasted—on programs advancing a US-centric agenda that alienated a once strongly pro-Western Russian constituency by its arrogance, ignorance, and insensitivity to Russia's real problems and prospects. It is little wonder then that the positive public-diplomacy impact of many laudable programs was outweighed by the negative effect of so much wasteful, ham-fisted, often hypocritical activity sponsored by the US government and administered by legions of bureaucrats or "professional development experts" who were frequently anything but expert on Russia and its unique post-Soviet conditions.

"Hypocrisy" is a strong charge, yet it is what many Russians came to perceive not only in America's larger foreign policy ("You must respect international law, but we are above it") but also in specific instances of US activity with respect to market- and democracy-building efforts in Russia. Many cases of rigged contracts and petty if not major fraud contradicted in deeds the values of honesty, open competition, and respect for law loudly proclaimed in America's words (Wedel 2000). A far more critical test of principles came just over a year into Russia's "shock therapy" when in the summer of 1993—as societal misery and hence public opposition to the "reforms" soared—President Boris Yeltsin responded to opposition from the Russian parliament with the flagrantly unconstitutional step of shuttering parliament and announcing new elections (as well as promulgating a new "superpresidential" constitution). A majority of parliamentary deputies denounced these measures while a militant minority prepared for armed confrontation. Goaded by Yeltsin, they "took the bait" in October with an assault to break out of their besieged parliament headquarters and seize key government buildings. The army, at Yeltsin's orders, responded with overwhelming force (tanks shelling the parliament, a commando raid to neutralize remaining opposition) at the cost of several hundred casualties. Russia was in shock as Yeltsin pushed ahead with early elections and a referendum on his new constitution. Tellingly, at least insofar as Russian opinion was concerned, the new parliament was even *more* conservative than the one just disbanded. Paradoxically, however, the constitution was simultaneously approved, though subsequent investigation revealed that this was fraudulently achieved.[8] Thus, less than two years into Russia's post-Soviet transition, not only the government's US-backed reforms but that government itself lost much of its popular—and arguably its legal—legitimacy.

We recall this episode not only because it was quickly forgotten in the West—though it was an absolutely searing experience, a turning point in outlook for many Russians—but also because that active forgetting reflects a flagrant example of the corrosive hypocrisy noted above. At the time, though US officials "regretted" the violence, they also uniformly blamed Yeltsin's elected opposition for the confrontation, pooh-poohed the unconstitutional closure of parliament and fraudulent passage of a new constitution, and pressed ahead with "business as usual," although even some Yeltsin admirers later admitted that "election fraud tarnished the results" (McFaul 2001). In other words, seemingly oblivious to popular opinion in Russia, the most fundamental violations of the rule of law were excused through a positively Leninist "the ends justify the means." Sadly, not only Western statesmen but also many Western NGOs, aid officials, and prominent Russia experts/consultants either openly or tacitly took the same position on the fateful drama of September–December 1993.[9] It was a shameful episode in both official and public diplomacy that they would like to—but many Russians could not—forget.

This is not to tar the efforts of many individuals and groups engaged in rule-of-law and democracy-promotion projects in Russia. Though frequently marred by the bureaucracy, cultural insensitivity, and US-centric focus criticized above, their sponsors were generally honest, well meaning, and hardly responsible for the hypocrisy of their government's larger Russia policy. But in the eyes of many Russians, including those activists struggling to promote liberal reforms *against* the corruption and cronyism of Yeltsin's regime, the distinction was often lost and US public diplomacy suffered a grievous setback.

Laboring under this cloud, public diplomacy efforts in the 1990s faced an uphill struggle that were only further complicated by various other early decisions. Robert Strauss, a longtime Democratic Party operative who possessed no Russian expertise and no professional diplomatic experience whatsoever, initially replaced the remarkable Matlock as ambassador. "Sensitive people felt the difference as Spaso's cavernous rooms less frequently hosted intellectual soirees. People grumbled that delegations of crass businessmen would entirely displace Russian artists and scientists" (Mayers 1995, 253). The US Congress initially cut cultural and other exchange programs by nearly half as emphasis shifted from understanding, informing, and persuading both elite and ordinary Russians to implementing a largely US-designed agenda for change. Post-1993 aid to the tune of several billion dollars was heavily weighted toward business and trade. US officials spoke of giving Russia "the spinach treatment"—"Eat it, *we* know what's good for you!"—showing callousness in the face of deep and prolonged public suffering (Talbott 2002). Russians developed a growing distaste for the "Bill and Boris Show," that is, the Clinton administration's personification of Yeltsin as the only hope for reform while largely ignoring the colossal corruption of his regime (Ermarth 1999; Wedel 2000). This was only heightened by US intervention in his flawed reelection in 1996—actions that ranged from overt cheerleading and campaign assistance to turning a blind eye to Yeltsin's blatant media and campaign-finance violations (Mendelson 2001; Wedel 2001; also Weir 1996).

Since the depths of the early to mid-1990s, public diplomacy efforts have revived or been rejuvenated in notable ways. The United States has increased support for many local initiatives (including small-scale grants programs) together with expanded representation throughout Russia; new consulates, libraries, and "American corners" now number more than two dozen (Dolinsky 2008). Russian-language publication of books and magazines has grown as well, along with renewed support for the VOA and Radio Liberty, while embassy outreach to the public through speakers, interviews, concerts, and other cultural events continues. Yet these efforts have met only modest success. Whether measured by listenership, website visits, or the popularity of such publications as the quarterly *Otkroi Ameriku* ("Discover America"), they evoke only modest interest (in comparison with their counterparts of the 1960s, 1970s, and 1980s) in today's Russia of far more diverse sources of information and entertainment (Dolinsky 2008). The success of the *New York Times* Russian-language online articles and blogs, to cite just one example, makes many government-sponsored initiatives seem almost quaint in a society where Internet access has grown rapidly and Russians have so many alternative sources of information and virtually unlimited digital access to Western cultural and media products (some 43 percent of Russians are now online and the growth rate is a rapid 20 percent per year).[10]

Yet it is not only the competition, but also the "sales technique" that is still problematic. Consider the "Stalin question," that is, attitudes toward the brutal dictator and his epoch in Soviet state-building and foreign policy of the 1930s–1950s. Many analysts agree that perceptions of Stalin—whether as a murderous and imperialistic tyrant whose legacy was overwhelmingly negative, or as a wise leader who strengthened his country against domestic and foreign threats alike—tell something important about the state of civil society and democratic attitudes in general. Yet the late 1990s–early 2000s growth in positive Russian attitudes about Stalin has been interpreted in different ways, with very different proposed responses. One, more alarmist and short-sighted, sees the public "failing" a crucial "Stalin test" with dire implications for Russia's future (Mendelson and Gerber 2006). Another, more judicious and far-sighted, sees instead an understandable backlash against the degradation of the 1990s as well as a normal emotional response to the vilification, especially from abroad, of the society that millions spent much of their lives building (Sherlock 2011). The former prescribes a US-led "mass education campaign." The latter, recognizing that it is precisely the foreign imposition of demands for rapid societal transformation that causes backlash, calls instead for a patient, long-term effort of scholarly-historical cooperation. These divergent prescriptions for addressing the same "illness" reflect two sharply different and highly consequential approaches to *all* aspects of societal transformation—including diplomacy—in post-Soviet Russia.

Perhaps paradoxically, public diplomacy fares better when it struggles in the shadows against official opposition than when there is little resistance.

Perhaps it is better received when it is the work of highly dedicated individual scholars, journalists, activists, and specialist-diplomats—not a vast government-funded and bureaucratically managed campaign. Of course, the US image was better when it was the imagined, not the real, America that Russians pondered. This may reflect a general tendency to idealize the unknown, the forbidden, with disillusion inevitable when it becomes real and familiar. Postcommunist transition was always going to be a harder road than most citizens living under state socialism imagined, with disappointment widespread even in the most successful transition states. All the same, as Cohen (2011) has so eloquently argued, Russian disillusion with America is based on much more. A country long respected as the linchpin of international fairness and justice, which then flagrantly thumbs its nose at international opinion and law, has heedlessly tarnished its own image. A country that long denounced Soviet torture of political prisoners, but then itself illegally "renders" and imprisons right-less suspects that it also tortures, has debased itself in the eyes of those who once looked to it for inspiration. And a country that once encouraged Gorbachev's withdrawal from Eastern Europe with the promise of a "new world order" without military blocs, but that then expands its own bloc right up to Russia's doorstep while arguing "We never *really* promised" via a technicality, is in many Russian eyes little more than a hypocritical bully. Those who would improve America's image in Russia confront a most difficult task. It is, indeed, as much the product as the sales technique that needs improving (Seib 2011).

Notes

1. Root, whose hectoring about continuing the war effort made him "as welcome in Russia as smallpox," recommended the United States establish a program of political lectures and YMCA-sponsored recreational activities to burnish America's image and stiffen Russian soldiers' spines (Mayers 1995, 78). While these could be viewed as public diplomacy of a sort, such efforts must be at least minimally cognizant of their intended audience—and the larger political context—to have any chance of success. Root's ill-founded and supremely ill-timed proposals were anything but.

2. A prescient warning to this effect by Felix Cole, the US consul in Archangel, was suppressed by the anti-Semitic and Germanophobic David Francis, America's leftover ambassador to the tsarist court. Francis banned contacts with the Bolsheviks, whom he saw as part of a German-Jewish plot; Lockhart, the experienced British consul in Moscow, skeptically quipped that "Old Francis doesn't know a Left Social-Revolutionary from a potato" (Mayers 1995, 78–85—quote on 78).

3. For a superb summary of wartime attitudes see Kennan (1961, 349–369).

4. From the gullible book by Joseph Davies, who succeeded Bullitt as ambassador during the terror of the late 1930s; see Hough (1999, 272).

5. Space does not permit justice to a large literature on the vital impact of many other diplomats, exhibition and tour guides, broadcasters, businessmen, and other official and "unofficial" public diplomacy practitioners. See for example Cautes (2005) and Wilford (2009) among many memoirs and studies.

6. This paraphrases the authors' argument (Brooks and Wohlforth 2007); see also Sestanovich 1988.

7. Cohen attracted broad interest well before perestroika. His book had been translated into Russian and circulated underground in the prereform USSR and was even read by Gorbachev at the outset of perestroika (see the Russian edition of Cohen 1980).

8. Via faked results, since the 50 percent participation necessary to validate the constitutional referendum was evidently not reached.

9. Examples include positions on the 1993 crisis taken by Amnesty International (AI) and Human Rights Watch (HRW). The former, citing its limited mandate, simply noted that "President Boris Yeltsin dissolved parliament" with no judgment of the move's legality, and limited its concern to the treatment of prisoners while stating that "we have no position on the banning of specific publications or parties" (Amnesty International 1993). The latter was more clearly partisan, blaming the parliament for the crisis because it had "undermined President Boris Yeltsin's reform program and executive power" (Human Rights Watch 1994) while ignoring the fact that it was the elected parliament's right to oppose policies with which it disagreed and that President Yeltsin, under the existing constitution, could as easily have been charged with "undermining legislative power." "Yeltsin's reform program" was hardly sacrosanct, but in HRW's view opposition to it somehow automatically impugned the parliament. Further, they wrote, the parliament "attempted to seize power" with no explanation that Yeltsin had first shuttered and then physically besieged that parliament (surrounding it with troops when it refused to disband itself and cutting off power, water, and sanitation). Human Rights Watch admitted that parliament's closure "violated key articles of the Russian constitution" but this was justified because "Yeltsin was supported in his action by the heads of state of many democratic governments including the United States" (ibid). But that is precisely the point—a profoundly undemocratic action was endorsed by many democratic states! Rather than legitimizing Yeltsin's actions, as HRW seemed to imagine, this delegitimized the authority and prestige of those who justified it: first, those democratic states who compromised their bedrock principles, and second, those NGOs and other groups who supported this fateful compromise. An ultimate irony is that it was the new, fraudulently approved, "superpresidential" constitution designed to enhance Yeltsin's power that Putin later legally employed to further centralize executive authority—a centralization that the same democracy and human rights advocates now decry. Yet one searches in vain for such advocates' admission that is was their own compromise of the rule of law, for the rule of one man, which has now come home to roost.

10. Internet World Stats (2011); accessed at http://www.internetworldstats.com/.

References

Alexeyeva, Liudmilla. 1986. *US Broadcasting to the Soviet Union*. New York: US Helsinki Watch.

Amnesty International. 1993. *Russia: Amnesty International Closely Monitoring Situation*, AI News Service 126/93 (5 October) and *Amnesty International Concerned at Reports of Ill-Treatment of Political Opponents in Moscow*. AI News Service 130/93 (11 October).

Bohlen, Charles E. 1973. *Witness to History, 1929–1969*. New York: World Book Promotions.

Brooks, Stephen G. and William C. Wohlforth, 2007. "Power, globalization, and the end of the Cold War." In *Explaining War and Peace: Case Studies and Necessary Condition Counterfactuals*, Gary Goertz and Jack S. Levy, eds. 195–236. New York: Routledge.

Brown, Archie. 1996. *The Gorbachev Factor*. Oxford: Oxford University Press.

Cautes, David. 2005. *The Dancer Defects: The Struggle for Cultural Supremacy During the Cold War*. Oxford: Oxford University Press.

Chaplowe, Scott and Ruth B. Engo-Tjega, 2007. "Civil Society Organizations and Evaluation." *Evaluation* 13:2, 257–274.

Cohen, Stephen F. 1980. *Bukharin and the Bolshevik Revolution: A Political Biography 1888–1938*. Oxford: Oxford University Press.

——. 1980. *Bukharin i bolshevistkaia revoliutsiia, politicheskaia biografiia, 1888–1938*: Royal Oak, Michigan: Strathcona Publishing.

——. 2001. *Failed Crusade: America and the Tragedy of Post-Communist Russia*. New York: W.W. Norton.

——. 2011. "Obama's Russia 'Reset': Another Lost Opportunity?" *The Nation*. June 20, 2011, 11–18.

Dolinsky, Aleksey. 2008. *British and US Public Diplomacy in Russia*. Tufts University Public Diplomacy Council, accessed at: http://publicdiplomacycouncil.org/tufts-papers

English, Robert. 2000. *Russia and the Idea of the West: Gorbachev, Intellectuals, and the End of the Cold War*. New York: Columbia University Press.

Ermarth, Fritz W. 1999. "Seeing Russia Plain: The Russian Crisis and American Intelligence." *The National Interest* 58, 5–14.

Evangelista, Matthew. 1999. *Unarmed Forces: The Transnational Movement to End the Cold War*. Ithaca, NY: Cornell University Press.

Fagan, Adam. 2005. "Taking Stock of Civil Society Development in Post-Communist Europe." *Democratization* 12:4, 528–547.

Friedrich, Carl J. and Zbigniew K. Brzezinski, 1956. *Totalitarian Dictatorship and Autocracy*. Cambridge, MA: Harvard University Press.

Funk, Nanette. et al., 1993. "Feminism and Post-Communism." Special symposium in *Hypatia* 8:4, 85–128.

Goldman, Marshall I. 1997. "Ignore Sovietology at Your Risk." *Demokratizatsiya* 5:4, 515–521.

Henderson, Sarah L. 2002. "Selling Civil Society: Western Aid and the Nongovernmental Organization Sector in Russia." *Comparative Political Studies* 35, 139–167.

Heitlinger, Alena. 1996. "Framing Feminism in Post-Communist Czech Republic." *Communist and Post Communist Studies* 29: 1, 77–93.

Hough, Jerry F. 1988. *Russia and the West: Gorbachev and the Politics of Reform.* New York: Simon & Schuster.

Human Rights Watch. 1994. *Human Rights Watch World Report: Russia.* Accessed at: http://www.hrw.org/legacy/reports/1994/WR94/Helsinki-18.htm#P555_166288

Kennan, George F. 1961. *Russia and the West Under Lenin and Stalin.* Boston: Little, Brown & Co.

———. 1967. *Memoirs, 1925–1950.* New York: Pantheon Books.

———. 1972. *Memoirs, 1950–1963.* New York: Pantheon Books.

———. 1988. "The Gorbachev Prospect." *The New York Review of Books.* January 21.

Kennan, George F. and Lukacs, John. 1997. *George F. Kennan and the Origins of Containment, 1944–1946: The Kennan-Lukacs Correspondence.* Columbia, MO: University of Missouri Press.

Leites, Nathan. 1953. *A Study of Bolshevism.* Glencoe, IL: The Free Press.

Matlock, Jack F., Jr. 1995. *Autopsy on an Empire: The American Ambassador's Account of the Collapse of the Soviet Union.* New York: Random House.

Mayers, David. 1995. *The Ambassadors and America's Soviet Policy.* New York: Oxford University Press.

McFaul, Michael F. 2001. *Russia's Unfinished Revolution: Political Change from Gorbachev to Putin.* Ithaca, NY: Cornell University Press.

McIntosh-Sundstrom, Lisa. 2002. "Women's NGOs in Russia: Struggling from the margins." *Demokratizatsiya* 10, 207–229.

Mendelson, Sarah E. 2001. "Democracy assistance and political transition in Russia." *International Security* 25:4.

Mendelson, Sarah E. and John K. Glenn, 2002. "Transnational Networks and NGOs in Post Communist Societies." In *The Power and Limits of NGOs: A Critical Look at Building Democracy in Eastern Europe and Eurasia,* Sarah E. Mendelson and John K. Glenn, eds. 1–28. New York: Columbia University Press.

Mendelson, Sarah E. and Theodore P. Gerber, 2006. "Failing the Stalin Test: Young Russians and their Dictator." *Foreign Affairs* 85:1, 2–10.

Nichols, T. M. 2002. "Russia's Turn West: Sea Change or Opportunism?" *World Policy Journal* 19:4, 13–22.

Noakes, Stephen. 2008. "Applied Research on Support to Civil Society." *Centre for the Study of Democracy.* Queen's University, Kingston, Ontario, Canada. Accessed at http://www.queensu.ca/csd/publications/Support_to_Civil_Society_Overview.pdf

Ottaway, Marina and Carothers, Thomas. 2000. *Funding Virtue: Civil Society Aid and Democracy Promotion.* Washington, D.C., Carnegie Endowment.

Reddaway, Peter and Glinski, Dmitri. 2001. *The Tragedy of Russia's Reforms: Market Bolshevism Against Democracy.* Washington, D.C.: US Institute for Peace.

Richmond, Yale. 1987. *US-Soviet Cultural Exchanges, 1958–1986: Who Wins?* Boulder, CO: Westview Press.

———. 2000. *Cultural Exchange and the Cold War: Raising the Iron Curtain.* University Park, PA: Penn State University Press.

Richter, James. 2002. "Evaluating Western Assistance to Russian Women's Organizations." In *The Power and Limits of NGOs: A Critical Look at Building Democracy in Eastern Europe and Eurasia.* Sarah E. Mendelson and John Glenn, eds. 54–90. New York: Columbia University Press.

Rotblat, Joseph, and H. Alfren, 1972. *Scientists in the Quest for Peace: A History of the Pugwash Conferences.* Cambridge, MA: MIT Press.

Schweizer, Peter. 1996. *Victory: The Reagan Administration's Secret Strategy That Hastened the Collapse of the Soviet Union.* New York, Atlantic Monthly Press.

Seib, Philip. 2011. "Russia is a Testing Ground for US Public Diplomacy." *The CPD Blog-USC Center on Public Diplomacy.* Accessed at http://uscpublicdiplomacy.org/index.php/newswire/cpdblog_detail/russia_is_a_testing_ground_for_us_public_diplomacy/

Sestanovich, Stephen. 1988. "Gorbachev's Foreign Policy: A Diplomacy of Decline." *Problems of Communism* 37:1, 1–15.

Sherlock, Thomas. 2011. "Confronting the Stalinist Past: The Politics of Memory in Russia." *The Washington Quarterly* 34:2, 93–109.

Shiraev, Eric, and Vladislav Zubok. 2000. *Anti-Americanism in Russia: From Stalin to Putin.* New York: Palgrave Macmillan.

Stavrakis, Peter J. 1996 "Bull in a China Shop: USAID's Post-Soviet Mission." *Demokratizatsiya* 4:2, 247–270.

Stiglitz, Joseph E. 2003. *Globalization and its Discontents.* New York: W. W. Norton.

Talbott, Strobe. 2002. *The Russia Hand: A Memoir of Presidential Diplomacy.* New York: Random House.

Thomas, Daniel C. 2001. *The Helsinki Effect: International Norms, Human Rights, and the Demise of Communism.* Princeton, NJ: Princeton University Press.

Tucker, Robert C. 1972. *The Soviet Political Mind: Stalinism and Post-Stalin Change.* New York: W.W. Norton & Co.

———. 1982. "Memoir of a Stalin Biographer." *University: A Princeton Magazine.* November.

———. 1990. *Stalin in Power.* New York: W.W. Norton & Co.

Tucker, Elizabeth. 1996. "The Russian Media's Time of Troubles." *Demokratizatsiya* 4:3, 422-438.

Ullman, Richard. 1999. "The US and the World: An Interview with George Kennan." *The New York Review of Books.* August 12.

Wedel, Janine R. 2000. "Tainted Transactions: Harvard, the Chubais Clan and Russia's Ruin." *The National Interest* 59, 23–34.

———. 2001. *Collision and Collusion: The Strange Case of Western Aid to Eastern Europe.* New York, NY: Palgrave.

Weir, Fred. 1996. "Betting on Boris." *Covert Action Quarterly* 38:41.

Wilford, Hugh. 2009. *The Mighty Wulitzer: How the CIA Played America.* Cambridge, MA: Harvard University Press.

Yanov, Alexander. 1995. *Weimar Russia—And What We Can Do About It.* New York, Slovo-Word Publishers.

2   CHINA

American Public Diplomacy and
US-China Relations, 1949–2012

Robert S. Ross

RELATIONS BETWEEN THE UNITED STATES AND CHINA since 1949 have been characterized by periodic swings between enmity, cooperation, and traditional Great Power competition. In June 1950 the Korean War ushered in a twenty-year period of unremitting hostility. Multiple crises in the Taiwan Strait and the wars in Indochina exacerbated mutual threat perception, and each side engaged in protracted preparation for a US-China war. But in the early 1970s, with increased Sino-Soviet tension and the beginning of the US retreat from the wars in Indochina, China and the United States finessed the Taiwan issue to focus on the common security concern—the growing power of the Soviet Union, which led to heightened threat perceptions of the Soviets. For nearly twenty years until 1989, China and the United States expanded diplomatic relations and established the foundation for enduring bilateral economic and cultural relations. Then, in 1989, the rapid demise of Soviet power and the end of the Cold War eliminated the underlying strategic imperative of US-China cooperation. The Chinese leadership's violent repression of China's democracy movement on June 4, 1989 removed the expectation of a common US-China interest in ongoing Chinese political reform. Since then, the two countries have settled into a traditional Great Power competitive relationship, characterized by strategic competition in East Asia and periodic crises and episodes of heightened strategic tension and economic conflict, even while they continued to develop bilateral economic and cultural relations.

During each of these three post-1949 periods of US-China relations, American public diplomacy possessed distinct characteristics reflecting a combination of developments in US-China relations and in Chinese domestic politics. This chapter examines the impact of American public diplomacy on US-China relations during each of these periods. It addresses whether the absence or presence of American public diplomacy has affected the development of US-China conflict and the degree of bilateral cooperation. The chapter examines public diplomacy from two perspectives. First, for each post-1949 period it considers the influence of the US diplomatic presence in China and US-China ambassadorial relations on cooperation and conflict. Second, for each period it also examines the role of less formal and less direct US government efforts to shape US-China relations, including government outreach programs such as the Voice of America (VOA) and cultural programs. In so doing, the chapter assesses the impact of US public diplomacy on post-1949 US-China relations.

The Absence of Public Diplomacy: US-China Relations, 1949–1973

When the Chinese Communist Party (CCP) established the People's Republic of China (PRC) on October 1, 1949, the United States looked forward to recognizing the new government. Secretary of State Dean Acheson prepared for the fall of Taiwan to the PRC and planned to acknowledge the reality of a communist China. But Acheson's opportunity to recognize the PRC was constrained by multiple factors. First, the United States could not recognize the PRC until it had released Angus Ward, the US consul general in Shenyang, from prison in December 1949. Then, the signing of the Sino-Soviet treaty in February 1950 constrained Acheson's flexibility. Finally, the June 1950 North Korean invasion of South Korea removed any possibility of US recognition of the PRC (Accinelli 1996, chaps. 1–2; Tucker 1983). The communist bloc's use of force in East Asia demanded an immediate and resolute American military response against its Chinese adversary. In these circumstances, the United States not only retained its diplomatic relationship with the Republic of China (ROC), now located on Taiwan, but also bolstered US-Taiwan defense ties. In addition, Washington encouraged the armed Tibetan independence insurgency (Knaus 1999).

From 1949 until 1973, when the United States and China established lower-level liaison offices in each other's capitals, the United States had no diplomatic presence in the PRC. Diplomatic communication between Washington and Beijing was limited to infrequent and tightly controlled ambassador-level meetings held in Warsaw, Poland. Nor did the United States have a cultural or economic presence in China. American communication with Chinese society was limited to VOA broadcasts. Yet even this "offshore" instrument was ineffective, insofar as the CCP frequently jammed US government radio broadcasts into China.

The absence of a US diplomatic presence in Beijing and minimal direct US-China communication had a negligible impact on the onset and development of the US-China Cold War. With North Korea's invasion of South Korea, the foundation of US-China hostility was well established (Jervis 1980). The formal US diplomatic relationship with Taiwan was firmly embedded in US security policy and the development of US regional alliances was well underway, reflecting post–June 1950 assumptions of Sino-Soviet regional ambitions. The United States' involvement in the Vietnam War in the early 1950s and its commitment to South Vietnam similarly reflected these early Cold War developments. The US involvement in the Indochina war in the 1960s and 1970s reflected concern for its regional credibility and the stability of its alliances should it "abandon" South Vietnam, rather than any immediate assessments of Chinese ambitions for regional hegemony. On the contrary, despite the absence of direct diplomatic communication, the United States understood China's limited ambitions in the Vietnam War, its cautious approach to US power, and its many differences with both its North Vietnamese ally and the Soviet Union. Furthermore, long-distance and indirect communication contributed to mutual US-China restraint in Indochina and to containing the escalation of the war ("CIA Secret Report" 1983; Hershberg and Jian 2006).

Equally important, even in the absence of diplomatic relations and direct diplomatic communication through embassies, the United States and China were able to manage difficult diplomatic issues. In 1962, Chinese threat perceptions vis-à-vis a potential coordinated US-Taiwan attack on the mainland escalated in the context of rising Sino-Soviet tension, Sino-Indian border conflicts, and Taiwanese military exercises. As China considered the possibility of war with Taiwan, it raised its concern at the Warsaw talks. The United States responded with assurances that it had no intent to use force against China and that it would restrain Taiwan. US assurances eased Chinese concern and the cross-strait tension quickly subsided (Tucker 1994). Similarly, the absence of diplomatic relations did not impede US-China rapprochement from 1969 to 1972 and the negotiations leading to Richard Nixon's 1972 visit to China to negotiate the Shanghai Communiqué, which established the framework for US-China cooperation before the establishment of diplomatic relations in 1979. The Warsaw talks; indirect communication through third parties, including through Pakistan (so-called back-channel negotiations); and Henry Kissinger's secret July 1971 visit to Beijing were all effective devices for the United States and China to communicate their respective interests and expectations, thus enabling a significant transition in both US-China relations and in the global balance of power (Ross 1995).

In addition, even if the United States had established diplomatic relations with China before the Korean War and maintained an embassy in Beijing, the impact of the American ambassador on subsequent Chinese policy making and on Cold War US-China relations would have been negligible, at best. In Mao Zedong's totalitarian China, access by an ambassador and his staff to Chinese foreign ministry and party officials was tightly controlled. Moreover, because Mao firmly controlled China's foreign policy and his foreign policy preferences were fixed, and because he exercised absolute political control over his lieutenants and other policymakers, Chinese diplomats possessed minimal ability to consider alternative policy options or to bring new and unexpected information to bear on policy making (see, e.g., the failed 1963 effort to moderate Mao's foreign policy, known as *sanhe yishao*, in MacFarquhar 1999, 269–274, 297–302). Similarly, in Maoist China ambassadors from Western bloc countries did not have access to the Chinese media or to public forums to promote "goodwill," understanding, and cooperation between their respective countries and China. Access to Chinese society throughout this period by an American ambassador or other US embassy officials in China would have been especially limited.

The United States' public diplomacy programs conducted by embassy public affairs officers also would have been ineffective. Although many American embassies develop cultural programs in host countries to disseminate knowledge about US society, politics, and foreign policy, any US embassy effort in this period to develop such programs would have been unknown to the Chinese people. The Chinese media would not have covered such programs and the American embassy could not have publicized the program. Moreover, even if a few Chinese had been aware of such programs, they would not have participated. Any effort to enter an American embassy and any possession of US materials would have exposed a Chinese person to the likelihood of extensive "political reeducation," charges of espionage, and jail. Communist party totalitarian controls over Chinese society also significantly undermined Cold War VOA broadcasts. Not only did the CCP jam US broadcasts, but apart from government intelligence collection, listening to the VOA was a dangerous activity for all Chinese. The Cultural Revolution in the 1970s was a particularly ideological era, but party controls over Chinese communication with Western countries in the early years of the PRC were no less strict.

Finally, even assuming the best, given the extent of conflict between the United States and China, opportunities for public diplomacy to affect relations was nearly nonexistent. Once the United States established its containment policy on China's periphery in June 1950 and involved itself in China's civil war through its recognition of the ROC and the negotiation of the US-ROC Mutual Defense Treaty, the PRC would forcefully resist the regional status quo wherever there was US forward presence on China's borders, and the United States would be determined to resist. The issue no longer entailed understanding but rather deeply entrenched conflicts over vital security interests. In this respect, it is significant that the United States and China improved relations only after the United States was on the verge of defeat on China's borders in Vietnam and was thus prepared to modify its Taiwan policy. The erosion of US security in the post–Vietnam War era and shared US-China interests vis-à-vis the Soviet Union, not better communication, were the prerequisites to improved US-China relations. The absence of American public diplomacy did not contribute to US-China Cold War conflict, and public diplomacy was not necessary to establish US-China rapprochement.

The one possible exception to this trend was US-China diplomacy before China's entry into the Korean War in October 1950, four months after the war began. In the brief period between January and June 1950, the United States had the opportunity to recognize the PRC and restaff its embassy in Beijing. It would have been a difficult move for Washington, insofar as China had only recently released Consul General Ward in December 1949, and Mao was in Moscow from late December to early February, where he concluded the negotiations with Joseph Stalin for the Sino-Soviet security treaty. During this same period, Chinese hostility toward the Western presence in China increased (Goncharov, Lewis, and Litai 1993). Nonetheless, if the United States had recognized China and restaffed its embassy, the opportunity for direct bilateral diplomatic communication might have averted the US advance to the Yalu River and Chinese entry into the Korean War in October (Christensen 1996, 174–176).

After US forces landed at Inchon and encircled and defeated the overextended North Korean People's Army, US forces moved unimpeded toward the 38th parallel, the prewar division between North and South Korea. In the absence of US-China diplomatic relations and direct communication channels, the new Chinese government used its official media and third-party channels to signal to the United States its resolve to intervene in the war should US forces cross the 38th parallel and endanger Chinese border security. But the United States, confident in Chinese respect for US military superiority and the effectiveness of its deterrent posture, and doubtful of the credibility of the third-party interlocutors, especially India, discounted the seriousness of Chinese warnings. Thus, Washington ignored Chinese signaling and its overextended and overconfident forces moved across the 38th parallel, unaware of the impending Chinese invasion. Had the United States recognized the PRC in 1949 or early 1950 and established a diplomatic presence in Beijing, direct US-China official communications may have established the credibility of Chinese warnings and contributed to effective Chinese deterrence of a US military advance beyond the 38th parallel. If such were the case, the US-China war in Korea could have been averted.

There are too many ifs in this possible "lost chance" to warrant confidence that US recognition of China and an embassy presence in Beijing would have enabled Washington to better understand Chinese intentions and thus avert a US-China war in Korea. The lack of an embassy in Beijing hindered US communication with Chinese policymakers, but US overconfidence and reluctance to exhibit strategic weakness toward China also contributed to the US decision to advance to the Yalu River (Stueck 1997, 235–241). It is also important to recognize that even if war had been averted, the North Korean invasion of South Korea and the subsequent intervention of US forces in the war had already firmly entrenched the Cold War in East Asia and established the basis for a long-term US military presence south of the 38th parallel and the ensuing decades of Great Power tension on the Korean Peninsula. The avoidance of major loss of life on the Korean Peninsula from October 1950 until the Korean armistice in July 1953 might have been a significant benefit of US-China diplomatic relations, but the impact of this possible "lost chance" on the course of US-China relations and East Asian international politics should not be exaggerated.

From October 1949 through May 1973, when the United States and China established liaison offices in each other's capitals, there was no US diplomatic representation in Beijing and, with the exception of Voice of America broadcasts, the United States had no public diplomacy program directed at the People's Republic of China. The absence of formal US-China diplomatic relations, however, had at best a negligible impact on the onset of the Cold War in East Asia and the development and intensity of the US-China conflict.

US Public Diplomacy during the Era of US-China Strategic Cooperation, 1973–1989

Once China and the United States established their common interest in resisting Soviet power, they quickly terminated the Sino-American Cold War, developed language to manage the Taiwan issue, pursued strategic cooperation, and developed diplomatic contacts. This trend in cooperative strategic relations enabled greater potential for US public diplomacy. But US-China cooperation through 1989 transcended two distinct periods in Chinese politics: the final years of the Maoist totalitarian era and the onset of Deng Xiaoping's authoritarian leadership. This political transition opened Chinese society to Western access with significant implications for US public diplomacy. These two periods also differed with respect to the level of US diplomatic representation in Beijing following the normalization of US-China relations in January 1979, with equally significant implications for US public diplomacy.

Maoist Totalitarianism, US-China Strategic Cooperation, and US Public Diplomacy

President Richard Nixon's February 1972 visit to China and the US-China Shanghai Communiqué established the political and strategic foundations for the development of US-China cooperation against the Soviet Union. Within this context of Great Power cooperation, China and the United States sought expanded diplomatic contacts. But as long as the United States recognized the ROC as the legal government of China, exchange of embassies and diplomatic personnel was impossible. Thus, in July 1973 the two sides agreed to establish liaison offices in each other's capitals. Apart from the ambassadorial talks held in Warsaw, these offices provided the first opportunity since 1949 for Chinese and US diplomats to engage in direct communication. Only after January 1, 1979, when the United States recognized the PRC as the sole legal government of China and shortly thereafter opened an embassy in Beijing, did the presence of a US embassy in China enable the United States to develop public diplomacy toward China.

During the initial stage of this period, when diplomatic contact was limited to communication through the liaison offices, the United States could not develop a robust public diplomacy program directed at Chinese society. US officials could not serve in China and there were political constraints on the size of the embassy staff. Nonetheless, it is highly unlikely that if Washington had recognized China at this early date and established a diplomatic presence in China, it could have carried out effective public diplomacy. Despite the improvement in US-China relations, Mao continued to rule China from 1973 to September 1976, and he kept firm totalitarian control over the Chinese media and access to Chinese society by foreign officials and citizens, regardless of whether China had diplomatic relations with a country. Moreover, Mao continued to wage the Cultural Revolution, and he and his followers demanded strict ideological and political conformity from every Chinese. Any Chinese that interacted with US liaison office personnel, attended events there, or possessed US materials (or listened to VOA) risked becoming the focus of brutal "struggle sessions" and imprisonment. In this respect, despite the advent of US-China strategic cooperation and establishment of liaison offices, the Chinese domestic political context had not changed since 1949, and it continued to significantly limit opportunities for US public diplomacy, regardless of the status of diplomatic relations.

These same Chinese domestic politics limited the effectiveness of the directors of the US liaison office and their staff seeking to communicate with Chinese society. Although as merely the directors of the liaison office, unofficial US representatives could not readily meet with Chinese diplomats and party officials, during the last years of the Maoist era Chinese political conditions were far more significant in determining their access to Chinese decision makers. Excessive friendliness with US officials could be grounds for criticism. Premier Zhou Enlai was criticized for alleged excessive eagerness to expand US-China cooperation. He and his foreign ministry staff thus limited their interaction with the directors of the US liaison office. The liaison office directors' contact with Chinese society was similarly constrained. The best that Director George H. W. Bush could do during his tenure at the liaison office was to ride his bicycle in Beijing. This enabled him to observe from a distance a thin slice of Chinese society and to make a meager effort to signal US goodwill. Other than his bicycle rides, Bush's insight into Chinese politics and foreign policy was based on the US liaison office's analysis of the official Chinese media, which was also being analyzed by many agencies in Washington, and on his contact with other foreign diplomats in Beijing who faced similar constraints on access to information (Bush 1987). Similarly, in Mao's China the Communist Party tightly controlled media coverage of Kissinger's many visits to China, the 1972 Nixon visit to China, and President Gerald Ford's December 1975 visit.

It is also important to note that the absence of an official US diplomatic presence in Beijing did not interfere with the development of US-China strategic cooperation. Until the end of the Maoist era, which coincided with the end of the Ford presidency, the president and Henry Kissinger, both as national security advisor and later as secretary of state, tightly controlled US-China policy. Kissinger insisted that liaison office officials refrain from holding policy discussions with Chinese officials (Bush 1987). He also bypassed State Department officials in Washington in managing China policy. After the establishment of liaison offices, Kissinger preferred to communicate with Huang Zhen, the director of the Chinese Liaison Office in Washington, and to make frequent trips to Beijing to hold direct discussions with Mao, Zhou Enlai, and Deng Xiaoping. Kissinger's personal diplomacy enabled the United States to negotiate the opening of the liaison offices and then to coordinate policy toward the Soviet Union, license US technology transfers to China, and negotiate the 1975 US-China summit and the summit joint statement (Ross 1995).

Moreover, despite the near irrelevancy of the US liaison office in Beijing to US-China relations, during this early era of US-China cooperation the United States established the foundation for later public diplomacy activism. The Shanghai Communiqué called for US-China cooperation in science, technology, culture, sports, and journalism in which "contacts would be mutually beneficial," and for each side to "facilitate . . . such contacts and exchange" (US Department of State 1972). Before Nixon's visit to China in February 1972, approximately ten American scientists, engineers, and physicians had visited China since 1949. By the end of 1972, approximately 100 scientists and scholars had visited China. In May 1973 a delegation from the US Committee on Scholarly Communication with the People's Republic of China (CSCPRC), a US government–sponsored program established in 1966 by the National Academy of Sciences, the American Council of Learned Societies, and the Social Science Research Council, traveled to Beijing and negotiated an agreement with Chinese Premier Zhou Enlai to carry out exchanges in nine scholarly fields, all in the natural sciences (Wang 2002, 213–214; Jin 2003,

3–4). US cultural diplomacy also began during this period. In March 1973, following the opening of the liaison offices in Beijing and Washington, the Philadelphia Orchestra traveled to China. It was the first visit to China by an American ensemble. The orchestra was welcomed by China's Central Philharmonic Chorus singing "America the Beautiful" in English.

US-China Strategic Cooperation and US Public Diplomacy during the Deng Xiaoping Era

The death of Chairman Mao Zedong on September 9, 1976 and the rapid emergence of Deng Xiaoping as China's paramount leader led to the political transition of China from a nonporous totalitarian state to an authoritarian state interested in expanding US-China economic cooperation. Then, on January 1, 1979, the United States established diplomatic relations with the PRC. These two developments combined to create significant opportunities for expanded American engagement with the Chinese government and society and also for American public diplomacy.

The first stage in the expansion of post-Mao US diplomatic activity in China occurred in 1978 during the negotiations for the normalization of US-China relations. For the United States, normalizing diplomatic relations with China was a strategic response to Soviet expansion in the developing world. For China, normalization of relations would be an immediate strategic asset as it prepared to invade Vietnam, an ally of the Soviet Union, in response to Vietnam's expected invasion of Cambodia. The Americans and Chinese were thus prepared to undertake the difficult negotiations required to normalize relations.

In contrast to the Nixon administration, the Carter administration preferred to work through the US liaison office in Beijing to conduct its China diplomacy. In part this was because the director of the office was Leonard Woodcock, who had a long-standing personal relationship with President Jimmy Carter. Woodcock's presence in Beijing was very valuable in the normalization process (Solomon and Quinney 2010, 26). First, in early 1978 he was able to use his personal relationship with the president and his understanding of developments in China to undermine State Department resistance to expedited normalization of relations. In the fall of 1978 the United States and China began detailed normalization negotiations. The US liaison office took the lead in conducting the negotiations for the United States. As the negotiations addressed sensitive issues, Woodcock's personal relationship with the president gave him credibility in China, and his frequent meetings with Chinese officials enabled detailed negotiations leading to normalization of relations. In the final days before normalization, Woodcock's meetings with Deng Xiaoping not only facilitated the final agreement on the text of the normalization communiqué but also enabled the president to clearly communicate US postnormalization policy regarding ongoing US arms sales to Taiwan, thus preventing possible US-China misunderstanding and a potentially disruptive controversy in US-China relations (Vogel 2011, 327–332; Ross 1995, 136–138). In 1978, direct US-China communication in Beijing was critical to the rapid pace of the normalization negotiations and to the avoidance of US-China misunderstanding.

During this same period, the political thaw in post-Mao Chinese politics and Deng Xiaoping's commitment to economic modernization created an opportunity for expanded US-China cooperation in the natural sciences. In July 1978, President Carter's Science Advisor Frank Press led a large delegation of US officials to Beijing to assess China's interest in cooperation in science and technology. Press's visit led to agreements in October 1978 on US-China exchanges in agriculture, space technology, and of students and scholars. That same month Secretary of Energy James R. Schlesinger traveled to China and reached agreements on US-China cooperation on a wide range of energy issues (Jin 2003, 4–5).

Once China and the United States normalized relations, they quickly expanded their nascent public diplomacy. One high-profile aspect of US public diplomacy was President Carter's December 1978 invitation to Deng Xiaoping to visit the United States and Deng's subsequent January 1979 visit. Deng was a master of public relations and his visit to the United States won China widespread American admiration. His discussions with members of Congress, his tour of the Boeing Company plant in Seattle, Washington, and his attendance at a Texas rodeo wearing a Texas-sized cowboy hat made a major contribution to America's reevaluation of communist China and to American readiness to participate in Chinese economic development (Vogel 2011, 333–343). Deng's visit would not have been possible without US recognition of the PRC as the sole legal government of China.

Normalization of relations also allowed opportunities for the United States to consolidate its nonofficial public diplomacy program by negotiating official agreements with China for education and cultural exchanges. During Deng Xiaoping's January visit to Washington, he and President Carter signed an agreement on cooperation in science and technology, and they agreed to establish the US-China Joint Commission on Science and Technology Cooperation. By the end of the Carter administration in 1980, the United States and China had signed fourteen protocols in science and technology cooperation and nearly every US technical agency had begun cooperation with its Chinese counterpart (Jin 2003, 5–6). President Ronald Reagan maintained the Carter administration's commitment to scientific cooperation with China. In 1983 Reagan explained that it was in the "fundamental interest" of the United States "to advance our relations with China" and that science and technology were an essential part of that relationship. In 1986 he reported to Congress that science and technology cooperation was a "cornerstone" of America's "expanding relations" with China. By this time, the US government's program for scientific cooperation with China had become America's largest and most ambitious bilateral scientific cooperation program (Jin 2003, 5–6).

Following the normalization of US-China relations and the gradual opening of Chinese society to Western voices, US public diplomacy programs and educational exchanges expanded beyond the natural sciences and thus played a more active role in communicating trends in American domestic and foreign policies and in translating American society to Chinese society. During the Carter administration the United States negotiated agreements with China to develop a Fulbright scholars program and a Peace Corps program. The United States also stationed VOA reporters in China. Moreover, American cultural and scholarly exchange programs established in the 1970s greatly expanded their activities. American-sponsored exchange programs included frequent visits to China by artists and musicians. Similarly, academic programs, such as the CSCPRC, expanded academic cooperation with China. Between 1979 and 1983 the number of Chinese students and scholars visiting the United States reached nearly 20,000 (Lampton 1986, 32, 39). Over the next decade, such visits continued to expand and Chinese scholarly visits gradually evolved beyond the natural sciences to include cooperation in the social sciences and humanities. In 1992–1993 approximately 45,000 Chinese studied in the United States. By 1995 approximately 130,000 Chinese had studied in the United States and more than 15 percent returned to China. Returned students and scholars contributed to research communities in Chinese scholarly institutions and to administrative offices in higher education institutions throughout China, especially showing their influence in the 2003 proposal for far-reaching reforms at Peking University (Li 2005, 78–79, 91–97, 99–101; Zheng 2005, 136–140).

But despite the significant changes in post-Mao China, the CCP retained absolute control over the media and continued to use the media to support party power and government policy. Ongoing party dominance of Chinese politics constrained the ability of US officials to talk directly to the Chinese people and engage in public diplomacy. To the extent that the Chinese media covered US embassy activities following normalization of US-China relations, including speeches by the ambassador and other US diplomats, it selectively reported only those statements and activities that reinforced existing Chinese policies. Within these constraints, during the 1980s, because both Deng Xiaoping and President Carter sought to expand US-China foreign policy and economic cooperation, the Chinese media widely reported US embassy activities. In this respect, the normalization of US-China relations and the US diplomatic presence in China contributed to US efforts to cooperate with China, in opposition to the Soviet Union, and to cooperate with Chinese economic reform and political liberalization.

In China's authoritarian political system, uncensored US government access to Chinese society primarily occurred through VOA broadcasts. The VOA enabled unfettered US reporting not only of US politics, foreign policy, and society but also of developments elsewhere in the world, including in China. Although such reportage might have enhanced Chinese appreciation for the US political system and social values, the ultimate effect of VOA broadcasts was likely detrimental both to US-China cooperation and to long-term Chinese political liberalization, especially in the aftermath of the 1989 Tiananmen incident.

Through the 1980s, as Chinese people, especially young people, became increasingly exposed to Western societies, they adopted many of these societies' values, including their fashions and various leisure activities, and they became emboldened to voice criticism of government policies. In response to these rapid changes in post-Mao Chinese society, Chinese conservatives resisted social and political liberalization. They first launched in 1981 the campaign against "bourgeois liberalization" and then in 1983–1984 the campaign against "spiritual pollution." But Chinese social change proceeded. A little more than five years later, tens of thousands of Chinese students amassed in Tiananmen Square to demand greater political liberalization and a more accountable government. The CCP could not tolerate a public mass challenge to its absolute opposition to independent political organization and to its absolute control over Chinese politics. The June 3–4, 1989 violent CCP suppression of the student movement was not inevitable, nor was it was surprising (Fewsmith 1994; Fewsmith 2001; Baum 1994).

American public diplomacy during the George H. W. Bush administration became enmeshed in the domestic politics of the Tiananmen demonstrations. As students amassed in Beijing and elsewhere in China, the CCP controlled the content of the Chinese media, trying to contain the student movement and to create conditions to bring the demonstrations to a rapid conclusion. Voice of America broadcasts, however, provided an independent source of information about both the demonstrations and developments in CCP politics, including divisions in the leadership regarding the party's response to the demonstrations. The VOA also broadcast US leaders' and diplomats' expressions of sympathy for the students' demands. The VOA's coverage of the Tiananmen demonstration and of US government statements thus undermined the CCP's attempt to manage China's political and social crises.

Deng Xiaoping and other Chinese leaders believed that Voice of America, and by extension the United States, had encouraged the demonstrations and prolonged student resistance to the leadership of the CCP (Suettinger 2003, 70; Vogel 2011, 636). In this context, conservative criticism of China's political opening gained credibility. In the aftermath of the CCP's June 3–4 suppression of the Tiananmen demonstration, Chinese leaders launched the campaign against "peaceful evolution," an alleged American plot to undermine the Chinese communist system through American nongovernmental penetration of Chinese society by American political and social values. Chinese scholars and officials were criticized and frequently punished for their alleged adoption of Western values. Moreover, VOA involvement in Chinese politics led to a backlash against broad-based US-China cooperation. China expelled the VOA director from China, suspended the Fulbright scholar program, and postponed the inauguration of the Peace Corps program in China (Ross 2001; Vogel 2011).

Direct US involvement in Chinese domestic politics occurred during President Bush's February 1989 visit to Beijing, just as the demonstrators were amassing in Tiananmen Square. The public diplomacy associated with the US-China summit significantly contributed to the erosion of US-China cooperation. The United States' inclusion of the scientist and political dissident Fang Lizhi on the invitation list for the US reciprocal banquet angered Chinese leaders, who accused the United States of interfering in Chinese domestic affairs. Deng Xiaoping was especially hostile to Fang and his political activities. Only after extensive negotiations and mutual compromise did Chinese leaders agree that Fang could attend the banquet. When Chinese security officials later attempted to arrest Fang in the aftermath of the June 4 Tiananmen demonstrations, he took refuge in the US embassy. Fang had become a Chinese fugitive and his residency in the US embassy had created a significant obstacle to post-Tiananmen restoration of US-China cooperation. According to James Lilley, US ambassador to China during the Tiananmen demonstrations, Fang's presence at the US Embassy was a "constant reminder" of the US involvement in China's Westernization and made the embassy "enemy number one" in Beijing. Chinese officials boycotted the US embassy for more than a year while Fang took refuge there (Lilley and Lilley 2004, 332–334, 351–364; Suettinger 2003, 25–29). Not until June 25, 1990, after Chinese leaders assured the United States that Fang would be allowed to leave China, could he leave the embassy and travel to the United States.

American government association with China's 1989 student movement through VOA broadcasts of US expressions of support and the US role in the Fang Lizhi affair undermined US interests in broad-based US-China cooperation and in the liberalization of the Chinese political system. Not only did US public diplomacy suffer setbacks after the suppression of the student movement, but US government association with the student movement bolstered Chinese conservative opposition to Deng Xiaoping's prior tolerance of political liberalization more generally and also for Deng's effort to reform China's economic system. In 1992 Deng regained dominance over Chinese policy making and reestablished China's economic reform policies (Fewsmith 2001; Zhao 1993). Nonetheless, more than twenty years after the 1989 demonstrations, the Chinese leadership's suspicion of US public diplomacy has not diminished, and the degree of political liberalization in China has still not returned to pre-1989 levels. Chinese internal dynamics have been critical to the political trends in China's authoritarian system, but US public diplomacy contributed to the deterioration in US-China cooperation and to China's post-1989 conservative resurgence.

American public diplomacy during the era of US-China strategic cooperation has a mixed record. On the one hand, the establishment of an American diplomatic presence and the opening of a US embassy in China have facilitated the successful negotiation of many important agreements, including the normalization of US-China relations and many bilateral public policy agreements fostering nongovernmental cooperation in academic and cultural affairs. Since 1973 US government–sponsored programs have contributed to robust US-China societal and cultural exchanges, and these exchanges have developed a self-sustaining momentum. Since their inception, these programs have contributed to greater US-China understanding and have created a web of societal interactions that has withstood the frequent instability in bilateral political relations and the development of a competitive strategic relationship. The establishment of diplomatic relations has also enabled frequent US-China summitry, which has contributed to greater societal awareness of each country's successes and problems and the importance of cooperation. Moreover, from normalization of relations until the 1989 Tiananmen incident, when the Chinese police and social systems experienced significant post–Cultural Revolution reforms, the VOA played a constructive role in reaching out to the Chinese people. It was a credible and popular source of news about both America and the world, and it contributed to popular Chinese support for US-China cooperation.

On the other hand, the record of US public diplomacy during this same period also indicates that the combination of greater public policy access to a political system and cooperative security relations do not guarantee a successful public diplomacy program. Regardless of the status of the bilateral political relationship, authoritarian governments will retain control over the media and place priority on domestic political stability. They will use their unchecked power to resist US government promotion of American political and social values as challenges to the power of the ruling elite. During periods of political instability, authoritarian elites will hold the United States' involvement in public diplomacy programs responsible for societal challenges to their power and cut back those programs that promote nongovernmental bilateral cooperation. The record of direct US public diplomacy efforts during this period, especially during and after the 1989 Tiananmen demonstrations, suggest that it is in the long-term interest of American public diplomacy directed at authoritarian states to be sensitive to the domestic conditions of the target country, which determines the effect of public diplomacy programs on cooperation among states, and to minimize direct US government participation in public diplomacy. The United States should primarily rely on government funding for indirect, less sensitive, and more effective unofficial exchange programs.

US Public Diplomacy during the Era of
US-China Great Power Competition, Post-1989

The role of US public diplomacy in China in the post-Tiananmen era fundamentally changed during the first decade of the twenty-first century. This change reflected five important developments in Chinese politics, US-China relations, and communication technologies. The combined effect of these changes has undermined the effectiveness and reduced the importance of US government-led public diplomacy in China while simultaneously presenting new and more effective nongovernmental instruments for carrying out public diplomacy. In this context, US government support for public diplomacy can be most effective by limiting its involvement to supporting American cooperation with China involving cultural exchanges between US nonprofit institutions.

First, since the June 1989 crackdown on the Tiananmen reform movement, China's authoritarian government has consistently prioritized domestic stability over reform and opening. It has thus resisted any political reforms that would loosen the party's control over politics, and it has maintained effective control over the Chinese media. Moreover, since 2008 the leadership's insistence on complete control over information has grown as increased economic problems and a rise in social media technologies have challenged the party's ability to maintain the legitimacy of party rule and social stability (Yang 2009; Qiang 2011a; Wines 2012).

In this Chinese domestic context, the VOA has become an increasingly ineffective instrument of US public diplomacy in China. In addition to the small number of radio listeners in China, Chinese leadership hostility to the VOA has grown, deterring popular Chinese use of the VOA as a source of news, and China continues to monitor and jam VOA broadcasts (US Department of State 2010, 15, 17). The Chinese leadership's insistence on absolute political control has also interfered with US efforts to use US-China summitry to advance US values. Presidents Clinton, Reagan, and Obama each sought to use summitry to secure a public platform in China to speak directly to the Chinese people. China responded by either refusing the president's request for a public platform or by censoring the president's comments. In either case, the US presidents' public diplomacy efforts not only failed to advance the mission of public diplomacy but also interfered with the development of cooperative US-China diplomacy by contributing to diplomatic tension and suspicion.

Second, a succession of US-Chinese incidents has contributed to Chinese suspicion of US foreign policy intentions. They have also led many Chinese to adopt a harsh, realist "zero-sum" perspective on the United States and US-China relations. The resulting heightened US strategic competition has combined with heightened popular Chinese confidence from the rise of China and its growing role in world affairs and anti-American nationalism to make the United States an increasingly suspect source in China for news and information.

The 1996 Taiwan Strait confrontation persuaded many Chinese that the United States was determined to use its advanced military capabilities to prevent China from realizing the unification of Taiwan with the mainland. Then in 1999, during the war in Bosnia, the United States accidentally bombed the Chinese embassy in Belgrade. In 2001 a US military surveillance aircraft operating near Chinese coastal waters collided with a Chinese military jet. The Chinese jet crashed in the South China Sea, killing the pilot (Gries 2005). These incidents elicited significant popular Chinese hostility toward the United States. Exacerbating this trend is the widespread view that after thirty years of Chinese economic and military modernization, the United States is now the primary obstacle to China's emergence as a global power. Moreover, such Chinese anti-American nationalism is no longer confined to urban youth and Chinese military officers, but has spread to all sectors of urban society, including businesspeople, academics, and political elites (Rosen 2003; Gries 2004; Shirk 2007; He 2007; Callahan 2010). By 2010 Chinese nationalism had become fully focused on the United States, so that dispassionate Chinese analysis of American policy is now routinely squelched in public discussions (Ross 2013).

In this transformed Chinese environment, except for a small number of specialists on US politics and foreign policy, US public diplomacy—including State Department and embassy video and audio reports, print publications, and leadership speeches—is routinely dismissed as self-serving American propaganda that merely seeks to prevent the rise of China and sustain US hegemony. Direct US public diplomacy is thus not only ineffective but also can be detrimental to advancing support for US-China cooperation and to developing widespread appreciation of American values. It is also a waste of limited financial resources that could better serve US public diplomacy if they were directed at public diplomacy activities that entailed less overt US involvement.

The third major change in US-China relations reflects the success of prior US public diplomacy. By the end of the Cold War and the emergence of post-Tiananmen US-China tension, postnormalization US public diplomacy programs had contributed to the development of dense and broad-based US-China societal-level cooperation. The United States' and China's cultural and educational institutions had already developed active channels of cooperation that were no longer dependent on US government initiative or diplomatic assistance. In the twenty-first century, American and Chinese artists, musicians, and scholars now routinely visit each other's countries, and they benefit from close personal and professional relationships. These activities frequently rely on US government financial assistance. But because this is indirect public diplomacy, the programs do not incur the hostility and suspicion associated with direct US public diplomacy activities that are tainted by the politics of bilateral relations, which can undermine official diplomatic cooperation.

The dense network of informal professional and personal relationships has enabled the United States to communicate American societal and political values to the Chinese that contribute to formal diplomatic cooperation. Thus, despite the difficulties in the increasingly competitive US-China political relationship, young Chinese who are China's future leaders aspire to attend universities in the United States. Many Chinese who have attended American universities return to China having developed an appreciation for US political and cultural institutions (Han and Zweig 2010; Zweig, Chen, and Rosen 2004). Hollywood movies may often be seen by Chinese as US propaganda, but they are also the most popular movies in China. Hollywood communicates American political and cultural values to an ever-larger proportion of Chinese society (Wan and Kraus 2002). More recently, Chinese tourism in the United States has exposed China's growing middle class to individual Americans and to American societal institutions. Tourism has also exposed Chinese to US political institutions and thus enables them to makes contrasts between US democracy and China's authoritarian political system. Between 2003 and 2010 the number of Chinese tourists visiting the United States increased by more than 400 percent (US Commerce Department 2010). This too benefits US diplomacy.

The fourth major change that contributes to the diminished importance of US public diplomacy in China is the digitalization of Chinese society. By the end of 2011 more than 500 million Chinese had access to the Internet and more than 155 million Chinese households were connected to the Internet (Zhang

2012). Despite increasing government monitoring, information is now disseminated by individuals through Internet websites, including social network sites. Digital communication technologies also allow Chinese access to international sources of Chinese domestic and international news (Qiang 2011b). For example, Chinese-language media originating in Hong Kong and Taiwan are accessible to mainland Chinese via the Internet (Jacobs 2012; "It's All Right, Ma" 2012).

In this digital communication environment, VOA radio broadcasts have become nearly obsolete instruments of American public diplomacy in China. The VOA has responded by developing Internet-based programming for the Chinese audience, including programs for China's growing number of mobile smart-phone users (US Department of State 2012, 9, 11–12, 14). Original programming on contemporary popular issues in US society and politics, and Chinese-language discussions of political issues among Americans and Chinese experts, can offer insights into US political and cultural values and policy debates. Similarly, online translations of influential US books and other literature can reach a large Chinese audience (Landler 2011).

Fifth, the expansion of Western print journalism into China and the emergence of digital communication technologies have reduced the importance of the government in US public diplomacy. Whereas Hollywood films once dominated private-sector dissemination of American culture, there has been a proliferation of corporate interests that widely diffuse American culture, so that the dissemination of knowledge about the United States and of American values is an increasingly apolitical, private-sector activity. Nongovernmental, private-sector public diplomacy via the media comes in many forms. Nearly all US news companies have a digital and print presence in China. Despite frequent Chinese government blocking of US websites, the *Washington Post*, the *Los Angeles Times*, and Fox News, for example, all have websites that are mostly accessible in China. The CNN website posts a weekly video of a Chinese-language news program. American sporting events are available at ESPN.com and other Internet websites. Market forces have encouraged American weekly newsmagazines, such as *Time* and *Newsweek*, to print mainland Chinese-language editions and to develop local websites. American popular television entertainment, including situation comedies and dramas, are available online without a fee from US network and cable providers. American fiction and nonfiction books are available through amazon.com and barnesandnoble.com, for example, and popular American music is accessible through such websites as itunes.com and mtv.com. Chinese-language American popular culture magazines, such as *Vogue*,

Elle, GQ, Men's Health, and *Sports Illustrated,* are readily available throughout China at sidewalk newspaper kiosks.

Given the mostly negative record of direct US government involvement in public diplomacy in China, the ongoing political sensitivity and stigma in China associated with US government information programs, and popular Chinese cynicism toward US government policy statements, American reliance on the private sector for public diplomacy may best serve American public diplomacy objectives. The US government can form partnerships with the private sector to advance public diplomacy. The Obama administration's 2009 "100,000 Strong" initiative sought private-sector support for US education exchanges with China. The initiative elicited significant private-sector funding for independent "student ambassadors" to study in China and for US college graduates to teach English in China, and soon transitioned into the independent nonprofit 100,000 Strong Foundation (US Department of State 2011; US Department of State 2012).

In terms of the three basic variants of public diplomacy described in the book's Introduction, the China case reveals a skeptical view of the effectiveness of traditional government-sponsored and -conducted public diplomacy (the editor's "traditional State Department" variant), but most significantly offers support for public diplomacy based more on nongovernmental and private efforts (definition 3). This conclusion raises the intriguing conceptual question of whether such nongovernmental efforts constitute "public diplomacy," "cross-cultural communication," or private-sector "market-driven people-to-people diplomacy"?

Nonetheless, there are limits to the value of all the variants of US public diplomacy in reaching Chinese society. The Chinese Internet firewall effectively censors all forms of foreign material that cover politically sensitive subjects. Chinese authorities block popular access to the Internet more easily than they interfere with popular access to VOA radio broadcasts (US Department of State 2012, 11–12). Chinese censors routinely block access to politically sensitive television broadcasts, such as CNN coverage of China. And the Chinese print publication industry is strictly governed by propaganda officials.

Conclusion

The post-1949 history of US public diplomacy toward China reveals many important lessons for public policy priorities. First, from 1949 through 1971, when the United States treated China as an adversary, the absence of a US diplomatic presence in China had a negligible impact on bilateral relations. The deep-seated conflicts of interest, the wars on the Korean Peninsula and in Indochina, and the crises in the Taiwan Strait did not allow for public diplomacy to either diminish hostility or increase cooperation. This dynamic affects the role of public diplomacy in any adversarial relationship. Second, the absence of opportunities for public diplomacy in adversarial relations is not an obstacle to cooperation when political conditions allow for change. When US-China strategic conditions changed in the late 1960s, the United States and China quickly moved to establish cooperative relations. Third, US public diplomacy dissemination of information to totalitarian states, such as China, has a negligible effect at best. Totalitarian political systems interfere with the transmission of public diplomacy, and the totalitarian political environment deters citizens from listening to US radio broadcasts, for example. This dynamic affected US diplomacy toward China when the United States and China were first strategic adversaries and then strategic partners, following Richard Nixon's visit to Beijing in 1972. The resistance of totalitarian states to US public diplomacy affects US efforts toward not only communist states but all ideological/religious totalitarian states as well. Fourth, public diplomacy can frequently undermine cooperative state-to-state relations. The Fang Lizhi affair and US-China friction over summit activities reveals that less active public diplomacy can better serve cooperation. Fifth, direct US government association with public diplomacy can undermine the effectiveness of public diplomacy. In the Chinese case, even after the end of totalitarian rule and the emergence of some social space, post-1989 Chinese nationalism and widespread popular suspicion of American motives creates skepticism toward direct efforts of US government public diplomacy. In this environment, US government support for indirect people-to-people diplomacy and private people-to-people diplomacy, such as tourism, can be the most effective instrument of public diplomacy. Sixth, in the digital era, private-sector transmission of US societal values can be far more effective than any US government program and it costs the taxpayer nothing.

The seventh lesson of post-1949 US public diplomacy toward China is the most important lesson. The most effective method to promote cross-cultural understanding and to convey US societal and political values across state boundaries is to build societal institutions that become self-sustaining, regardless of changes in political relations. The thick web of US-China cooperation that has transcended the end of the Cold War, China's violent suppression of the June 1989 democracy demonstration, and the emergence of US-China Great Power competition owes its extensiveness to the first tentative steps in the late 1970s and early 1980s to develop US-China cultural and educational exchanges. At that time, US diplomats took advantage of an opening window of opportunity to develop public diplomacy initiatives that rapidly developed into an important foundation of twenty-first-century US-China cooperation. The contemporary dense network of US-China societal exchanges is what distinguishes contemporary US-China Great Power relations from the US-Soviet relationship. More than thirty years after the normalization of US-China relations and the expansion of US diplomacy activities in China, self-sustaining people-to-people relations obstruct the development of US-China Cold War societal hostility.

References

Accinelli, Robert. 1996. *Crisis and Commitment: United States Policy toward Taiwan, 1950-1955*. Chapel Hill, NC: University of North Carolina Press.

Baum, Richard. 1994. *Burying Mao: Chinese Politics in the Age of Deng Xiaoping*. Princeton: Princeton University Press.

Bush, George H. W. 1987. *Looking Forward: An Autobiography*. New York: Bantam Books.

"CIA Secret Report on Sino-Vietnamese Reaction to American Tactics in the Vietnam War." 1983. *Journal of Contemporary Asia* 13/2: 261–277.

Christensen, Thomas. 1996. *Useful Adversaries: Grand Strategy, Domestic Mobilization, and Sino-American Conflict, 1947–1958*. Princeton: Princeton University Press.

Callahan, William A. 2010. *China: The Pessoptimist Nation*. New York: Oxford University Press.

Donglin, Han and David Zweig. 2010. "Images of the World: Studying Abroad and Chinese Attitudes towards International Affairs." *China Quarterly* 202.

The Economist. 2012. "It's All Right, Ma." January 21 at http://www.economist.com/node/21543197.

Fewsmith, Joseph. 1994. *Dilemmas of Reform in China: Political Conflict and Economic Debate*. Armonk, NY: M.E. Sharpe.

———. 2001. *China since Tiananmen: The Politics of Transition*. New York: Cambridge University Press.

Goncharov, Sergei N., John W. Lewis and Xue Litai. 1993. *Uncertain Enemies: Stalin, Mao and the Korean War*. Palo Alto, CA: Stanford University Press.

Gries, Peter Hays. 2004. "Popular Nationalism and State Legitimation in China." In

State and Society in 21st Century: Crisis, Contention and Legitimation, Peter Hays Gries and Stanley Rosen, eds. New York: RoutledgeCurzon.

———. 2005. *China's New Nationalism: Pride, Politics, and Diplomacy*. Berkeley: University of California Press.

He, Yinan. 2007. "History, Chinese Nationalism and the Emerging Sino-Japanese Conflict." *Journal of Contemporary China* 16/50.

Hershberg, James G. and Chen Jian. 2006. "Informing the Enemy: Sino-American Signaling and the Vietnam War, 1965." In *Behind the Bamboo Curtain: China, Vietnam and the World Beyond Asia*. Priscilla Roberts, ed., 193–257. Palo Alto: Stanford University Press.

Jacobs, Andrew. 2012. "Taiwan Election Stirs Hopes Among Chinese for Democracy." *New York Times* January 16 at http://www.nytimes.com/2012/01/17/world/asia/taiwan-vote-stirs-chinese-hopes-for-democracy.html?_r=1

Jervis, Robert. 1980. "The Impact of the Korean War on the Cold War." *Journal of Conflict Resolution* 24/4.

Jin, Xiaoming. 2003. "The China-US Relationship in Science and Technology," paper presented at conference on "China's Emerging Technological Trajectory in the 21st Century." Lally School of Management and Technology, Rensselaer Polytechnic Institute, Troy, New York, USA. Available at http://www.law.gmu.edu/nctl/stpp/us_china_pubs/6.5_China-US_relationship_in_Sci_Tech.pdf

Knaus, John Kenneth. 1999. *Orphans of the Cold War: America and the Tibetan Struggle for Survival*. New York: Public Affairs.

Lampton, David M. 1986. *A Relationship Restored: Trends in US-China Educational Exchanges, 1978–1984*. Washington, D.C.: National Academy Press.

Landler, Mark. 2011. "A New Voice of America for the Age of Twitter." *New York Times*, June 8 at *http://www.nytimes.com/2011/06/08/world/08voice.html?pagewanted=all*.

Li, Cheng. 2005. "Coming Home to Teach: Status and Mobility of Returnees in China's Higher Education." In *Bridging Minds Across the Pacific US-China Educational Exchanges, 1978–2003*. Li Cheng, ed. 78–79, 91–97, 99–101, 136–140. Lanham, MD: Lexington Books.

Lilley, James and Jeffrey Lilley. 2004. *China Hands: Nine Decades of Adventures, Espionage and Diplomacy in Asia*. New York: Public Affairs

MacFarquhar, Roderick. 1999. *The Origins of the Cultural Revolution, Volume 3: The Coming of the Cataclysm*. New York: Columbia University Press.

Qiang, Xiao. 2011a. "The Battle for Chinese Internet." *Journal of Democracy* 22/2.

———. 2011b. "The Rise of Online Public Opinion and its Political Impact." In *Changing Media, Changing China*. Susan L. Shirk, ed. New York: Oxford University Press.

Rosen, Stanley. 2003. "Chinese Media and Youth: Attitudes Toward Nationalism and Internationalism." In *Chinese Media, Global Contexts*. Jinquan Li, ed. New York: RoutledgeCurzon.

Ross, Robert S. 1995. *Negotiating Cooperation: The United States and China, 1969–1989*. Palo Alto, CA: Stanford University Press.

———. 2001. "The Diplomacy of Tiananmen: Two-Level Bargaining and Great Power Cooperation." *Security Studies* 10/2.

———. 2013. "Domestic Instability and Chinese Nationalism: Instability in US-China Relations." In *Across the Divide: The Domestic and Global in Politics and Society.* Rosemary Foot, ed. Oxford: Oxford University Press.

Shirk, Susan L. 2007. *China: Fragile Superpower: How China's Internal Politics Could Derail Its Peaceful Rise.* New York: Oxford University Press.

Solomon, Richard and Nigel Quinney. 2010. *American Negotiating Behavior.* Washington, D.C.: United States Institute of Peace.

Stueck, William. 1997. *The Korean War: An International History.* Princeton, NJ: Princeton University Press.

Suettinger, Robert L. 2003. *Beyond Tiananmen: The Politics of US-China Relations.* Washington, D.C.: Brookings.

Tucker, Nancy Bernkoph. 1983. *Patterns in the Dust: Chinese-American Relations and the Recognition Controversy.* New York: Columbia University Press.

———. 1994. *Taiwan, Hong Kong, and the United States, 1945–1992.* New York: Twayne Publishers.

US Department of Commerce. 2010. http://tinet.ita.doc.gov/outreachpages/download_data_table/2010_China_Market_Profile.pdf.

US Department of State. 1972. *Shanghai Communiqué. http://history.state.gov/historicaldocuments/frus1969–76v17/d203.*

———. 2011. *U.S.-China CPE Cooperation on the 100,000 Strong Initiative.* http://www.state.gov/r/pa/prs/ps/2011/04/160615.htm.

———. 2012. 100,000 Strong Educational Initiatives. http://www.state.gov/100k/.

United States Department of State and the Broadcasting Board of Governors. 2010. *Report of Inspection: Voice of America's Chinese Branch.* Report ISP-IB-10–53. http://oig.state.gov/documents/organization/145823.pdf.

Vogel, Ezra F. 2011. *Deng Xiaoping and the Transformation of China.* Cambridge: Harvard University Press.

Wan, Jihong and Richard Kraus. 2002. "Hollywood and China as Adversaries and Allies." *Pacific Affairs*, 75/3.

Wang, Zuoyue. 2002. "Chinese American Scientists and US-China Scientific Relations: From Richard Nixon to Wen Ho Lee." In *The Expanding Roles of Chinese Americans in US-China Relations.* Peter H. Koehn and Xiao-huang Yin, eds., 213–14. Armonk, NY: M. E. Sharpe.

Wines, Michael. 2012. "China Expands Program Requiring Real-Name Registration Online." *New York Times*, January 18.

Yang, Guobin. 2009. *The Power of the Internet in China: Citizen Activism Online.* New York: Columbia University Press.

Zhao, Suisheng. 1993. "Deng Xiaoping's Southern Tour: Elite Politics in Post-Tiananmen China." *Asian Survey* 33/8.

Zhang, Yixuan. 2012. "Number of Netizens Reaches 500 million in China." *People's Daily* (online) at *http://english.peopledaily.com.cn/90882/7704757.html.*

Zheng, Shiping. 2005. "Sino-US Educational Exchanges and International Relations Studies in China." In *Bridging Minds Across the Pacific US-China Educational Exchanges, 1978-2003*. Li Cheng, ed. 78–140. Lanham, MD: Lexington Books.

Zweig, David, Chen Changgui and Stanley Rosen. 2004. "Globalization and Transnational Global Capital: Overseas and Returned Scholars to China." *China Quarterly* 179.

3 NORTH KOREA

Engaging a Hermit Adversarial State

Scott Snyder

THE ADVERSARIAL RELATIONSHIP BETWEEN THE
United States and the Democratic People's Republic of Korea
(DPRK) is arguably the longest-running hostile relationship in the modern
era. The relationship itself was shaped by the US-Soviet confrontation early
in the Cold War, and it has been mirrored by an absence of formal diplomatic
relations and, consequently, the use of public communication via various
kinds of actors. The global US-Soviet rivalry was compounded by an inter-
Korean competition for legitimacy between two Korean leaders, backed by
American and Soviet patrons, who were dead set on the task of Korean reunification. It was this rivalry, enabled by what was envisioned to be the temporary division of the Korean Peninsula into US and Soviet zones of occupation
at the end of World War II, that set the stage for the outbreak of the Korean
War in 1950. The establishment of two competing governments in the DPRK
and the Republic of Korea (ROK) in 1948 deepened the division. To some
degree, it is possible to argue that US–North Korean hostility predated the
establishment of the DPRK itself.

The outbreak of the Korean War cemented US-DPRK enmity and left a
legacy of hostility that lasted for decades. North Korea's June 1950 surprise
attack on the South precipitated a strong international response, including
a US-led effort to condemn North Korea and to mobilize an unprecedented
multinational response under United Nations (UN) authorization (a response
made possible by a Soviet boycott of the UN Security Council). Following

three years of hostilities, the UN Command, the DPRK, and the Chinese People's Volunteer Forces concluded the negotiation of a ceasefire and an armistice treaty on the Korean Peninsula. The armistice signified an inconclusive outcome of the war and became a vehicle for preserving US-DPRK hostilities, even in the context of dramatic changes in the international environment. Because of the UN role in the conflict, North Korean perceptions of its relationship with the United States carry additional connotations for North Korean perceptions of its role in and relationship to the international community. The Military Armistice Commission, tasked with the technical details of maintaining the peace, was for decades the only window for formal diplomatic communication between the United States and North Korea.

These technical contacts in the service of armistice implementation quickly (d)evolved into a set-piece dialogue that ritualized the ongoing confrontation (Downs 1998). Both sides preferred to use the venue as a proxy for military conflict by focusing on propaganda and one-upmanship. The Military Armistice Commission, as a mechanism led by military representatives with the primary purpose of addressing armistice violations, had a limited capacity to serve as a viable channel for political dialogue. The propaganda war also continued across the Demilitarized Zone (DMZ) through each side's setup of loudspeakers, leaflet drops, and other psychological operations designed to criticize the political and economic system of the other side. Thus, the main form of public messaging toward North Korea during this period was negative: both sides demonized the other in forms that became deeply embedded in their respective popular cultures. This situation was sustained until the waning days of the Cold War, even through periods of US-Soviet détente and Sino-US rapprochement in the 1970s. Despite periodic North Korean efforts to reach out to the United States following the thaw of US-Soviet and Sino-US relationships, it was not until the mid-1980s that a low-level channel for political dialogue was established between the United States and North Korea through political counselors at the US and DPRK embassies in Beijing. The technique of authorizing diplomatic talks held in a "neutral setting" through diplomatic representatives stationed in a third country had been instrumental in opening Sino-US diplomatic ties. The authorization of a "modest initiative" for dialogue, accompanied by a loosening of restrictions on cultural, humanitarian, and financial exchanges, was intended as a clear signal, authorized by the Reagan administration's Assistant Secretary of State for East Asian and Pacific

Affairs Gaston J. Sigur Jr., of US willingness to open diplomatic dialogue with North Korea (Berridge and Gallo 1999; Wit 2001).

Because of the domestic origins of the Korean War and the Cold War context of Great Power confrontation, the role and scope of opportunity for public diplomacy (which will be treated broadly within this chapter to address both nongovernmental efforts and government attempts to influence the public and therefore the policies of the target state) in the US-DPRK relationship has been inhibited to a greater degree than in many other cases. This situation was exacerbated due to the following reasons: (1) the two sides continue to be officially in a state of war, with the Military Armistice Commission and the UN Command still the primary vehicles for managing technical issues associated with the armistice between the two sides (however, this dialogue channel is insufficient to manage broader political issues, particularly in the post–Cold War context); (2) during most of this period, North Korea was wrongly perceived to be a client of China and the Soviet Union and, thus, the imperative for direct engagement was lessened as a result of a view that incorrectly gauged the level of autonomy North Korea preserved for itself in the management of its international relations; (3) management of the US-DPRK relationship continues to be influenced by the US alliance with South Korea, which in turn requires that attention be paid to the state of inter-Korean relations as a factor, constraining the range of possibilities for improving the US-DPRK relationship; and (4) the preexisting division and state of war on the Korean Peninsula was made even more intractable as a result of the United States' post–Cold War concerns with nuclear nonproliferation that emerged at the same time that North Korea's security vulnerabilities drove it to pursue nuclear development to compensate for its conventional military weakness compared to the United States and South Korea. These obstacles to engagement limited meaningful contact between the United States and North Korea, effectively constraining the environment for meaningful public diplomacy. Without an on-the-ground diplomatic presence in Pyongyang and with limited channels for direct communication, public diplomacy consisted primarily of public messaging designed to support diplomatic initiatives and a range of track two initiatives—private efforts to facilitate official contacts and communication indirectly, often with the knowledge and/ or endorsement of the governments concerned—designed to facilitate contacts between the United States and the DPRK.

The core issue between the two sides remains the legacy of mutual hostility from the Korean War, but issues related to the war have been overshadowed by a post–Cold War US focus on global nonproliferation as a priority concern and by North Korea's ongoing efforts to build a nuclear capability, at least in part to offset its conventional disadvantage with South Korea and the United States, and to provide deterrence against external intervention that might be used to destabilize North Korea's political system. In this context, public diplomacy provides an adjunct to limited channels of official communication and can be used to amplify disagreements as well as to signal affirmation of understandings that may develop through limited channels. The differing relationships of the respective governments with media and the desire to target multiple audiences also may heighten potential for misinterpretation or miscommunication between the two sides.

Following a further examination of factors limiting US-DPRK political engagement during the Cold War, this chapter will focus primarily on the range of public diplomacy opportunities between the two countries that have emerged in the context of warming inter-Korean dialogue and the establishment of bilateral US-DPRK channels for high-level political dialogue in the post–Cold War period. The case illustrates how—in the absence of formal diplomatic relations over an extended period and where the information environment is heavily controlled by one side—traditional "government to foreign public" public diplomacy is almost nonexistent. Under such circumstances, this chapter shows how nontraditional diplomatic instruments and indeed nongovernmental communication, or what is described in the book's Introduction as "new public diplomacy" channels, can be helpful in lessening tensions between intractable adversaries. The chapter will further examine South Korean sensitivities as a constraint on US public diplomacy toward North Korea, the range of nongovernmental public diplomacy tools and channels used to supplement initial steps toward an official government-to-government dialogue, and the various ways in which the two governments have attempted to signal their positions through public messaging on global media platforms on various issues in a context of ongoing, limited direct communications between the two governments.

US-Soviet Détente and Nixon's Visit to Beijing, but No US-DPRK Rapprochement

Cold War developments in the 1950s and 1960s made life simple for the United States and North Korea, who were pitted against each other in an ongoing stalemate that included regular small-scale skirmishes and intrusions across the DMZ. The US-ROK alliance deterred a full-scale confrontation, but it was unable to deter a wide range of smaller-scale confrontations including the EC-121 spy plane incident in 1969; a North Korean infiltration and assassination attempt on South Korean President Park Chunghee that was stopped yards from the Blue House in Seoul; and the North Korean capture of the US spy ship the USS *Pueblo*, through which the captain and crew were detained and tortured for almost a year (Michishita 2010). During this period, North Korea's own politics were in a militant phase contemporaneous with China's Cultural Revolution, North Korea had clear military and economic superiority over the South, and the United States was escalating its efforts in Vietnam and wary of North Korean attempts to take advantage of US distraction. In fact, North Korea was so isolated that Robert Jenkins and several other US soldiers made the fatal miscalculation that they could avoid a transfer to the warfight in Vietnam by deserting from South Korea to the North and then seeking repatriation via Moscow (Jenkins 2009).

This level of US-DPRK hostility precluded almost all forms of diplomacy but created conditions for a strategic shift at the global level occasioned by US-Soviet détente and President Richard Nixon's move to develop Sino-US relations as a counter to Soviet power. The latter move provided a great shock in Asia that reverberated through Tokyo, Seoul, and Pyongyang. The most immediate influence on the peninsula was to force both Park Chunghee and Kim Il Sung to grapple with a changed context that shook up their worldview and sowed doubts about alliance reliability as a result of the shift by their primary major-power patrons. In their attempts to deal with Nixon's visit to Beijing, both Korean leaders sought secret contacts with each other, leading to an unprecedented inter-Korean joint declaration on July 4, 1972 (Oberdorfer 1999). This inter-Korean declaration emphasized the importance of seeking reunification through Korea's own efforts and signaled an apparent easing of the inter-Korean confrontation, although in reality the move was primarily a tactical effort to avoid being undercut by new developments in Asia's regional security environment.

Sino-US rapprochement also broke the ice in terms of Korean thinking about the potential for developing new relationships across Cold War lines. Sino–South Korean contacts remained limited but were facilitated by sports diplomacy and management of specific incidents that required communication links between Seoul and Beijing (Chung 2008). For their part, the

North Koreans began probing, both publicly and privately, for opportunities to improve relations with the United States. The North made public bids to open channels with the United States through appeals for a dialogue on peninsular peace with the US Congress, signals of openness to relations with the United States through foreign media interviews with Kim Il Sung, and other efforts designed to achieve the strategic objective of a new relationship with the United States. For instance, the North Koreans attempted to use private exchanges, such as a 1976 hosting of a ping-pong delegation to Pyongyang, which was carefully explored as a potential vehicle for opening an official dialogue with the United States on the model of Sino-US ping-pong diplomacy. The US delegation, however, was purely private and was not a signal of a US desire for improved relations (Linton 2003a; Linton 2003b).

During this period, there were a number of constraints that clearly inhibited prospects for the opening of direct US-DPRK contacts. As suggested earlier, one major obstacle was opposition from America's allies in Seoul. Although the 1972 Joint Declaration seemed a promising step forward, it was short-lived, as the two Koreas resumed a global competition for legitimacy during the 1970s that included international organizations and stretched to Africa. Having watched the Nixon opening to China, South Koreans worried that American contact with North Korea could lead to an unwelcome surprise breakthrough in US-DPRK relations. As long as South Korea viewed US bilateral contacts in any form with the North as an act of betrayal, there would be high costs to the initiation of diplomacy with North Korea.

A second major obstacle was that the US administration viewed North Korea's leadership as inveterately militant, hostile, and irrational. This view was reinforced by North Korea's handling of the *Pueblo* incident and the axe murder incident at Panmunjom in 1976, in which the United States mobilized an aggressive military counter-response to North Korea's shocking and brutal attack on an American military tree-trimming crew. The likelihood of the United States pursuing a diplomatic breakthrough with such a militant and isolationist regime was low, particularly in the absence of a compelling strategic rationale on par with that faced by the United States when Nixon sought better relations with China as a counter to the Soviet Union.

Informal Contacts as a Bridge to Official Diplomacy:
The End of the Cold War, US-DPRK Direct Dialogue

The end of the Cold War brought about changes both in the strategic context surrounding the Korean Peninsula and in the views of the key parties about the limits of interaction across previously unbridgeable diplomatic divides. In addition, South Korea enjoyed rapid economic development throughout the 1980s, took advantage of new diplomatic opportunities occasioned by its hosting of the Olympics in Seoul in 1988, and underwent a relatively peaceful transition from military authoritarian rule to democracy. These developments provided South Korea with the opportunity to establish new diplomatic relationships with countries on the other side of the Cold War divide, including Hungary, Czechoslovakia, and even the Soviet Union in September 1990. The policy of trying to reach out to former Eastern bloc countries—known in South Korea as "Nordpolitik"—led to the admission of North and South Korea to the United Nations as separate states and to the establishment of a high-level inter-Korean dialogue in 1990. The dialogue eventually resulted in the negotiation of the landmark December 1991 Agreement on Inter-Korean Reconciliation, Nonaggression, Exchanges, and Cooperation, and then to Sino–South Korean normalization in August 1992.

South Korea's efforts to reach out to the North and break the North's diplomatic isolation created opportunities for the United States to establish direct diplomatic contact with the DPRK. In response to these changes, in 1988 the Reagan administration authorized the "modest initiative," through which a low-level diplomatic channel was established between political counselors of the DPRK and US embassies in Beijing. These talks went on sporadically through the early 1990s and provided the opportunity to exchange background information on the two parties' main concerns and objectives, but the talks were held at too low a level to be able to make substantive achievements. As the Chinese government became more actively involved in discussions of diplomatic normalization with South Korea, some Chinese senior officials revived the idea of "cross-recognition," whereby China would normalize with Seoul while the United States would normalize with Pyongyang, but that idea faltered as China's economic ties with South Korea grew while the United States focused on North Korea's suspected nuclear weapons program.

These developments marked a promising but short-lived window of opportunity for progress in US-DPRK relations from 1990 to 1992. Various types of informal and public channels were used on both sides to signal the possibility of an improved diplomatic relationship. These tools included non-official track two discussions hosted by the North Koreans in Pyongyang with a range of American interlocutors, including a number of former offi-cials who had had direct experience managing Asian security issues, public statements by American and North Korean officials designed to send positive signals to the other side, and limited diplomatic contacts designed to signal an openness on both sides to improved relations. For instance, former Reagan National Security Council (NSC) official James Kelly, Center for Strategic and International Studies (CSIS) vice president William Taylor, and University of California, Berkeley professor Robert Scalapino all led delegations to Pyong-yang during this period to discuss prospects and conditions for improved US-DPRK relations at the invitation of the Institute of Disarmament and Peace (IDP) (Asia Society 1992; Asia Society 1993). It was very clear during these visits that North Korea was utilizing these opportunities to collect as much information as possible about official US government positions in advance of the launch of formal US-DPRK contacts designed to improve the official relationship. For instance, almost all of the interlocutors at IDP subsequently went on to become involved in almost every important bilateral negotiation between the two sides over the course of the past two decades. Among the visitors to Pyongyang during this period was Billy Graham, the American evangelist with ties to many American presidents and whose wife Ruth Gra-ham had attended a missionary school based in Pyongyang before World War II. With DPRK permission, Graham brought CNN cameramen with him to record the visit, which provided opportunities for US and DPRK leaders to exchange private messages of reassurance designed to support an improved US-DPRK relationship. Starting from that trip, the North utilized invitations to CNN on several occasions during the 1990s to send signals to the United States about conditions in North Korea or to promote improvements in US-DPRK relations (Chinoy 2008, 4–11).

North Korea's decision to actively invite a range of American think tanks to send delegations, consisting of academic specialists and former officials, to Pyongyang clearly signaled a desire on the part of the North Koreans to explore possibilities for an improved relationship with the United States. The Foreign Ministry–affiliated IDP hosted these delegations, which provided an opportunity for in-depth conversations on the range of issues that would have to be resolved to enable a high-level dialogue. Delegation officials provided reports back to State Department colleagues regarding these conversations, a process that served to inform both governments regarding their thinking on sensitive issues and next steps in improving the relationship.

American officials tried to work in tandem with developments in inter-Korean relations during this period, using the warming inter-Korean relations as a basis upon which to open US-DPRK dialogue. One significant global development that diplomats were able to use effectively on the Korean Peninsula was President George H. W. Bush's announcement of the withdrawal of all land-based nuclear weapons from foreign soil in 1990. This announcement was accompanied by an offer on the part of the Bush administration to have a high-level meeting with North Korea if Pyongyang were to take steps to sign an International Atomic Energy Agency (IAEA) safeguards agreement, which the DPRK did in January 1992. These communications set up an unprecedented meeting in New York between Undersecretary of State Arnold Kanter and the DPRK Worker's Party Secretary for International Affairs Kim Young Sun. The meeting provided an opportunity for a direct exchange of views but did not lead to a sustained dialogue. Despite apparent political momentum during this period in US-DPRK and inter-Korean relations, the conduct of IAEA discussions and discovery of apparent discrepancies between the DPRK's report on its reactor operations and data collected by IAEA inspectors in the summer of 1992 created the conditions for the first North Korean nuclear crisis. Tensions over the history of North Korea's nuclear facilities led to a stalemate with the IAEA, the breakdown of implementation of the Inter-Korean Basic Agreement, and North Korea's March 1993 announcement that it would withdraw from the nuclear Nonproliferation Treaty (NPT) (Wit, Gallucci, and Poneman 2005).

During this period, track two diplomacy helped form the basis for apparent progress in US-DPRK relations, although that progress was short-lived. The combination of President Bush's announcement of the nuclear weapons withdrawal abroad and ROK President Roh Tae Woo's subsequent confirmation that no US nuclear weapons were in South Korea sent a clear public signal to North Korea that the United States was ready to meet at high levels if the North would reciprocate by signing and implementing its IAEA safeguards obligations. This series of steps, reinforced by a breakthrough in inter-Korean relations, provided the basis for the first high-level political contacts between the United States and North Korea since the end of the Korean War. This development signaled only the beginning of diplomatic contacts and was accompanied by a moderation of North Korea's anti-American propaganda, which was another signal of North Korea's desire to improve relations with the United States, but the scope for other forms of public diplomacy beyond the utilization of respective media to signal commitment to negotiations remained quite limited (Mazarr 1995).

US-DPRK Nuclear Negotiations in the Absence of Diplomatic Relations: Geneva Agreed Framework

The period during the negotiation and implementation of the 1994 Geneva Agreed Framework under President Bill Clinton has proven to be the most significant and effective period of direct engagement between the United States and North Korea to date. But even that period of relatively intense diplomatic engagement provides a public diplomacy record that is almost entirely limited to the transmittal of public messages on either side designed to send signals to the counterpart government in support of building diplomatic channels for US-DPRK relations. Major forms of nongovernmental or private engagement and public diplomacy during this period consisted of quiet diplomacy and the calculation of delicate prior understandings and diplomatic sequencing designed to build trust and encourage reciprocal steps between the two sides; the moderation of propaganda and use of public statements by selected DPRK government representatives signaling the prospect for progress in diplomatic negotiations; and the use of nongovernmental and track two efforts in support of the diplomatic process as a means by which to provide public and financial support for unfolding official negotiations. However, mechanisms for the conduct of public diplomacy remained limited to a signaling function related to official diplomatic activity, especially given the continued absence of a US diplomatic presence in North Korea, the constrained presence in New York of North Korean officials stationed at the DPRK Mission to the United Nations, and the ongoing desire of North Korea to maintain exclusive control over messages aired in the North Korean media.

The negotiation of the Geneva Agreed Framework in the mid-1990s also represented a rare opportunity for the United States and North Korea to build stronger diplomatic ties since the framework included both a pathway for the implementation of North Korea's denuclearization and a roadmap toward US-DPRK diplomatic normalization. These objectives were to be sought in tandem, but the focus on denuclearization and the construction of more proliferation-resistant light water reactors became the main preoccupation of the United States as it related to the agreement's implementation. Despite efforts to implement the provisions of the agreement related to establishment of liaison offices as part of the Geneva Agreed Framework, those negotiations were hung up over a number of issues, including the price of property in Washington, American insistence on having diplomatic pouches delivered securely to Pyongyang via the DMZ should a liaison office be established, and apparent hesitations in the North Korean military/security apparatus about the effects of having an American presence in Pyongyang. As a result, efforts to implement the envisioned roadmap for improved diplomatic relations as part of the Geneva Agreed Framework stalled and implementation of the denuclearization portion of the agreement became the main focus for both sides. However, the existence of the Agreed Framework provided the foundation for an exchange of high-level visits involving DPRK National Defense Commission Vice Chairman Cho Myung-rok and Secretary of State Madeleine Albright in the waning days of the Clinton administration, visits that came the closest to influencing US and DPRK public views of the two countries' relationship. The following sections examine specific ways in which public communication was used by both sides to facilitate official negotiations as part of the Geneva Agreed Framework.

(A) Back Door Diplomacy; The Delicate Choreography of Replacing Hostility with Cooperation

In large part because of the relative lack of channels for high-level communication and the seriousness of the confrontation over North Korea's announcement that it would leave the NPT and expand its production of weapons-grade plutonium, the North Korean nuclear crisis quickly came to a head in the summer of 1994. Lower-level efforts to choreograph a return to diplomacy in early 1994 failed to bring the parties back to negotiation. North Korea began to unload fuel rods from its five-megawatt reactor before IAEA inspectors were present in Pyongyang to observe the process, despite a US warning not to do so. As tensions escalated, several efforts to mobilize private interlocutors materialized in an attempt to forestall the crisis. Scholar Selig Harrison of the Carnegie Endowment for International Peace visited Pyongyang in May 1994 to hold discussions with North Korean interlocutors, subsequently conveying North Korean thinking back to Washington. Senators Richard Lugar and Sam Nunn were also approached to make a visit to Pyongyang, offering a higher-level and more credible quasi-official channel through which the United States and DPRK might communicate ideas that might moderate the crisis. But ultimately it was former President Jimmy Carter who dramatically intervened with private diplomacy, playing a key role in changing the trajectory of US-DPRK relations from escalating confrontation to negotiations during his June 1994 visit to Pyongyang (Creekmore 2006).

There is no need to retell the well-known story of Carter's high-level intervention since it has been recounted on many occasions, including in a memoir by one of Carter's aides who accompanied him on the Pyongyang visit (Creekmore 2006), but it is worth noting the following points in this remarkable intervention by a former president:

- President Carter correctly analyzed that a show of respect from a former US president had the potential to sweep away growing tensions and alter the path of the US-DPRK relationship from an escalation of the crisis to renewed negotiations over North Korea's nuclear program.
- Carter's visit and announcement of the results of his conversations with Kim Il Sung averted the likely recommendation of a US troop augmentation in South Korea that might have further inflamed tensions and heightened prospects for military confrontation.
- By bringing a CNN television camera crew with him, Carter was able to set parameters for renewed negotiations publicly, even without a mandate to lay down specific conditions for a return to negotiations. This had the effect of binding both governments from further escalatory steps and committed both sides to renewed negotiations.
- Carter's visit and intervention was also reported in the North Korean media, cutting through the boilerplate image of the United States as an enemy and providing the North Korean people with a rare alternative image of the United States as a potential diplomatic partner rather than as an adversary.

Carter's intervention clearly changed the course of events on the Korean Peninsula and brought the United States and North Korea back to the negotiating table. This turn of events enabled the negotiation of the Geneva Agreed Framework, through which the North Koreans agreed to shut down their nuclear reactor in return for the provision of 500,000 tons of heavy fuel oil per year and construction of two 1,000-megawatt proliferation-resistant nuclear reactors in North Korea. The United States, South Korea, and Japan attempted to address this through the Korean Peninsula Energy Development Organization, founded in March 1995 following the Agreed Framework, along with the efforts of its first executive director, Stephen Bosworth. Although that agreement would become politically contested on Capitol Hill and Congress would withhold financial support for its part of the project to pressure President Clinton to certify that North Korea was abiding by its commitments, the agreement capped North Korea's ability to pursue a full-blown nuclear weapons capacity. However, it did not prevent covert efforts by North Korea to pursue a uranium-based path to the development of nuclear weapons, a factor that proved to be the undoing of the agreement in 2002 during the George W. Bush administration.

(B) The Moderation of Propaganda and Selected Use of Public Statements to Reinforce Negotiations

Once negotiations were able to resume, the two sides used public statements on key occasions during the negotiation process to reinforce diplomatic messages and signal concessions designed to move the process forward. On the North Korean side, North Korean ambassadors abroad have been used by the DPRK to send public messages at critical points in international negotiations with the United States. There were a number of examples of this in the 1990s where ambassadorial statements might be used to signal concessions or adjustments of the North Korean position on important issues that might be taken up in negotiations. In the case of the United States, senior officials appeared to make public statements designed to affirm and validate specific points of discussion as the negotiation process unfolded. This use of public messages reinforced critical points being discussed in the negotiations, affirmed areas where it would be possible to make progress, and set markers designed to show the limits beyond which it would not be possible to make concessions.

In the case of North Korea, one consistent complaint of diplomats serving in Pyongyang has been the extent to which the DPRK government controls and limits their access to senior-level officials in the capital. One way of dealing with restrictions on the ground is to use high-level visitors who are able to meet at a level above that which is available to permanent representatives on the ground. However, the timing of the high-level visit is also a smart tactic that must be deployed in pursuit of multiple objectives. Experience suggests that returns on investment of time spent in North Korea have been perceived as marginal, making it even more difficult to sustain a strategy designed to capture higher-level insights regarding the North.

(C) Track Two Efforts

Following the negotiation of the Agreed Framework, there was a need for ongoing consultations on a number of issues related to implementation of the framework and possible improvement of US-DPRK relations. During this period, a variety of nongovernmental organizations (NGOs) sought to engage with North Korean visitors in an attempt to expose them to the views of a broader group of Americans beyond US government officials. Facilitation of broader exposure to a variety of unofficial American views would provide North Korean officials with a better understanding of the complexity of influences on the US foreign policymaking process while also providing more Americans with the opportunity to hear and understand North Korean positions on a range of issues. Another motive for engaging in track two activities during this period on the part of the North Koreans was related to their own financial conditions in the context of a famine that struck North Korea in the mid-1990s. Financing of diplomatic activities within the foreign ministry itself had become difficult, so American private financial support for North Korean diplomats to travel to the United States for a combination of governmental negotiations and NGO activities helped to facilitate more frequent diplomatic interaction between the United States and DPRK.

One of the main nongovernmental actors that provided funding at that time in support of North Korean delegations to visit the United States was the Washington-based Atlantic Council, which received a major grant from the Department of Energy to facilitate track two diplomacy between the United States and North Korea. The grant was administered by Tony Namkung, a longtime facilitator of US-DPRK informal contacts. In addition to the Atlantic Council, other groups were asked to support part of the cost of travel as cosponsors for DPRK delegations. By the late 1990s the Atlantic Council had dropped from the scene, but Stanford University's John Lewis and the National Committee for American Foreign Policy's Don Zagoria maintained active efforts to keep track two diplomacy alive with North Korea throughout the Bush Administration (Chinoy 2008).

In response to North Korea's famine, American NGOs justified US government support for an NGO response beyond contributions to the UN World Food Programme by appealing both to American humanitarian spirit and the public diplomacy benefits of establishing people-to-people contacts, which could serve as a tangible signal to the North Korean people that Americans were willing to respond to the North's humanitarian need. The American private voluntary consortium of aid organizations organized in the late 1990s ended in failure as a result of infighting, incomplete monitoring, and the unwillingness of the North Koreans to conform to international standards for the monitoring of humanitarian assistance; but the experience laid the groundwork for a more successful effort by American NGOs in 2008–2009 (Snyder and Flake 2003). According to Mercy Corps President Nancy Lindborg, who served as coordinator of that effort, the involvement of US NGOs in the monitoring program "demonstrated the spirit and goodwill of the people of the United States toward the people of North Korea" (US Senate Foreign Relations Committee 2009). This effort was reportedly even more successful than that of the UN World Food Programme, and was once again justified on the basis of the need to promote ties with the North Korean people.

(D) Exchange of High-Level Visits and Public Messaging About US-DPRK Relations

Toward the end of the Clinton administration in the late 1990s, there were three notable high-level exchanges between Pyongyang and Washington that had the potential to influence American public attitudes toward US-DPRK relations. The first visit, by former Secretary of Defense William Perry, who served as coordinator for policy toward North Korea at that time, was part of an effort to formulate new guidelines for US policy toward North Korea, which had been a subject of particular contention on Capitol Hill. Secretary Perry's May 1999 visit was designed to open communications and test North Korea's intentions regarding opportunities for improved dialogue between the two countries. His visit was also designed to facilitate discussions over a controversial site near the village of Keumchangri where the US intelligence community suspected North Korea was conducting additional nuclear activities. The American delegation was received at a relatively modest level in Pyongyang and the group did not have a chance to meet with North Korea's top leadership, but conversations held during the visit informed Perry's policy approach and recommendations, which included advocacy of continued diplomatic engagement with North Korea on nuclear and missile issues. The visit (and US pledges of additional food aid) facilitated an agreement to hold inspections of the suspect site, which did not show any sign of nuclear-related activities. The Perry visit provided credibility within the community of US policy specialists and on Capitol Hill, so the impact of the visit on public perceptions was targeted and limited but not inconsequential. The report laid the foundation for a much more dramatic series of exchanges in 2000, including the exchange of visits between National Defense Commission Vice Chairman Cho Myung-rok, the senior-ranking military official in the DPRK leadership hierarchy, and Secretary of State Madeleine Albright.

The Cho Myung-rok visit to Washington in October 2000 had a bigger impact on public perceptions of North Korea since Cho was the highest-ranking DPRK official ever to visit the United States. The delegation visited the West Coast and Washington, DC, for a series of meetings that included a meeting with President Clinton in the Oval Office. The exchange carried with it potentially significant symbolic implications because it affirmed the Clinton administration's willingness to recognize and have dialogue with senior leaders from Pyongyang in Washington. As a senior military officer and vice chairman of the National Defense Commission, Cho made an important political statement when he chose to wear his uniform to his meeting with President Clinton, signaling a symbolic willingness of the DPRK military and senior leadership to end hostilities and establish a new relationship with the United States. Cho's public visit to the White House suggested to both North Koreans and Americans the possibility of an improved diplomatic relationship between the two countries. But the decision to wear the uniform was also mildly controversial among some quarters in the United States for precisely the same reasons, given that the armistice was still in place and hostility between the two sides had not been fully overcome.

Shortly afterward in October 2000, Secretary of State Albright visited Pyongyang following the historic June 2000 inter-Korean summit and reciprocating Cho's visit weeks earlier. Albright had extensive discussions with Kim Jong Il. Her visit had a mixed impact on public perceptions in North Korea and the United States. The visit of an active US secretary of state to Pyongyang itself showed an unprecedented level of recognition and respect for the DPRK and provided an opportunity for direct communication between the two governments. The Secretary of State showed respect for DPRK institutions, including a visit to the Keumsusan Memorial Hall where the remains of North Korea's founder, Kim Il Sung, are displayed. In addition, Kim Jong Il took the unusual step of joining Secretary Albright for a mass games performance held in her honor before a crowd of more than 100,000 people in Pyongyang, a powerful public symbol of the DPRK's desire to improve relations with the United States. During Albright's visit, there were extensive discussions about the possibility of a visit by President Clinton and about the issues in the relationship that would have to be resolved to enable such a visit. The main issue on the agenda was North Korea's missile program, and a subsequent round of missile negotiations was held in early November, but the negotiations made little progress. However, the possibility of a visit by President Clinton to Pyongyang was upended by the controversy over the outcome of the 2000 US presidential elections.

Although President Clinton did not ultimately visit the DPRK as president, he did visit Pyongyang in August 2009 on a diplomatic mission to secure the release of two American journalists who had been captured and detained on the North Korean side of the border while conducting research for a story on North Korean refugees. Although the potential influence of former presidents as envoys had been clearly illustrated during his own administration by President Carter's diplomatic intervention with Kim Il Sung, President Clinton's role during the Obama administration was highly circumscribed by instructions from the Obama White House, in which his wife, Hillary Clinton, was serving as Secretary of State. President Clinton essentially played the role of messenger by securing the release of the two American journalists who had been held in North Korea and sentenced for illegally crossing the border into North Korea. Although Clinton met with Kim Jong Il and had private talks, it appears that neither side was able to use the opportunity to facilitate a diplomatic opening. The Obama administration handled former President Clinton's North Korea visit with a great deal of political caution, perhaps as a result of the Clinton administration's experience with former President Carter. When President Carter visited North Korea in the spring of 2011 with a delegation of eminent global figures known as The Elders, the Obama administration actively distanced itself from the visit to the extent that Kim Jong Il failed to meet the group and Carter could not gain high-level appointments for briefings following his visit. Although there are political risks attached to the use of former presidents as envoys, they also have provided unique opportunities for direct access to Kim Jong Il, who, like Kim Il Sung before him and Kim Jong Un today, was the only consequential decision-maker in Pyongyang. In contrast, US public official channels have consistently been handled at lower levels and limited to foreign ministry officials such as Kim Kye-gwan and Kang Sokju.

The Second North Korean Nuclear Crisis:
Public Diplomacy Remains Constrained

The George W. Bush administration entered office with a different attitude and approach to North Korea. The Bush administration's public signals toward North Korea were negative. President Bush's characterization of North Korea as part of an "axis of evil" was evidence of a tone that reinforced hostility. Special envoy Jim Kelly's October 2002 visit to Pyongyang and his accusation that North Korea was pursuing a covert uranium enrichment program led to the unraveling of the Agreed Framework, the dismantling of the Korean Peninsula Energy Development Organization (KEDO), and North Korea's expulsion of IAEA inspectors from the Yongbyon facility. The Six Party Talks were established in 2003 as a vehicle by which to persuade North Korea to return to the path of denuclearization. But the talks made little progress as the United States resisted direct dialogue with North Korea even under the rubric of the Six Party Talks.

Though in her confirmation hearing in early 2005 Secretary of State Condoleezza Rice referred to North Korea as an "outpost of tyranny," she sent a different signal the following May in an effort to rejuvenate the talks, stating that the United States recognized North Korea as a sovereign state. Shortly thereafter, Assistant Secretary of State Christopher Hill met with North Korean counterpart Kim Kye-gwan in Beijing, signaling US willingness to negotiate directly with North Korea. This sequence of events enabled the resumption of the Six Party Talks and an intense negotiation that led to a September 2005 Joint Statement among all the parties that emphasized the common objectives of denuclearization, normalization of relations, peace, and economic development. But the opportunity to build on that statement was short-lived as a result of the announcement of a US advisory against Banco Delta Asia, a Macao-based bank that handled North Korean accounts and was suspected of money laundering and counterfeiting. This process stalled the talks for over a year, until North Korea's first nuclear test catalyzed passage of UN Security Council (UNSC)Resolution 1718 and then a resumption of the Six Party Talks. Following an inconclusive round of talks in Beijing in December 2006, the United States and North Korea held bilateral talks the following month and negotiated the outlines of a deal with North Korea. That agreement was formalized in the six-party implementing agreement of February 2007. North Korea agreed to disable and dismantle its facilities at Yongbyon in return for one million tons of heavy fuel aid and removal from the US terrorism list. However, implementation of the agreement was drawn out and eventually fell apart at the end of the Bush administration over North Korean refusal to accept verification of its declaration about its nuclear facilities under the agreement.

During this period of regression in US-DPRK relations, prospects for public diplomacy were limited; other than specific signals designed to reinforce diplomatic messages, the environment for effective public diplomacy was constrained. The Bush administration resisted private efforts to facilitate renewed diplomacy such as those by ambassadors Donald Gregg and Don Oberdorfer to facilitate contacts in November 2002, immediately following the US presentation of allegations to North Korea regarding its covert uranium-based nuclear program. Another effort to promote public diplomacy during this period was the arrangement by the Korea Society of a concert by the New York Philharmonic Orchestra in Pyongyang in February 2008. This was a potentially pathbreaking event that followed the pattern of using cultural diplomacy to expand cultural contacts in the early stages of normalization between the United States and China. However, the Bush administration showed ambivalence toward this effort, which ultimately did not result in a reciprocal visit or broadening of channels for public diplomacy with North Korea (Chinoy 2008).

The environment for public diplomacy efforts toward North Korea has not changed under the Obama administration, despite President Obama's promise in his inaugural speech to greet with an outstretched hand those who will unclench their fists. Instead, North Korea's provocations in the early part of the Obama administration have forestalled diplomatic engagement and extended the confrontation between the two sides while limiting prospects for expanded forms of public diplomacy between the two countries. The Obama administration mobilized UN sanctions and the passage of UNSC Resolution 1874 in response to North Korea's April 2009 multistage rocket launch and June 2009 nuclear tests, while North Korea's alleged sinking of the South Korean warship *Cheonan* in March 2010 and its artillery shelling of Yeonpyeong Island in November 2010 raised tensions and minimized diplomatic space for direct dialogue. The 2014 release of a strongly critical report on North Korean human rights by the United Nations Commision of Inquiry as well as the controversy over *The Interview*, a motion picture comedy that criticized North Korea's leadership, further decreased the space for effective public diplomacy between the two countries.

Shortly following Kim Jong Un's assumption of power following his father's death in December 2011, the United States and DPRK negotiated a "Leap Day understanding" through which both governments announced a deal in which North Korea would suspend its provocative nuclear and missile tests in return for hundreds of thousands of tons of grain from the United States, but this understanding broke down weeks later when North Korea announced preparations for a multistage rocket launch that failed on April 12, 2013. Prospects for negotiations were further stalled following a December 2012 rocket test launch that led to UNSC Resolution 2087 and, after the February 2013 nuclear test, UNSC Resolution 2094.

Under Kim Jong Un, one of the most unusual participants in "public diplomacy" with North Korea emerged in the form of Dennis Rodman, a former National Basketball Association (NBA) star with the Chicago Bulls who visited North Korea and met with Kim during a Harlem Globetrotters basketball exhibition game in Pyongyang in January 2013. Following Rodman's visit, he publicly stated that Kim Jong Un wanted Obama to call him and made multiple return visits to Pyongyang over the course of the following year including for the staging of an exhibition game held in Pyongyang with former NBA stars and the North Korean national team on Kim Jong Un's birthday. However, Rodman's involvement brought mixed impact on public perceptions of North Korea and did not have any impact on the official US-DPRK relationship.

US Propaganda Instruments: Radio Free Asia and Voice of America

Another aspect of the US public diplomacy strategy that developed in the late 1990s was the establishment of Radio Free Asia (RFA) and its Korean service, which was accompanied in turn by the expansion of Voice of America's (VOA) Korean service in the early 2000s. This development was greeted vociferously by the North Korean government, but appears to have had a relatively limited initial impact on North Korea (leadership and citizenry) due to the limited bandwidth and hours of the broadcast service, limited availability of radio receivers in North Korea, and the extensive restrictions and punishments average North Koreans face if they are caught attempting to listen to foreign media. In recent years, there is evidence, based on surveys of refugees who have left Korea, that the influence of radio broadcasts targeted at

North Koreans has broadened, presumably as a result of increased ownership of receiving technologies, loosening social practices, and the North Korean authorities' limited enforcement capacity.

North Korean criticism of RFA at the time of its founding suggests that North Korean authorities had a genuine fear regarding the potential impact of foreign broadcasting efforts on their population. This fear is further evidenced by the extent to which the DPRK government attempts to control the messages and information available to its people. Efforts on the part of RFA and VOA, in combination with growing South Korean efforts to broadcast news to the North Korean people, appears to have had an impact on North Korean society. For instance, North Korean official reporting on important events appears to have been influenced to some degree by foreign news coverage of certain issues, suggesting that foreign information is penetrating inside North Korea (Beck 2010). Surveys of refugees from North Korea suggest that the influence of foreign radio and television programming (disseminated secretly via DVDs or USB drives) has gradually grown inside North Korea, presumably as the state loses the battle to control information as new technology seeps into North Korea and marketization of North Korea's domestic economy is increasingly spreading throughout the country. But these surveys show that the greatest source of information threat to the regime remains word-of-mouth transmission of information, despite the state's effort to control information from the outside. However, from the second year of Kim Jong Un's rule more efforts have been taken by the state to limit telecommunications and radio frequencies traveling across the Sino–North Korean border, limiting the amount of information seeping into the country.

Inter-Korean Confrontation as an Obstacle to Direct US-DPRK Contact

For many decades a major factor inhibiting US direct engagement with the DPRK has been consideration of the attitudes of America's alliance partners in South Korea. As a practical matter, South Korea's concern about being left out of or negatively affected by US-DPRK direct interaction has been greater during periods when the inter-Korean relationship has not been good, while US opportunities for enhanced diplomatic engagement have generally been most successful during positive phases in inter-Korean relations. For example, high-level inter-Korean dialogue in the early 1990s eased the environment for a parallel US-DPRK high-level meeting in 1992 that was used to address American concerns about North Korea's nuclear programs. Similarly, Secretary of State Albright's visit to Pyongyang came in the wake of the June 2000 inter-Korean summit.

Conversely, US-DPRK direct dialogue became a focus of concern or anxiety in South Korea during periods of difficulty in inter-Korean relations. South Korean President Kim Young Sam felt very uncomfortable with US-DPRK bilateral negotiations that led to the Geneva Agreed Framework precisely because South Korea did not have a seat at the table for negotiations that would have a direct impact on South Korea's security. Kim worried that North Korea would take advantage of the United States at the expense of South Korean interests in negotiations as a result of perceived American ignorance regarding North Korean tactics and negotiating style.

During periods of inter-Korean engagement, however, the United States found little support from South Korea for efforts to broaden the availability of alternative information sources to the North Korean people. RFA and VOA were unable to place a transmitter in South Korea under the progressive administrations of Kim Dae Jung and Roh Moo-hyun, which were both focused on expanding inter-Korean engagement and dialogue and feared such a tactic would damage their apparent progress.

US Presence in South Korea and Messages to the North

The US embassy/ambassador in South Korea has a role in public diplomacy that is primarily targeted at South Korea but also has an indirect impact on the North, if for no other reason than that the US ambassador's statements in Seoul are closely monitored and reported in the South Korean press, and the South Korean press is accessible to high-level North Korean authorities and may have an influence in framing North Korean interpretation and understanding of the outside world. This creates a particularly challenging task for the ambassador, as remarks on peninsular issues have dual audiences and impacts on both the public in South Korea and the North Korean government's understanding of sensitive issues in the relationship.

Representation on the Korean Peninsula complicates and facilitates the ability of the United States to monitor the situation in North Korea. Since the 2000 inter-Korean summit, ambassadors of third countries are increasingly dual-accredited to Seoul and Pyongyang, providing opportunities for the sharing of on-the-ground impressions among diplomats not permanently based in Pyongyang. While Pyongyang-based counterparts share their observations, they provide only indirect views of current developments in North Korea. Permanent representatives also have the impression that the North Koreans try extremely hard to keep diplomats accredited to Pyongyang in a bubble; there are not many opportunities for informal interactions with North Korean high-level officials that might help to explain the context for political developments in North Korea (Hoare 2007).

Conclusion: Transforming the Propaganda Message and the Limits of Public Diplomacy in a Hostile Environment

Public diplomacy remains hostage in the North Korean case to limited bandwidth for engagement. While NGO/track two opportunities and exchanges designed to enhance North Korean understanding of the outside world might be desirable, one limit is the apparent inability to gain direct access to the North Korean public. As the North Korean government's control over its people declines, it may be possible to expand access to the public, but it is also likely that the DPRK government will increasingly see expanded public diplomacy efforts toward North Korea as hostile or, at best, double-edged. The ongoing atmosphere of hostility (and lack of diplomatic representation) between the two sides is a major obstacle to expanded public diplomacy toward North Korea, and North Korea's own domestic political constraints suggest that the prospects for fashioning an effective message that can reach the North Korean people remains premature. Most public diplomacy activities have been geared toward facilitation of expanded communication and toward enabling changes in the official relationship between the two governments as a prerequisite for expanded contacts. At the same time, some US NGOs have been successful in establishing relationships and programs on the ground, in areas such as humanitarian and health/medical assistance, development, and education/training, on a limited basis despite the absence of official relations between the two governments. Politically, this kind of engagement with isolated states is to be welcomed, but conceptually there may well be some dispute as to whether such relations can be called "diplomacy" in the strict sense or rather serve as a form of transnational communication that facilitates formal diplomacy, including its public dimension. Former presidents Carter and Clinton are arguably (public) diplomacy actors, but (in)famous basketball stars such as Dennis Rodman perhaps are not. The nuclear issue has overall been a dampening factor on the development of official relations as well as on public diplomacy efforts to facilitate negotiations, despite the public roles of skillful nonresident special envoys such as Robert Gallucci and Christopher Hill. A factor unique to the North Korean case is the need to improve US-DPRK relations in tandem with progress in inter-Korean reconciliation. Thus, US public diplomacy toward its isolated longtime adversary in the North needs to take close account of its ally in the South and key regional partners such as Japan.

Some observers saw Kim Jong Un's activities when he assumed power after his father's death in 2011 as a signal that the United States might be able to increase its public diplomacy in North Korea. However, as he consolidated power, such hopes proved unwarranted. Kim Jong Un appears to want to control all outside influences, including the media and telecommunications, and he has avoided interaction with any foreign leadership, even the leaders of DPRK's longtime ally, China. Whether a high-level envoy, such as a former US president, would have the pull to arrange a meeting with Kim Jong Un has yet to be tested, but until the regime sends signals that it is interested in engaging with South Korea or the United States, the opportunities for US public diplomacy toward North Korea remain extremely limited.

References

Asia Society. 1992. *Divided Korea*, New York: The Asia Society.

———. 1993. *Divided Korea II*. New York: The Asia Society.

Beck, Peter. 2010. Conference presentation. Conference on Nontraditional Security in North Korea, Kyungnam Institute of Far Eastern Studies. July 14.

Berridge, G.R. and Nadia Gallo. 1999. "The Role of the Diplomatic Corps: The US-North Korea Talks in Beijing, 1988–1994." In *Innovation in Diplomatic Practice*, Jan Melissen, ed., 214–230. New York: Macmillan.

Chinoy, Mike. 2008. *Meltdown: The Inside Story of the North Korean Nuclear Crisis*. New York: St. Martin's Press.

Creekmore, Marion. 2006. *A Moment of Crisis: Jimmy Carter, The Power of a Peacemaker, and North Korea's Nuclear Ambitions*. New York: Public Affairs.

Downs, Chuck, 1998. *Over the Line: North Korea's Negotiating Behavior*. Washington, DC: American Enterprise Institute.

Hoare, James L. 2007. "Diplomacy in the East: Seoul, Beijing, and Pyongyang, 1981–2002." In *The Diplomatic Corps as an Institution of International Society*, Paul Sharp and Geoffrey Wiseman, eds., 105–124. New York: Palgrave MacMillan.

Jae Ho Chung. 2008. *Between Ally and Partner: Korea-China Relations and the United States.* New York: Columbia University Press.

Jenkins, Charles Robert. 2009. *The Reluctant Communist: My Desertion, Court-Martial, and Forty-Year Imprisonment in North Korea.* Berkeley: University of California Press.

Linton, Stephen. 2003a. Congressional Testimony, House Foreign Affairs Committee, June 5.

———. 2003b. Personal communication with author, June.

Mazarr, Michael. 1995. *North Korea and the Bomb: A Case Study in Nonproliferation.* New York, St. Martin's Press.

Michishita, Narushige. 2010. *North Korea's Diplomatic Campaigns, 1966–2008.* New York: Routledge.

Oberdorfer, Don. 1999. *The Two Koreas: A Diplomatic History.* New York: Basic Books.

Snyder, Scott and L. Gordon Flake, eds. 2003. *Paved With Good Intentions: The NGO Experience in North Korea.* New York: Praeger.

US Senate Foreign Relations Committee. 2009. Statement of Nancy Lindborg. June 11.

Wit, Joel S. 2001. "North Korea: The Leader of the Pack." *The Washington Quarterly.* 24/1: 77–92.

Wit, Joel, Robert Gallucci and Dan Poneman, 2005. *Going Critical: The First North Korean Nuclear Crisis.* Washington, DC: Brookings.

4 VIETNAM

American and Vietnamese Public Diplomacy, 1945–2010

Mark Philip Bradley and Viet Thanh Nguyen

THE MORNING AFTER PRESIDENT WILLIAM JEFFERSON Clinton announced the United States had lifted its decades-long economic embargo against Vietnam, a giant inflated facsimile of a Pepsi-Cola can hovered over the busiest intersection in Ho Chi Minh City (Shenon 1994). The very public struggle for the Vietnamese cola market in 1994 marked a moment in which the more than thirty-year-long state of war between Vietnam and the United States began to fall away. The wars for Vietnam had been long and savage. They were at once a colonial war, civil war, cold war turned hot, and war of memory. From 1945, when Ho Chi Minh proclaimed a postcolonial Vietnamese state, to 1975, when North Vietnam defeated South Vietnam, Vietnam remained in a state of war: first in an eight-year French war supported by the United States and then in the more than twenty-year-long American war. Some 58,000 Americans lost their lives in Vietnam. Three million Vietnamese were killed. In the aftermath of war, fierce mutual animosities lingered for another two decades. Only in 1995, some fifty years after the first sustained Vietnamese-American encounter, were diplomatic relations between the two countries normalized. The neoliberal global economic order and shared concerns about a rising China replaced the Cold War battleground as the centerpoint of Vietnamese-American relations.

This chapter explores the place of public diplomacy in that history. It adopts an especially capacious understanding of the actors and processes that make up public diplomacy, one that reflects the complexities of agency and structure in the modern history of Vietnamese-American relations. At the state level, we consider the perceptions and policies of American and Vietnamese diplomats, though on the Vietnamese side that requires taking into account not only the northern and southern regimes (the leadership of the latter shifted markedly over time) but also the National Liberation Front (NLF). Like other quasi-state actors in this period such as the Algerian *Front de Libération Nationale* and the African National Congress, the NLF joined with its more traditional state counterparts in the employment of public diplomacy. The nonstate level offers a more varied constellation of actors, from nongovernmental organizations *avant le lettre,* such as the short-lived Vietnamese-American friendship associations of the 1940s and 1950s, to the more familiar Smithsonian Institution, Ford Foundation, and New York Philharmonic. We also consider the Vietnamese American community as a critical actor in the making of public diplomacy, as well as specific writers and artists from Vietnam, the United States, and the diaspora. In this history, both state and nonstate actors turned to political, economic, and cultural forms of public diplomacy at times as tools of war but more often, and more successfully, to seek legitimacy from international publics or reconciliation among themselves.

Foregrounding such historical actors as the Ford Foundation and the NLF, we reflect the broader turn that Wiseman identifies in the Introduction, from "traditional government to foreign public" initiatives to a "new public diplomacy" involving both state and nonstate actors. In its sustained focus on a disaggregated Vietnam rather than simply on US policy, our approach also aligns with an emerging consensus that public diplomacy is most usefully studied in dialogic rather than monologic terms. Moreover, in places we go beyond the "new public diplomacy" view in that we include actors (such as antiwar activist Jane Fonda, journalist Harrison Salisbury, and novelist Graham Greene) who helped shape public perceptions, but who some would classify as simply individuals engaging in communication between two countries and thus not "true" public diplomacy actors. An additional framing point underscoring our very broad view of public diplomacy is that we are using the terms "public diplomacy" and "propaganda" interchangeably, while being aware of the latter's negative connotations. Public diplomacy did not win or lose the wars for Vietnam, though it played a sustained instrumental role in the wider strategies of all the protagonists. But in the postwar period, public diplomacy in its broadest sense has been an essential part of the confidence-building mechanisms that eventually allowed Vietnam and America to move from war to peace.

Public Diplomacy in the Vietnam Wars

Shortly after Ho Chi Minh proclaimed Vietnam free of French colonial rule and established the Democratic Republic of Vietnam (DRV) in September 1945, the new Vietnamese government oversaw the organization of the Vietnamese-American Friendship Association (Hoi Viet-My Than Huu). The Association aimed to promote improved economic and cultural relations with the United States through public lectures, translation of books, language courses, and publication of a monthly magazine. Its leaders came from Hanoi's business community who had ties with the new Vietnamese government and were especially interested in US commerce, mass culture, and technology. As one wrote hopefully in an early 1946 issue of the Association's magazine, "Vietnam will be a new market for American manufactured goods, and what is more, we do not see any reason why the Americans should not build a Ford plant in our country" ("About Future Relations" 1945–46, 18). The Association played host to delegations from several leading US firms with interests in Vietnam's economy, including the oil companies Standard-Vacuum and California-Texaco, General Motors, Harley-Davidson, and New York–based insurance underwriters. It also ushered in a return of American film, which had been extremely popular among urban Vietnamese during the colonial period, at cinemas in major Vietnamese cities. These films, the Association's magazine told its readers, "[remind us] the USA . . . is a grand and lovely country and the Americans a nice people" (ibid., 17).

The Association's activities grew out of a broader effort by the DRV to seek more official ties to the United States. The Viet Minh, a World War II–era nationalist coalition led by Ho Chi Minh through which the DRV came to power, cultivated members of the US Office of Strategic Services (OSS) first in southern China and later in Vietnam itself when OSS officers came there to oversee what was anticipated to be an imminent Japanese surrender during the waning days of the war. Ho himself had spent a brief period of time in the United States before World War I, and he drew on these experiences in making overtures to the Americans. Archimedes Patti, the officer who led the OSS mission in Hanoi, was close enough to Ho Chi Minh that Ho invited him to review his independence day speech to ensure his quotations from the

American Declaration of Independence were accurately rendered. Through Patti and later General Philip E. Gallagher, who served as the senior US military adviser in Vietnam in the fall of 1945, Ho sent a series of messages to President Harry Truman and Secretary of State James F. Byrnes asking for US support of the DRV. In one message to Byrnes, Ho suggested the Vietnamese were "keenly interested in things American" ("Ho Chi Minh to James Byrnes" 1971) and asked to send a delegation of fifty Vietnamese students to the United States to undertake training in agriculture, engineering, and other applied sciences. Meanwhile representatives of the DRV in the South told Americans there that the government looked forward "to the opportunity of cooperating with American industrial [sic] and businessmen" (Thach 1945; also see Bradley 2000, 107).

Nothing, in the end, came of these initiatives. None of Ho Chi Minh's letters to Washington in 1945 and 1946 were answered, and indeed with the formal outbreak of war between France and the DRV in December 1946 the United States took a position of pro-French neutrality. But as the war escalated, the United States began its own public diplomacy campaign in Vietnam. The US Information Service opened a reading room and library in late 1946 in Saigon that featured books, magazines, and films focused on US political history and technological prowess, and it began to broadcast American music on a local radio station. The French viewed these modest efforts by its erstwhile ally with considerable suspicion, suggesting privately that "the exaltation of American power and ideals of democracy" were an effort to bring Vietnam "into the American orbit" (Rapport 1946; also see Statler 2009). Meanwhile DRV diplomats in Southeast Asia and India established the Vietnam News Service and participated in several regional conferences aimed at drawing on the common experiences of colonialism and decolonization to build support for the government. The DRV mission in Bangkok also sought out former OSS officers working in Thailand to urge American mediation of the French war and to build cultural ties with the United States, including the establishment of joint scientific organizations, funding for a chair in American literature at the University of Hanoi, and scholarships for Vietnamese students at American universities (Bradley 2000, 146).

By 1950, with the coming of the Cold War in Asia, the Truman administration fully backed the French war effort, eventually paying as much as 80 percent of its cost. At the same time, the Soviet Union and People's Republic of China extended diplomatic recognition to the DRV, with the Chinese sending increasingly larger numbers of military advisers and substantial amounts of military equipment and supplies to support the Vietnamese war effort. Public diplomacy between the DRV and the United States, beyond hostile Cold War polemics, largely came to an end, though American information activities continued in French-controlled areas of the country. But in fact most American officials had indifferently received the DRV's substantial public diplomacy initiatives toward the United States even before the Cold War came to intensify broader and unfavorable American perceptions of the Vietnamese. Americans during World War II and its immediate aftermath encountered the Vietnamese through a racialist lens that rendered them as a backward and primitive people incapable of self-government and susceptible to external direction. These sentiments and the dangers they posed eventually layered onto and shaped American Cold War concern about Soviet dominance of the DRV. As one State Department observer from the period argued in what was then common parlance, the "Annamese are attractive and even lovable" but "essentially childish" and "under the present government . . . [Vietnam] would immediately be run in accordance with dictates from Moscow" (Saigon Consulate 1947). Neither racialized nor Cold War perceptions were especially hospitable optics for American reception of DRV public diplomacy. For their part, the Vietnamese may have misperceived the ambiguous American professions of anticolonialism and believed that the United States would serve as a reliable wedge against French efforts to reconstitute its imperial order.

Against hardening Cold War tensions, the 1954 Geneva Accords brought an end to the French war dividing Vietnam at the 17th parallel. With North Vietnam preoccupied by internal development of its economy in the mid- to late 1950s, the renewal of Vietnamese-American public diplomacy initially focused on the US-backed South Vietnamese government under Ngo Dinh Diem. Similar to the Ho Chi Minh government view during the French war, the fledging Diem government saw public diplomacy as a way to build international legitimacy. Though some efforts were made regionally and in Western Europe, Diem was especially keen to cement ties with the United States and to keep flowing what would eventually become billions of dollars in US military and economic aid to South Vietnam by the early 1960s. In doing so, Diem built upon ties he had established during the French war when he lived in a Maryknoll seminary in New York from 1950 to 1953 and forged relationships with such influential American political figures as Senator John F. Kennedy,

Senate Majority Leader Mike Mansfield, Supreme Court Justice William O. Douglas, and Cardinal Spellman (Miller 2004, 443–447).

Diem's public diplomacy also benefited from his triumphant official visit to the United States in 1957, during which *Life* magazine proclaimed him "the miracle man of Southeast Asia," and less directly from the attention Vietnam received in Thomas Dooley's bestselling book *Deliver Us from Evil*, which vividly chronicled the exodus of Vietnamese Catholics from the north after the signing of the Geneva Accords. Dooley's widely disseminated writing and his hugely popular Sunday radio broadcasts from Laos in the late 1950s—what one might characterize as nonstate public diplomacy aimed at marshaling support for Dooley's Cold War humanitarian projects in the region—may have been the most important single influence in shaping the perceptions held by ordinary Americans of Vietnam and Southeast Asia in this period (Fischer 1997; Jacobs 2004, 221).

The Diem government's own efforts began in earnest in 1955 when South Vietnam signed a contract with Harold Oram and Associates, an American public relations firm, to oversee the state's information and propaganda campaigns in the United States. Oram, a founding member of the American Friends of Vietnam (AFV), which sought to promote Diem to American officials, organized conferences, distributed political tracts, and wrote editorials for American newspapers and magazines (Morgan 1997; Jacobs 2004, 217). At the same time, the Vietnamese embassy in Washington submitted editorials to the American press, sent books and pamphlets to American libraries, and organized symposia at a variety of college campuses. A major exhibit on Vietnamese culture at the Smithsonian organized by South Vietnam with the cooperation of the United States Information Agency (USIA) was among the most visible of these efforts to, in the words of one official, make "a definite contribution to American-Vietnamese understanding." It featured traditional Vietnamese art and handicrafts, but also conveyed a clear political message. Visitors to the exhibit were not only greeted by a large photograph of Diem and several of the regime's propaganda tracts but were given a guidebook, written by the South Vietnamese ambassador to the United States Tran Van Chuong, that emphasized a historical narrative linking Diem with celebrated Vietnamese emperors and their patriotic resistance to the Chinese over a millennium of Vietnamese history. After leaving Washington, the exhibit reached a considerable audience as it traveled to a dozen American cities (Masur 2009, 304–308).

These efforts by the Diem regime to win the goodwill of the American population spoke to the importance of culture as an arena of public diplomacy. The Vietnam War would eventually become known as the first television war, indicating how much influence media would have over the debate in the United States about the war and on the direction of the war. But even in the 1950s, cultural texts were having an impact on how Vietnamese and Americans were being perceived. *The Ugly American*, a 1958 novel by Eugene Burdick and William Lederer, depicts American efforts against Communism in a fictitious Southeast Asian country. The central figure in English novelist Graham Greene's 1956 southern Vietnamese–based novel *The Quiet American* is Alden Pyle, who for Greene represents the American character: he believes in the ultimate goodness of American intentions in Vietnam and the wider world and in the necessity of stopping communist influence at all costs. Led morally astray by his ideals, Pyle ends up sponsoring bombings that kill Vietnamese civilians. At the time, Americans read the novel as an anti-American critique, so much so that the 1958 Hollywood film adaptation changed the ending to depict Pyle as a hero. But by the 1960s, the consensus even among American readers was that Greene was prescient, and his novel became required reading for Americans coming to Vietnam. Like the ugly American, the quiet American also became a type of character that would be recognized in discussions over the war and American foreign policy.

In this context of swaying public opinion internationally, the Diem government and subsequent northern and southern governments would undertake various cultural efforts to try and shape that opinion. Perhaps the most quixotic undertaking by the Diem government to bolster its legitimacy was the promotion of international tourism. South Vietnam's National Tourism Board, founded in 1957 with the motto "make the country better known and thus better loved," began a marketing campaign in the United States that combined orientalized descriptions of Vietnam's "exotic" charms and potted histories of the Vietnamese past with reminders that South Vietnam was a devoted member of the "American" family of free nations. The AFV helped disseminate the Tourism Board's lavishly illustrated *Visit Fascinating Vietnam* and *Guide to Viet-Nam*, including them in their "Kit for Teachers" that received wide distribution to American elementary and secondary teachers. These initiatives drew upon what Christopher Endy in his work on Cold War tourism characterizes as broader efforts by the American state to encourage international travel as a patriotic commitment to its Cold War allies. To an extent the campaign worked: international arrivals in Vietnam went from 13,250 in 1957 to 37,783 in 1961 with Americans representing the largest group of visitors (Endy 2004; Laderman 2009, 15).

But the larger message of the southern government's public diplomacy, aimed at convincing the American public that "Diem was the rightful leader of a legitimate nation deserving of American support," floundered as the war in the south intensified. The Smithsonian exhibition opened in 1960 just as Diem's generals staged a failed coup against him, and as the American press began to report more critically on the repression, corruption, and nepotism that characterized his regime. The government shifted to a more covert and aggressive form of public diplomacy, seeking through its embassy in Washington to shape the tone of American news coverage by arranging for what it saw as "objective" journalists to travel to South Vietnam. These efforts too collapsed during the Buddhist Crisis of 1963 as images from the streets of Saigon of the self-immolation of monks who were protesting the dictatorial nature of the Diem government shocked audiences around the world. The very public and ultimately undiplomatic comments of Madame Nhu, the wife of Diem's brother and the unofficial first lady of South Vietnam, about the self-immolations did not help the regime. In a letter to the editor of the *New York Times*, she wrote that "I would clap hands at seeing another monk barbecue show, for one cannot be responsible for the madness of others," telling the world press, "let them burn and we clap our hands" ("Mrs. Nhu Defends Stand," 14 August 1963). As South Vietnam's former prime minister and vice president Nguyen Cao Ky eventually remarked, the South Vietnamese had a poor understanding of how to engage diplomatically with American public opinion. For Ky, who held office from 1965 to 1973, public diplomacy would have included a campaign in public relations, mass media, and popular culture, aimed at supplementing traditional diplomatic efforts. "I should have visited America often," he said, "not to go to the White House or the Congress or the Pentagon, but to speak with the people of America as I did with the people of Vietnam" (Ky 2002, 252). Whether such efforts would have saved the southern war effort, as he suggests, is debatable but they testify to the importance of cultural efforts in diplomatic work.

Thus, even after the Diem government fell in 1963 and as the American war dramatically escalated in the 1960s, South Vietnam's tourism campaign continued. In December 1973, when travel writer Paul Theroux was in Saigon to ride the local train, the Tourism Board was still making its pitch. Meeting with the heads of the board, Theroux pointed out that "tourists might be a bit worried about getting shot." His hosts quickly dismissed the idea, even though, as he notes, 70,000 people had been killed since the cease-fire declared earlier that year. "Places like Bangkok and Singapore are just commercial," the Tourist Board's deputy commissioner told Theroux. "That's not interesting. We can offer spontaneity and hospitality, and since our hotels aren't very good we could appeal to the more adventurous. . . . These people can go back to the States and tell their friends they saw where this or that battle was fought" (Theroux 2006, 243–244).

Along with these efforts at cultural persuasion, the Diem government and the subsequent southern regimes sought to build relations with the United States by sending military officers, students, and diplomats to study and work in America. Officers, paratroopers, and pilots trained at various forts and bases throughout the United States in the 1950s and 1960s, acquiring the tactical, technical, and linguistic skills that would be crucial in implementing American-style military strategy and handling US weapons, vehicles, and planes (Wiest 2008). College students attended universities throughout the country and in at least a couple of instances, at Michigan State University and Southern Illinois University at Carbondale, these schools not only provided a standard education but became involved in training Vietnamese bureaucrats and technocrats in support of the southern regime. As the involvement of the United States in Vietnam deepened, and the war became more controversial both in the United States and in Vietnam, the Vietnamese student population likewise became caught up in political struggles. Some students endorsed the southern regime, some the northern regime or the NLF, and some were antiwar or prodemocracy; and inevitably the different factions came into conflict with each other. Activist Vietnamese students became representative of the revolutionary struggle for the American antiwar movement and in that way fulfilled an informal diplomatic function. They were viewed as voices of authenticity by antiwar activists and sometimes invited to be a part of teach-ins during the war to comment on Vietnamese politics (Emerson 1976; Pham 2002).

The formation in 1960 of the NLF, the public face of the growing communist insurgency in southern Vietnam, ushered in another form of wartime Vietnamese public diplomacy. Much of the NLF's activities were directed at challenging the South Vietnamese state and winning support in rural and urban Vietnam, first through political struggle and later through guerilla and more conventional warfare. But the NLF created a Foreign Relations Commission in 1962 to aggressively take its message beyond Vietnam. The NLF's embrace of neutralism as the centerpiece of its diplomatic strategy drew upon the spirit of the 1955 Bandung Conference and the emergence of the Non-Aligned Movement. In doing so, its public diplomacy built upon and deepened an emergent global symbolic theater of quasi-state diplomacy in the 1960s. As Matt Connelly has argued, the Algerian War unleashed a diplomatic revolution that fundamentally challenged the state-based scaffolding upon which the Cold War international order rested. In part, this was the result of the Algerian liberation movement, the *Front de Libération Nationale*, being treated in the postcolonial world and beyond as possessing the attributes and legitimacy previously accorded only to states. This shift in perception of the power and significance of liberation movements contributed to the increasing importance of the African National Congress in South Africa, al Fatah in the Palestinian diaspora, and similar groups in Angola and East Timor in the international politics of decolonization after 1962. It did the same for the NLF (Connelly 2002, 3–13, 276–287).

The skillful propagandists of the NLF's diplomatic service were well-educated and urbane southern Vietnamese who traveled the world in the early 1960s to meet with governments and the Western media, including the *New York Times* and American journalists, to press their agenda of neutralism. They received expressions of support from the Soviet bloc, Mao's China, some in the Non-Aligned Movement including the Indonesian leader Sukarno and Cambodia's Prince Sihanouk, the UN Secretary General U Thant, and Charles de Gaulle's France. In what would become common practice as the American war escalated, the NLF also began to send its diplomats to Eastern Europe, Africa, and Cuba with photographs of suspected communists being tortured by the South Vietnamese secret police and of Americans using chemical defoliants in the Vietnamese countryside. Throughout the war, NLF diplomats engaged in various forms of public diplomacy to promote a pacific resolution of the war, to drive a wedge between Washington and its Saigon allies, and more generally to shape international public opinion in opposition to the South Vietnamese state and American intervention in Vietnam (Brigham 1998). In some cases, the diplomatic effort was more covert. The legendary spy, Pham Xuan An, who would socialize and work with the most influential circles of American journalists and the South Vietnamese leadership, was dispatched by the NLF to study in California in the 1950s (Berman 2008;

Bass 2009). The NLF also covertly inserted its agents into the highest ranks of President Nguyen Van Thieu's southern government, including Thieu's special adviser and the congressman charged with leading a congressional delegation to the United States in 1975 to ask for more emergency aid to fight off the final northern assault, which NLF agents ensured that the southern government did not receive (Engelmann 1990, 306–307). Although the NLF presented the public fiction that it operated independently of North Vietnam, in fact the North was present at its creation and would increasingly dominate and control its activities as the war continued. Nor were the interests of the NLF and the North always the same, and the growing suspicions and hostilities between the two groups, while never made public during the war, prompted the North to largely push aside the NLF's leadership when the war ended in 1975.

The North Vietnamese state also employed public diplomacy during the war, with mixed results. Its more ham-handed efforts to have American POWs held in the North speak out against the war through carefully controlled public broadcasts tended to inflame rather than win over American public opinion toward the war. More successful was its effort to reach out to the American press, including Harrison Salisbury, whose influential 1967 *Behind the Lines—Hanoi* was one of the rare examples of American wartime reportage from inside northern Vietnam. The antiwar movement was also sympathetic and some of their representatives, most notably Jane Fonda and Susan Sontag, came to visit Hanoi and speak out against American policy (Wells 1996; Wu 2013). Although the North tended to overestimate the ability of the antiwar movement to affect US domestic politics, it had some successes, most notably with the 1968 Tet Offensive's impact on American public opinion (Braestrup 1977). While the Tet Offensive failed militarily, it was a diplomatic success, turning American public opinion decisively against the war. While antiwar sentiment was not the same as pro-left or pro–North Vietnamese sentiment, there was a clear convergence for some Americans, as in Peter Davis's Oscar-winning 1974 documentary *Hearts and Minds*. Davis's controversial film laid the blame for a failed war at the feet of American and South Vietnamese politicians and generals, and represents one way in which cinema was used as a political intervention during the American involvement in Vietnam.

Another area of diplomatic success for the North and the NLF occurred with progressive minority groups in the United States. The idea of gender equality among Vietnamese revolutionaries and the image of Vietnamese women participating in the revolutionary war effort were important to a resurgent American feminist movement. Pacifist religious groups such as the Quaker American Friends Service Committee and the Mennonite Central Committee combined antiwar activism at home with programs beginning in 1966 to provide medical supplies and equipment for civilians and children in both North and South Vietnam. Meanwhile, the radicalization of minority civil rights movements in the United States owed a great deal to the Vietnamese revolution, which shaped the anti-imperialist language of the antiwar movement. A self-conscious Asian American movement emerged from a combination of antiwar, antiracist, and anti-imperialist sentiments among Asian Americans. Meanwhile, the Black Panthers not only invoked Mao and his Little Red Book but also paid attention to Vietnam, where they considered the war to be an imperialist venture that contradicted black interests (Maeda 2009; Wu 2013). Huey Newton, cofounder of the Black Panthers, offered to send Black Panthers to fight with the Viet Cong (Newton 1992, 133–136). Whether serious or rhetorical, his effort was symbolic of the larger success that the Vietnamese revolution had on the world stage among the global antiwar left and anticolonial revolutionaries. Che Guevara put it this way: "How close and bright would the future appear if two, three, many Vietnams flowered on the face of the globe. . . . Our every action is a call for war against imperialism and a cry for the unity of the peoples against the great enemy of the human species: the United States of North America" (Guevara 1967, 15).

The final defeat of the South Vietnamese government on April 30, 1975 brought an end to the thirty years' war in Vietnam. Another twenty years would pass before the newly reunified Vietnam and the United States established diplomatic relations. In the slow road to normalization of relations and in its aftermath, public diplomacy in a variety of forms would often play a critical role.

Postwar Public Diplomacy and the Road to Normalization

The immediate postwar years saw little diplomatic contact, traditional or public, between the United States and Vietnam. Efforts to normalize diplomatic relations floundered on sharp mutual hostilities after 1975. The United States established an embargo on commerce and travel to Vietnam as soon as the war ended, and in the fall of 1975 it vetoed Vietnam's application for membership in the United Nations. Quickly the demand for a full accounting of American POWs/MIAs, and the perceived Vietnamese reticence to do so, further soured American attitudes toward Vietnam and over time would come to serve as the biggest domestic obstacle to normalization. This demand was a historical novelty: far fewer MIAs were unaccounted for in the aftermath of the American war in Vietnam (fewer than 3,000) than following World War II or the Korean War, and no similar call emerged in the wake of those wars. Moreover, the Vietnamese had their 300,000 MIAs along with 1.4 million people disabled from the war and some 500,000 war-induced orphans. But the grassroots efforts of POW/MIA families, their championing by conservative political leaders, and the sting of America's first wartime defeat combined to produce a domestic political culture that insisted upon full accounting as the *sine qua non* of any future relations with Vietnam. The POW/MIA movement's success in shaping the political conversation about Vietnam was and is symbolized in the black flag the movement created, which is still flown in many public spaces alongside American and state flags (Allen 2009).

In the often desultory talks between the two sides in late 1970s, Vietnam demanded that the United States lift the embargo and make good on President Richard Nixon's promise at the time of the 1973 Paris Peace Accords to provide more than $3 billion in reconstruction aid to Vietnam. A brief thawing of American attitudes toward Vietnam and a drive toward diplomatic recognition under the Carter administration stumbled in the wake of the 1978 Vietnamese invasion of Cambodia and the warming of relations between China and the United States, as well as divisions within the administration's own foreign policy team. The Reagan administration did not create an especially auspicious domestic political environment to renew efforts at diplomatic recognition, with the president pushing hard on the cultural politics of the POW/MIA issue, and insisting that the American war in Vietnam had been a noble and necessary one to beat back the menace of international communism.

Part of the important evidence for this narrative came from the creation of a Vietnamese diaspora in the United States. When South Vietnam collapsed in 1975, the United States extracted about 150,000 South Vietnamese, many of them members of the political and military classes, or otherwise affiliated or aligned with the American presence, and accepted them as refugees. From the American perspective, this was a rescue operation that saved the Vietnamese from communist persecution, a story that overlooked American culpability in the division of Vietnam and its own deep involvement in the war. Such a story also overlooks the radically insufficient nature of the rescue, hobbled by inadequate planning and lack of coordination, given that South Vietnam had a million men in its armed forces alone, not to mention implicated civilians (Snepp 1977; Butler 1986; Engelmann 1990; Bon Tempo 2008). Ironically, the American military came to rescue those who arguably would not have needed such a rescue if it were not for American military and political strategies. This irony was driven home by the refugees being taken along a route tracing the expansion of American geopolitical influence. Airlifted or boatlifted from South Vietnam by the US Navy and Air Force, the refugees were taken to a Marine base in Guam or Clark Air Force Base in the Philippines, both in the American sphere of influence due to American efforts in the early twentieth century to establish control of the Pacific. As Yen Le Espiritu argues, this was a "militarized rescue" that served the interests not only of the refugees but also of the United States, intent on continuing a diplomatic fight about the perils of communism and the promises of democracy (Espiritu 2014).

The South Vietnamese were themselves ambivalent about their militarized rescue, for many felt they had been abandoned by the United States after participating in a war that was determined largely by the United States. Such sentiments, however, were generally not uttered outside of the refugee community. Aware of their dependency on American goodwill, the refugees were more likely to engage in a "politics of gratitude" that was essentially an act of public diplomacy with the American public. This politics of gratitude was already visible by the time the refugees reached American shores, where they were routed through one of four US military bases to an eventual settlement that was dependent on having an American sponsor outside of the bases. Gratitude to the United States and to individual American sponsors was crucial to settlement. Settlement of the refugees was uneven, with some Americans hostile to their presence and others welcoming, but the overall narrative attributed to Vietnamese Americans, which many themselves would adopt and promote, was one of the fulfillment of the American Dream (Nguyen 2009). Having fled from communism and come to the United States with little, the refugees seized American educational and economic opportunities and became productive, even exemplary, American citizens, or so the story goes in such popular Vietnamese American–authored books as Andrew Lam's *Perfumed Dreams* or Le Ly Hayslip's memoirs *When Heaven and Earth Changed Places* and *Child of War, Woman of Peace*. Mainstream news accounts featured success stories of Vietnamese valedictorians, Ivy League graduates, military officers, and attorneys like Viet Dinh, assistant attorney general for the US and coauthor of the Patriot Act. But the coverage of Vietnamese Americans revealed some ambivalence as well, as the stories of Vietnamese Americans also involved welfare dependency, domestic violence, poverty, and gang violence. The struggle over how to tell the story of Vietnamese Americans had diplomatic implications regarding whether they would be perceived as a "model minority" that supported the uplifting narrative of American possibility or as unwanted refugees who brought with them seemingly Third World problems in which the United States was implicated.

Throughout the 1980s, this Vietnamese American population swelled, first with additional refugees who fled by boat from Vietnam, second with Amerasians whose fathers were Americans, and third with former southern Vietnamese soldiers released from Vietnamese reeducation camps. The Vietnamese American population would eventually reach a total of about two million, the largest community of Vietnamese outside of Vietnam. The public politics of this community were deeply anticommunist, a perspective that resonated with mainstream American politics throughout the 1980s. Vietnamese Americans created their own ethnic economy, newspapers, and television shows; their own civic and paramilitary organizations; and their own mass entertainment media, all of which facilitated the sense of a Vietnamese American nation-in-exile that espoused what Phuong Nguyen calls a "refugee nationalism" steeped in nostalgia for South Vietnam. With strongholds in several American states, most visibly in California and specifically the de facto capital of the nation-in-exile, Orange County, Vietnamese Americans sought to make their collective anticommunist voice heard in ongoing debates and disputes over the US relationship with Vietnam. Sensitive to these types of politics, the Vietnamese state regarded the overseas Vietnamese with ambivalence if not outright hostility during this decade.

The Vietnamese state's intransigence toward some of the obstacles to diplomatic recognition with the United States waned in the mid-1980s as the Vietnamese began to deal with a severe postwar economic crisis through a move toward market economic reforms. The war-ravaged Vietnamese economy suffered from low agricultural and industrial output, high unemployment, and, in the South, rampant inflation. Faced with the postwar economic embargo by the United States that was honored by most of the developed world, and limited economic assistance from the socialist world, Vietnam was largely on its own in dealing with these serious economic problems. Vietnam's postwar efforts at creating a socialist economy in the postwar South and the failures of agricultural collectivization in the North further mired the country in dire poverty. Grain shortages forced the government to institute food rationing amid reports of spot famines. High unemployment persisted and increased. International development indicators placed Vietnam as the third poorest country on earth in the early 1980s (Duiker 1989, 41–70; Hardy 2003; Kerkvliet 2005, 143–189).

These economic problems and Vietnam's continuing postwar tensions with the United States were intensified by the state's postwar foreign policy toward Cambodia and China. April 1975 not only marked the end of the American war in Vietnam but also brought Pol Pot's Khmer Rouge ascension to power in Cambodia, which quickly launched a genocidal terror that claimed the lives of more than one million Cambodians. Tensions between the Vietnamese and Khmer Rouge centered less on the genocide, whose scope was not yet fully apparent, and more on Khmer Rouge purges of Vietnamese-trained communists, massacres of ethnic Vietnamese living in Cambodia, and border raids into Vietnam. They were heightened by the deterioration of Sino-Vietnamese relations. The Chinese were strong supporters of the Khmer Rouge and had been angered by Vietnam's decision to align with the Soviet Union in the postwar period. The Vietnamese launched a full-scale invasion of Cambodia in late 1978 and quickly put into place a puppet government, beginning what would become a ten-year military occupation. To punish the Vietnamese for attacking its Khmer Rouge clients, China invaded the northernmost provinces of Vietnam in February 1979. After seizing several provincial capitals and encountering heavy Vietnamese resistance, the Chinese withdrew their forces in late March. Both the war with China and the long occupation of Cambodia deepened Vietnam's economic crisis (Kimura 1989; Thayer 1994). The Chinese invasion seriously damaged northern Vietnam's industrial base while the Cambodian occupation kept the military from undertaking economic reconstruction at home and diverted limited government revenues from investments in infrastructure, education, and public health. Moreover, many demobilized veterans of the Cambodian war and occupation returned home to face under- or unemployment, further increasing dissatisfaction with the policies of the regime. The growing warmth of Sino-American relations and vigorous US opposition to the Cambodian government installed by the Vietnamese also linked foreign policy concerns to the need for economic reform (Chanda 1988).

To arrest the stagnation and poverty that was engulfing the nation, Vietnam undertook a radical economic transformation in 1986 by adopting the policy of *doi moi* or renovation. Abandoning socialist economics but not the one-party Leninist state, *doi moi* marked the introduction of market reforms into the Vietnamese economy. Failing agricultural collective and state industrial enterprises were replaced by household agricultural farms and an opening up to foreign investment to build the industrial and service economies (Ljunggren 1993; Turley and Seldon 1993). *Doi moi* also brought significant foreign policy shifts, including a willingness to withdraw Vietnamese forces from Cambodia, efforts to repair relations with China, and new expressions of interest in reopening diplomatic relations with the United States. These domestic and international dimensions of *doi moi* intensified after the collapse in 1991 of the Soviet Union, which had been Vietnam's most important source of foreign aid in the postwar period.

The move toward *doi moi* brought into play two broad ideational currents in the leadership of the communist party in Vietnam, whose importance in shaping the dynamics of its public diplomacy persists to the present day. Integrationists or modernizers (most of whom were associated with the Ministry of Foreign Affairs and their allies in the growing Vietnamese private sector and emergent professional classes) advocated for a more open economy, enmeshing Vietnam in the neoliberal global economic order, as well as closer ties to the United States. More hardline conservatives (largely in the state's powerful security apparatus with allies in the still substantial state-owned sectors of the economy) resisted the policies of the integrationists, fearing their impact on their own state interests, and have tended to favor stronger relations with China rather than the United States. The debates and differences between the two groups have little to do with regime change (the integrationists are not democrats) but rather competing visions of how best to keep the party in power (Thayer and Ramses 1999; Gainsborough 2010; Hayton 2011). Vietnamese Foreign Minister Nguyen Co Thach was the most visible leader of the integrationist camp in the late 1980s and early 1990s, leading efforts to bring the Vietnamese occupation of Cambodia to an end, promote closer economic ties with and membership in the Association of Southeast Asian Nations (ASEAN), and court American officials.

In these renewed Vietnamese initiatives to normalize relations with the United States in the 1980s, nonstate American actors and public diplomacy played an important role. While the US economic embargo continued, travel restrictions began to loosen, allowing more Americans and Vietnamese to travel between the two countries. The Quakers and the Mennonites, who developed ties with the North during the American war, set up offices in Hanoi with programs focused on public health and community development. Private educational exchanges, such as those organized by the US-Indochina Reconciliation Project and Harvard University, began to take place, and individual American scholars received access to Vietnamese research sites for the first time since the war ended. While none of these developments drove the formal processes of normalization, they were especially important in terms of confidence building at the elite level in Vietnam.

The early 1990s brought a significant shift in official American attitudes toward relations with Vietnam. At a geopolitical level, it reflected the final collapse of the Cold War international order after the fall of the Soviet empire in Eastern Europe and the end of the Soviet Union itself. But the changing domestic politics around normalization were more directly shaped by the successful efforts of the first Bush administration and Congress to better manage the POW/MIA issue. A softening of its hardline stance toward Vietnam late in the Reagan administration put this shift in motion and produced an agreement with the Vietnamese on joint searches for American MIAs. The Bush administration slowly intensified these efforts, offering the Vietnamese a road map for normalizing relations in early 1991. The first step was the establishment of a US POW/MIA office in Hanoi. Meanwhile in Congress, Senator John Kerry, a Vietnam War veteran, chaired a newly established Senate Select Committee on POW/MIA affairs whose final report convincingly argued there was no credible evidence of POWs being held in Vietnam, a longtime if fanciful claim of the American hard right, and detailed increasing Vietnamese cooperation on MIA remains. The report in large measure took the POW/MIA issue off the table as the major stumbling block for normalization.

Between 1991 and 1995, the thawing Vietnamese-American relationship brought an incremental series of steps toward normalization. Initially the United States lifted restrictions on nongovernmental and nonprofit relief organizations to work in Vietnam, and the USIA began a modest project to administer humanitarian aid for war victims. As the policies of *doi moi* began to attract more foreign investors to Vietnam, the American business community successfully lobbied for the lifting of the economic embargo in early 1994. About the same time, the United States cleared the way for the International Monetary Fund and the World Bank to begin lending in Vietnam. In

July 1995, the Clinton administration and Vietnam announced an agreement to exchange ambassadors and open embassies in Washington and Hanoi. In these gradual moves toward normalization, perhaps one of the most important steps was the decision in 1991 to permit Vietnamese Americans to wire money directly to their relatives in Vietnam. Over time the overseas Vietnamese (*Viet kieu*) would become among the most important "foreign" investors in Vietnam. By 2004 they had sent $3.8 billion to Vietnam through official channels, and even more unofficially; total direct foreign investment in 2004 was just over $4 billion, making overseas Vietnamese remittances as important to the economy as top investors such as Singapore, Taiwan, Hong Kong, South Korea, and the United States (Bainbridge 2005; MFA 2011).

Public Diplomacy after Normalization

Since normalization, public diplomacy between Vietnam and the United States continues in a variety of political, economic, and cultural arenas. Its broader contours are undoubtedly shaped by the fact that the United States has become an important provider of bilateral aid, an increasingly significant trading partner, and a leading foreign investor in the Vietnamese economy. Diplomatic relations received a significant boost with the appointment of Pete Peterson, who had been held as a POW by Hanoi during the war, as the first postnormalization US ambassador to Vietnam. Shortly after his return to Vietnam, he met and married Vi Le, the Vietnamese-born Australian trade commissioner in Hanoi. Peterson and Le had especially high visibility in Vietnam, and Peterson made postwar reconciliation a major priority. Formal security relations moved forward more gradually, though recently there have been tentative conversations about security issues, including flying high-ranking Vietnamese officials to US aircraft carriers off Vietnam's central coast. These talks are largely prompted by shared Vietnamese and American concerns with increasingly vigorous Chinese claims to the strategic and potentially oil-rich Spratly and Paracel Islands. Cam Ranh Bay, a major American base and supply center during the war, has been opened again to foreign navies, and the US Navy has made port calls there and in Danang. Most symbolically dramatic was the arrival of Commander Hung Ba Le, the first Vietnamese American to command a US naval destroyer and whose father held a significant position in the South Vietnamese navy, in a 2009 formal port call in Danang ("US Navy Officer" 2009). As China seeks to expand its clout in Asia, the United States has cultivated its relations with countries that might be able to contain Chinese power, notably Japan, Korea, Taiwan, and the Association of Southeast Asian Nations, including Vietnam. Still, tensions between Vietnamese and the United States persist, most often over American pressures about human rights and religious freedom. Moreover, the still raw memories of the American war could make Vietnam toxic in US domestic politics, as the "swift-boating" of Democratic presidential candidate John Kerrey in the 2004 election demonstrated.

In Vietnam itself, tensions between hardliners and integrationists persist and color policy toward the United States. In part the United States offers a potential balance to what the Vietnamese see as dangerous Chinese pressures not only over the Spratly and Paracel Islands but also on northern land border issues and Chinese plans for damming the Mekong River. Both hardliners and integrationists also look for other geopolitical counterweights to both the United States and China, including Russia (for military supplies), India (for strategic balance with China), Japan (investment aid), the European Union and its member states (as foreign investors and trade partners, and a leading source of development assistance), and ASEAN (strategically and economically). Taiwan and South Korea are the top two foreign investors in Vietnam, giving them an especially important role in Vietnamese diplomacy. Meanwhile, Vietnam continues to seek its own sphere of influence in Southeast Asia via its relations with Cambodia and Laos, both of which were wartime allies and are now, reluctantly or otherwise, political, economic, and military partners with Vietnam.

In this mix there is a space for public diplomacy, although its vectors on the Vietnamese side are often more heavily focused at the economic and cultural levels on South Korea rather than on the United States. The most extensive state and nonstate public diplomacy between the United States and Vietnam has been in the realm of educational exchanges. From almost zero in 1990, the State Department estimates 13,000 Vietnamese were studying in the United States in 2009. Many are Fulbright scholars, with the Fulbright exchange initiated in 1992 several years before formal diplomatic relations. Ever larger numbers of American scholars and US undergraduates are now studying in Vietnam. Measuring the impact of educational exchange is difficult, but on the Vietnamese side it would appear to increase the constituency within the elite for a more integrationist foreign policy. The Ford Foundation was the first major American philanthropic organization to return to Vietnam after normalization, opening its offices in Hanoi in 1996, and has made grants of more than $70 million for education, development, and public health projects. Numerous foundations and American-based nongovernmental organizations have followed suit (Ford Foundation 2006).

Public diplomacy of the Internet and Twitter varieties encounters more obstacles. Vietnam first connected to the Internet only in November 1997, after six cautious years of experimentation with more basic forms of electronic communication. The state's national firewall, though not impregnable, is relatively easy to maintain as the three Internet gateways are controlled by companies owned by the state, including one by the Ministry of Defense. In 2007 there were almost 18 million Vietnamese Internet subscribers, up from 165,000 in 2001, but given state control of gateways the content of privately owned Internet suppliers is easily filtered. State control is extensive, especially for sites dealing with politics or religion, though to a large extent the Vietnamese Internet population self-censors its own access to such sites. Low-level harassment of potential dissidents, whose numbers are quite small but who receive outsize state attention, is common. Shortly before the 2006 Asia-Pacific Economic Cooperation summit meeting in Hanoi (President George W. Bush was slated to attend), homes were raided, computers confiscated, computer disks and memory drives seized, and activists detained by the security services (Hayton 2011, chaps. 6–7). Traditional modes of cultural exchange are considerably more robust, among them a recent visit by the New York Philharmonic to Hanoi, ongoing collaborations between leading museums in Vietnam and the American Museum of National History and the Asia Society in New York, and the growing visibility of contemporary Vietnamese art in the American and global art markets (American Museum of Natural History 2003; Wakin 2009; Asia Society 2010; Taylor forthcoming).

On the cultural front, overseas Vietnamese (or at least their politically active leadership) continue to be significant agents of public diplomacy, although their political focus has shifted quite dramatically in orientation over time. Anticommunism still dominates the public discourse of the community, with elected Vietnamese American officials and civic organizations striving to have a voice in political and diplomatic issues concerning what they see as the dangers of Vietnamese communism. In 2004, for example, Vietnamese American officials in Orange County led the drive to declare the "Little Saigon" of Westminster and Garden Grove a "Communist Free Zone" in order to forbid a visit by Vietnamese officials. Anticommunist demonstrations were common throughout the 1990s and 2000s, sparked by incidents such as art exhibitions that featured communist iconography, the public display of pictures of Ho Chi Minh, and the visit of artists from Vietnam who, besides their citizenship, had no relationship to communism in their art. April 30, the anniversary of the fall of Saigon, became the occasion to mark "Black April" in various Vietnamese American communities. In Orange County, where Vietnamese American civic groups in conjunction with local government created the first memorial dedicated to the memory of South Vietnamese soldiers, Black April became an annual gathering at the memorial of thousands of veterans and community members. The existence of Little Saigon itself is evidence of a kind of public diplomacy, as the Vietnamese American community of Orange County declared itself to be an alternative to the current regime of Vietnam and evoked the memory of the lost South Vietnam (Aguilar-San Juan 2009). But the politics of public diplomacy would also prove to be as divisive as it was unifying, as the experience of the Vietnamese American community in San Jose, California, the second-largest in the country, showed. In 2008, this community was deeply fractured over arguments over whether to officially name the Vietnamese American business enclave "Little Saigon" or "Saigon Business District" (Woolfolk 2011). While the differences between such names might be opaque to outsiders, for some in the Vietnamese American community the politics of using "Saigon Business District" spoke of reconciliation with communism and the current Vietnamese regime. In contrast, "Little Saigon" evoked the Saigon of the Republic of Vietnam.

While the electoral, civic, and economic politics of the Vietnamese American community continue to be dominated by anticommunist concerns, cultural politics are more diverse and play an important part in how Vietnamese Americans represent themselves and are seen by the American public and Vietnam. As had other Asian and minority immigrants who came before them, Vietnamese Americans who created Vietnamese American stories were often seen as "cultural ambassadors" between the general American public and an unfamiliar new minority. Some Vietnamese Americans actively embrace that informal diplomatic role, such as Le Ly Hayslip, who not only wrote her memoirs (made into a film by Oliver Stone) but also created a foundation to perform charity work in Vietnam and promote reconciliation between Vietnamese and Americans. Many other Vietnamese American cultural works are simply read as ambassadorial texts that reveal little-known histories or perspectives to American audiences, for better or for worse. Cinematically,

Vietnamese American directors have addressed topics they consider to be underserved or neglected in American culture: the war from a South Vietnamese point of view (Ham Tran's *Journey from the Fall*, a sentimental favorite in the Vietnamese community), boat people (Minh Nguyen's *Bolinao 52*), adoption and orphans (Tammy Nguyen's *Operation Babylift*), and numerous others of concern to Vietnamese Americans. In literature, Vietnamese American authors are increasingly successful, winning national acclaim and readership as they draw portraits of Vietnamese people not defined only by the war (Monique Truong's *The Book of Salt*), or still dealing with the damages inflicted by the refugee experience (lê thi diem thúy's *The Gangster We Are All Looking For* and Andrew X. Pham's *Catfish and Mandala*). Official consecration of the Vietnamese American presence in the United States happened in 2004, when the Smithsonian Museum inaugurated the Vietnamese American Heritage Project. Fifty years after its first exhibit on American-Vietnam relations, the new Smithsonian project had a different but related focus: "to commemorate the thirty plus years of mass Vietnamese migration to the United States, telling the story of challenge, sacrifice, and change—an ongoing journey that is changing the face of America" (The Smithsonian Vietnamese Heritage Project 2011). The importance of culture as a front for public diplomacy was not lost on other populations affected by the long war. Some of the earliest advocates for reconciliation were American veteran authors such as W. D. Ehrhart, Larry Heinemann, Wayne Karlin, and Bruce Weigl, who wrote about their hopes for peace in their books, and who also traveled to Vietnam to meet with their North Vietnamese counterparts—soldiers who became writers, such as Le Minh Khue. While these efforts were marginalized in mainstream American culture, Robert Olen Butler won the Pulitzer Prize in 1992 for his efforts to imagine the stories of Vietnamese refugees to the United States in *A Good Scent from a Strange Mountain*. The work of these peace-minded American writers could be contrasted with Hollywood, which in the 1970s and 1980s waged the war one more time on celluloid via popular films such as *The Deer Hunter* (1978), *Apocalypse Now* (1979), *Platoon* (1986), and *Full Metal Jacket* (1987). In these films, Vietnam was war and the Vietnamese were faceless enemies or doubtful friends. Given Hollywood's global reach, it could be argued that American culture functioned diplomatically by exporting one version of American memory to the rest of the world in a way that Vietnam could not compete with. Not until 2002, with Mel Gibson's *We Were Soldiers*, did Hollywood show much interest in depicting the

Vietnamese perspective. By then, such a reconciliatory gesture would have to be placed within a larger context of how the United States as a whole had striven to contain the memory of the Vietnam War as a misguided adventure or failed but noble endeavor (McMahon 2002).

The Vietnamese state also saw culture as a vehicle for reconciliation, an effort realized most recently and spectacularly around *The Diaries of Dang Thuy Tram*. Tram was a young North Vietnamese doctor killed by American troops, who also seized her diaries. When an American officer returned the diaries in 2005 to Tram's family, the event and their publication was a cause célèbre. The diaries became a bestseller in Vietnam. They were translated in the United States using a title, *Last Night I Dreamed of Peace*, chosen by the family that focused on only one message in Tram's writing, a desire for peace without Americans or the southern Vietnamese government present in Vietnam. Dang Nhat Minh, Vietnam's premier director, amplified the possibility of a larger reconciliation by turning her story into the epic film *Don't Burn* (2010). Shot both in Vietnam and the United States, the film incorporated the story of the return of the diaries by the American officer and became a narrative ultimately about the reconciliation of former enemies. His gesture of public diplomacy, however, would not be the only kind. Of equal and probably greater magnitude is the writing of Duong Thu Huong, northern veteran and celebrated—or notorious—dissident against the Communist Party. Disillusioned by the consequences of the war and the behavior of what she saw as a corrupted party and its cadres, Huong wrote a series of novels that were translated and celebrated in the West, depicting the evils of the Communist Party. For this, her books were banned in Vietnam. She was put under house arrest and eventually forced into exile. These political acts demonstrate how culture's political potential was still feared by the Vietnamese state.

The state has tried to manage the political dimensions of another important aspect of culture-as-diplomacy, namely the country's tourism industry. The seeds of such management of travelers were already evident during the war, as the southern government tried to nurture an actual leisure industry in tourism, while the northern government sought to control the image of the country and revolution presented to sympathetic political visitors. The tension between promoting Vietnam as a tourist destination and the reality of the war would continue and be complicated for the next thirty years, as postwar Vietnam continued to acknowledge the war's history as one of its major tourist selling points while also arguing that Vietnam was the name of a beautiful country, not a terrible war (Kennedy and Williams 2001). Some foreign tourists insist that Vietnam is both things, and sometimes see themselves as engaged in diplomatic efforts. For example, numerous American veterans or even Americans with some vested interest in Vietnam have returned or come to Vietnam on personal missions of reconciliation or as part of groups intent on doing various kinds of work seeking to heal the legacies of the war: providing health care, demining, reforestation, education, and the like (Bleakney 2006; Schwenkel 2009). But it is arguably the case that the more conventional modes of tourism promoted by the state for purposes of leisure also function diplomatically, since they are supposed to embody the fruits of the revolution. Still, even as the country has built bigger and more luxurious hotels, beach resorts, and golf courses, one of the most popular tourist sites in the country remains Ho Chi Minh City's War Remnants Museum and the nearby Cu Chi Tunnels. The Tunnels were the site of a drawn-out, intense struggle between the US military and NLF guerrillas who literally lived underneath American-controlled areas in subterranean complexes. Visitors to the Tunnels are supposed to be impressed by the dedication and tenacity of NLF guerrillas, and so the Tunnels play a role in keeping alive the memory of the struggles of the Vietnamese people to unify the nation (even as they disavow the fact that many NLF guerrillas were nationalists rather than communists). Likewise, the War Remnants Museum commemorates the many decades of revolutionary struggle that toppled the French and the Americans and is most notorious for its graphic display of photographs depicting atrocities committed against the Vietnamese people. Public diplomacy's role is explicitly acknowledged in the museum, where a wing is dedicated to remembering the international solidarity of global antiwar movements.

In a similar way to how official diplomacy must often negotiate the contradictions of a country's policies, Vietnam's public diplomacy in regards to culture must balance messages that are often in tension with each other. On the one hand, the Vietnamese state wants to stress its revolutionary heritage of discipline, dedication, and sacrifice, which is what justifies its legitimacy. On the other hand, the state wants to build capitalist markets and attract foreign capital, which raises uncomfortable questions about whether capitalism and communism can be reconciled and whether foreign capital, both in terms of investor funding and tourist money, compromises revolutionary ideals about being an independent nation of equality and moral purity. Foreign capitalists may present the lures of collaboration, while foreign tourists may introduce or encourage the "social evils" of drugs, prostitution, and liberated or loose sexuality that the state periodically attempts to purge (Nguyen-Vo 2008). Both foreign capitalists and foreign tourists represent the possibility of greater equality, with their promises of wealth and/or more democratic ideas, as well as the possibility of greater inequality. That is, the lifestyles of capitalists and tourists may reflect the interests of the growing monied class in Vietnam rather than the working class, which serves those interests or is excluded from them. The public diplomacy the Vietnamese state engages in is therefore aimed not solely at foreigners but also at its own people. On the cultural front, the state must negotiate the same mixed messages about revolutionary heritage and capitalist promise to its own citizens, who are increasingly themselves tourists to destinations in their own country and outside.

An "Overdue Alliance"?

This case suggests that in attempting to understand American efforts to influence its Vietnamese adversary, via what might loosely be called "public diplomacy," it is necessary to analyze an even broader range of actors than those Wiseman discusses in the Introduction. It is true that traditional government units (notably the State Department and its embassies in Saigon during the war and in Hanoi after normalization), the military's wartime public communication activities, and nongovernmental actors funded or facilitated by the US government all played a role in Vietnamese-American public diplomacy. This assemblage of actors resembles the third ("new public diplomacy") definition mentioned at the outset of this chapter and in the book's Introduction. However, we have also included another set of factors: namely, civil society actors with little or no direct connection to government, such as the Vietnamese diaspora in the United States, religious groups such as the Mennonites, Hollywood films, and individual activists (opposed to government policy). Moreover, we have given weight to Vietnamese public diplomacy, signaling our view that public diplomacy among adversaries is a highly interactive, dialogic practice. In moving beyond the "new public diplomacy" approach, our more expansive view suggests perhaps a fourth "people-to-people" alternative be added. We recognize that this approach invites challenging analytical questions such as where to draw the line between public diplomacy and cross-cultural communication or transnational activism, and who exactly should be considered a public diplomacy actor. The Vietnam case cannot answer these conceptual questions on its own, but it is a vital one in addressing them in the context of the effectiveness of US diplomacy with publics in adversarial states when diplomatic relations between governments are absent or limited.

The complex legacies of the multilayered nature of public diplomacy between the United States and Vietnam continue to hover over the claims that may come to bind the two countries closer together in the future. In the wake of shared American and Vietnamese anxieties about escalating Chinese aggression in the South China Sea during the spring and summer of 2014, Tuong Lai, an informal adviser to the Vietnamese state, wrote an op-ed for the *New York Times* arguing for the pressing need to bring into being "Vietnam's overdue alliance with America." Identifying the United States as "the key ally for Vietnam today . . . when our priority is to defeat our present day enemy: China," Lai recalled Ho Chi Minh's use of the American Declaration of Independence in 1945 and his letters to President Truman seeking diplomatic relations to urge the establishment of the "sort of close economic and military relations with the United States that Ho wanted after World War II" (Lai 2014). Seventy years on, and with the Obama administration's pivot to Asia, this reprise of public diplomacy as historical parable may yet find a receptive American audience.

References

"About Future Relations between Vietnam and the USA." *Viet-My Tap Chi [Vietnamese-American Friendship Association Review]*. Christmas and New Years ed., 1945–46, 18.

Aguilar-San Juan, Karin. 2009. *Little Saigons: Staging Vietnamese in America*. Minneapolis: University of Minnesota Press.

Allen, Michael J. 2009. *'Until the Last Man Comes Home': POWs, MIAs and the Unending Vietnam War*. Chapel Hill: University of North Carolina Press.

American Museum of Natural History. 2003. "Vietnam: Journeys of Mind, Body, and Spirit." Accessed August 22, 2011. *http://www.amnh.org/exhibitions/vietnam*

Asia Society. 2010. "Arts of Ancient Vietnam." Accessed August 22, 2011. *http://sites.asiasociety.org/vietnam*

Bainbridge, Bill. 2005. "Once Cursed, Vietnamese Welcomed Home." *International Herald Tribune*, March 18.

Bass, Thomas. 2009. *The Spy Who Loved Us: The Vietnam War and Pham Xuan An's Dangerous Game*. New York: Public Affairs.

Berman, Larry. 2008. *Perfect Spy: The Incredible Double Life of Pham Xuan An*. New York: HarperCollins.

Bleakney, Julia. 2006. *Revisiting Vietnam: Memoirs, Memorials, Museums*. New York: Routledge.

Bon Tempo, Carl. 2008. *Americans at the Gate: The United States and Refugees during the Cold War*. Princeton: Princeton University Press.

Bradley, Mark P. 2000. *Imagining Vietnam and America: The Making of Postcolonial Vietnam, 1919–1950*. Chapel Hill: University of North Carolina Press.

Braestrup, Peter. 1977. *Big Story: How the American Press and Television Reported and Interpreted the Crisis of Tet 1968 in Vietnam and Washington*. Boulder: Westview Press.

Brigham, Robert K. 1998. *Guerilla Diplomacy: The NLF's Foreign Relations and the Viet Nam War*. Ithaca: Cornell University Press.

Butler, David. 1986. *The Fall of Saigon*. New York: Dell.

Chanda, Nayan. 1988. *Brother Enemy: The War after the War*. New York: Free Press.

Connelly, Matthew. 2002. *A Diplomatic Revolution: Algeria's Fight for Independence and the Origins of the Post-Cold War Era*. New York: Columbia University Press.

Duiker, William J. 1989. *Vietnam Since the Fall of Saigon*. Athens: Ohio University Monographs in International Studies/Southeast Asia.

Emerson, Gloria. 1976. *Winners and Losers: Battles, Retreats, Gains, Losses and Ruins from the Vietnam War*. New York: Harvest/HBJ.

Endy, Christopher. 2004. *Cold War Holidays: American Tourism in France*. Chapel Hill: University of North Carolina Press.

Engelmann, Larry. 1990. *Tears Before the Rain: An Oral History of the Fall of South Vietnam*. New York: Oxford University Press.

Espiritu, Yen Le. 2014. "Militarized Refuge: A Critical Rereading of Vietnamese Flight to the United States." In *Transpacific Studies: Framing an Emerging Field*, Janet Hoskins and Viet Thanh Nguyen, eds., 201–224. Honolulu: University of Hawaii Press.

Fischer, James T. 1997. *Dr. America: The Lives of Thomas A. Dooley, 1927–61*. Amherst: University of Massachusetts Press.

Ford Foundation: Vietnam. 2006. New York: The Ford Foundation. Accessed August 5. *http://www.ngocentre.org.vn/ingodirectory*.

Gainsborough, Martin. 2010. *Vietnam: Rethinking the State*. London: Zed Books.

Guevara, Che. 1967. *On Vietnam and World Revolution*. New York: Merit Books.

Hardy, Andrew. 2003. *Red Hills: Migrants and the State in the Highlands of Vietnam*. Honolulu: University of Hawaii Press.

Hayton, Bill. 2011. *Vietnam: Rising Dragon*. New Haven: Yale University Press.

"Ho Chi Minh to James Byrnes, 1945, November 1." Reprinted in *United States-Vietnam Relations, 1945–1967*, vol. 1. *Vietnam and the United States States, 1940–1950*. US House of Representatives, Committee on Armed Services. Washington, DC: US Government Printing Office, 1971: C95–96.

Jacobs, Seth. 2004. *America's Miracle Man in Vietnam: Ngo Dinh Diem, Religion, Race and US Intervention in Southeast Asia*. Durham: Duke University Press.

Kennedy, Laurel B. and Mary Rose Williams. 2001. "The Past Without the Pain: The

Manufacture of Nostalgia in Vietnam's Tourist Industry." In *The Country of Memory: Remaking the Past in Late Socialist Vietnam,* Hue-Tam Ho Tai, ed. 135–163. Berkeley: University of California Press.

Kerkvliet, Benedict J.T. 2005. *The Power of Everyday Politics: How Vietnamese Peasants Transformed National Policy.* Ithaca: Cornell University Press.

Kimura, Tetsusaburo. 1989. *The Vietnamese Economy, 1975–1986.* Tokyo: Institute of Developing Economies.

Laderman, Scott. 2009. *Tours of Vietnam: War, Travel Guides and Memory.* Durham: Duke University Press.

Ljunggren, Börje ed. 1993. *The Challenge of Reform in Indochina.* Cambridge: Harvard Institute for International Development.

Masur, Matthew. 2009. "Exhibiting Signs of Resistance: South Vietnam's Struggle for Legitimacy, 1954–1960." *Diplomatic History* 33.2: 293–313. Quoting "Show of Vietnamese Art," 17 January 1961, Box 8, Folder 43, Douglas Pike Collection. Vietnam Archive, Texas Tech University.

Maeda, Daryl J. 2009. *Chains of Babylon: The Rise of Asian America.* Minneapolis: University of Minnesota Press.

McMahon, Robert J. 2002. "Contested Memory: The Vietnam War and American Society, 1975–2001." *Diplomatic History,* 26, 2: 159–184.

MFA. Vietnam Ministry of Foreign Affairs. 2011. "Foreign Investment into Vietnam." Accessed July 11, 2014. *http://www.mofa.gov.vn/en/tt_baochi/nr041126171753/ns050223104952.*

Miller, Edward. 2004. "Vision, Power and Agency: The Ascent of Ngo Dinh Diem, 1945–54." *Journal of Southeast Asian Studies,* 35.3: 443–47.

Morgan, Joseph. 1997. *The Vietnam Lobby: The American Friends of Vietnam, 1955–1975.* Chapel Hill: University of North Carolina Press.

"Mrs. Nhu Defends Stand: Diem's Sister-in-Law Reiterates Views on Buddhists," Letters to the Times, *New York Times,* 14 August 1963, 32.

Newton, Huey P. 1992. "Letter to the National Liberation Front (With Reply)." In *Vietnam Documents: American and Vietnamese Views of the War,* George Katsiaficas, ed. 133–136. New York: M.E. Sharpe.

Nguyen Cao Ky with Marvin J. Wolf. 2002. *Buddha's Child: My Fight to Save Vietnam.* New York: St. Martin's Press.

Nguyen, Phuong. 2009. "The People of the Fall: Refugee Nationalism in Little Saigon, 1975-2005." PhD diss., University of Southern California.

Nguyen-Vo, Thu-huong. 2008. *Ironies of Freedom: Sex, Culture and the Neo-Liberal Governance in Vietnam.* Seattle: University of Washington Press.

Pham Ngoc Thach. 1945. "Some Notable Characteristics of the Revolution in August 1945." October 1945, Box 1, Records of Consular Posts, Hanoi, 1950–52, US Department of State, RG 84, National Archives, Washington, D.C.

Pham, Vu Hong. 2002. *Beyond and Before the Boat People: Vietnamese American History Before 1975.* Ph.D. dissertation, Cornell University.

Rapport, 9 January 1946, Folder: "Indochine-Amérique, 1945–11/48, E170-3,"

Indochine, Asie Oceanie, 1944–1955. Archives due Ministère Étrangères Diplomatique, Paris, France.

Saigon Consulate, Confidential Records of. Memorandum of Conversation between Bullitt and Ogden, 29 May 1947, Box 4, Record Group 84, National Archives.

Schwenkel, Christina. 2009. *The American War in Contemporary Vietnam: Transnational Remembrance and Representation.* Bloomington: Indiana University Press.

Shenon, Philip. 1994. "New Vietnam Combat: Coke vs. Pepsi." *New York Times.* February 7.

Snepp, Frank. 1977. *Decent Interval: An Insider's Account of Saigon's Indecent End.* New York: Random House.

Statler, Kathryn C. 2009. *Replacing France: The Origins of American Intervention in Vietnam.* Lexington: University of Kentucky Press.

The Smithsonian Vietnamese American Heritage Project. 2011. Accessed July 21. *http://vietam.si.edu/about.asp.*

Taylor, Nora. Forthcoming. *Exhibiting Vietnam: Vietnamese Visual Culture in the Era of Globalization.*

Thayer, Carlyle A. 1994. *The Vietnam People's Army under Doi Moi.* Singapore: Institute of Southeast Asian Studies.

Thayer, Carlyle A. and Ramses Amer, eds. 1999. *Vietnamese Foreign Policy in Transition.* Singapore: Institute of Southeast Asian Studies.

Theroux, Paul. 2006. *The Great Railway Bazaar.* New York: Mariner Books.

Tuong Lai, 2014. "Vietnam's Overdue Alliance with America." *New York Times,* July 11.

Turley, William S. and Mark Seldon, eds. 1993. *Reinventing Vietnamese Socialism.* Boulder, CO: Westview Press.

"US Navy Officer Who Fled Vietnam as a Boy Returns." 2009. *New York Times,* November 9.

Wakin, Daniel. 2009. "Philharmonic Plans Trip to Vietnam." *New York Times,* January 12.

Wells, Tom. 1996. *The War Within: American Battle over Vietnam.* Berkeley: University of California Press.

Wiest, Andrew 2008. *Vietnam's Forgotten Army: Heroism and Betrayal in the ARVN.* New York: New York University Press.

Woolfolk, John. 2011. "Vietnamese leaders celebrate Little Saigon monument in San Jose." *San Jose Mercury News,* May 5. Accessed July 20. *http://www.mercurynews.com/politics-government/ci_18106258.*

Wu, Judy. 2013. *Radicals on the Road: Third World Internationalism and American Orientalism during the Vietnam Era.* Ithaca: Cornell University Press.

5 LIBYA

The United States and the Libyan Jamahiriyya:
From Isolation to Regional Ally, 1969–2011

Dirk J. Vandewalle

SINCE THE CREATION OF THE KINGDOM OF LIBYA AT the behest of the Great Powers in 1951, relations between the North African country and the United States have witnessed a number of wrenching changes: from a warm and supportive US role during the monarchy (1951–1969) to an increasingly skeptical and then antagonistic stance toward the Muammar Qadhafi regime, which resulted in a cutoff of diplomatic relations, a US military attack on Tripoli and Benghazi in April 1986, and a US economic embargo. After December 2003, when Libya *inter alia* publicly renounced programs to seek weapons of mass destruction (WMD), a new lukewarm relationship developed that was followed, ultimately, by US support for an international effort to remove the Qadhafi government from power when the country's civil war erupted in February 2011. This chapter delineates US diplomacy and its public expressions (what many call "public diplomacy") toward Libya during the Qadhafi period, from the 1969 military coup until the country's 2011 uprising against the dictator.[1]

Libya's tumultuous interactions with the United States after 1969, a deteriorating relationship starting in the mid-1970s, and Qadhafi's firm internal control meant that the possibilities for US public diplomacy in Libya were severely limited. Moreover, a good deal of what counts as "traditional diplomacy" (a government seeking to directly influence the views of another sovereign state's government) was conducted in private, generally shaded by the penumbra of public hostility. For almost four decades since the Qadhafi government assumed power in September 1969, much of the world stood transfixed as the small North African oil exporter turned itself into a confrontationist state that used its oil riches to confront the West as well as its regional and internal enemies. At the height of that confrontation Libya found itself diplomatically isolated from the international community—much of the energy for that international ostracism coming from the United States—and subject to a combination of some of the most stringent US and multilateral economic sanctions witnessed in recent decades against any country. Yet, by the end of 2008, three years before an internal revolt would remove the regime, Libya had witnessed the visit of the American secretary of state to Tripoli, as well as what superficially looked like a normalization with the United States and the international community. Conceptually, US public diplomacy toward Libya under Qadhafi, until normalization in 2003, was less about strategies and programs to influence the Libyan mass public (or even its attentive and opinion-forming elites) and more about using public platforms to communicate with the Qadhafi regime and indeed to discredit it internationally.

Since 1969, and particularly during the 1970s and 1980s, the Qadhafi regime's use of anti-Westernism and of a highly charged symbolic rhetoric that in part focused on what the Libyan leader considered to be the obsolescence of traditional diplomacy was, as in all self-proclaimed revolutionary regimes, part and parcel of Libya's response to the United States and arguably a form of revolutionary public diplomacy (Sharp 2005, 110–114). It provided a *leitmotif* that many of the regime's neighbors, as well as the international community, found difficult to understand or to come to terms with. Perhaps no other country found it more difficult to do so than the United States, whose privileged position in the country during the monarchy had left it unprepared for the confrontations and diplomatic tussles that were to emerge soon after the military leadership assumed power and whose diplomatic tradition of how to deal with "rogue" regimes favored ostracism over engagement.

From friend and economic partner, Libya after 1969 quickly turned into an activist state that in its public utterances portrayed the West, and in particular the United States, as enemies of Libya and the Arab world. Upon coming to power, Qadhafi had repeatedly claimed to represent the future of pan-Arabism and Arab nationalism in the Middle East. The fact that Libya remained forever too inconsequential a player on the regional political scene to pursue and implement such ambitions, and also that the Libyan leader's exhortations for Arab unity were routinely dismissed with derision and scorn in the Arab world, was of little comfort to Washington. To American leaders, Qadhafi's pronouncements and actions were increasingly seen as meddling and, eventually, as potentially destabilizing to several regional regimes and governments it supported, as well as, simultaneously, a threat to its own interests that had changed from essentially strategic during the period of the monarchy to commercial by the mid-1970s.

Before 1969, Libya and the United States had traditionally considered themselves special partners in development. The expansion of the Libyan oil industry had in large part been tied to the presence of US companies whose removal during the period of economic sanctions in the 1980s and 1990s against the *jamahiriyya*—a term coined by Qadhafi meaning Libya's rule by the masses and adopted as part of the country's official name in 1977— put a temporary halt to the special relationship. Many Libyan policymakers complained nostalgically as the country became increasingly isolated. This isolation was first led by the United States and then by the international community under United Nations (UN) sanctions, which were aggressively promoted and pursued by Washington starting in the mid-1970s.

A quarter of a century later, a process of formal and informal diplomacy, spearheaded by Great Britain and eventually supported by the United States, brought Libya back into the international fold and then, ironically perhaps, elevated the country to a partner in the US struggle against terrorism.

Relations between Libya and the West illuminate the depths to which diplomatic, political, and economic relations between former allies can sink. The subsequent process of rehabilitating Libya also pinpoints, however, the mechanisms by which such relations can slowly and painstakingly be reconstructed by using a combination of formal, informal, and public diplomacy; nongovernmental intermediaries in the diplomatic process; a combination of unilateral and multilateral economic sanctions, refraining from politicizing the diplomatic negotiation process; and use of a carrot-and-stick approach that ultimately persuaded the Libyan government to "come in from the cold."

1969–1973: Laying the Groundwork for International Agitation

From the first day of his "revolution" it was clear that Qadhafi seemed determined to chart a new political course for Libya in the Arab world and the world at large—a course that would test many of the precepts of traditional international diplomacy and views about influencing foreign publics. Qadhafi, like other young Arab nationalists who had followed the ideological debates and struggles in Arab nationalism, viewed Egypt's Gamal Abdel Nasser as a dedicated Arab revolutionary who could return to the Arab world much of the grandeur and power it had once possessed. That Nasser cloaked much of his vision in language that took the West to task only added to his appeal for the new Libyan leaders, who viewed the presence of British and American military bases as an unacceptable compromise made by a corrupt monarchy.

To Qadhafi, the possibility for renewed respect and power for the region had not yet been exhausted, and Libya's oil revenues could serve as part of a strategy of renewal. Qadhafi was willing to commit his country's resources to the pursuit of unity with other Arab countries, thus establishing a precedent that would remain a guideline for the next two decades—and led the country into conflict with the United States.

No doubt, in other Arab capitals where revolutions and popular upheavals had already taken place decades earlier, Qadhafi's often naïve speeches were received by an older generation with disbelief. To many of them, who had dealt with the West since the independence of their countries in the inter-war period, his speeches and exhortations often seemed anachronistic. But this was a new era—or at least so Libya's new rulers believed. Qadhafi and his young revolutionaries represented a dramatic change from the conservative and timid generations before them, and a concrete embodiment of what the Egyptian journalist and Nasser confidant Muhammad Heikal called the "post-setback [i.e., 1967] generation."

Qadhafi's repeated public references to the disastrous legacy of Italian colonialism and to the "neocolonial arrangements" imposed on Libya after World War II—Qadhafi would forever refer to 1951 as a "false independence" and to September 1, 1969, as Libya's true independence day—provided a backdrop to a much larger historical tapestry into which he skillfully wove his vision for a new Libyan society. The confrontation with the West—still exclusively verbal during this initial phase—formed a theme in his search for personal legitimacy, and for the legitimacy of his revolution, from which Qadhafi would never waver for more than three decades.

There was, as yet, no hint of the open confrontation with the West that would emerge full-blown within a decade, and diplomatic relations between the two countries remained cordial. Though cautious, Washington hoped that Libya could be kept outside the Soviet orbit and that Libya's close business

ties to the United States, and their earlier special relationship, could be maintained. As the single most important donor for Libya's development since its
independence, and as the country that had played the single largest role in
constructing Libya's oil industry, the United States clearly did not favor a confrontation with the new regime.[2]

The existence of US and UK bases on Libyan soil, however, provided an
easy target for the Qadhafi regime that resonated with the wider ideological
pursuits of its revolution. Qadhafi quickly seized upon the bases as yet one
more sign of the monarchy's collusion with Western interests. Their abandon-
ment soon after the 1969 coup was portrayed as a victory for Libya's revolutionaries. Simultaneously, the regime skillfully extended leverage over its oil
industry, relying on mechanisms for confronting the international companies
that had been developed during the monarchy. Throughout 1970 and 1971,
Qadhafi increased royalties and taxes with seeming impunity. The rapidly
growing revenues in the wake of higher posted prices for Libyan crude oil
added to the conviction that Qadhafi's emphatic call for greater economic and
political sovereignty could be fulfilled.

For most of the first half-decade after the coup, however, Libyan-US relations remained characterized by caution and pragmatism on both sides. The
Libyan government, despite the nationalization of some US and UK oil interests in 1973, showed no inclination toward an open confrontation with the
West. Its opposition remained a rhetorical tool used primarily for mobilization purposes inside Libya. Gradually, however, opposition to the West came
to assume a larger role within the revolution during the 1970s and 1980s.

1973–1986: The Everlasting Revolution

The long decade between 1973 and early 1986 forever became the symbol of
Qadhafi's confrontation with the United States, and of his attempt to do away
with the niceties of international diplomacy in his pursuit of the country's
regional and international policy goals. One example was Qadhafi's attempt
to destabilize neighboring Tunisia, which led to a more open confrontation
with France and the United States. In January 1981 the French government
refused to implement a contract between the oil parastatal Elf-Aquitaine
and Lipetco, Libya's official investment company, and France became more
openly aligned against Libya following the latter's renewed invasion of Chad.
The period between 1973 and 1986 also led to an increasingly acrimonious

public confrontation between Libya and the United States that would eventually result in a complete rupture of diplomatic relations—and US sanctions against the *jamahiriyya*.

After 1973, Libya increasingly focused on countering US public accusations. The United States by then had started to accuse Libya of supporting terrorism, engaging in subversion in sub-Saharan Africa and beyond, boycotting the Middle East peace process and, eventually, attempting to produce WMDs. The assassination of Israeli athletes at the 1972 Munich Olympics and the 1973 killing of the US ambassador to Sudan raised the first, albeit still unsubstantiated, questions about Libya's involvement with terrorist groups. These concerns were heightened as the regime increasingly and openly expressed support for radical Palestinian groups, with the Abu Nidal group, the Popular Front for the Liberation of Palestine-General Command, and Palestinian Islamic Jihad finding a home in the *jamahiriyya*.[3] Libya also attempted to ship weapons to the Irish Republican Army. In 1989 Washington accused Libya of supporting roughly thirty international terrorist and revolutionary movements worldwide.

Libya's rhetoric in speeches and government statements against Israel at home and in various international fora remained uncompromising as Qadhafi opposed US efforts to resolve the Arab-Israeli conflict, culminating in the Libyan leader's public condemnation of the Camp David Accords. Worried about these developments and about the growing Soviet presence in Libya, the Carter administration in 1978 prohibited the sale of all military equipment to Libya. By the end of 1979, Libya was put on the list of state sponsors of terrorism, which extended the ban to include most economic assistance to the country. On February 15, 1980, the United States closed its embassy in Tripoli.

In several ways, Libya's confrontation with the United States became a rhetorical duel as Qadhafi and successive US presidents portrayed each other as outcasts in the international community. President Reagan's denunciation of Qadhafi as the "mad dog of the Middle East" allowed the latter to deflect much of whatever internal criticism was gingerly voiced against his policies at home, creating the image of a highly hypocritical antagonism that the Libyan leader exploited. President George W. Bush's later statement that Libya's actions posed an unusual and extraordinary threat to the United States only added to the David-versus-Goliath image that Qadhafi used for his own internal purposes.

The transfer of power in Washington from the Carter to the Reagan administration in January 1981 marked a significant threshold for US-Libyan diplomatic relations. From this time, attempts by both adversaries to influence the other's publics (and world opinion for that matter) can hardly be described as *public diplomacy*, which would imply some mutual expectation of accommodation and cooperation, but rather as *public relations*, which would imply a one-way advantage with the stronger power stereotyping the smaller state as a renegade and the smaller state countering by labeling the stronger power as an imperialist. President Reagan, in part eager to demonstrate US strength in the region in the wake of the 1979 Soviet invasion of Afghanistan, viewed Libya as a worthy target for his new policy of opposing regional adversaries. The United States moved with determination to further contain Libya. Arguing that the *jamahiriyya* was actively engaged in the destabilization of local regimes and the promotion of international terrorism, the administration in May 1981 closed the Libyan People's Bureau (embassy) in Washington. Relations continued to worsen when Washington accused Libya of attempting to assassinate US officials. In August 1981 the confrontation took an even more ominous turn when the US Sixth Fleet shot down two Libyan jet fighters over the Gulf of Sirte, which Libya claimed as territorial waters but which Washington viewed as an international waterway. The skirmish provided further evidence for the regime of US imperialist goals. In December 1981 US citizens were prohibited from traveling to Libya, and Reagan urged all Americans to leave Libya. Soon afterward, in March 1982, all crude oil exports from Libya were embargoed and exports of sophisticated oil and gas equipment prohibited. On April 17, 1984, personnel at the Libyan People's Bureau in St. James' Square in London shot and killed Yvonne Fletcher, a local policewoman who was on duty during an anti-Qadhafi demonstration. Reaction to the murder marked the beginning of more concerted efforts by the Europeans to isolate Libya diplomatically, although, much to Washington's consternation, the Europeans proved unwilling to impose economic sanctions, with some even keeping their embassies in Tripoli.

The United States' actions were further extended in November 1985 when President Reagan banned the import of refined petroleum products from Libya. A month later, terrorist attacks at the Rome and Vienna airports were linked to the Abu Nidal organization, which had close ties to Libya. In January 1986 President Reagan invoked the International Emergency Economic Powers Act that halted all loans and credits to Libya, prohibited all financial transactions by US citizens with Libya, and froze Libyan foreign assets in the United States. In a message that showed how personalized the conflict had become, Reagan warned that the United States was willing to take further and more decisive steps if Qadhafi did not modify his behavior (Reagan 1986). That next step—the bombing of Tripoli and Benghazi in April 1986—would prove a decisive turning point in the US-Libyan confrontation and marked the beginning of a slow change and internal reappraisal of Libya's policies.

From the outset, Reagan attempted to destabilize the Qadhafi regime through public denunciations and covert actions in addition to pinprick military confrontations over the Gulf of Sirte. Libyan opposition groups in the West and in Chad, where the US administration supported the Chadian government of Hissen Habre in the war over the Aouzou strip, enjoyed US support in an effort to destabilize the regime. The covert efforts increased after a June 1984 CIA assessment that asserted that the overthrow of Qadhafi would be necessary to halt Libyan aggression (Woodward 1985). That the regime's domestic upheavals and embroilment in foreign adventures produced relatively little internal dissent was due in large part to the way in which the regime exercised control throughout the country—making individuals prefer exit to the uncertainty of any concerted opposition. It was also due to the fact that most Libyans, as direct or indirect beneficiaries of economic largesse, had become largely depoliticized despite the revolutionary fervor for mobilization. Despite all the excesses and uncertainties he had introduced, many Libyans continued to identify with the Libyan leader and agreed with his basic ideological precepts—if not his tactics. Consequently, any US public diplomacy efforts directed at Libyans were ineffective.

This worsening relationship with the United States, highly politicized by both sides for the sake of each country's political purposes, put increasing pressure on US oil companies to review their investments in Libya after the Reagan administration came to power. Exxon, which was represented in Libya by Esso Standard Libya and Esso Sirte, on November 4, 1981 announced that it would withdraw their operations. On March 10, 1982, the US government adopted a measure that prohibited the import of all Libyan oil and started to restrict the flow of US goods to the *jamahiriyya*. In January 1983 Mobil followed suit and withdrew its operations after months of unsuccessful negotiations with Libyan officials (*Middle East Economic Survey* 1982). By that time, several other companies had reviewed their own presence and, as in the case of the French parastatal Elf-Aquitaine, decided to at least temporarily halt the implementation of earlier signed contracts.

Thus, between the oil crisis of 1973 and the US bombing of Tripoli and Benghazi in April 1986, Libya's increasingly activist foreign policy had brought the regime into an open confrontation with the West, and in particular with the United States, which more and more favored a direct confrontation with Libya that gradually narrowed and then halted diplomatic interactions between the two sides. Within its ideological framework, the confrontation with the West for Libya became a tool the Qadafi regime used to vindicate its own actions.

The rupture of diplomatic relations with the United States and Great Britain was the culmination of a period of escalating confrontation between Libya and the West that left the country diplomatically and economically isolated after 1986 (St. John 2002). As Libya headed even further into a headlong confrontation with the United States, Washington assiduously pursued its regional diplomatic and more covert efforts to limit Libya's behavior in several distinct areas, seeking to oppose its support of extremist and terrorist groups, curtail its foreign policy adventurism, halt its unwavering opposition to US-sponsored attempts to settle the Arab-Israeli conflict, and prevent its attempts to acquire or produce nonconventional weapons and WMDs.

In the years between 1979, when the US State Department put Libya on its first list of state sponsors of terrorism, and the 1986 US bombing of Tripoli and Benghazi, several developments in the deteriorating US-Libyan relationship took place, including the closure of the US embassy in Tripoli and of the People's Bureau in Washington; the embargo of crude oil and then of refined petroleum products from Libya; and, in January 1986, the comprehensive trade embargo. The April 1986 bombing of Tripoli and Benghazi marked the apex of the confrontation, the exhaustion of diplomacy, and the beginning of a period of growing economic upheaval in Libya that ultimately, in retrospect, proved to be a significant turning point for Qadhafi's revolution. The mutually vitriolic public nature of this adversarial relationship left little room for public diplomacy in the traditional meaning of the term.

1986–2003: International Isolation, Economic Sanctions, and the Beginning of Rapprochement

The direct impact of US unilateral sanctions between 1986 and 1992 was relatively small. Its importance was not in influencing Libyan economic decisions directly, but rather in heightening the country's vulnerability to the multilateral sanctions that were to follow, forcing Libya to conclude deals with economic partners, particularly in the oil industry, it would normally have eschewed.

Similarly, the 1986 freeze of all Libyan foreign assets in the United States was relatively benign, since Libya had been careful not to make substantial investments in the country and had shifted most of its liquid assets to other venues in anticipation of US measures. It was estimated that less than 2 percent of Libya's total overseas investments of roughly $5 billion were affected (Economist Intelligence Unit 1986). US pressure on international lending agencies to avoid extending loans to Libya also proved at best a minor irritant since the *jamahiriyya* was either not eligible to borrow from the World Bank because of its relative wealth, or simply refused to do so. Hence Libya's foreign debt remained small throughout the 1980s and into the 1990s.

Greater damage was done by US sanctions on Libya's investment patterns. Since the early 1980s, Libya had started to invest considerable amounts of money in oil downstream activities in Europe, acquiring a network of gasoline stations across Western and Eastern Europe, Egypt, and Malta, in addition to refineries for its oil. These investments had been made partly in anticipation of, and partly as a reaction to, the US ban to guarantee that the country would be able to find steady outlets for its oil. There was also a political dimension to these investments: Tripoli thought they would solidify closer relations with Europe. Once the US ban had been expanded to all exports to Libya, the impact became more onerous as the country faced the withholding of aviation technology, airplane parts, and other types of high technology for its oil industry.

Overall, the US sanctions on Libya's oil sector by themselves had an almost negligible direct impact. It is unlikely that Libya would have had the capability to produce substantially more oil during the 1980s even absent the sanctions. The regulations under the Iran Libya Sanctions Act (ILSA) of 1996 proved of marginal value in deterring investment. Investment patterns in Libya hardly changed, due in large part to the fact that the country, except for a major overhaul of some of its infrastructure, did not need any substantial investments that would have exceeded the $40 million limit imposed by ILSA. Companies also simply amended old contracts to accommodate new investments and avoided signing new contracts that could have triggered ILSA regulations. But the combination of ILSA and previous sanctions created an environment in which the long-term prospects for Libya's oil industry became more closely circumscribed, and the earlier set of US sanctions made the country's economy overall more sensitive (if not vulnerable) to additional pressures that would soon materialize in the form of multilateral sanctions.

In many ways the US sanctions magnified the overall existing problems in Libya's oil sector, creating greater uncertainty in the process.

The seven-year period of multilateral sanctions (April 1992 through April 1999) against Libya, combined with existing internal conditions, proved much more damaging than the US sanctions. Libya's economy grew only 0.8 percent a year and the country's per capita GDP fell from $7,311 to $5,896 between 1992 and 1999 (Economist Intelligence Unit 2001). In 1998 alone, Libya's export earnings dropped to roughly $7 billion, the lowest since the 1986 oil price crash. Shifting Libyan assets away from vulnerable locations, as in the case of the US unilateral sanctions, mitigated the financial impact of the multilateral sanctions. But, as a result, Libya's ability to earn income abroad hampered its ability to pay foreign companies. In the more restrictive economic climate of the 1990s this proved a much bigger irritant than it had been in the previous decade, forcing Libya to further limit trade and making it more difficult to secure short-term credit at a time when oil prices further declined.

Undoubtedly, the multilateral trade sanctions proved the most difficult to deal with. Adjusting trade patterns, as Libya had done previously, no longer proved possible. The ban on imports affected particularly Libya's downstream oil operations and its aviation industry. Its inability to obtain equipment for the maintenance of its refineries forced Libya to search for substitute technology and parts (often on the black market) that were often suboptimal and more expensive than normal international market prices. It also made it necessary for Libya to forgo upgrading its refineries, making it impossible to produce more gasoline for domestic consumption. This also meant that Libya had to spend increasingly scarce foreign reserves purchasing lighter fuels abroad rather than using its own best-quality crude for producing more lucrative high-end fuels. Libya's airline industry was also dramatically affected: with a halt in passenger traffic, a shortage of spare parts, and a deteriorating technical capability, the damage went far beyond the estimated financial loss of $900 million during the period (Economist Intelligence Unit 1997; O'Sullivan 2003, 381, n 89).

The uncertainty surrounding the sanctions made matters worse, and Washington was acutely aware of this situation. Subject to review by the UN Security Council every four months, the fear of additional more stringent measures, as well as the continued US pressure for such actions, proved a deterrent in several ways. The value of the Libyan dinar declined, and inflationary pressures were exacerbated by the fact that all commodities had to be brought into Libya overland or by sea along with the growing pressure of a burgeoning black market. The sanctions also forced Libya to maintain an unnecessarily high level of reserves, not knowing whether additional sanctions would be imposed. With domestic investment virtually halted, the government was forced to curtail development projects, and Libya suffered shortages of foreign exchange. In addition, the continuing uncertainties, lack of international flights into the country, sheer inconvenience of gaining access to the country, and lack of financial resources forced Libya to forgo developing several sectors it had marked for that purpose under economic liberalization strategies adopted earlier.

The oil fields that had been taken over from US companies by the Libyan National Oil Company (LNOC) slowly declined in production as Libya struggled to manage them with increasingly outdated US equipment. Production from LNOC-operated fields declined on average 8 percent annually after the takeover. Finally, Libya also hoped to exploit its enormous, and largely unexploited, natural gas reserves primarily for the European market, but also to substitute natural gas for oil on the domestic market. Although several companies expressed an interest, it was clear that such interest would remain limited as long as the sanctions were in place.

In 1993 LNOC signed a $5.5 billion joint venture for development of the Western Libyan Gas Project with one of its oldest customers, Italy's Agip-ENI. Agip-ENI argued that, since the original contract had been signed in 1993, it was exempted from ILSA. The controversy surrounding the contract, however, ensured that further development of Libya's enormous natural gas fields would remain suspended until more propitious times made international investments possible again. Libya was careful to ensure that US companies that had left retained "suspended rights" to their concessions under so-called standstill agreements.

President Reagan's warning in the wake of his invocation of the International Emergency Economic Powers Act in early 1986—that Washington would take additional steps to confront the Qadhafi regime if needed—quickly became reality. A bomb explosion on April 4, 1986 at a discotheque in West Berlin frequented by US servicemen was blamed on Libyan operatives. Two weeks later, on April 15, the United States bombed Tripoli and Benghazi, allegedly leaving one of the Libyan leader's adopted daughters dead. The raid on Libya—code-named Operation El Dorado Canyon—came hours after the European Union reached an agreement to reduce the number of Libyan diplomats in Europe and to dramatically reduce their own number in Libya. As part of their agreement, they also adopted more restrictive visa requirements for Libyans traveling to Europe.

International cooperation to act against Libya, forcefully underpinned by US diplomatic efforts, came within two weeks after the US bombing when the leaders of the Group of Seven (G7) issued a declaration at their Tokyo meeting to fight terrorism, singling out Libya as the main culprit. The declaration involved limits on arms to Libya, further limits on diplomatic activities of countries involved in terrorism, and improved extradition procedures for bringing suspected terrorists to trial. However, European countries resisted further economic sanctions against Libya, much to Washington's chagrin. Despite the 1984 killing of Yvonne Fletcher, even Britain's Prime Minister Margaret Thatcher, a close ally of the US fight against terrorism, demurred on the grounds that other countries could readily circumvent an embargo.

The bombings marked the apotheosis of the US-Libyan confrontation. It was clear to most close observers that the US and multilateral sanctions, accompanied by a muscular US diplomatic effort to keep Libya tainted and isolated, had taken a heavy toll on the regime. In response, through a number of diplomatic initiatives aimed overwhelmingly initially at Europe, Qadhafi attempted to break the country's isolation by introducing countermeasures that the regime would never have considered during its so-called revolutionary phase of the 1970s and early 1980s. In 1987, after a humiliating defeat by Chadian forces just north of the Aouzou strip, Libya withdrew from Chad and agreed to submit its claim to the contested territory to the International Court of Justice. Qadhafi participated in the creation of the Arab Maghreb Union in 1989, meant to construct an economic community among the North African countries. In speeches when he finally reappeared in public after the bombing, Qadhafi announced the country's intention to discontinue its earlier activism, clearly aiming at an international audience.

Subsequently, President Reagan's successor, George H. W. Bush, temporarily adopted a less confrontational policy with Libya while maintaining the economic pressure. After what seemed like a temporary lull, in September 1988 the United States accused Libya publicly (reinforced in traditional diplomatic briefings in other capitals) of manufacturing chemical weapons at Rabta, a charge that soon would be extended to an accusation that Libya was pursuing WMDs.

However, it was the bombing of Pan Am Flight 103 over Lockerbie, Scotland on December 21, 1988, followed by the September 19, 1989 explosion

of the French UTA Flight 772 airliner over Niger, that propelled the antagonism between the West and Libya to a new, more coordinated level (on the
legal issues involved, see Joyner and Rothbaum 1993). In late 1991 the United
States and Great Britain indicted two Libyan security officials, Abdel Basset
Ali Muhammad al-Megrahi and Al-Amin Khalifa Fhimah, for their alleged
involvement in the Pan Am bombing. Joined by France, which indicted four
Libyan intelligence officers in the UTA bombing, the three countries asked for
the surrender of those charged. In January 1992, under the chairmanship of
Great Britain, the UN Security Council unanimously passed Resolution 731,
calling on Libya to comply with the three countries' demands for the suspects'
extradition. Several weeks later the Security Council passed Resolution 748
once more requesting the handing over of the suspects, threatening further
sanctions if Libya failed to do so within two weeks. When Libya rejected the
demands as a violation of its national sovereignty, the Security Council on
April 15, 1992 banned all international flights to Libya and embargoed all
arms sales. The sanctions could only be lifted if Libya surrendered the Lockerbie suspects and ceased all forms of support for terrorism. The resolution also
called on Libya to pay compensation for the victims if the suspects were found
guilty. Reinforcing its strong public statements, behind the scenes the United
States played a powerful diplomatic role in moving these additional measures
forward.

When Libya resolutely refused to turn over the accused, UN sanctions were
renewed on a three-month basis. In the United States, Congress—urged on by
a number of groups, including the Families of Pan Am Flight 103—exerted
pressure on the Clinton administration to extend US sanctions even further.
In November 1993, the Security Council finally passed Resolution 883 that
included additional bans on the sale of certain oil technologies and equipment
to Libya. Significantly, however, the United States had been unable to include
a total embargo of Libyan oil exports. But in August 1996, the US Congress,
in the most damaging measure so far, adopted the Iran and Libya Sanctions
Act (ILSA). It further constrained international trade with the *jamahiriyya*
and included provisions for sanctions against foreign companies dealing with
or investing more than $40 million in Libya's oil industry, leading to a dispute
with Europe over the legality of the ILSA provisions (Gray 1996).

The unease of the European countries and the gradual violation of the ban
on flights into Libya, particularly by African leaders, indicated that by 1998
the international isolation of Libya was slowly starting to crumble. The loss

of enthusiasm by African countries in general was due less to the success of Qadhafi's attempt at portraying Libya as a victim than to longstanding African aversion to Western-led boycotts against members of the Organization of African States (OAS). In September 1997 the Arab League similarly asked its members to take measures that would alleviate the sanctions against Libya, while in June 1998 the OAS announced that its members would no longer enforce UN sanctions unless the United States and Great Britain agreed to hold the trial of the Lockerbie suspects in a neutral country—one of the conditions under which Libya was willing to compromise. In August 1998 the United States and Britain, seeking a compromise and in order to stem the erosion of the sanctions, agreed to have the trial in The Hague. After some additional wrangling, in April 1999 Libya handed over the two suspects to the Netherlands.

The pressure from the Lockerbie families—which could not by itself be regarded as public diplomacy but as public pressure—proved highly effective in the United States, but was viewed by several countries as emblematic of, and an extension of, a history of poor US-Libyan relations that long predated the Lockerbie incident. As Libya publicly promised compensation for the victims of UTA Flight 772, compensation to Yvonne Fletcher's relatives, and incentives to international investors, the United States intensified pressure on Libya to meet its other demands, including taking responsibility for its officials' actions in the Lockerbie bombing and providing adequate compensation for the Lockerbie victims. The United States acquiesced to the suspension of UN sanctions, but ruled out having the US sanctions lifted until all its conditions were met. Pressure from Congress led to the renewal of ILSA legislation and, temporarily, rendered moot any further debate on improving US-Libyan relations. This state of affairs remained until after September 11, 2001.

As intractable as the impasse between Libya and the West may have appeared by 2000, relations between the two sides had started to change slowly. After Libya turned over the Lockerbie suspects in April 1999 and UN sanctions were lifted, several indicators hinted at the possibility of a rapprochement. Backchannel conferences and talks, initially between Great Britain (which by then had an embassy in Tripoli) and the *jamahiriyya*, were slowly laying out the differing talking points that would inform the reconciliation process and lead to a December 2003 agreement. In June 1999, Libyan and US officials met for the first time in eighteen years in an official capacity to discuss the UN sanctions. In March 2000, US State Department officials visited Libya to assess lifting the existing travel restrictions to Libya. The main challenge for British and US policymakers was to move UK and US domestic public opinion in the rapprochement direction, and less so on moving Libyan public opinion. The foreign policy goals of the UK and US governments led to a form of a two-level game focusing on their own peoples (a public affairs challenge), rather than a public diplomacy issue involving the Libyans, who were already supportive of improved relations.

Domestic constituencies within the United States, particularly the Pan Am 103 families, continued to press for Libya's marginalization and punishment. Consequently, US policymakers saw little urgency in restoring any relationship with Libya. The US Congress in April 2000, in a Sense of the Senate resolution, advised the president not to lift travel restrictions and to consult with the Senate on US policy toward Libya. In November 2000 the State Department renewed the travel ban, and the president reauthorized ILSA in August 2001. After Libya turned over the Lockerbie suspects, and after the UN sanctions were lifted in September 2003, however, it became more difficult for the United States to restrain Libya—as part of a containment strategy—by enlisting international cooperation in pursuit of justice for the Lockerbie victims. While the United States retained its unilateral sanctions in the wake of the Lockerbie verdict, and insisted that Libya meet all UN demands before the suspension of the multilateral sanctions could be extended formally into lifting them, it was clear that the dynamics and the interaction between Libya and the international community were caught in a maelstrom of change, and that the United States needed to reexamine its previous policies and its diplomacy toward Libya as well.

From a US perspective, unilateral sanctions did not make much sense when the international community was welcoming Libya back into the fold. Could a sanctions-led policy retain the purpose it had during the 1990s when multilateral cooperation was assured and when the threats emanating from Libya were tangible? The answer had seemingly changed in the wake of the Lockerbie settlement. Washington could encourage the positive changes in Libyan behavior, knowing that retaining the country's isolation looked increasingly problematic and impractical, or insist on keeping the regime isolated only to find itself marginalized given the gradual reintegration of Libya into the international community.

Libya's support of US efforts in its worldwide campaign against international terrorism in the wake of the September 11, 2001 attacks on the World

Trade Center and the Pentagon added to Washington's dilemma. Qadhafi quickly condemned the attacks publicly and described the US intervention in Afghanistan as a justified act of self-defense, labeling the Taliban regime "Godless promoters of political Islam" (Economist Intelligence Unit 2002). While the United States kept insisting on the need for Libya to fulfill all its obligations under UN resolutions and continued to highlight the country's pursuit of WMDs, a number of trilateral talks between Britain, the United States, and Libya, as well as negotiations between US and Libyan lawyers over the details of compensation for the Lockerbie victims, quietly began.

At the same time, Libya's earlier activist policies changed. In early 2000 US officials acknowledged that Libya had distanced itself from involvement in terrorism and from supporting groups involved in terrorism. The Abu Nidal organization and several other groups had to leave Libya. Ronald Neumann, Deputy Assistant Secretary of State for Near Eastern Affairs, argued that Libya's actions in regard to the Abu Nidal organization were "not window dressing but a serious, credible step" (Neumann 2000).

Slowly, Qadhafi's rhetoric regarding a solution to the Arab-Israeli conflict moderated, in effect questioning—via the medium of his own, often idiosyncratic, brand of public diplomacy—the tactics and the rationale of what had once been one of the *jamahiriyya*'s ideological cornerstones. Qadhafi's earlier public dismissal of the Camp David agreement and of the 1993 Israeli-PLO Oslo Accords gradually yielded to a previously unknown pragmatism—one admittedly met by some skepticism among those who argued that, here as elsewhere, it represented nothing but a cynical ploy to attract investment into Libya and to reshape the country's image internationally (Schneider 1999).

Many of Libya's foreign policy initiatives, particularly in sub-Saharan Africa, also began to change considerably in scope and nature. From its earlier destabilizing adventures in Uganda, Chad, Tunisia, and Egypt, the regime gradually distanced itself from direct and indirect involvement in most of the regional insurgencies it had previously supported. When the International Court of Justice (ICJ) ruled in favor of Chad over the Aouzou strip dispute, Libya accepted the ruling. Relations with Egypt turned cordial after years of open hostility, with both countries embarking on collaborative efforts to find a solution for neighboring Sudan's longstanding civil war. The effort resulted in Sudan's acceptance of an Egyptian-Libyan peace plan that nevertheless left the conflict festering. In April 1999, Qadhafi brokered a peace accord between Uganda and the Congo, sending Libyan troops to Uganda to help implement it.

Unbeknown to virtually anyone at that time, Libya engaged in "quiet diplomacy" with Britain. Telling for what was unfolding in Libya, the talks with the British now included Saif al-Islam al-Qadhafi, Qadhafi's second son, as well. Saif thought that a chance existed for Libya to emerge from its diplomatic and economic isolation. European and other foreign investors were slowly making their way back to Tripoli. Only a complete lifting of the US sanctions, however, could deliver the kind of economic resurgence and the necessary international diplomatic imprimatur that the regime sought. For that, the *jamahiriyya* needed to be removed from the State Department's sponsors-of-state-terrorism list.[4]

The round of negotiations, informal meetings, and off-the-record conferences initiated by Britain steadily grew in scope eventually to include Libyan activities in sub-Saharan Africa, the Fletcher shooting, Lockerbie, Libya's cooperation in illegal migration toward Europe, and a number of smaller issues. Libya agreed to settle the Lockerbie issue by promising to adhere to a tiered process of compensation for the victims' families. This, in turn, would eventually lead to the suspension of US sanctions against Libya and the removal of the *jamahiriyya* from the State Department's terrorism list.

But Washington proved initially highly skeptical about engaging Libya, preferring to stand on the sidelines until it became clear that Libya was willing to move forward in good faith, especially concerning WMDs. Throughout the 1980s, Washington had watched Libyan efforts to acquire such weapons with increasing concern, devoting considerable attention to gathering intelligence on Libya's progress. The ongoing controversy in the 1980s and 1990s over the Rabta chemical facility and the Tarhuna industrial complex accelerated US efforts to deny Libya any technology or imports that could be used for WMD purposes.

In 1997, the CIA concluded that the *jamahiriyya*'s efforts to acquire unconventional weapons had slowed, a conclusion that was later confirmed for chemical weapons, but not for Libya's attempts at obtaining further missile and nuclear technology (*Jane's Defence Weekly* 1998; O'Sullivan 2003, 382–383, n 115). When the UN sanctions were suspended, however, Washington's concern focused on the fact that Libya would now be able to purchase the technology and components necessary to resume its quest for nonconventional weapons.

Libya's willingness since 1999 to adopt reforms, however, had clearly resonated with the British and US governments. The US administration viewed an agreement on WMDs with Libya as an important step that would send the right signal to other proliferating countries, and it was willing to expend considerable diplomatic capital to reach an agreement. There was a realization in Washington that its policy of isolating Libya—through private and public diplomacy—was increasingly counterproductive as Britain and other European countries were willing to reengage diplomatically and economically with Libya and its people in the wake of the Lockerbie trial and following the Libyan government's willingness to settle victims' claims. In April 2003 the Atlantic Council—an organization hardly friendly to Libya—issued a report titled *US-Libyan Relations: Toward Cautious Reengagement*. The report advocated "A New Strategy for a New Context" and aptly summarized the new realities of the US-Libyan relationship faced at the end of the millennium (Atlantic Council 2003).

2003–2011: Rehabilitating a "Rogue Regime" and Normalization

In December 2003, the Libyan regime made a spectacular announcement that it was willing to give up its WMDs following negotiations with Washington and London. The announcement not only captured attention worldwide but also represented the end of the period of quiet, background diplomacy that had started in 1999. After decades of confrontation with the West, the Libyan decision to cooperate on the WMD issue marked the apotheosis of a process of reappraisal that the country's leadership had embarked upon. As described above, the agreement came at the end of a period of protracted negotiations and backchannel diplomacy that had started—almost exclusively at first at the behest of the British government—between Libya, Great Britain, and the United States. In the end, it was a process of careful and sustained traditional diplomatic negotiations conducted behind closed doors, holding out both carrots and sticks to the Libyan side. In sum, public diplomacy played no part in this process.

For Western policymakers and academic observers alike, the agreement raised many questions. If the Libyan government appeared increasingly pragmatic in the years leading up to the WMD announcement, much of that pragmatism was seen as having been forced upon the country's leadership by the impact of the sanctions and by the general isolation Libya found itself in during most of the 1990s. How genuine therefore was Libya's newfound willingness to play by internationally accepted norms of state behavior? Was the pragmatism part of a process of adjustments to a number of economic and political realities that could in the future be reversed? Or was it simply a means to ensure a return of international investment, a use of diplomacy for larger strategic purposes? The United States in particular was anxious that there would be no backtracking on Libya's promises, and the step-by-step negotiations, disentangling but linking progress on the issues under negotiation, were made in part to convey to the Libyans that all issues were part of a larger settlement from which it could not simply pick and choose.

Although the WMD announcement captured a dramatic moment in Libya's political life, its underlying pragmatism was based on a number of developments that had started to worry Qadhafi over a much longer period, developments that prompted the *jamahiriyya* to come to terms with the sanctions' economic effects. By the time of the Atlantic Council study, Libya had already taken corrective measures to break the isolation caused by the sanctions and had started to reform its economy. The country's economic liberalization and attempt to settle all outstanding issues with the West not surprisingly coincided. By the time the WMD agreement was formally announced, Libya had already embarked for almost two years on economic reforms.

Once Libya had signed the agreement on WMD, a flurry of public diplomatic and economic activity followed, indicating the eagerness of the West and Libya to settle whatever issues were left outstanding. Then, in February 2004, the United States lifted its travel ban to Libya. The following month the first US congressional delegation visited Tripoli. In April, British Prime Minister Tony Blair paid an official visit to Libya while the United States lifted most of its economic sanctions. Later that month the Libyan leader flew to Brussels for an official visit to the European Union. In June the United States and Libya formalized the emerging new relationship by officially reestablishing diplomatic relations, by exchanging diplomatic missions in respective capitals, and with Secretary of State Condoleezza Rice visiting the country in 2008. By then the United States had removed all of the country's nuclear weapons program's equipment and had started to eliminate the country's chemical weapons (DeSutter 2004). In a further astonishing reversal, Libya quietly became a partner in the US war on terror. In short, Libya's economic and political isolation, and the protracted diplomatic process to rehabilitate the country back into the international community, had come to an end. Although the

United States had fully restored formal diplomatic relations with Libya, it was clear that despite cooperation on a number of issues, particularly the war on terror, relations between the two countries remained cool and were marked by suspicions on both sides about the intentions of the other. Despite the Obama administration's initial reluctance to take sides when the country's civil war started in February 2011, it joined and then forcefully supported an international effort that led to the removal of Qadhafi in October 2011.

Libya and US Diplomacy

This chapter has focused on relations between Libya and the United States during the Qadhafi regime—a single, prolonged period during which the United States dealt in varying ways with a highly authoritarian regime whose behavior often flouted many of the conventions of diplomacy. The 1969–2011 period is particularly instructive in demonstrating how Libya, originally flouting international diplomatic conventions, eventually adhered to international norms of state behavior and renounced WMD, the most powerful bargaining chip at its disposal. As this chapter demonstrated, Libya's changing behavior represented the outcome of a long process of coordinated diplomatic actions by the United States, Great Britain, and, eventually, the international community. Despite an initial lack of vulnerability to unilateral US sanctions, multilateral, UN-sponsored sanctions became instrumental in bringing Libya to the bargaining table. Conversely, the worry about a deteriorating international sanctions regime against Libya spurred the United States on in its dealings with the *jamahiriyya*.

In this process, the intermediation of Great Britain, whose negotiators wisely chose to keep the talks away from the public spotlight, proved crucial. The British role as a credible intermediary was enhanced by the fact that, despite its own grievances and public condemnations of Libyan behavior, it never allowed those issues to become overly politicized. The British approach contrasted strongly with what occurred in the United States, where negotiating with the Libyans became (perhaps understandably) a public (or at least highly publicized) debate on how to deal with the Qadhafi regime.

The US unilateral diplomatic isolationist strategy initially hardened the position of the Qadhafi regime, in part because of how US antagonism could be "sold" domestically—and even regionally—as one more example of US imperialism. This became immeasurably more difficult when the international community, including the Arab world and the sub-Saharan region, became involved, showing some sympathy for the evolving Libyan position and skepticism about apparent US inflexibility. It was also clear that informal confidence-building measures (a kind of second-track diplomacy that involved technocrats without clear, official links to either the Libyan or Western governments) on several occasions pushed forward the debate on what was acceptable to all sides. Most participants at those informal gatherings knew that although there was no link to ongoing (or initially not yet existing) formal talks, they were all linked one way or another to a more official "audience" on both sides. It was clear from the shifting agenda points discussed at successive meetings that some feedback, reflecting particularly the Libyan government, was involved.[5] The more informal meetings were also useful in explaining to the Libyan side—often frustrated by delays or by the politicized nature of the debate in the United States—how the process was evolving.

Looking back at the period covered in this chapter, it is clear that persistent US diplomatic efforts at isolating Libya, particularly when joined by multilateral actors and supplemented by stringent embargoes, did have a noticeable effect on the Libyan leadership and public. But this was really a victory for traditional, behind-the-scenes diplomacy or, perhaps more accurately, coercive diplomacy. Public diplomacy—in its government to foreign public, whole-of-government, or "new" multiactor forms—played a limited part. It is unlikely that without continuous pressure on the regime that gradually narrowed its own diplomatic and economic options, Saif al-Islam and the small band of reformers around him would have found much traction at home, no matter how ill-considered their reforms were in the end. It was particularly these younger regime elites who were eager to restore the luster that a US diplomatic presence in Tripoli (and Benghazi) would bring. Ultimately, the tortuous path of US-Libyan diplomatic relations demonstrated the usefulness of international support for pressuring so-called rogue states such as Libya to accept widely accepted norms of behavior. But it also demonstrates that US strategic policy persistence, often in the absence of effective in-country diplomacy for dealing with Libya, was critical in that process and in generating the international consensus that ultimately proved effective in convincing the Libyan regime to change. A new form of diplomatic persistence will now be required in the wake of Libya's latest revolution. Whether, and how, to use resident diplomatic missions in Libya deploying public diplomacy instruments that effectively engage Libya's people will be a challenge for the country's international partners—managing the shift from Libya as an isolated, intractable adversary to Libya as an engaged, if struggling, regional ally. The Benghazi killing of US Ambassador Christopher Stevens in September 2012 and the evacuation of the US embassy in July 2014 underscore both the need for persistence and the magnitude of the challenges ahead.

Notes

1. For the post-Qadhafi period, see Vandewalle (2012).

2. Interview with David Mack, 12 November 2004. Mack was a junior political officer at the US embassy at the time.

3. For Libya's involvement in terrorism, see the annual volumes of the Office of the Coordinator for Counterterrorism, US Department of State's *Patterns of Global Terrorism* (until 2003) and *Country Reports on Terrorism* (since 2004) (Washington, DC: Government Printing Office).

4. Libya remained on the list in 2005, in part because of an alleged attempt by the regime to assassinate Crown Prince Abdullah of Saudi Arabia in 2004.

5. The appearance of Saif al-Islam al-Qadhafi for dinner at one of the final meetings of the informal group testified to this fact.

References

Atlantic Council of the United States. 2003. *U.S.-Libyan Relations: Toward Cautious Reengagement.* Vol. 7. Washington, DC: Atlantic Council.

Central Intelligence Agency. 2000—2001. *Unclassified Report to Congress on the Acquisition of Technology Relating to Weapons of Mass Destruction and Advanced Conventional Munitions, 1 January through June 2000,* February 2001.

DeSutter, Paula A. 2004. Assistant Secretary of State for Verification and Compliance before the subcommittee on International Terrorism, Nonproliferation and Human Rights. 22 September. Washington, DC: Federal Document Clearing House Media.

Economist Intelligence Unit. 1983. *Country Report: Libya,* Third Quarter 15.

———. 1986. *Country Report: Libya,* First Quarter 13.

———. 1997. *Country Report: Libya,* Third Quarter 15.

———. 2001. *Country Profile: Libya* 25.

———. 2002. *Country Report: Libya* 12.

Gray, Jerry. 1996. "Foreigners Investing In Libya or in Iran Face U.S. Sanctions." *New York Times,* 24 July.

Jane's Defence Weekly. 1998. "Libya Hampered by Decade-Old U.N. Ban, Says CIA." August 12: 7.

Joyner, Chris C., and Wayne P. Rothbaum. 1993. "Libya and the Aerial Incident at

Lockerbie: What Lessons for International Extradition Law?" *Michigan Journal of International Law* 14, no. 2: 222–261.

Middle East Economic Survey. 1982–1983. 25, no. 41 (July 26, 1982); 3–4; 25, no. 42 (August 2, 1982): 3.

Neumann, Ronald E. 2000. "Testimony on US Policy toward Libya before the Subcommittee on Near Eastern and South Asian Affairs, Senate Foreign Relations Committee, 106th Congress, second session, 4 May 2000 (GPO 2002)." *Libya: A U.S. Policy Perspective. Middle East Policy* 7: 142–145.

O'Sullivan, Meghan. 2003. *Shrewd Sanctions: Statecraft and State Sponsors of Terrorism.* Washington, DC: Brookings Institution Press.

Office of the Coordinator for Counterterrorism, Department of State. *Patterns of Global Terrorism* (until 2003) and *Country Reports on Terrorism* (since 2004). Washington, DC: US Government Printing Office.

Reagan, Ronald. *Public Papers of Presidents: Ronald Reagan, 1986.* Washington, DC: US Government Printing Office, 1988, 1:18.

Schneider, Howard. 1999. "Libya, Seeking Investors, Moves from Fringe toward Mainstream." *Washington Post,* 20 July, A13.

Sharp, Paul. 2005. "Revolutionary States, Outlaw Regimes and the Techniques of Public Diplomacy." In *The New Public Diplomacy: Soft Power in International Relations,* Jan Melissen, ed. Basingstoke, UK: Palgrave Macmillan.

St. John, Ronald B. 2002. *Libya and the United States: Two Centuries of Strife.* Philadelphia: University of Pennsylvania Press.

Vandewalle, Dirk. 2012. "After Qaddafi." Foreign Affairs 91, no. 6 (November/December): 8–15.

Woodward, Bob. 1985. "CIA Anti-Qaddafi Plan Backed: Reagan Authorizes Covert Operation to Undermine Libyan Regime." *Washington Post,* A1.

6 IRAN

Public Diplomacy in a Vacuum

Suzanne Maloney

A
T FIRST GLANCE, IRAN WOULD SEEM TO BE THE poster child for the future of American public diplomacy. After all, the Islamic Republic represents a critical national security priority for Washington, and yet it has gone without official American diplomatic relations for more than three decades. As a result of this estrangement, public diplomacy increasingly assumed the role that traditional diplomacy serves in the relationship with almost every other country in the world. Rhetoric, messaging, and direct engagement with the Iranian people constituted critical tools of American policy toward Iran. The paucity of other mechanisms and the legacy of historical sensitivities between the two countries mean that Washington's public discourse with Iran—directed at both the political leadership and the general public—plays a decisive role in shaping the bilateral dynamic and context for US policy.

The growing centrality of public diplomacy vis-à-vis Iran comes at a historical moment when technological advancement and the widespread dispersal of information and communications have fundamentally altered the environment of international relations. The advent of the Internet and the proliferation of both the equipment and the knowledge to exploit it have rendered the conditions of the Iron Curtain—isolation, incomprehension, and the corresponding lack of empowerment in civil society—functionally impossible to replicate. As the dramatic upheavals in Tunisia and Egypt underscore, even a state with repressive policies on speech and assembly, and the capabilities and willingness to foreclose access to the Internet, can find itself intensely vulnerable to social forces mobilized through the public media. In such a context, official interest in public diplomacy as a means of enhancing American influence seems to offer great potential and possibilities.

Yet the case of Iran also highlights some of the pitfalls of a diplomatic approach that is overly dependent on the instruments of public diplomacy. Even in this era of global interconnectedness, there are limitations on a government's ability to advance policy objectives through public diplomacy, particularly when the most effective instruments of public diplomacy tend to inflame the suspicions of intended recipients. Public diplomacy may provide effective tools for influencing public opinion in a constructive fashion, although evidence from Iran raises questions about its utility even for that secondary interest. However, it is simply inadequate for advancing hardcore security interests such as nonproliferation and, more generally, for overcoming the hurdles of official animosity and isolation. Deployed prudently, the tools of public diplomacy can help shape a positive long-term context for bilateral relations, but as the 2013–2014 negotiations on Iran's nuclear program underscore, resolving the most urgent disputes between Washington and Tehran will require a reversion to the traditional tools of formal diplomacy, especially direct negotiations.

Historical Factors Shaping US-Iranian Diplomacy

Throughout most of the early interaction between the United States and the country that would eventually be known as Iran, traditional diplomacy represented the least significant dimension of the relationship. Formal relations began during the middle of the nineteenth century, but for the next hundred years, until it became caught in the vortex of World War II, Iran remained a relatively unimportant concern within American foreign policy. Before 1940, to the extent that contact existed, it transpired within the realm of unofficial engagement between individual Americans and an Iran that was experiencing the final gasps of a fading monarchy and the struggle for authority and legitimacy in its aftermath. During this period, several US citizens earned considerable gratitude within Iran for their service to the country as missionaries, as educators, as financial advisers pressing for modernization, and even as democratic partisans during the aborted Constitutional Revolution. Their contributions combined with deep-seated suspicions of the aims of the dominant foreign powers in Iran—Russia and Britain—helped elevate the United States to the position of a much sought-after counterweight. With the exception of the secondment of several important financial advisers such as Morgan Shuster, traditional American diplomacy was negligible.

This situation changed radically after the German invasion of the Soviet Union in 1941. Iran emerged as a crucial transshipment link between the United States and the Soviet Union, a vital sea-lane in the incipient international oil industry, and a battleground for influence among the contesting world powers and eventually among the Allies themselves. Reza Shah appealed to Washington in protesting the British and Russian invasion of his country in August 1941. However, while official US messages offered modest reassurance on the preservation of Iranian sovereignty, Washington acceded to Reza's forced abdication in favor of his son and eventually joined the occupation of Iran after entering the war. The postwar crisis over Moscow's refusal to withdraw from northern Iran drew the first major commitment of American diplomatic capital on Tehran's behalf, but Washington was not yet wholly persuaded to expand its political investment in Iran. Economic and military assistance remained modest over the course of the 1940s, and the Iranian political elite joked with frustration about American unreliability (Rubin 1980, 50).

The second major milestone that intensified American interest in Iran was the attempted nationalization of the Anglo-Iranian Oil Company in 1951 and the Cold War–inspired fears of Iran moving into the Soviet orbit. The events of this period, including an international embargo of Iranian oil and the coup that eventually overthrew the popular prime minister who had engineered the nationalization, helped enmesh the monarchy and Washington in an ever-tighter embrace through spiraling strategic ties and assistance. The infamous US role in the 1953 coup that unseated Prime Minister Muhammad Mussadiq and reinstated the shah to the throne after his brief, ignominious flight to Italian exile helped crystallize a "conspiratorial interpretation of politics" that "permeates [Iranian] society, the mainstream as much as the fringe, and cuts through all sectors of the political spectrum" (Abrahamian 1993, 12). For the monarchy's opponents, memories of the 1953 coup fostered an obsessive resentment of the United States and a conviction that American domination of Iran and hostility toward its democratic aspirations was the root of their country's problems. "Iranians will never forget the 1953 US-supported coup," argues Akbar Ganji, a former revolutionary who has become Iran's best-known dissident, because it cost the country "one of its most important historical opportunities for the establishment of a democracy" (Ganji 2007).

Arguably, the relative attribution of culpability in the Mussadiq affair has been overstated by American scholars of Iran as well as by Iranians (Takeyh 2010). It is notable that the Islamic Republic has done relatively little to honor this secular nationalist figure, quickly rescinding a postrevolutionary move to affix his name to Tehran's largest avenue and otherwise minimizing his historical importance. Nonetheless, he remains a widely revered hero among Iranians, and the saga of a democratic movement aborted by the machinations of an external power continues to foster suspicion and hostility toward Washington, as distinct from the American people or American culture.

After 1953, the American-Iranian diplomatic relationship ballooned. Washington embarked on a program of generous technical and financial assistance to Iran, which enabled the shah to impose a higher degree of central control and reassemble the mechanisms of the state under his personal authority. Beyond economic assistance and military sales, Washington began to assert a more significant influence on the shah's domestic political agenda. Concerned about the implications of a destabilizing recession and the intensification of political unrest in Iran, the United States began pressing the shah for structural reforms. The White Revolution, as the shah's development program was initially called, began in 1962–1963 with land reform and import-substitution industrialization as its most prominent components. Other elements included the sale of state-owned factories, the establishment of voting rights for women, profit-sharing schemes for workers, a literacy corps, and nationalization of the forests.

The protests that erupted in response to the unveiling of the White Revolution among the Iranian clergy forged a leading role for Ayatollah Ruhollah Khomeini, and his thundering objections emphasized the role of Washington in shaping the shah's liberalizing agenda. A year later, Khomeini emerged from prison to confront the shah once again in vociferous fashion. The issue of the day was the government's decision to extend diplomatic immunity to American military personnel. In Khomeini's sermonizing, this concession symbolized a more profound betrayal of Iranian sovereignty. "They have sold us, they have sold our independence," he inveighed (Moin 1999, 123). In 1964, Khomeini was dispatched into exile, first to Turkey and eventually to Najaf, Iraq.

Iran's reform and the reactions of 1963 represented yet another turning point along the route to the epic events of the 1979 revolution, escalating the interdependence of America and the Pahlavi monarchy at the same time as it accelerated the alienation of vital sociopolitical constituencies. Over the course of the next fifteen years, the diplomatic relationship between Washington and Tehran grew apace, particularly after the explosion of Iranian oil revenues during and after the 1973 oil boom. Billions of dollars in unconditional arms sales, a vast official relationship underpinned by intricate interpersonal and informal ties, and an array of institutional cooperation between American and Iranian businesses, universities, and media organizations made for a robust official diplomatic interaction as well as an extensive bilateral cultural exchange.

Throughout the prerevolutionary period, nongovernmental interaction represented an important, if underappreciated, parallel dimension of the formal relationship. Some of the earliest ties between Americans and Iranians were in fact forged via cultural and medical institutions established in Iran by American educators and missionaries. These included Iran's first modern medical school (in Urmiyeh) and its first Western-style university (Alborz College, founded in 1873) with coeducational classrooms, laboratories, and a student-run newspaper. Americans also played a formative role in shaping the context that helped produce Iran's Constitutional Revolution—the first effort to promote representative democracy in the modern Middle East. An American school in Tabriz trained two of the most consequential figures in the push for a parliament, and one of the teachers at the school remains revered in Iran for fighting and dying alongside the Constitutionalists (Asgard 2010). Other American scholars engaged in independent efforts to document and promote Persian art and architecture as early as the 1920s, launching conferences, surveys, and cultural institutions that remained landmark cultural endeavors throughout the early Pahlavi period, when the official relationship was relatively anemic.

The US government began contributing to these transnational cultural exchanges considerably later, although eventually it came to subsidize a wide-ranging program of activities and institutions in what is traditionally termed "public diplomacy." Through embassy-sponsored poetry readings and English-language classes taught at the Iran-America Society (IAS), cultural affairs officers provided rare opportunities for contact between American officials and the artists and underprivileged within Iranian society whose relevance would come to the fore a few years later during the prerevolutionary mobilization. Cultural programming incorporated Iranian architecture, experimental cinema, jazz performances, stage productions of works that ranged from Shakespeare to Thornton Wilder, and even technical cooperation among librarians from both countries. The US Information Service translated dozens of books into Persian, operated public libraries in Iran, and stewarded such laudable programs as the Fulbright exchange, which brought more than 1,300 Iranians to the United States, and a broader official recruitment of students helped bring as many as 30,000 Iranians to study in the United States by the 1970s.

Broadcasting represented another important dimension of prerevolutionary American public diplomacy programming; the Voice of America (VOA) was established in 1942 and began operating in Iran the same year. It remained only an intermittent presence until the 1979 revolution because of opposition from the shah and some of his senior aides, and in fact had been on a thirteen-year hiatus at the time of the 1979 revolution. Also notable was the Peace Corps program, which sent more than 1,700 young Americans to Iran over fourteen years to teach English and assist with agricultural, environmental, and urban planning projects in collaboration with Iranians. Among the alumni of the Peace Corps program in Iran are former Secretary of Health and Human Services Donna Shalala and Ambassador John Limbert, who was one of the American diplomats held hostage and later served as deputy assistant secretary of state for Iran during the Obama administration.

Postrevolutionary Diplomacy

Iran's revolution did not in and of itself lead to an immediate rupture in the US-Iranian relationship. Established in the days after the shah's effective abdication and Khomeini's subsequent triumphal return, the Provisional Government in fact maintained "close and direct contact" with Washington on a host of issues (Bill 1988, 265). The United States recognized the new government, rebuffed entreaties of support from the many opponents of the new regime, and tried to rebuild constructive relations with revolutionary leaders. Iran's new bureaucracy included many moderates well known to Washington. Their interest in securing US intelligence and military spare parts paralleled Washington's understandable eagerness to gain a better understanding of the new leadership.

The November 1979 seizure of the American embassy in Tehran radically altered the context for bilateral relations, but notably Washington continued efforts to initiate a dialogue with Tehran throughout the hostage crisis (Limbert 2009). The event prompted the Provisional Government's resignation, eliminating Washington's primary channel to the new regime and forcing the United States to intensify contacts with other elements of Iran's fluid power structure. This sparse dialogue with the revolutionary clergy proved to be of limited utility, as Ayatollah Khomeini's endorsement of the embassy seizure made any hint of opposition tantamount to treason. Still, Washington continued to entertain openings to individual Iranian interlocutors seeking to advance negotiations. The receptivity to dialogue extended to the decision to keep the Iranian embassy in Washington open even as US diplomats remained captive in Tehran. It was not until April 7, 1980—a full five months into the crisis—that President Carter formally severed diplomatic relations with Tehran and banned American exports to Iran.

Throughout the 1980s, America's readiness to deal directly with Tehran persisted, even in the face of escalating regional tensions and US-Iranian naval skirmishes in the Persian Gulf. This receptivity helped inspire the Reagan administration's covert arms sales to the struggling Islamic Republic, in addition to the obvious short-term interest in enlisting Iranian assistance on behalf of Western hostages held in Lebanon. America's Israeli interlocutors, as well as some in the White House including National Security Advisor Robert McFarlane, were persuaded that direct contacts with Tehran could tip the balance within the Islamic Republic in favor of moderates who were opposed to Ayatollah Khomeini's rule (McFarlane and Smardz 1994, 106). For McFarlane and other US officials, the backchannel dealings with Iran were analogous to his predecessor's secret meetings with Chinese leaders prior to the Sino-American thaw.

Even in the disastrous aftermath of the Iran-Contra revelations, Secretary of State George Shultz tried to keep the door open to dialogue. Washington continued to meet with Iranian interlocutors through December 1986 and repeatedly requested meetings with various Iranian officials, including President Khomenei during his September 1987 UN visit. "We are prepared for a structured, authoritative dialogue with the Iranian Government at a responsible level, " senior State Department official Edward Djerejian told a *New York Times* reporter in November 1987. "We think direct communication between the US and Iran would be a step in the right direction in trying to resolve our differences" (Sciolino 1987). The administration balked, however, at Iran's insistence on delivery of prerevolutionary arms sales and the meetings never transpired. In 1987 congressional testimony, Shultz acknowledged that Washington had an "obvious stake in better relations with Iran" and acknowledging the Iranian revolution as a "fact of history" (Hunter 1990, 67). A year later, Washington responded positively to new backchannel inquiries from Tehran seeking a direct dialogue, but any contacts were precluded by the July 1988 accidental US downing of an Iranian passenger jet in the Gulf (Sciolino 1998).

The two central episodes of US-Iran diplomacy during the first decade following the revolution, the effort to resolve the hostage crisis and the Iran-Contra affair, helped to engrain a deep-seated disinclination toward backchannel diplomacy as a means of dealing with the Iranian leadership. This aversion reflects an understandable reaction to the frustrations of dealing with self-appointed intermediaries throughout the 444-day hostage ordeal, and the disastrous domestic political consequences that ensued for both sides from the Iran-Contra dealings. However, the reasonable reluctance to rely on clandestine or third-party contacts predictably created other problems; in particular, it propelled the lion's share of the diplomatic interaction between Tehran and Washington into the public domain. For formal US diplomatic representation in Tehran, communication via the Swiss embassy remained a semiroutine mode of official communications. On occasion an American administration might use the Omani government or a regional leader to convey a particularly sensitive message to Tehran. However, in the aftermath of Iran-Contra, the notion of seeking out or empowering intermediaries to engage in more serious or sustained dialogue has rarely been entertained in Washington. As a result, from the late 1980s until 2013, the overwhelming majority of US-Iranian dialogue has been carried out in the public domain through official rhetoric.

One of the most important examples of this tendency for public rhetoric being used as a means to communicate with other governments, replacing private diplomatic discourse, transpired at the outset of the George H. W. Bush administration. In his inaugural address, President Bush referenced American hostages held in Lebanon and said "assistance can be shown here, and will be long remembered. Good will begets good will. Good faith can be a spiral that endlessly moves on" (Bush 1989a). Iran replied in a public sermon by Ayatollah Khomenei that contained far less generosity.

> Now the new U.S. President has stated that he is ready to resume relations with Iran, subject to this and that. He is setting conditions! We do not accept

your conditions! You have nothing to say to us. We object, we do not agree to a relationship with you! We are not prepared to establish relations with powerful world devourers like you! The Iranian nation has no need of the United States, nor is the Iranian nation afraid of the United States. (cited in Fuller 1991, 255–256)

Still, sufficient positive signs emanated from Tehran, including an August 1989 direct appeal by President Rafsanjani, for the Bush administration to persist in pressing for Iranian assistance in freeing the hostages, albeit indirectly through the United Nations. The Bush administration remained receptive to dialogue with Tehran, including one embarrassing incident when President Bush himself accepted a telephone call from an imposter posing as Rafsanjani. Bush publicly appealed to Tehran repeatedly, saying, "we don't have to be hostile with Iran for the rest of our lives. We've had a good relationship with them in the past, they are of strategic importance . . . they would be welcome back into the family of law-abiding, non-terrorist-sponsoring nations" (Bush 1989b).

The administration also appeared to have briefly toyed with the notion of some positive post–Gulf War role for Iran. In February 1991 Secretary of State James Baker testified about plans for a Gulf security framework that would exclude no regional state, explicitly envisaging including Tehran "as a major power in the Gulf" (Friedman 1991). Instead, in the ensuing months, the launch of a new Arab-Israeli peace process at the October 1991 Madrid Conference positioned Tehran as the most vocal and violent adversary of Washington's hoped-for "new Middle East."

The Clinton administration entered office determined to avoid the disastrous Iranian entanglements of its predecessors. Secretary of State Warren Christopher's strong views on Iran were framed by his experience leading the contentious negotiations that freed the hostages. National Security Advisor Anthony Lake proposed a "dual containment" strategy, arguing that "Americans had a bad habit of being seduced by the siren song from Tehran and then [being] badly betrayed by it" (Pollack 2004, 259). Eventually, however, domestic developments within Iran prompted the White House to shift its approach and resume its predecessors' efforts to reach out to Tehran.

The catalyst was the unexpected 1997 election of a moderate president, Mohammad Khatami, and his subsequent gestures, particularly his January 1998 statements about respect for the "great American people" and "an intellectual affinity for American civilization" in a CNN interview (Khatami 1998). His rhetoric stood in sharp contrast to a speech only days before by Khamenei, who accused the West of using "guileful propaganda tricks . . . to bring about instability and insecurity in the nation" (*New York Times*, 1998). The interview ignited a storm of controversy within Iran, and Khatami quickly played down the significance of the interview and adopted harsher rhetoric toward Washington. Conservative opposition was driven as much by a self-interested aversion to rapprochement, implemented by a political rival, as by their longstanding ideological antipathy toward the United States.

In response, Secretary of State Madeleine Albright later publicly proposed parallel confidence-building steps that would enable cooperation in developing a "road map" for a new relationship (Albright 1998). Over the course of the next two years, as an epic internal power struggle raged in Iran, Washington again sent quiet overtures. The administration authorized the sale of airplane spare parts, lifted sanctions on food and medicine, and proposed opening a consular station in Iran. At an April 1999 White House event, President Clinton acknowledged Iran's historical grievances, adding that "we have to find some way to get dialog, and going into total denial when you're in a conversation with somebody who's been your adversary, in a country like Iran that is often worried about its independence and its integrity is not exactly the way to begin" (Clinton 1999). The administration also tried to develop a *modus vivendi* with Iranian reformers on terrorism via an August 1999 letter seeking cooperation in investigating the 1996 Khobar Towers bombing. Tehran apparently did not respond and news of the secret communiqué quickly leaked in Iran. In the end, yet another attempt at generating traction on engagement ended in mutual recriminations.

The Clinton administration's most dramatic opening to Iran came in March 2000, after an overwhelming reformist victory in Iranian parliamentary elections. In a speech commemorating the traditional Persian new year, Albright expressed regret for a range of previous American policies, acknowledged "Iran's importance in the Gulf," and offered to "deal directly with each other as two proud and independent nations and address on a mutual basis the issues that have been keeping us apart" (Albright 2000). As a first step, Albright announced the lifting of sanctions on caviar, carpets, and pistachios, and promised to expedite the settlement process on Iran's outstanding frozen assets. It was by far the most ingratiating overture of its kind, one that received effectively no response or reciprocity from Tehran.

Skeptical of the credibility and utility of Iranian reformists, President George W. Bush sought to propel a more dramatic transformation and pressed to align US policy with the Iranian people, rather than any faction of its political elite. Well before the September 11, 2001 attacks and the subsequent development of a broader philosophical and bureaucratic framework for the "Freedom Agenda," the Bush administration was taking a more activist posture vis-à-vis Iran's internal politics. In July 2002 the White House issued a statement of support to protesters marking the anniversary of student demonstrations that had rocked Iran three years earlier. The statement lamented the fact that Iranians' "voices are not being listened to by the unelected people who are the real rulers" and promising that "[a]s Iran's people move towards a future defined by greater freedom, they will have no better friend" than Washington (Bush 2002). Coming on the heels of Bush's inclusion of Iran alongside Iraq and North Korea as the "axis of evil" in his January 2002 State of the Union address, the President's forceful statement drew sharp rebukes from the Iranian regime, which depicted the statement as "open interference," as well as from an array of leading reformers (AFP 2002).

Zalmay Khalilzad, senior director at the National Security Council, described the Bush approach to Iran as "dual track" in its twin focus on pressuring the regime and supporting the Iranian people. "US policy is not to impose change on Iran but to support the Iranian people in their quest to decide their own destiny," Khalilzad said in an August 2002 speech to a Washington think tank. "Our policy is not about Khatami or Khamenei, reform or hard-line; it is about supporting those who want freedom, human rights, democracy, and economic and educational opportunity for themselves and their fellow countrymen and women" (Khalilzad 2002).

This repudiation of Iran's ruling elites and the conscious embrace of the generic "Iranian people" became the hallmark of Bush administration policy toward Iran. In particular, this determination informed the administration's decision in 2003 to cut off a quiet official dialogue with Tehran on Afghan issues and preclude any further official contacts, a move that contradicted all prior American administrations' efforts to start a dialogue with Tehran. The early success of the Iraq war, as well as events within Iran such as the serious student unrest that erupted in June 2003, validated the view that the Iranian regime was vulnerable and that any contact with official Iran would "legitimize" and even strengthen the clerics' precarious hold on power. This conviction framed the skepticism and apparent disinterest that was the Bush administration's response to a 2003 backchannel overture from mid-ranking Iranian officials interested in exploring the possibilities for a "grand bargain" between the two governments. In May 2006, however, Washington shifted its stance with an offer to join Britain, France, and Germany, which together with the European Union were engaged in direct negotiations with Tehran on the nuclear issue. The offer remained stillborn for several years because Tehran rejected the stipulation within it regarding a prior suspension of uranium enrichment originally agreed upon with the Europeans. Still, the Bush administration remained committed to negotiations on the nuclear issue and continued to test opportunities for talking with Tehran in its final years in office.

The Obama administration placed great emphasis on a new Iran policy from the earliest days of the campaign, when the now-president promised to meet with any Iranian leader—a pledge that elicited opposition from his then rival (now Secretary of State) Hillary Clinton. The first major initiative of the new administration's policy of engagement was a masterful piece of public diplomacy, a videotaped broadcast of President Obama himself extending greetings to commemorate the Iranian New Year (or *Noruz*) in March 2009. While the gesture itself was not truly innovative—the tradition of White House *Noruz* greetings dates back at least to the Clinton administration—the personal investment of the president and the use of rhetoric that was clearly designed to appeal to regime elites as well as to regular citizens drew considerable positive attention in the media as well as within Iran.

Over the course of the next several months, Washington reportedly engaged in other less public overtures toward Iran, including direct communications from President Obama to the Iranian supreme leader, an unprecedented step. Despite plaudits from some Iranians and external analysts, Washington's latest efforts at engagement produced little more than the more provocative approach of its predecessor, and by the end of the first year of the Obama presidency, US policy toward Tehran had reverted to the familiar terrain of economic sanctions and talk of "dual-track" tactics—an improvement in the lexicon but not, unfortunately, in the efficacy of longstanding carrot-and-stick measures to persuade Tehran to adopt more constructive policies in the region.

Even as Iran's domestic politics hardened, the Obama administration took pains to reiterate its willingness to talk with Tehran on issues of mutual concern, beginning with the nuclear issue. Washington has engaged in a few modest gestures toward Tehran, including the November 2010 designation of a Baluchi insurgent group as a terrorist organization. However, the early nuclear negotiations between Iran and the international community, including Washington, after President Obama took office produced frustration. Obama insisted from the outset that engagement efforts would not be indefinite, and so by the end of his first year, Washington had begun to seek new forms of leverage through strengthened economic pressure. These efforts were strengthened by newfound support from Europe and elsewhere, particularly after 2009, when internal upheaval in Iran and new revelations on the nuclear program deepened international mistrust of the Iranian leadership.

The result was a multilayered framework of economic sanctions, consisting of both unilateral and multilateral measures that had a devastating impact on the Iranian economy. These sanctions created profound disruptions for Iranian consumers and heightened debate within the Iranian elite over the system's approach to the world and nuclear negotiations. In 2013, Iranians elected Hassan Rouhani as president; Rouhani openly campaigned on resolving the nuclear impasse and quickly revived the dormant negotiating process after he took office. It is worthwhile to note, however, that even before Rouhani's election—and even at the least promising points in Iran's domestic evolution—the Obama administration continued to seek diplomatic openings with Tehran, including an October 2009 confidence-building proposal on the nuclear issue and 2013 backchannel discussions with Iranian interlocutors in Oman.

In addition to his popular mandate, Rouhani has apparently been accorded considerable room for maneuver on the nuclear issue. This helped generate a series of unprecedented events in the postrevolutionary bilateral US-Iranian relationship—including a September 2013 telephone conversation between the presidents of the two countries; the November 2013 interim nuclear accord, which was intended as a stepping-stone toward a permanent and more comprehensive agreement; and routinized diplomatic engagement between Iranian and American officials in the context of ongoing negotiations on the nuclear issue. As of late-2014, these contacts had not facilitated a broader dialogue or realistic prospects for a rehabilitation of the bilateral relationship, but the productivity of direct interaction on the nuclear issue over the course of 2013 and 2014 will make it difficult for both sides to revert to a complete rupture, even in the event that the negotiations themselves do not resolve the nuclear impasse.

Postrevolutionary Public Diplomacy

Just as it ruptured the official relationship, the Islamic Revolution and its aftermath produced an abrupt termination of the public diplomacy efforts of the US government and a sharp decline in any kind of unofficial cultural interaction between the two countries. Many of the leading institutions of American-Iranian cooperation came under direct attack during the unrest both before and after the shah's ouster; the IAS's Tehran center was bombed in 1978, and its final director, Kathryn Koob, was among the hostages seized by prorevolutionary students in November 1979 and held hostage along with fifty-one diplomats and other US public servants until January 1981. Ironically, some of these facilities of prerevolutionary cultural exchanges were expropriated by the revolutionary regime but retained their basic focus; the IAS center in Tehran is now headquarters of a state-affiliated agency that conducts foreign-language programs across the country.

In the aftermath of the long hostage siege, public diplomacy toward Tehran did not rank particularly high on the agenda of US policymakers in seeking avenues for shaping Iranian policy. As suggested above, the primary framework for American policy toward Tehran during the first decade after the revolution comprised modest diplomatic pressure and episodic efforts to engage directly with the Iranian leadership, largely shaped by expectations that Iran's revolutionary fever would eventually abate. Moreover, faced with the restrictions on direct contact between Iranians and Americans during the 1980s as a result of the diplomatic estrangement and the war with Iraq, and deprived of the most obvious institutions or instruments for implementing public diplomacy programming, both the Reagan and George H. W. Bush administrations did not invest significant funds or focus on any efforts to reach Iranians beyond the leadership itself.

Washington's interest in a more wide-ranging approach to Iran began to heighten by the 1990s, however, largely as a result of the dramatic shifts in the international context with the demise of the Soviet Union, the end of the Cold War, and the prospect of a meaningful breakthrough in the Arab-Israeli peace process. In this new environment, the opportunity of reaching out to the Iranian people appeared to gain currency, particularly among Republicans in Washington. Meanwhile, the American interest in countering Iran's polices as Tehran began seeking ways to expand its own influence in a more subtle fashion took on a new urgency. As a result, the past two decades have seen a steady increase in efforts to communicate with Iranians, particularly as shifts in Iran's internal politics have elevated the salience of a broader bilateral discourse.

Throughout this period, official American public diplomacy toward Iran has primarily been composed of four main strands: broadcasting; democracy promotion and other civil society programming; people-to-people exchanges; and technical cooperation and communication.

Broadcasting

Broadcasting has become an increasingly central component of US public diplomacy toward Iran for decades. This importance can be directly attributed to the Iranian revolution; the change in government facilitated a revival of VOA's Farsi Service, as it was then known, which had been shelved for thirteen years due to the shah's discomfort at its broadcasts. No longer constrained by deference to a prickly ally, broadcasting quickly assumed greater importance within American cultural diplomacy and information provision toward Iran.

More importantly, the developments that produced revolution provided dramatic illustration of the vital role of the media in shaping political outcomes. A variety of media outlets and programs contributed to the coalescing of the amorphous forces against the shah into something resembling a coherent opposition movement and became particularly vital to the basic exchange of information among Iranians as a result of a prolonged strike by the domestic media. Among them were cassette tapes of Khomeini's sermons smuggled into the country to promote his ideas. Consistent with storied Iranian tradition, pamphlets, leaflets, *elamieh* (announcements), and *shabnameh* (night letters) were distributed to publicize developments and accusations against the shah. Meanwhile, opposition leaders "became adept at feeding information to the BBC correspondent" to the extent that the shah took to jamming the BBC during his final months. And despite an engrained aversion to the media, Khomeini himself shrewdly utilized the international press corps during the final months of his exile in Paris to solidify his role as the revolution's leader (Srebeny-Mohammadi and Mohammadi 1994).

The Islamic Republic has banned satellite dishes since 1995, and the official state television and radio networks under the auspices of the Voice and Vision of the Islamic Revolution nominally retain a monopoly over broadcast services within the country. As the beneficiary of these restrictions, state broadcasters remain the most important source of news and information for the vast majority of the population. As a result, the management of the state broadcasting authority has remained a highly prized post within the Iranian political hierarchy, although a long-running debate among various political factions over its lack of objectivity, routine use of bullying tactics, and relatively low-quality production values particularly for entertainment has produced little in the way of constructive improvements over the years. Iran's conservatives have routinely stonewalled efforts to liberalize this sector through greater competition or to provide more effective parliamentary oversight.

By the same token, the broadcast media offer a tempting target for external groups and governments seeking to influence Iranian opinion. The satellite ban is enforced with almost cursory infrequency, particularly as the advent of the Internet and other forms of communications technology revolutionized access to and dispersion of information. Every available measure shows that satellite access in Iran continues to expand (a recent discussion in the Iranian parliament cited a 30 percent growth in satellite dishes).

As a result of the dichotomy between the official ban on satellites and its minimalist enforcement, a cottage industry of foreign broadcasts into Iran emerged in the 1990s, mainly relying on the talents of former journalists and entertainers from the Pahlavi era, many of whom were based in the Los Angeles area by virtue of the region's long historical association with Iran. Several of the channels were either explicitly or tacitly associated with expatriate political factions, such as the Mojahideen-e Khalq and the Iranian Communist Party (*Tudeh*). Many Iranians also tune into programming offered in other languages, including Turkish, Arabic, and English.

At the same time, VOA expanded its broadcasts to include satellite television. Frustrated with what it saw as insufficient commitment to promoting change in Iranian politics and policies, a Republican-dominated Congress persuaded the Clinton administration to establish a Persian-language radio station under the auspices of Radio Free Europe/Radio Liberty (RFE/RL). The intended parallels between the new station and US broadcasting efforts to undermine communist regimes in Eastern Europe during the Cold War were not lost on the Iranians, who vociferously denounced the move as an "act of aggression" against Iran (BBC 1998).

Radio Azadi was established in 1998 as a joint venture operated by VOA and RFE/RL. Having originally resisted congressional pressure to establish the station, the Clinton administration named Steven Fairbanks, longtime State Department Iran analyst and former Peace Corps volunteer in Iran, to lead the service, a move viewed widely as a hedge against its deployment as a tool of heavy-handed propaganda. Radio Azadi was retooled in 2002 as part of a broader post-9/11 rethink of American programming toward the Muslim world; it was rebranded as Radio Farda or "Radio of Tomorrow" and its broadcast hours were expanded. Today, Farda streams live twenty-four hours a day, with a website that generates ten million hits per month, an active presence on social media sites such as Twitter and Facebook, and extensive interactive text messaging, according to the station. Now run solely by RFE/RL, Farda's mission is to focus on news and developments within Iran, as differentiated from VOA that per its charter offers a broader menu of news and information about America.

For its part, VOA has also engaged in a significant expansion and revamping of its broadcasting into Iran and maintains a website and five hours of radio programming a day. In recent years, its television service has been renamed the Persian News Network, with broadcasts of original and simulcast programming twenty-four hours a day (Izadi 2009). In 2006, nearly half the $66.1 million appropriated by Congress in response to a new State Department initiative for promoting democracy in Iran was used to expand VOA broadcasts into Iran. With this infusion of resources and official support for its mission, VOA has upgraded its capabilities and expanded its reach considerably. Over the past four years, the website has incorporated interactive lessons in colloquial English and applications to facilitate downloading of broadcasts onto mobile phones. It has the largest combined audience of all the international broadcasting outlets in Iran, reaching approximately 20 percent of the population on a weekly basis according to its own surveys.

VOA has also made a substantial effort to modernize its programming, move away from reliance on longtime diaspora figures as guests, and attract a younger audience. For a time, viewers could tune into the highly regarded political satire show, *Parazit (Static)*, as well as listen to commentary by former Islamic Republic officials turned opposition activists such as Mohsen Sazegara. Before it was taken off the air, *Parazit* drew 45,000 hits weekly on YouTube and had 200,000 Facebook fans (Bahrampour 2011). While Parazit's host, Kambiz Hosseini, moved onto other programs, including one distributed on Radio Farda, VOA has continued efforts to reach young Iranians through more relevant programming, including another award-winning satire show, OnTen (Antenna)

In early 2011 Ramin Asgard, a veteran State Department officer with long experience dealing with Iran policy, was named to direct VOA's Persian-language news service. It was hoped that Asgard's familiarity with US policy concerns together with his Persian-language skills might boost the credibility and quality of an operation that is still struggling to find its footing amid rapid expansion and high expectations among its advocates in Congress and the Obama administration. Asgard left a year later, and was eventually replaced by Setareh Derakhshesh, who previously served as deputy director and as lead anchor of the daily news program.

Both the Bush and Obama administrations have made an effort to cultivate their connections with the Persian-language media not only as a means of boosting the profile of VOA and other US government–affiliated assets but also in hopes of expanding the reach of Washington's efforts to counter official Iranian propaganda on key issues such as the nuclear dispute. The president himself participated in a BBC Persian interview in the fall of 2010, a move praised as savvy by a key Mahmoud Ahmadinejad aide because of the BBC's sway and audience (BBC 2010). The entrance of the BBC into the Persian-language television market in 2009 has widely been perceived as a direct threat to VOA's market share.

Still, as tensions between Washington and Tehran have intensified over the years, criticism of VOA and Radio Farda has similarly heightened, with some advocating that Washington should use these tools more explicitly to promote American values and policy positions. In 2002, when Radio Azadi was transformed into Radio Farda, some critics questioned the wisdom of scaling back the station's news focus in favor of music and other programming intended to attract a younger audience (Fathi 2002). These critiques echo a broader debate about US broadcasting, as stalwart VOA defenders have expressed concerns about the dilution of both VOA's brand and its standards by the establishment of different services for Persian, Arabic, and other audiences.

At the same time, achieving high-quality programming during a period of considerable expansion of its Persian-language broadcasting has created challenges for VOA. In a report by the State Department's Office of the Inspector General (OIG), questions were raised about the utility of its radio broadcasts, which apparently reach a very small audience mainly composed of an elderly demographic (US Department of State 2009). The report also highlighted profound problems with the work environment for VOA's Iran programming staff. Other critics continue to flog the VOA operation as retrograde and insufficiently nimble for a fast-paced news environment. In the aftermath of the 2009 Iranian presidential election, for example, VOA's Persian News Network ended live programming after reporting initial results. At a moment when many Iranians were seeking an independent view of the controversial election results, VOA was showing prerecorded material (Sheridan 2009).

Getting the political balance right while expanding coverage has proven to be a challenge for American Persian-language broadcasters, and much of the intermittent scrutiny from Congress and political watchdogs has not generated positive feedback. At times, analysts as well as expatriates saw VOA's approach as overly accommodating of the Iranian government and individual leaders, earning Radio Azadi the sarcastic epithet "Radio Khatami." Meanwhile, others—both in the diaspora and within Iran itself—countered that the VOA hallmark of ideological objectivity has been sacrificed to advance an anti–Islamic Republic agenda, citing an interview with a Baluchi guerilla leader, Abdulmalek Rigi, as an irresponsible American embrace of violent regime change. The March 2009 OIG report flagged concerns about objectivity and credibility, although the question of political orientation is off-limits for its assessment. In addition, there have been several publicized incidents involving critiques by former employees about the political content of VOA programming.

Beyond its formal US government broadcasting capabilities, Washington has invested in a broader effort to enhance American communications with Iran. The State Department launched a Persian-language website in 2003 and in the past several years has greatly intensified its use of social media for communicating with Iranians. In 2011 a Persian-language spokesperson was appointed and, in an explicit policy shift, Washington approved regular interaction with the Iranian press. Then Deputy Assistant Secretary of State Philo Dibble explained that "[f]or years, private sector studies have shown that the majority of Iranians—upwards of 80 percent—get their news from government-owned media. We are offering those media appearances by US official spokespersons on live Iranian TV and radio in Farsi. We hope that by engaging with all aspects of Persian-language media—private, Western, Iranian state-owned and, of course, Radio Farda and VOA Persian—we will expand what Iranians hear about U.S. foreign policy and enable them to hear messages directly from U.S. sources" (Esfandiari 2011). The diplomat appointed to the post, longtime foreign service officer Alan Eyre, has established a large

and enthusiastic following on various forms of social media and has successfully bridged the gap between public and traditional diplomacy as a valued
member of the American nuclear negotiating team.

Later that year, in her first-ever interview with a Persian-language television program (VOA's now-defunct program *Parazit*), Secretary of State Hillary Clinton announced the establishment of "Virtual Tehran Embassy," an
effort designed to facilitate more routinized and more accurate communication with Iranians on issues related to US policy and consular matters (RFE/
RL 2011). The site can be viewed in English as well as Persian, and by the time
of its one-year anniversary, the Virtual Embassy had received nearly two million page views.

In addition to the embassy's online presence, the State Department has
created a Persian-language Twitter account (more than 81,000 followers as of
December 2014), a Google+ account (7,072 followers and over 5,224,598 page
views), and a Facebook page (more than 451,728 likes), under the branding
USAdarFarsi ("USA in Persian"). USAdarFarsi also has a YouTube channel
that provides viewers a variety of viewing material with Farsi subtitles, such
as US State Department briefings, President Barack Obama's *Noruz* messages,
sports diplomacy, and the latest world news, as well as the popular online
program "Ask Alan," which gets an average of 4,000 views per month and
provides Iranians an opportunity to pose questions to the Persian-language
spokesman. The Virtual Embassy maintains an official blog in Persian that
posts regularly about American history and culture, as well as regular contributions by the Persian-language spokesman.

Civil Society and Democracy

A second component of American public diplomacy toward Tehran encompasses formal US support for civil society and democracy promotion. Ironically, this dimension of American policy assumed greater primacy within the
Washington debate on Iran after the advent of a reformist movement within
the Islamic Republic in the late 1990s. Before that time, there was only episodic US interest in trying to influence the internal political dynamics of the
postrevolutionary regime, and that interest focused on elite machinations
within the regime itself. However, the emergence of Iran's reformers only
exacerbated partisan differences on Iran policy within the US government.

Iran has also featured prominently in the post-9/11 movement toward a
more substantive US government role in efforts to advance democracy in the

Middle East. In 2004, frustrated with the administration's failure to include Iran-related programming in broader regional initiatives, Congress used a soft earmark of $1.5 million to require the State Department to award "grants to educational, humanitarian and nongovernmental organizations (NGO) and individuals inside Iran to support the advancement of democracy and human rights in Iran" (Katzman 2006). The Bureau of Democracy, Human Rights and Labor used the earmark to support programs at the National Endowment for Democracy and to establish a center that would document Iranian human rights abuses along the lines of a similar initiative by Iraqi exiles before Saddam Hussein's removal.

The earmarks doubled in 2005 and expanded to $10 million in 2006, although the projects and individuals who received this funding were classified out of concern for their safety. Meanwhile, several senators and representatives tabled legislation proposing exponentially larger bonanzas for Iran's expatriate media and opponents of the Iranian regime. Once again, Iranian internal dynamics helped play a part, with the 2005 election of a provocative new president, Ahmadinejad, only strengthening American interest in efforts to foster change in Iran.

In February 2006, Secretary of State Condoleezza Rice launched her annual budget testimony with a surprise request for an additional $75 million to "begin a new effort to support the aspirations of the Iranian people." Ultimately, Congress appropriated $66.1 million, with more than half designated for the US Broadcasting Board of Governors to expand Persian-language radio and television programming and smaller sums for exchange programs, Persian-language Internet resources, and democracy programs (US Department of State 2006). Subsequent budget requests for democracy programming were even higher.

The Obama administration continued the democracy programming, in part because of continued enthusiasm for the program on Capitol Hill. The scope of overall funding for support to civil society organizations continues to expand. However, the State Department has sought to deemphasize the singularity of the Iran program by requesting funds more broadly for Middle East democracy programming with the implicit understanding that a substantial proportion would be devoted to Iran programming. The funds are allocated by the State Department's Near East Affairs Bureau, in cooperation with the US Agency for International Development, which handles grant administrations. Altogether, the Congressional Research Service estimates that approximately $60 million was allocated for Iran democracy programming between 2004 and 2010 (Katzman 2011).

It remains effectively impossible to evaluate the quality and effectiveness of American efforts to support civil society and develop conditions conducive to democratic development within Iran due to the secrecy associated with the program. The recipients of the funding are classified as secret in all communications with congressional funders, and other efforts are taken to avoid exposure either of any Iranian participants in US government–funded programs, or of partner organizations in the United States or around the world. As a result, almost no publicly available information exists as to the specific activities and/or programs undertaken through this strand of American public diplomacy.

In 2008 Undersecretary of State for Political Affairs Nicholas Burns described the programming in general terms, indicating that the US-supported activities were designed "to support different parts of Iranian society by promoting basic human rights and religious freedoms; building civil society; improving justice, accessibility and the rule of law; and promoting a deeper understanding of our culture, values, and ideas." Only a few recipients, including Freedom House, the International Republican Institute, and the Connecticut-based Iran Human Rights Documentation Center, have publicly acknowledged receiving US government support, and then only after their proposals for additional funding were rejected by the Obama administration's State Department (Feith and Weiss 2009).

People-to-People Exchanges

A third avenue of American public diplomacy toward Iran involves NGOs' cultural activities, which was perceived by Washington as the most viable means of reviving the once-robust connection between the two countries, in part because of the official encouragement from Iranian reformists during the late 1990s. In his groundbreaking January 1998 CNN interview, President Khatami specifically endorsed "the exchange of professors, scholars, authors, journalists, and tourists" on grounds that "[n]othing should prevent dialogue and understanding between two nations, especially between their scholars and thinkers" (Khatami 1998).

For nearly a decade after Khatami's invitation, direct diplomacy between American and Iranian institutions flourished. Academic exchanges involving individual scholars and university presidents, as well as institutions such as the American Institute of Iranian Studies, resumed for the first time since the revolution. The American Bar Association, the Academy of Motion Picture Arts and Sciences, and other professional organizations sent and received delegations of their Iranian counterparts. The National Geographic Society and the Meridian International Center presented a joint art exhibit that had showings in Washington and Tehran.

Sporting events in both countries drew fans of soccer, wrestling, table tennis, weight lifting, water polo, and basketball to cheer at matches with visiting teams. The athletic exchanges have not been limited to men; the Iranian women's table tennis team was included in a 2008 US visit.

Scientific exchanges drew some of Iran's leading physicians, including its renowned and outspoken expert on AIDS, and enabled Iranian medical professionals to meet their counterparts at Harvard Medical School and the Centers for Disease Control. Many of these endeavors were privately funded, but a critical mass received both financial and logistical support from both of the governments in question, with the US Information Agency and later the State Department's Bureau of Educational and Cultural Affairs providing funding and the impetus for fulfilling the vision endorsed by Khatami in his 1998 interview.

One interesting dimension of the direct diplomacy between Iranians and Americans has been its utilization as a surrogate for formal relations. Several leading think tanks and foundations have maintained regular track two sessions that have endured for a decade or more, involving former senior officials from both sides. In October 2004 the head of the Library of Congress, James Billington, traveled to Tehran; his trip followed several years of informal contacts with an Iranian nonprofit established by Khatami to promote his dialogue-among-civilizations initiative. The sensitivity of these contacts remains intense and unpredictable, however, and many planned exchanges have collapsed due to security and political concerns. After the 2009 upheaval in Iran, the flow of exchanges in both directions declined precipitously, and the 2013 election of a more moderate president has only just begun to revive some of these contacts.

For years, there were active efforts on both sides to initiate exchanges between members of Congress and their counterparts in the Majlis. After the election of a reformist-dominated parliament in 2000, informal meetings took place between Iran's parliamentary speaker, Mehdi Karrubi, and several other MPs with a handful of US congresspeople, under the guise of a reception at the Metropolitan Museum of Art held during the United Nations General

Assembly. Shortly after Khatami's reelection in 2001, Tehran was abuzz about an exchange of letters between reformist MPs and US congresspeople, as well as reports that Khatami had established a high-level committee to study the possibilities for engaging with the United States (Iran 2001). Efforts on both sides involving political partisans from across the aisle in Washington remain active, and several MPs visited a retiring congressman in his office as recently as November 2008. All of these official meetings have entailed the necessity of plausible deniability on the part of the Iranian interlocutors.

The Bush and Obama administrations provided official US government support for the people-to-people diplomacy between Washington and Tehran as a central component of efforts to reach out to the Iranian people and expedite political change inside the country. Unfortunately, much of the hardline Iranian leadership has adopted a similar interpretation of the destabilizing purpose of direct diplomacy and has assiduously sought to impede its implementation and punish would-be participants. Since 2008, the arrest of several staffers employed by American NGOs that facilitate exchanges, as well as several high-profile participants in previous programs, has forced a cessation of nearly all officially sponsored US exchange activities with Iran, although many private organizations remain active on both sides.

Seizing Opportunities

Finally, US public diplomacy toward Iran has been deployed episodically to take advantage of particularly opportune moments. A prime case in point is the December 2003 earthquake that devastated the Iranian city of Bam, a major population center and home to a profoundly important historical site. Estimates suggested at least 30,000 Iranians were killed, another 30,000 injured, and additional tens of thousands were left homeless by the disaster. In this case, the administration communicated directly with Iran's UN representative on humanitarian assistance, and US policymakers worked around the clock over the holidays to create a facilitating climate for official and unofficial American aid to Iran. Official American contributions to the disaster relief effort involved an eighty-one-member disaster assistance team from the US Agency for International Development and a moratorium on sanctions restricting NGO donations to Iran.

Similar entrepreneurial measures have been undertaken in the aftermath of the June 2009 election protests to facilitate imports into Iran of technology that helps dissidents and opposition activists evade official monitoring and filtering. The 2010 Victims of Iranian Censorship Act drew bipartisan support in Congress for measures that imposed sanctions on companies selling technology to Tehran for the purpose of suppressing popular access to the Internet; the scope of these penalties was broadened in the July 2010 Comprehensive Iran Sanctions and Divestment Act. In part spurred by the evidence of the importance of technology during Iran's 2009 unrest, Secretary of State Hillary Clinton made cyberfreedom a signature initiative throughout her tenure. Her efforts included the establishment of the Office of Coordination of Cyber Issues, which reports to the secretary herself. The Obama administration has also issued new regulations to permit Iranians to download free American software that was previously illegal under US sanctions. Finally, reports suggest that the administration has provided support and/or licensing to antifiltering technology intended to enable Iranians to evade regime restrictions in accessing information on the Internet.

Challenges in Using Public Diplomacy to Impact Iran

In many respects, public diplomacy appears to offer a perfect mechanism for advancing American policy on Iran. The formal instruments of diplomacy are unavailable to Washington, and the spread of technology and innovative new forms of media enable the United States to reach the Iranian people in a much more direct and immediate fashion. Most significantly, copious anecdotal evidence and the relatively smaller data set of public opinion polling among Iranians suggests that interest in America, and in having access to more and more objective information about a wide range of subjects, remains higher than ever among Iranians today.

Approximately two-thirds of Iran's population is under the age of thirty, and a full 40 percent are under eighteen. The Iranian youth bulge has even more significance for Washington's approach toward Iran than even its neighbors with similarly disproportionately young populations, since Iran is the only country in which there is no official US representation. Young Iranians represent an eager audience for American cultural and public diplomacy.

The opportunity presented by Iran for innovative, meaningful public diplomacy is counterbalanced, however, by a series of challenges that, while hardly insurmountable, limit the overall efficacy of public diplomacy as an instrument for advancing American objectives vis-à-vis Iran.

Interpreting Iran from a Distance

It is difficult if not impossible to appeal to an audience without a minimal familiarity with its preferences, priorities, opinions, and even discourse. And yet the absence of any US government presence in Iran, which is compounded by the severe restrictions imposed on US officials with respect to contact or interactions with Iranians, means that Washington has had almost no substantive contact with Iranians for three decades. This absence inherently complicates the logistics and framing of American efforts to reach out to Iranians.

Without a direct, ongoing dialogue with a broad array of Iranians, it is impossible for US-based purveyors of cultural programming to achieve an effective discourse. Almost by definition, in the absence of formal diplomatic relations or significant bilateral unofficial contact, Americans are at a tremendous handicap to appreciate the vocabulary, metaphors, or humor of Iranian culture today. Moreover, some of the most ardent advocates of expanding official US public diplomacy efforts toward Iran appear to have a particularly limited background on Iran and as a result strike a surprisingly tone-deaf approach to Iran, as shown by the recommendation from two former Bush administration officials to deploy former actor and California governor Arnold Schwarzenegger in broadcast appeals to Iranian youth (Glassman and Doran 2010). Many of the critiques of VOA programming have focused on the unfamiliarity of US broadcasters with the preferences and vernacular of young Iranians.

To their credit, successive American administrations have recognized the impediments posed by the absence of US presence in and ongoing contact with Iranians. Since 2006, the State Department has considerably expanded its resources devoted to Iran, expanding language training and other opportunities for Foreign Service officers interested in Iran, and establishing specialized offices in Washington and Dubai as well as a string of "Iran watcher" positions stationed in cities with sizable Iranian populations. The Dubai office in particular has been deeply engaged in shaping US public diplomacy toward Tehran and has been described informally as serving as a kind of "shadow embassy" to mimic the broader diplomatic responsibilities of an in-country post from a short distance away from Iran. Other US government agencies, including the Defense Department, are investing heavily in the notion of strategic communications toward Tehran.

These are all laudable and worthwhile efforts; however, they cannot provide an adequate substitute for the kind of sustained, long-term interaction between peoples, with or without official involvement. Beyond the official lack of contact, the revolution and its aftermath have severely constrained all forms of contact between Americans and Iranians. Few US citizens have the opportunity to travel to Iran, with the exception of the approximately one million Americans of Iranian origin, although even for dual nationals, travel and contacts have become more risky in recent years. Over the past decade, Tehran has begun targeting Iranians with dual nationality, and several US and European citizens have endured lengthy detainments. This has deterred some Iranian Americans, especially those who work on political issues or have had previous relationships with Washington, from engaging even in personal travel to Iran. The heightened repression has also curtailed many of the exchange activities and other avenues for Iranians and Americans to engage in dialogue. And while more Iranian intellectuals and activists have left the country since June 2009, restrictive post-9/11 visa policies make it exceptionally difficult for them to come to the United States. Finally, the WikiLeaks release of thousands of official cables will inevitably have a chilling impact on the willingness of Iranians to engage in substantive conversations with US government officials, reducing the efficacy of the Dubai office and the "Iran watcher" positions elsewhere.

The bottom line is that American public diplomacy, in its diplomatic-messaging form, was until recently formulated in an environment that was almost entirely devoid of direct, ongoing dialogue with its intended audience. This stands in stark contrast to the capabilities available to the Iranian regime to counter American messages through both repression and official propaganda.

Overreliance on Public Messaging and Rhetoric
In reviewing the history of diplomatic interactions between the United States and Iran since the revolution, it is evident that official rhetoric has assumed a central dimension in shaping the overall dynamic between the two countries. The reliance on public messaging for what had always been private communications between governments began in dramatic fashion with the seizure of the US embassy in Tehran in November 1979. Suddenly, Washington was deprived of the standard mechanisms for communications and forced to rely heavily on media broadcasts for communicating authoritatively, as well as for information gathering. The Iranian students who seized the embassy actively courted the international media as a means of pressuring their own government as well as the Carter administration. For Washington, the centrality

of the media during the hostage crisis magnified their frustration over the impasse by reducing or even eliminating their ability to control the message or the means, timing, and context for delivering it (Karl 1982). This phenomenon has only intensified over the course of the ensuing three decades, as the world experienced an explosion in media and communications technology while the 24/7 news cycle has only increased attention on the major events of the day.

With the exception of a communications channel maintained by the Swiss embassy in Tehran, most official interaction between the two governments must take place not just indirectly but in an open setting. As a result, the past thirty-five years of American diplomacy have demonstrated a persistent reliance on public discourse and official remarks, formal statements read at a spokesperson's podium, congressional testimony, public appearances by senior officials, and engagement with the media. In the absence of an embassy and diplomatic representation, public diplomacy serves as a substitute for direct communication.

Unfortunately, however, public discourse and official remarks have not proven to be a particularly effective method for addressing the enduring deep differences between the two governments. The result of the primacy of public rhetoric has been that Americans and Iranians simply talk at one another, and any possibilities for nuance, interpretation, or a deeper appreciation of the viewpoint of the other side are simply absent from the exchange. Time and again, signals from one side or the other have been misread; rhetoric has inadvertently created expectations or fallen short of them; and the proliferation of official voices and, particularly in recent years, media outlets has exacerbated the dissonance and misunderstandings. Of particular note is the March 2000 Albright speech, crafted with intense effort by staffers with considerable insight into Iranian political dynamics. Yet it generated no traction or reciprocal gesture from Tehran, and has been criticized repeatedly for needlessly antagonizing Iranian decision-makers with references to Iran's "unelected leadership" and other jabs at the undemocratic elements of Iran's Islamic system of government.

The failure of the profoundly forward-leaning Albright speech leaves open an important question: Can public rhetoric by the US government achieve any progress in generating cooperation with Tehran, or even in laying the foundation for greater trust between the two governments? For example, the *Noruz* greeting broadcast by President Obama only weeks after he took office appears to have created more reason for skepticism about the utility of public rhetoric as a means of advancing diplomatic and security objectives. The broadcast received high marks from outside analysts and reportedly generated resoundingly positive responses among Iranians themselves. His efforts to avoid demonizing the Iranian regime did not generate any significant response from Tehran.

The corresponding dilemma associated with the centrality of public rhetoric is the disproportionate significance associated with any formal diplomacy between the two governments. For years, Tehran has utilized its reluctance to negotiate as a means of rectifying the inherent power imbalance. Defending the Iran-Contra arms purchases before a hostile parliament, Rafsanjani crowed in 1986 that the episode "demonstrated that the decision is with us. . . . When we desired, we talked. When we desired, we remained silent; we got everything we wanted" (Milani 1984). In similar fashion, the rarity of official dialogue means that any negotiations are cast into the cold, hard light of intense media speculation—raising the stakes, and the risks, for both sides. The collapse of a preliminary nuclear fuel exchange deal in October 2009 can be attributed at least in part to the necessity of carrying out such a politically precarious dialogue with real-time scrutiny from both capitals' fractious domestic politics. Ultimately, neither public rhetoric nor public diplomacy more broadly conceived can serve as an effective replacement for the more traditional elements of diplomacy, particularly for dealing with urgent security issues.

Historical Resentment of External Intervention

One of the particular difficulties of using public diplomacy to enhance American soft power vis-à-vis Iran is the extent to which these tools are viewed as interference or even subversion by the Iranian leadership. Suspicion of external influences has always featured prominently in the Iranian political psyche, and the instability that accompanied the revolution and the early years of the Islamic Republic's reign has exacerbated the insecurities of its leadership. As a result, a deep-seated aversion to the influence of external powers has become internalized within the postrevolutionary state and political culture. Fears of an American-orchestrated coup to reinstate the monarchy, along the lines of the 1953 Mossadeq affair, ran high during the regime's chaotic early months in power, and every subsequent shift in American policy has only appeared to confirm these suspicions.

Exacerbating these insecurities is the central role of culture for the post-revolutionary leadership's vision of their objectives. Culture has always been a critical battlefield for the postrevolutionary leadership. Discomfort about the omnipresent influence of American and Western ideas and values were a prominent part of the intellectual discourse among even secular critics of the monarchy during the 1960s and 1970s, and Ayatollah Khomeini was explicit about his interest in reshaping a truly Islamic society. One of the new regime's major initiatives involved wide-scale purges of the country's cultural and educational infrastructure.

It is important to note that for the Iranian leadership this perspective goes beyond mere posturing or counterpropaganda. Through its own rhetoric and propaganda, academic seminars, and active countermeasures and institution-building, the hardliners who dominated the Islamic Republic and its security forces have made it clear that they see information and cultural contact as weapons aligned against their own interests in preserving their hold on power. While the excesses of their approach reflect the paranoid fantasies of the hardliners, the resentment of Western cultural imperialism and mistrust of foreign governments' motives has long roots in Iranian society, which gives these fears greater reach within Iranian society.

As a result, initial efforts to expand American involvement with Iran's civil society and enhance Iranian efforts to promote democracy in their own country quickly ran into roadblocks in the form of official paranoia and repression, as well as a considerable amount of skepticism and disdain from the very activists whom the programs were designed to support. Tehran has vociferously objected to congressional appropriations for democracy programming as violations of US obligations under the Algiers Accords, the agreement that resolved the hostage crisis, to refrain from intervention in Iranian affairs. Through official rhetoric and propaganda, the regime pressed its case that US funding for democracy represented a nefarious ploy and a broader conspiracy to control the world by fomenting uprisings in adversarial states. For Iran's hardliners, US support of civil society cemented their conviction that Washington was intent on changing the Iranian government through a "soft revolution," and helped intensify their campaign of internal repression.

In the aftermath of the Bush administration's request for significantly increased funds for promoting democracy in Iran, the Iranian government harassed, detained, and explicitly prosecuted a growing number of its citizens as well as dual nationals on suspicion of involvement with American-funded programs. Although the recipients of US government funding were not publicly disclosed, this protective measure did not insulate Iranian participants or those associated with civil society in the least; instead, it enabled Iran's hardliners to level accusations indiscriminately without any possibility of exonerating evidence. Indeed, several of the first high-profile arrests made by the Iranians involved dual nationals with no known association with the American democracy program; both were targeted for their private efforts to promote dialogue and cooperation among the two countries.

Clearly, however, the Iranian regime watched the development of the programs closely, despite American efforts to avoid identifying participants or partners. Over the ensuing years, a number of staff and participants in US government–funded exchange programs found themselves under intense scrutiny from the regime, through interrogations, passport seizures to prevent travel, or even worse. Among the highest-profile targets were Arash and Kamiar Alaei, brothers who are physicians renowned for their work in treating AIDS patients in Iran. Two years after their participation in the first medical exchange organized by the State Department's International Visitors Leadership Program, they were arrested on charges of "communicating with an enemy government" and sentenced to long prison terms. Since their release (in 2010 and 2011), they live and work in the United States.

For their parts, Iranians with long experience in civil society activities initially voiced profound misgivings about the complications posed by public American support for or involvement with their work. Almost across the board, Iran's best-known activists decried the Bush administration's effort to expand funding for Iranian civil society and democracy programs, arguing that it played into the hands of a regime eager to taint their work as illegitimate and inspired by foreign conspiracies. They viewed Washington as heavy-handed and counterproductive to their efforts.

Nobel Peace laureate Shirin Ebadi inveighed against the funding, writing in a 2007 op-ed in the *New York Times* that reformists "believe that the best Washington can do for democracy in Iran is to leave them alone." She added, "no truly nationalist and democratic group will accept such funds" (Ebadi and Sahimi 2007). Ebadi blamed US funding for the increase in repression against Iranian activists and for undercutting the prospects of moderate factions within the regime. A range of other credible, established activists echoed Ebadi's sentiments.

These critiques complicated an already Herculean task of attempting to develop effective programs to strengthen Iran's indigenous civil society sector.

Very few American NGOs have any recent experience working in Iran or with Iranians, and while Washington boasts a range of institutions with strong track records of similar work elsewhere, identifying reliable partners on the ground in Iran as well as individuals capable of coordinating US-based sponsor organizations and Iran-based programming remains essential.

It should be noted that many advocates of intensifying US public diplomacy efforts see neither the critiques of Iranian activists nor the regime's repression as an argument for avoiding American involvement. To the contrary, many advocates and analysts see public diplomacy as the most effective means of either implementing regime change or, at a minimum, changing the character of the regime—which they see as inherently linked to Tehran's most objectionable policies. They also argue that the long track record of Iranian repression cannot be attributed to American policies but simply to the brutal tactics that the Islamic Republic is prepared to use to retain power.

Iran's Information Monopoly

Even though Iran's government since the revolution had attempted to control the flow of information into and within the country, during the Rafsanjani presidency the print media began to emerge as an alternative venue for veteran Iranian political figures, particularly those who had been sidelined from official positions, to advance their positions. After the 1997 election of Khatami, a more liberal permitting process helped generate an explosion in the number of daily newspapers.

For a brief, halcyon moment, newspapers served as the primary vehicles of an alternative form of political mobilization that, though not opposed to the ruling system, had an undeniably subversive quality. Reformist newspapers pushed the limits of permissible discourse, questioned ideological verities, engaged in robust, high-minded philosophical debates, and dabbled in innuendo, rumor-mongering, and thinly veiled accusations against many of the Islamic Republic's most established figures. Conservative defenders of the regime quickly caught on to the nascent power of the press and in April 2000 began a campaign of judicial terror targeting writers, editors, and publishers. The remainder of the reform period was dominated by a cat-and-mouse game between the liberal-leaning press, its tacit accessories in Khatami's executive branch, and the long arm of the judiciary.

For the same reason, politicians critical of the Iranian leadership have sought to expand their own media presence. However, in the wake of the conservatives' successful crackdown on the print media, reformist politicians began seeking more powerful media options. Mehdi Karrubi, a cleric who served as speaker of the reformist-dominated Seventh Majlis, tried to establish a Dubai-based satellite channel for the new political party he launched after the 2005 election of Mahmoud Ahmadinejad, but found little appetite among UAE officials for hosting a mechanism that the Iranian regime would view as provocative. Iran's hardline media alleges that some of Karrubi's aides, who have been forced to leave Iran since the 2009 unrest, have sought to amplify their political activities by joining forces with external satellite television stations (Javan 2010). In late 2010, the Green Movement announced via its website that it would launch a television station, initially via streaming Internet. Other opposition activists have pressed vocally for Washington and European governments to invest more resources in broadcasting and other mechanisms to expand the information flow to Iranians (Glassman and Doran 2010).

Having successfully restrained the domestic press, Tehran has focused its energies on restricting access to other media, in particular the Internet and foreign satellite coverage. Mass access to video technology arrived almost simultaneously with the new regime, and for a decade the revolutionary government outlawed the importation of VCRs (although the regime largely turned a blind eye to the private "video clubs" that enabled Iranians to rent movies through the black market). From the regime's perspective, the next great threat came from satellite television, which was the subject of informal and eventually legislated prohibition. In 1995, Interior Minister Mohammad Ali Besharati said that "the ban will immunize the people against the cultural invasion of the West" (*Washington Post* 1995). That prediction proved untrue; reliable figures are hard to come by, but even Ahmadinejad's cultural advisor Mehdi Kalkhor acknowledged that satellite dishes are "inseparable from people's lives" (Peterson 2010, 292).

Unable to forestall the proliferation of satellite dishes, the Islamic Republic has opted for other means of blocking public access to international news coverage and other forms of information. Tehran routinely jams the BBC (both English and Persian) and VOA Persian services in violation of the constitution of the International Telecommunication Union. The interference with the stations tends to intensify around public holidays and anniversaries of prior protests, suggesting that Tehran sees the capabilities of these stations to revive popular opposition to the government as episodic but significant. Most recently, Tehran jammed the BBC's Persian-language television station after a joint broadcast with its Arabic service enabled Iranian and Egyptian callers to exchange views about the January 2011 opposition protests in Egypt (Greenslade 2011). Materials published as a result of the WikiLeaks release of classified US government documents suggest that the British Foreign Office considered retaliatory action against Tehran's English-language channel, which maintains a sizable overseas staff.

Particularly in the aftermath of the unrest associated with the June 2009 presidential elections—when satellites, along with Internet-based social media and cell-phone texts provided crucial sources of information to the outside world—the foreign broadcast media have played a prominent role in Tehran's preferred narrative. In the conspiratorial view of the regime's hard-liners, satellite programming aimed at Iran is a crucial component in the "soft revolution" being orchestrated by Washington and the West as a means of removing the Islamic Republic. A book published by Iran's Ministry of Culture and Islamic Guidance accuses the management of the US government–funded Radio Farda of establishing Iranian-based "networks . . . to promote the project of creating instability in the country" and of coordinating the postelection protests (Tait 2010). The regime's paranoia extends beyond those productions that are directly funded by the US government, however; Farsi 1, a Dubai-based, Persian-language satellite station, which features only entertainment programs and is edited for a conservative Middle Eastern audience, has also been subject to cyberattacks and jamming by the Iranian government (Mac-Farquhar 2010).

Despite the important role that the BBC played during the revolution—or perhaps because of it—the postrevolutionary leadership has viewed its foray into satellite television with considerable suspicion. Upon the 2009 launch of BBC Persian's television service, Iran's intelligence minister declared that the channel would destroy Iran's security, while a hardline parliamentarian announced that the government had arrested Iranians involved in promoting a "velvet revolution" under the auspices of the BBC.

As a result, Tehran takes an almost obsessive interest in the coverage of BBC Persian as well as the VOA. Tehran hosts academic seminars and publishes books critiquing their work. Frequent assessment of their coverage in the hardline Iranian media accuse VOA and the BBC, as well as other expatriate stations, of association with vilified organizations such as the discredited expatriate opposition group Mojahideen-e Khalq, or persecuted religious minorities including the Baha'i faith, as a means of smearing their coverage and, presumably, their viewers (Javan 2009; FNA 2009). Beginning in 2007, Tehran also arrested individuals associated with foreign government broadcasting, and there have been anecdotal reports of the security services summoning Iranian relatives of individuals interviewed on BBC or VOA programs.

Ironically, Iranian authorities remain unwilling to take a relatively simple step to undercut the popularity of foreign broadcasts: opening the airwaves to domestic competitors. As Iranian advocates emanating from a variety of different political perspectives have suggested, even a modest liberalization that welcomed heavily vetted allies of the regime might divert some of the audience that currently exists for international broadcasting, and yet the regime's resistance suggests it recognizes the power of the platform itself. The situation is vaguely reminiscent of the final years of the monarchy, when the shah's prime minister acknowledged that the popularity of the BBC was a direct result of the politicization and censorship displayed by state television (Srebeny-Mohammadi and Mohammadi 1994).

As technology has progressed, Tehran has sought to maintain its capacity to repress information and deny access. Access to the Internet proliferated early and widely throughout Iran, and Persian was one of the most widely used languages in the early blogosphere, thanks to the efforts of bloggers who translated the coding instructions from English. Although the Iranian government was an early promoter of Internet usage and prominent political figures were among Iran's earliest adapters—the country's first email message was sent in 1993 by Mohammad Javad Larijani, a well-known conservative politician whose brothers currently serve as speaker of the parliament and head of the judiciary—the telecommunications sector evolved with some autonomy at the outset. Tehran saw the Internet as an ideal vehicle for a new era of export of the revolution, and state educational institutions helped popularize the technology with Iran's vast young population.

However, during the reformist era, it became clear that the Internet also posed a direct and compelling threat to the regime's aspiration to maintain a monopoly over information and authority. Dissidents began posting materials online that would never pass muster with the censors in the regime's Ministry of Culture and Islamic Guidance. Students used email and chat rooms to coordinate protests, as in the July 1999 demonstrations that the regime violently suppressed. Cell-phone cameras and blogging capabilities enabled ordinary citizens to publicize repression to both their fellow citizens and the world.

These developments provoked a series of countermeasures by the regime beginning in 2001. The Supreme Council for the Cultural Revolution began mandating filtering of all websites deemed to be antigovernment or contrary to Islam. In 2003, with the leadership's fears at perhaps the highest ebb since the revolution over international pressure on its nuclear program and the US invasion of Iraq, a much more severe crackdown was launched. Bloggers and journalists were arrested and harassed, and the government put in place much more intrusive surveillance technology to ensure that service providers were filtering "illegal" sites as mandated. Iran apparently uses pirated filters developed by a US firm and also deploys surveillance technology that enables the security forces to eavesdrop on cell-phone conversations and text messaging.

Information technology played a major role in the 2009 postelection protest movement, although some reports have suggested that the much-discussed Twitter effect was overstated. Still, it is clear that access to phone-based text messaging and social networking sites provided one of the most important tools in coordinating the massive, peaceful gatherings of Iranians in Tehran and other major cities. The government shut down all cell-phone networks in Iran during the days after the election, a move that may have been initially motivated by reports that former president Rafsanjani had funded an election-monitoring effort that relied on cell-phone input. The restrictions also hampered the ability of the world to monitor events in Iran, although many Iranians found their way around the filters to distribute videos and photos of the massive protests and security forces' abuse of peaceful demonstrators.

In the ensuing months, Tehran went on the offensive in its cyberwar with the outside world courtesy of a $500 million budget appropriated by the Majlis as well as by the purchase of a controlling share in the state telecommunications authority by a firm affiliated with the Revolutionary Guard. Iranian cyberoperatives apparently hacked Twitter in December 2009, and access to the Internet and/or specific social networking sites is routinely slowed or cut off entirely. In the aftermath of the 2009 protests, there were numerous reports of Iranians questioned or detained based on information posted to their Facebook accounts or a connection—even an indirect one—with satellite television coverage. The government's efforts to restrict access to the Internet continue, despite Rouhani's rhetorical support for greater openness; since his 2013 election, Iran's judiciary has blocked several social-networking sites including Viber, Tango, and WhatsApp.

Conclusion and Policy Recommendations

Public diplomacy has a proud and storied history within the array of US policy options for dealing with Iran. In recent years, successive American administrations have begun to invest more to gain the capabilities and garner the resources necessary to interact effectively with a country whose trajectory will shape the future of a key region of the world. Through dramatic expansions in broadcasting and other forms of communication into Iran, as well as civil society programming and measures to ensure Iranians have access to information through the Internet, US public diplomacy programs play an important role in advancing American interests vis-à-vis Iran.

However, ultimately relying on public diplomacy as a central instrument of US policy for influencing the Islamic Republic presents an obvious disconnect between objectives and capabilities. Overcoming three decades of animosity, and resolving profound differences on urgent security issues such as Iran's nuclear ambitions and its activities across the Middle East, requires a much broader mobilization of diplomatic instruments and resources. Public diplomacy can support that effort, but it cannot supplant the vital role of formal diplomatic engagement between governments for handling crises and thorny security dilemmas.

In this environment of tremendous flux within the regional balance of power and US policy options, there are several simple principles that should guide future American public diplomacy toward Tehran. First, the objectives and expectations of public diplomacy in an environment of hostility, repression, and limited information must be kept modest. Second, Washington should be equally eager to invest in formal diplomacy toward Tehran as it has demonstrated with regard to public diplomacy. Currently, besides the lack of reciprocal embassy presence, American-Iranian relations suffer as a result of the no-contact policies that exist for US officials. Such policies do little to undercut the authority of the Iranian regime and they perpetuate the crippling limitations on an understanding of Iranian political dynamics and culture that will be essential to any long-term solution to the estrangement. Finally, those who frame American public diplomacy toward Tehran should bear in mind that a three-and-a-half decade absence has somehow raised Iranian opinions of American culture and values. This suggests that the impact of public diplomacy must be assessed within a broader and ever-expanding spectrum of cultural interaction, even where direct contacts remain constrained.

References

Abrahamian, Ervand. 1993. *Khomeinism: Essays on the Islamic Republic.* London: I. B. Tauris.

AFP. 2002. "Iran's Rafsanjani Slams Bush's 'Flagrant Support' for Reformers." *Agence France-Presse.* July 15. Accessed March 18, 2015 at http://www.diplomatie.gouv.fr/en/country-files_156/iran_301/the-iranian-nuclear-question_2724/elements-of-revised-proposal-to-iran_5314.html.

Albright, Madeleine. 1998. Speech at Asia Society Dinner. New York, June 17. Accessed March 18, 2015 at http://www.usis.usemb.se/wireless/300/eur304.htm.

———. 2000. Speech before the American-Iranian Council, March 17. Accessed March 18, 2015 at http://secretary.state.gov/www/statements/2000/000317.html.

Asgard, Ramin. 2010. "US-Iran Cultural Diplomacy: A Historical Perspective." *Al Nakhlah* (Spring): 1–12.

Bahrampour, Tara. 2011. "'Daily Show'-type satire finds an audience in Iran, and a big enemy," *Washington Post,* January 1, A1.

BBC International Monitoring Service. 2010. "Iran president's advisor praises BBC Persian." Nov. 29. Accessed Aug. 8, 2012 at http://www.accessmylibrary.com/article-1G1-243114333/iran-president-advisor-praises.html

Bill, James. 1988. *The Eagle and The Lion: The Tragedy of American-Iranian Relations.* New Haven: Yale University Press.

Bowden, Mark. 2006. *Guests of the Ayatollah: The First Battle In America's War with Militant Islam.* New York: Atlantic Monthly Press.

Burns, R. Nicholas. 2007. Testimony before the Senate Foreign Relations Committee, March 29. Accessed March 18, 2015 at http://merln.ndu.edu/archivepdf/NEA/State/82374.pdf.

Bush, George H. W. 1989a. Inaugural Address of George Bush. Yale Law School Avalon Project Documents in Law, History and Diplomacy, January 20. Accessed March 18, 2015 at http://avalon.law.yale.edu/20th_century/bush.asx

———. 1989b. *New York Times.* Transcript. August 16. Accessed March 18, 2015 at http://query.nytimes.com/gst/fullpage.html?res=950DE6D61230F935A2575BC0A96F948260&sec=&spon=&pagewanted=all.

Bush, George W. 2002. "Statement on Iran." *Weekly Compilation of Presidential Documents.* Washington: 38 (28): 1184. July 15.

Clinton, William. 1999. "Remarks at the Seventh Millennial Evening at the White House." *Weekly Compilation of Presidential Documents* 35:15, 636–7. April 12. Accessed March 18, 2015 at http://frwebgate1.access.gpo.gov/cgiin/PDFgate.cgi?WAISdocID=503061450623+0+1+0&WAISaction=retrieve.

Ebadi, Shirin and Muhammad Sahimi. 2007. "The Follies of Bush's Iran Policy." *New York Times,* May 30.

Esfandiari, Golnaz. 2011. "State Department's First Persian-Language Spokesperson Could Appear In Iranian State Media." Radio Free Europe/Radio Liberty. April 9. Accessed March 18, 2015 at http://www.rferl.org/content/state_department_first_persian_language_spokesperson_could_appear_in_iranian_state_media/3552043.html

Fathi, Nazila. 2002. "US's powerful weapon in Iran: TV." *New York Times*, December 7, B7.

Feith, David and Bari Weiss. 2009. "Denying the Green Revolution". *Wall Street Journal*, October 24, A15.

FNA. 2009. "Mischief of BBC Persian TV and Voice of America on the sidelines of the Geneva conference (5+1)." *Fars News Agency*, October 1.

Friedman, Thomas L. 1991. "Baker Sketches Future Gulf Role." *New York Times*, February 7. Accessed March 18, 2015 at http://query.nytimes.com/gst/fullpage.html?res=9D0CE0D91030F934A35751C0A967958260&sec=&spon=&pagewanted=2.

Fuller, Graham. 1991. *The Center Of The Universe: The Geopolitics Of Iran*. Boulder: Westview Press.

Ganji, Akbar. 2007. "The View From Tehran: Changing Iran from Within." *Boston Review* May/June. Accessed March 18, 2015 at http://new.bostonreview.net/BR32.3/ganji.php

Gasiorowski, Mark. 1991. *US Foreign Policy and the Shah: Building a Client State in Iran*. Ithaca and London: Cornell University Press.

Glassman, James K. and Michael Doran. 2010. "The Soft Power Solution in Iran." *Wall Street Journal*, January 21, A23. Accessed March 18, 2015 at http://search.proquest.com/docview.lateralsearchlink_1:lateralsearch/pubtitle/Wall+Street+Journal/10482?t:ac=399141841/12D66026B834D94DB7A/1&t:cp=maintain/resultcitationblocks.32 (2) July/August: 44–47.

Hunter, Shireen. 1990. *Iran and the World Continuity in a Revolutionary Decade*. Bloomington: Indiana University Press.

Iran. 2001. "American Congress replies to the letter sent by the Association of Veteran Majlis Deputies." June 27. Accessed March 18, 2015 at http://www.iran-newspaper.com/1380/800406/html/politic.htm#PoliticCol2.

Izadi, Foad. 2009. "US International Broadcasting: The Case of Iran." *The Journal of Arts Management, Law and Society* 39 (2) Summer: 132–148.

Javan. 2009. "Unpublished details about a new media of the 'ring of pressure'." September 16.

———. 2010. "Karrubi, Musavi's negotiations with Afghan network." June 2.

Karl, Patricia A. 1982. "Media Diplomacy." *Proceedings of the Academy of Political Science*, 34 (4) *The Communications Evolution in Politics* 143–152.

Katzman, Kenneth. 2006. "Iran: US Concerns and Policy Response." CRS Report RL32048, June 2. Accessed March 18, 2015 at http://fpc.state.gov/documents/organization/67845.pdf.

———. 2011. "Iran: US Concerns and Policy Responses." Congressional Research Service Paper RL32048, February 14. Accessed March 18, 2015 at http://www.fas.org/sgp/crs/mideast/RL32048.pdf .

Kessler, Glen. 2002. "US changes policy on Iranian reform." *Washington Post*, A1.

Khalilzad, Zalmay. 2002. Speech to the Washington Institute for Near East Policy, August 2, 2002. Accessed March 18, 2015 at http://usinfo.state.gov/xarchives/display.html?p=washfile-english&y=2002&m=August&x=20020802184730pkurata@pd.state.gov0.9542963.

Khatami, Mohammad. 1998. *CNN*. Christiane Amanpour interview. January 7. Accessed March 18, 2015 at http://www.cnn.com/WORLD/9801/07/iran/interview.html.

Landler, Mark and Brian Stelter. 2009. "Washington Taps Into a Potent New Force in Diplomacy." *New York Times*, June 17, A12.

Limbert, John. 2009. *Negotiating with Iran*. Washington DC: US Institute of Peace Press, June 11, A19.

MacFarquhar, Neil. 2010. "Challenging Iran, With YouTube Views," *New York Times*, April 10, A9.

McFarlane, Robert C. with Zofia Smardz. 1994. *Special Trust*. New York: Cadell & Davies.

Milani, Mohsen. 1994. *The Making of Iran's Islamic Revolution: From Monarchy to Islamic Republic*. Boulder: Westview Press.

Moin, Baqer. 1999. *Khomeini Life of the Ayatollah*. New York: St. Martin's Press.

New York Times. 1998. "Spiritual Head of Iran Renews Attacks on US." January 3. Accessed March 18, 2015 at res=9E07E6D61630F930A35752C0A96E958260&scp=1&sq=khatami+cnn&st=nyt.

Peterson, Scott. 2010. *Let the Swords Encircle Me: Iran—A Journey Behind the Headlines*. New York: Simon & Schuster.

Pollack, Kenneth M. 2004. *Persian Puzzle: The Conflict Between Iran and America*. New York: Random House.

Powell, Colin L. 2003. Interview. *The Washington Post*. October 3. Accessed March 18, 2015 at http://www.state.gov/secretary/former/powell/remarks/2003/25139.htm.

Radio Free Europe/Radio Liberty. 2011. "In First Persian Media Interview, Clinton Announces U.S. 'Virtual Embassy' In Tehran." October 26. Accessed March 18, 2015 at http://www.rferl.org/content/hillary_clinton_announces_virtual_iran_embassy/24372464.html

Reich, Bernard. 1980. "The United States and Iran: An Overview." *Economic Consequences of the Revolution in Iran: A Compendium of Papers*. Submitted to the Joint Economic Committee, Congress of the United States. Washington, DC: US Government Printing Office, 18.

Rubin, Barry. 1980. *Paved with Good Intentions The American Experience and Iran*. Oxford: Oxford University Press.

Schweid, Barry. 1999. "Iran Said To Reject US Overtures." *Associated Press*, December 3.

Sciolino, Elaine. 1987. "US Asserts Iran Rebuffed Offers of Direct Talks." *New York Times*, November 2. Accessed March 18, 2015 at http://query.nytimes.com/gst/fullpage.html?res=9B0DE0D61631F931A35752C1A961948260&sec=&spon=&pagewanted=1.

———. 1988. "Shultz Says Iran Made Overtures." *New York Times*, July 6. Accessed March 18, 2015 at http://query.nytimes.com/gst/fullpage.html?res=940DEEDA103AF935A35754C0A96E948260&scp=607&sq=shultz+iran&st=nyt.

———. 1998. "Iranian Leader Dismisses All Hopes of Early Political Thaw." *New York Times*, Sept. 23.

Sheridan, Mary Beth. 2009. "Persian News Network finds new life in contested Iranian election". *Washington Post*, June 18, A8.

Sreberny-Mohammadi, Annabelle and Ali Mohammadi. 1994. *Small Media, Big Revolution: Communication, Culture, and the Iranian Revolution.* Minneapolis: University of Minnesota Press.

Tait, Robert. 2010. "Radio Farda An Agent Of The West's 'Soft War' Against Iran, Book Says." August 9. Accessed March 18, 2015 at http://www.rferl.org/content/Radio_Farda_An_Agent_Of_The_Wests_Soft_War_Against_Iran_Book_Says/2122663.html.

Takeyh, Ray. 2010. "Clerics responsible for Iran's failed attempts at democracy." *The Washington Post*, August 18. Accessed March 18, 2015 at http://www.washingtonpost.com/wp-dyn/content/article/2010/08/17/AR2010081704944.html.

US Department of State. 2006. *Summary and Highlights International Affairs Fiscal Year 2008 Budget Request.*

———. 2007a. "Update on Iran Democracy Promotion Funding." June 4. Accessed March 18, 2015 at http://www.state.gov/r/pa/prs/ps/2007/jun/85971.htm.

———. 2007b. "Sports Initiatives with Iran." Accessed March 18, 2015 at http://exchanges.state.gov/sports/index/images/iran2.pdf.

———. 2008. "Dispelling Myths and Making New Friends: US—Iranian Table Tennis Friendship Tour." Accessed March 18, 2015 at http://exchanges.state.gov/sports/visitor/072408.html.

US Department of State and Broadcasting Board of Governors. 2009. *Report of Inspection: Voice of America's Persian News Network*, Report Number ISP-IB-09-27, March.

Washington Post. 1995. "Iran to Dismantle Privately Owned Satellite Dishes." April 18.

7   SYRIA

Public Diplomacy in Syria: Overcoming Obstacles

William Rugh

I N THE SYRIA CASE, THIS BOOK'S FRAMING QUESTIONS can be synthesized into two questions that apply here: First, since Syria and the United States are in an adversarial relationship, what can American public diplomacy do, if anything, to help shape the context in which the Syrian government makes decisions of importance to US interests? And second, what difference does the presence of an embassy and ambassador make and what options are available to US public diplomacy given the ongoing civil war and the Syrian government's restrictions on US public diplomacy operations?

In this chapter, the term "public diplomacy" refers to the efforts by officials of the United States government—mainly, foreign service officers from the former US Information Agency (USIA) now in the public diplomacy career track in the Department of State, plus various broadcasting services—to support American national interests by communicating directly with the Syrian public through a variety of instruments. The instruments at normal diplomatic posts include print publications, radio and television broadcasting, social networking media, press conferences and media appearances, public statements (rhetoric), libraries and cultural centers, cultural performances, English teaching, and student counseling, as well as educational and professional exchanges and personal contacts.[1]

Before the 2011 uprising that by 2012 turned into full-blown civil war, leading to the withdrawal of the US embassy in Damascus, the American-Syrian adversarial relationship was symbolized by the fact that there was no US ambassador in Syria for most of the time since 2005. Drawing partly on interviews with American officials, this chapter argues that although the problems in carrying out US public diplomacy were exacerbated by the absence of an American ambassador, the problems were basically the result of a number of other factors on both sides of the relationship. (The United States blamed Syria for the disputes, but Syria regarded actions by the United States including Congress as unfairly hostile.)

Bilateral Diplomatic Relations

Bilateral relations between Syria and the United States have been characterized by decades of tension and disagreement with periodic confrontations over a number of policy issues (Enderlin 2002; Kissinger 1979, 1982; Lesch 2005; Ma'oz 1995; Norton 2007; Quandt 1977, 1988; Seale 1986, 1988; Sultan 1995; Tillman 1982; Woodward 1991). Since 1946 when the United States first established diplomatic relations, there have been seven years of broken relations (1967–1974) because of Syrian objections to US support for Israel, and another eighteen years with no US ambassador to Syria for various reasons.

Throughout the Cold War and especially after 1963 when the Baath Party came to power in Syria, bilateral relations were strained because of Syria's close military and political relationship with the Soviet Union. Since the end of the Cold War, several political problems remain between the two countries. The George W. Bush administration withdrew the American ambassador in 2005 over issues relating to Lebanon, and although the Obama administration filled the post in 2011, serious bilateral tensions remained, and they soon worsened.

There have been periods of thaw but they have not been sustained (Tabler 2009c). In 1990 Syria joined the United States in a coalition that expelled Iraq from Kuwait, and in 1991 Syria joined a US-brokered Middle East peace conference with Israel. However, during the Clinton administration Syria stayed out of the peace process, and President George W. Bush imposed new economic sanctions on Syria (OIG 2010; Tabler 2010a; US Embassy Damascus 2010).

There are seven major enduring policy issues of importance to the United States on which Washington has been very critical of Damascus. A senior US official described US concerns about Syria in 2010 as follows: "[O]ur agenda in the Middle East includes some of the most challenging and urgent policy issues facing the United States today: countering terrorism, stabilizing Iraq, preventing Iran from acquiring a nuclear weapon, facilitating Middle East peace, stopping the proliferation of weapons of mass destruction, and expanding respect for human rights and democracy. The United States remains a strong supporter of Lebanese sovereignty and independence. Syria figures prominently in each of these issues—often as part of the problem, and potentially as part of the solution" (Feltman 2010). Each issue is complex and has a history. Below is a summary of the seven issues:

1. The Israeli-Arab conflict: This is the most important and longest-lasting US-Syrian dispute. The United States has for decades been Israel's primary international patron, but since the establishment of the Israeli state, Syria has been a leader among the Arab states in supporting Palestinians and fighting wars and encouraging guerrilla actions against Israelis. Syria has consistently accused the United States of unfairly taking Israel's side and enabling Israeli occupation with massive assistance. President Bashar Al-Assad demands that Israel withdraw from occupation of the Golan Heights, but says he is ready for peace (Al-Assad 2010). An Obama administration official summarized the US view this way: "While we are working to develop the regional conditions conducive for re-launching Middle East peace talks, Syria threatens to play its traditional role as a spoiler" (Ford 2010).

2. Iran: The United States has been in confrontation with the Iranian government since 1979, when Grand Ayatollah Ruhollah Khomeini overthrew the shah and the US embassy was occupied. Syria has established a close strategic relationship with Iran, which supported Syria against the uprising, and the United States has accused Syria of helping to "promote Iran's destabilizing policies" in the Middle East (Feltman 2010; Ford 2010).

3. Lebanon: The United States regards Syrian influence in Lebanon as an unacceptable intrusion in a friendly sovereign nation, while Damascus sees Lebanon as a vital neighbor. After the 2005 assassination of former Lebanese Prime Minister Rafiq Hariri Syria withdrew its troops from Lebanon, but its influence remained.

4. Terrorism: Syria supports Hamas, Hezbollah, and the Palestinian Islamic Jihad. The US government officially designates all three as terrorist organizations and consequently has put Syria on the list of state sponsors of terrorism. One US official warned that without significant changes in its policy, Syria will remain on the US terrorism list "for the foreseeable future"

(Feltman 2010; Ford 2010). President Assad responds that Syria supports Hamas because it is a political organization for Palestinians whose land is occupied, and he supports the Palestinian view that they have a right to their own state and regain the land they lost in 1967 (Al-Assad 2010).

5. Iraq: Washington regards Syria as unhelpful in efforts to establish security and stability in Iraq, a charge Damascus has denied (Al-Assad 2010; Ford 2010).

6. Weapons of mass destruction: Washington accuses Syria of violating the Non-Proliferation of Nuclear Weapons Treaty that it signed, and of carrying out development of chemical weapons and a domestic missile production program (Feltman 2010).

7. Human rights: The United States has criticized Syria on human rights grounds, but Syria rejects criticism of its internal affairs (Feltman 2010; Ford 2010).

President Obama's Engagement Effort

During his election campaign and soon after he took office, President Barack Obama called for engagement with Syria. In February 2009 for example, he said, "the United States will pursue principled and sustained engagement with all of the nations in the region, and that will include . . . Syria" (Obama 2009). He began by sending official envoys to Damascus. In March 2009 Acting Assistant Secretary of State Jeffrey Feltman and National Security Council (NSC) Senior Director of Near Eastern Affairs Dan Shapiro visited Syria and met with Syrian Foreign Minister Walid Muallim. They were the first senior American officials to visit Damascus since the US ambassador was withdrawn in 2005,[2] and they returned again in May. President Obama's Special Middle East Envoy, Senator George Mitchell, went to Syria in June and met with President Assad, the first senior administration official to do so since 2005 ("Mitchell Cites Syria's Role" 2009). Shortly thereafter, the United States informed Syria that Obama would appoint a new ambassador to Damascus, and when Senator Mitchell returned to Syria in July, Secretary of State Hillary Clinton told the press that the Obama administration intended to pursue engagement with Syria (Baghdadi 2009; BBC 2009).

In February 2010, President Obama announced the appointment of Robert S. Ford as ambassador to Syria. Ford, an Arabic-speaking career foreign service officer with experience in the region, was approved by the Senate Foreign Relations Committee, but eight Republican senators led by Tom Coburn

(R-OK) put a hold on his confirmation before the whole Senate could vote on it.[3] They explained that the Syrian government conducts a hostile foreign policy and has a "horrific and worsening" human rights record. They said the United States should not lend "even a modicum of international legitimacy to a regime like Syria's" (US Senate 2010).

At his Senate confirmation hearing, Ford made the case for engagement in detail. He said:

> a sustained and principled dialogue with the Syrian government at the ambassadorial level does not promise fast results, but it is in our national interest and will move us closer to achieving our goals . . . so far . . . , we have only . . . spoken directly to the top Syrian leadership when high-level American delegations have visited Damascus . . . at a time when the Middle East confronts increasing regional tensions, we must be talking every day and every week with top-level officials who have influence and decision-making authority. They need to hear directly from us, not from the media or third-party intermediaries, what are our bottom lines and the potential costs to them—and to the region—of their miscalculations. (Ford 2010)

A senior official added, "[T]he United States and Syria have been substantially at odds over a broad range of issues for some six decades. The decision of our President to draw on a full inventory of diplomatic tools at his disposal does not anticipate instant success but the initiation of a sustained effort to succeed where we have failed to succeed in the past" (Feltman 2010).

On December 29, 2010, after the Senate had gone into holiday recess, President Obama used his authority to announce a "recess appointment" to send Ambassador Ford to Syria. He had decided to wait no longer to engage the Syrian government, but to go around the Republican bloc on Ford's assignment. Ford arrived in Damascus on January 15, 2011, filling a post that had been vacant for six years since the departure of Ambassador Margaret Scoby in February 2005.[4] (American congressional hostility to Syria, however, remained a burden on US diplomacy and public diplomacy that the US government had little control over.)

In addition, by executive order Obama eased some of the economic sanctions that the Bush administration had imposed on Syria. In March 2009, for example, some sanctions on the transfer of information technology and civil aviation parts were lifted (UPI 2009). Most of the Syria sanctions, however, remained in force because they were based in US law or because there were strong voices in Congress that supported sanctions (*BBC* 2009; Otterman 2009).

Effect of the Popular Uprising

The Syrian popular uprising against the Assad government that began in 2011 led to a dramatically heightened level of confrontation between Washington and Damascus, and effectively stalled Obama's engagement policy.

As street protests erupted in other Arab countries, Syrian citizens began to show their disapproval of the Assad regime, first as a small demonstration in the town of Dera'a on January 26, 2011, and then as mass protests in other cities. Most protesters were nonviolent but they were met with brutal repression by Syrian security forces using tanks, snipers, and other forceful means. Army defectors were executed and whole towns were besieged. By April 2014 estimates of those killed in the fighting exceeded 150,000 ("War Deaths Top 150,000" 2014).

The United States, along with the Arab League, the Gulf Cooperation Council, the Islamic Conference, Turkey, and even Iran criticized the Assad regime. American official condemnation of the Syrian government gradually increased until President Obama on August 18 took the major step of calling for Assad to resign, saying, "For the sake of the Syrian people, the time has come for President Assad to step aside" and at the same time imposed additional punitive economic sanctions on Syria (Phillips 2011). Assad rejected the demands from the United States and others, claiming that foreign agents and thugs were responsible for the violence.

Although President Obama had sent Ambassador Ford to Syria in January 2011, the US embassy and Ambassador Ford himself were increasingly threatened as the uprising escalated in the spring and summer of 2011. For example, in July 2011, government supporters attacked the US embassy, climbed onto the roof, and raised the Syrian flag there. The United States condemned the government for facilitating the attack. White House spokesman Jay Carney denounced "an ongoing campaign to intimidate and threaten diplomats attempting to bear witness to the brutality of the Assad regime" (Jackson 2011). Ambassador Ford made public appearances in support of the demonstrators, but by October 2011 this had become dangerous. The Obama administration recalled him to Washington, because there had been "credible threats to his safety," and clearly blamed the Syrian government for being behind a campaign of intimidation against Ford (Blanford 2011; Shadid 2011).

Meanwhile on October 3, 2011, the Senate formally confirmed Ford as ambassador to Syria, in effect expressing approval of his aggressive public diplomacy efforts while in Syria ("SYRIA: U.S. Senate Approves Robert Ford" 2011), but this was too late to be helpful. Then in February 2012 the US closed its embassy, citing "serious concerns" that it was "not protected from armed attack" (Shadid 2012).

The US-Syrian adversarial relationship had reached a new level, creating additional challenges to US diplomacy and public diplomacy on top of the ones that existed before the uprising began.

Syrian Restrictions on US Public Diplomacy Operations

American officials believe that public diplomacy is an essential tool in Syria, despite all the problems, although its impact is very difficult to measure. According to Foreign Service officer and public diplomacy specialist Charles Hunter, who was Deputy Chief of Mission (DCM) and at times chargé d'affaires in Damascus, American officials were painfully aware of significant Syrian obstacles to carrying it out effectively, both direct and indirect, even when the embassy remained open (Hunter, author interview 2010).

Restrictions on Educational Programs

The Syrian authorities have for decades restricted US public diplomacy operations, and these restrictions increased during the last years of the Bush administration. In 2007, the Syrian minister of higher education banned Americans from Damascus University by sending a confidential instruction to all university deans and faculty (but not to the embassy) not to have any contact with foreign embassies and especially with the American embassy. This had serious negative repercussions on US programs. The embassy had in the past arranged Fulbright programs through Damascus University but that had to stop. Consequently, in order to recruit Syrian students to the Fulbright program, the embassy had to place ads in Syrian newspapers announcing the program, quietly interview candidates, and then ask successful candidates to obtain their own permissions to go. The minister's order also meant that embassy personnel could no longer have access to the "American Corner" facility (see below) that they had set up inside the university. The minister did not directly inform the embassy, but American officials obtained a copy of his letter. Pamela Mills, cultural affairs officer at the US embassy from 2007–2009, has noted that the minister himself has an American education—a PhD from the University of Texas—so it seemed clear to embassy officials that he was acting on instructions from higher authorities (Mills, author interview 2010).

Also, because of these governmental restrictions, Syrians noticed that if they accepted an American grant to travel to the United States, when they returned to Syria they were often unable to get a job; word of this spread and dissuaded some Syrians from accepting an American grant. In the past, an American education or professional visit to the United States was usually career-enhancing (Mills, author interview 2010).

For years, American exchange students funded by the embassy studied at Damascus University, which sponsored their visas. The government's 2007 ban on contact with the university also adversely affected American study-abroad students. Some exchange students came to Syria anyway on tourist visas, because they regarded living in Syria as a worthwhile educational experience. But because tourist visas are only issued for a limited period, the American students had to apply frequently for new visas. Since the extension process usually took a long time and was often arbitrary, many of them left the country temporarily (usually to go to neighboring Jordan) to get new visas outside. But some who did that were denied reentry, so the public diplomacy staff advised the others to apply for renewal in Damascus (Mills, author interview 2010).

In 2003, the State Department started the Youth Exchange and Study (YES) Program to bring foreign teenagers to the United States for a year of high school study. It was implemented in Syria, administered for the embassy by Amideast (see below), and functioned for two years, from 2003 to 2005, with the cooperation of the Syrian Ministry of Education that made the nominations. The public diplomacy section organized meetings and social sessions for the YES students when they returned to Syria, and these became effective contact groups for the Americans because the returnees were enthusiastic about their American experience and active supporters of improved US-Syrian relations. They even organized campaigns to write letters to officials urging a relaxation in Syrian hostility toward America. But in 2005 the ministry stopped cooperating with the YES program, and it was clear that the government did not want it to continue, so it ceased. In the judgment of the public diplomacy staff, the returnees were attracting too much negative attention and undermining the government's confrontational policy toward the United States (Mills, author interview 2010).

The Syrian government has offered grants for study abroad to its own students. In the past, some of these grants were approved for study in the United States, but in recent years, the practice has been for the government to send students only to Western Europe and not to America (Mills, author interview 2010).

Restrictions on Official Contacts

Syria has for years regularly restricted contacts by American officials, which significantly hampered public diplomacy operations. Syrian authorities do not permit US officials to meet with officials of the military or of the Baath Party. These restrictions have existed for years, and often non-American diplomats—for example from the Soviet Union during the Cold War—have not been so restricted (Mills, author interview 2010). Also, the Ministry of Culture has issued instructions to all embassies not to have contact with any Syrians under the age of eighteen (OIG 2010; Mills, author interview 2010). During the period when there was no US ambassador in Syria, 2005–2011, Charles Hunter, the chargé d'affaires who headed the mission, was never able to meet with the Syrian president, and no senior officials visited from Washington so the United States never had an opportunity to interact with him directly (Hunter, author interview 2010).

Moreover, all contact with Syrian officials required official approval by the Ministry of Foreign Affairs (MFA), and application for such meetings had to be made through diplomatic note. Sometimes the request was denied and sometimes it was ignored. Syrian rules can be arbitrary and capricious; for example, the Syrian MFA canceled a Fulbright briefing session at the American school the day it was to be held, although the Ministry of Education had approved it (Mills, author interview 2010).

Restrictions on Media

Syria has also hampered US public diplomacy efforts based offshore by discouraging American government–sponsored broadcasting aimed at the Syrian public. The primary American public diplomacy broadcast instruments intended for Syrian audiences are Radio Sawa and Alhurra television, both in Arabic, and both operated by the Broadcasting Board of Governors (BBG). The Voice of America (VOA) English Service is barely audible in Syria, and the VOA Arabic Service that existed for half a century was canceled by the BBG in 2002. Although several Arab governments have concluded agreements with the BBG to relay Radio Sawa locally, Syria refused to do so. Some Syrian radio listeners can hear Radio Sawa broadcasts intended for neighboring Arab countries, and they can pick it up on the Internet. As for Alhurra, theoretically the nearly one million satellite TV viewers in Syria can see it, or people can watch it on the Internet, but the Syrian authorities have not allowed it to advertise in Syria (OIG 2010). The Alhurra program is not popular in the Arab world, and although viewer surveys are unavailable because Syria does not permit that kind of polling, Alhurra is unlikely to have a large audience. As for social media that are used by public affairs officers (PAOs) in many other countries, in Syria the authorities block most of them, although some Syrians have found ways to work around the censors and gain access (Mills, author interview 2010).

PAOs at US embassies abroad normally cultivate contacts with key media editors and reporters, but the PAO in Syria has routinely been denied that access. Tracy Roberts, the PAO who was at the Damascus embassy from 2007 to 2010 and speaks fluent Arabic, was never able to meet with any editor of any government-owned media outlet. Clearly the media have been under instructions to deny such access. She did however meet privately with bloggers and with journalists from small private media outlets (Mills and Roberts, author interviews 2010).

All Syrian media are tightly controlled by the regime (OIG 2010). Syrian media have been described as "mobilization" media because the regime actively uses them to mobilize support for its policies, so their content conveys policy messages (Rugh 2004a). After he came to power in 2004, Bashar al-Assad allowed a few private publications to appear, but they do not publish any news or views that contradict or challenge the official government line. News selection and editorials in all media consistently portray US policy in a negative light. Syrian media often purposely ignore advertisements or news about programs organized by US public diplomacy staff in Syria (OIG 2010; Mills, author interview 2010).

Restrictions on American Institutions

The Syrian authorities have restricted American institutions located in Syria, all of which have served US public diplomacy in various ways. In 2006 the Syrian authorities closed the American nongovernmental organization (NGO) Amideast, and in November 2008 they ordered the closure of the American Cultural Center (ACC), the American Language Center (ALC), and the Damascus Community School (DCS) (OIG 2010; Mills, author interview 2010).

Amideast: In November 2006, the Syrian authorities ordered the closure of the American NGO Amideast, which for fifty years had provided Syrians with educational services such as student counseling, testing, and college placement. These services have been financed in part by the State Department as an essential public diplomacy activity.

Within a month of the closure, Ambassador Theodore Kattouf, the president of Amideast, went to Syria to reopen the office. Kattouf, an Arab American, was the US ambassador to Syria from 2001 to 2003 and had excellent relations with President Assad and the foreign minister. On that 2006 visit, he met with the minister of social affairs and the chief of Syrian intelligence and made the case to them to allow Amideast to reopen. He failed, but he made another visit to Syria in early 2007 to try again. He met with Foreign Minister Walid Muallim and with the minister of information, whose son had studied English in the Amideast-run American Language Center. Kattouf made the case to both ministers to allow Amideast to reopen; but again he failed, and Amideast remained closed. His strategy in February 2011 was to ask the new American ambassador to make the case with the Syrians (Kattouf, author interview 2010), but because of the uprising that was impossible.

Amideast conducted some student advising and testing sessions temporarily in the DCS although DCS was also formally closed (see below) (OIG 2010). On one occasion, the embassy offered to conduct interviews with Fulbright candidates at DCS, and cleared the proposal with the Education Ministry, but chargé d'affaires Charles Hunter recalls that the Foreign Ministry ordered the interviews canceled at the last minute (Hunter, author interview 2010). This illustrates the ambivalence of the Syrian government toward such US activities and the difficulty of carrying out a consistent program. Presumably the Syrian authorities tolerated this activity at DCS occasionally because influential Syrian families lobbied to permit such activities, but the authorities did not always agree (Mills, author interview 2010).

The American Cultural Center: The ACC, operated by the US Embassy, had for several decades been the major platform for US public diplomacy programming in Syria. Located in a building outside the embassy compound with minimal security, Syrian students and professionals could find American books and periodicals at the ACC that were unavailable elsewhere. It was also a place where they could meet less obtrusively with American officials. The ACC's weekly showing of American films attracted capacity audiences. Because of the Syrian ban on contact with any Syrian under eighteen years of age, the staff was careful to turn young people away, although IDs were not required. The Syrian government ordered the ACC closed in November 2008, and even the sign on the door had to be taken down (OIG 2010; Mills, author interview 2010).

The American Language Center: The ALC, located in a building next to the embassy, opened in Damascus in 1986. In its early years it was managed directly by the US embassy's public diplomacy section, and more recently it has been managed by Amideast in cooperation with the embassy. Syrians considered it by far the best place in the country to learn English, and each quarter it had enrollments of more than 2,000 students and professionals, turning away hundreds more for lack of space. Syria closed it in November 2008. It was able to reopen four months later, in March 2009, following representations by US officials, but it had to close again in December 2011 (see below) (OIG 2010; US Embassy Damascus 2012).

The Damascus Community School: The DCS was founded in 1957 as a nonprofit independent school offering pre-K–12. Since its beginning, DCS has been the school of choice for the children of all Americans in Syria, as well as most foreign diplomats and many Syrians. Governed by an independent board of directors, it has however always had the close support of the US embassy, and the deputy chief of mission is traditionally chair of the board. The Syrian authorities closed it in 2008, but in the fall of 2010 they agreed to allow it to reopen (Hunter, author interview 2010).

All four of these American institutions—the cultural center, language center, Amideast, and DCS—had supported the goals of US public diplomacy, and their closure hurt the public diplomacy effort. Syrian motivations for the closure of these four institutions are complex. In the case of Amideast, embassy officials suspect that the Syrian action resulted from the deteriorating condition of bilateral relations in 2006. Those in the Syrian regime who wanted to punish the Bush administration for its policies probably decided to close Amideast to show their displeasure with American policy, and in selecting a private institution that the US government supported for public diplomacy purposes, they probably felt they could make this symbolic gesture at little cost to Syria. According to the author's interview with a knowledgeable source, such Syrian official gestures are usually carefully calibrated (Anonymous B, Knowledgeable official, author interview B).

As for the other closures, the ostensible reason was a Syrian response to an incident on the Syrian-Iraqi border in which US forces were accused by Syria of entering sovereign Syrian territory near the town of Sukkariya and killing Syrian personnel (Tabler 2009a). The American action at the border was in the context of American efforts to combat terrorists entering Iraq from Syria. In the embassy's judgment, the Syrians took the step of closing three American institutions as the best way to show their displeasure over the border incident because they could take this step easily without going further and restricting the embassy itself. In an interview with the author, Charles Hunter, the chargé d'affaires at the time, pointed out that the Syrians wanted to "teach the Americans a lesson" (Hunter, author interview 2010).

There were probably other motives involved as well. Syrians in key positions in the regime who are fundamentally hostile to the United States probably resented the presence of these American institutions on Syrian soil. The embassy believes that officials in the Ministry of Education and Culture and the Baath Party saw the American cultural institutions as a threat. Also, in the case of the ALC, Syrian businesspeople who owned private language centers probably supported the ALC's closure to get rid of an effective competitor. Likewise, according to two officials posted at the embassy in Damascus, owners of private K–12 schools were happy for business reasons to see the DCS closed and probably supported the decision (Mills, author interview 2010; Roberts, author interview 2010). Finally, the legal status of the institutions allowed the government to close them because they were not officially and formally licensed, although they had operated without any problems in the past. In fact, when efforts were made in the past to obtain a license for the Amideast office, Syrian officials refused to issue one, simply saying a license was unnecessary because it was seen to be part of the embassy. This was not so, but in the event, this "assurance" did not protect it as relations deteriorated during the Bush administration.

Syria's Indirect Obstacles to American Public Diplomacy

In addition to the restrictions Syria has imposed specifically on US embassy operations, there have been obstacles to the conduct of American public diplomacy more generally arising from the Syrian government's foreign and domestic policies.

The Syrian government over the years has created a climate of hostility against American policy that all Syrians are very aware of and that indirectly affects US public diplomacy operations. The hostile climate is facilitated by Syria's strictly authoritarian political system, tightly controlled from the top by President Hafiz al-Assad and later by his son Bashar when he succeeded his father as president in 2000. The atmosphere of fear that prevails affects public diplomacy. Syrians are extremely careful about what they say on political issues, and who they say it to, because they are being watched by the omnipresent secret police, the *Mukhabaraat*.

How the Embassy Has Dealt with Obstacles to Public Diplomacy Operations

The US government has regarded public diplomacy as one of its most essential means of advancing American national interests in Syria, given the severe restrictions on both traditional diplomatic relations and economic and commercial ties (Hunter, author interview 2010). Although the impact is difficult to measure, diplomats know that efforts to communicate often have long-term effects. Embassy personnel therefore creatively found ways to deal with those obstacles over the years, and also in crisis situations like that presented by the 2011 uprising and subsequent civil war.

Creative Public Diplomacy during Past Decades
Over the years, the PAO and the public diplomacy staff at the embassy have developed ways to deal with the existing obstacles to public diplomacy operations. The embassy regards the following to be the five most important public diplomacy tools in this situation: cultural programming, educational exchanges, English teaching through the ALC, American Corners, and personal contact. Personal contact is the most important: the embassy's Mission Strategic Plan lists people-to-people contact as a high-priority goal, and since there are so few private Americans in Syria, this means essentially contact by embassy personnel (US Embassy Damascus 2012).

Cultural programming: Because any public effort by embassy personnel to conduct normal information outreach and policy advocacy has been impossible, the public diplomacy strategy has focused on cultural and educational programming, which is nonpolitical. The public diplomacy staff partnered with Syrian NGOs since they were easier to work with than government agencies. They also focused on projects the Syrians are interested in rather than what Washington wanted to promote. For example, during a six-month period in 2010 the embassy organized six major cultural and educational programs for Syria, including American music and film. The US embassy did not insist on labeling the programs as being sponsored by the embassy because the staff was more interested in successfully carrying out programs than in taking credit for them. Following are some examples of successful programs that were concluded with the support of Syrian institutions and individuals:

- Four American musicians gave a hip-hop and break-dancing show in a Syrian theater and then a workshop for local artists.

- Pianist Malek Jandali, a Syrian American, performed before a packed crowd at the St. Elian's Cultural Festival in the city of Homs where he was born. This was the first time the embassy was able to participate in that festival. In addition to his concert, Jandali gave a workshop and master classes.

- Three documentary filmmakers, one of whom was the Egyptian American Jihane Noujaim, spent ten days in Syria; they screened their films six times in Damascus including at a film festival and in two provincial cities, and each of them conducted master classes for Syrians.

- The Chris Byers Jazz Quartet played classics from the 1940s and 1950s as well as jazz versions of traditional Arab music in five concerts in Damascus and three provincial cities; they also gave workshops for Syrian musicians.

- A Muslim American country western singer gave a concert in Damascus.

- Professor Jill Williams of Kennesaw State University spent two weeks in Syria as a Fulbright Specialist speaking to teachers and education administrators about teaching children with disabilities. The US embassy arranged the program in cooperation with the Syrian NGO Amaal, an organization that is part of the Syrian First Lady's Trust for Development. This was the first time in five years that the embassy had worked directly with the Education Ministry.

- Mrs. Williams's husband, a journalist, conducted a specialized training program for Syrian journalists. The project was so successful that President Assad instructed Syrian officials to read the report's recommendations. This project worked because it responded to the needs of Syrians and because it was approved by the Syrian First Lady.

Opportunities for cultural programming opened up so well that the embassy had used all of its 2010 budget allotted for such programming by May 2010 and requested additional funds (US Embassy Damascus 2010a and 2010b).

Educational exchanges: As Syrian restrictions on local programming increased during the Bush era, the embassy substantially expanded its educational exchanges. In the years 2008–2010, when several American institutions were closed, the embassy sent more Syrians to America on the International Visitor Leadership (IVLP) program than in the previous several years. In 2009 the embassy sent thirty Syrians to the United States on the IVLP, involved twenty-six American and Syrian students and scholars in the Fulbright program and two others in the Humphrey Scholarship program, and engaged one Syrian foreign-language teaching assistant. For 2010, Washington responded positively to the embassy's request for IVLP slots for Syria, doubling the number from thirty-two to sixty-four. In addition, the embassy brought seven Americans to Syria to study Arabic under the critical language program (OIG 2010). The embassy was however careful not to try to generate media coverage for the individuals participating in the exchange program for fear it would put them in jeopardy with the authorities, and the candidates themselves have expressed concerns about receiving publicity (OIG 2010).

English teaching: The embassy has over the years made excellent use of the ALC. It is a very effective platform for public diplomacy operations under current circumstances because English-language lessons are popular with Syrians, and teaching English is a way to convey a great deal about American culture and society while seeming to be nonpolitical. It also allows contact between Americans and Syrians in a benign environment. The high enrollment of the ALC exceeds the goals of the Mission Strategic Plan (Mills, author interview 2010). The embassy hopes if one day it is able to reopen the ACC, it might consolidate its functions with the ALC because the ALC is so effective as a public diplomacy instrument and attracts less suspicion from the authorities (Hunter, author interview 2010).

American Corners: In some countries, American public diplomacy officials have tried a new innovation that puts American materials in a local institution without American staff, but they have not always been successful. In Syria, the embassy tried the technique and found it to be useful. American Corners have been established in the provincial cities of Dara'a (in a private English-language institute "Infinity") and Suwaida, near the Jordanian border. The embassy also studied the possibility of establishing an American Corner in a private university or English-language school in Aleppo, the northern city of four million people, and the State Department inspectors recommended that they do so (OIG 2010).

Personal contacts: Embassy personnel have quietly sought to establish and maintain active personal relations with any influential Syrians willing to talk to them. Because of Syrian restrictions on institutional contacts, embassy personnel consciously developed personal relations with key individuals in institutions they want to work with, since these individuals are often able to make arrangements for programs that would be impossible to achieve through the normal bureaucratic process.

Before the crisis began in 2011, the PAO and the rest of the public diplomacy staff had some success engaging with private-sector Syrians and a few Syrians employed in government agencies by arranging private meetings in Syrian homes, American homes, or restaurants. They even met with individual Syrians in the (closed) offices of the ACC, since the ACC is located in a building occupied by other embassy offices and the ACC meetings tend to go unnoticed by the authorities. They met with members of Syrian NGOs, who are less fearful of US contacts than government employees. In fact, members of the public diplomacy section of the embassy had considerably more success than other embassy officials because they were identified as cultural and information staff, which to most Syrians seems benign compared to political officers, who are often avoided. Moreover, since they work with student and professional exchanges, such personnel more easily develop contacts that can be deepened. For example, when Pamela Mills was the PAO, she arranged to meet regularly at her home with returnees from the YES exchange program, which became a useful contact group (Mills, author interview 2010).

Following the 2007 instruction from the minister of education banning university contact with Americans, the public diplomacy staff was no longer able to work directly with universities as institutions, so instead they worked quietly with individual university faculty members who were willing to try to arrange contacts and programs. In preparation for a program, public diplomacy officials routinely sent diplomatic notes to the government requesting permission, and if they did not receive a specific negative reply, they went ahead through private contacts, who, if asked, explained that the embassy had sent a note and was not denied permission. If the embassy was explicitly told not to do the program, of course it had to comply (Mills, author interview 2010).

Although US officials have not been able to have sustained discussions of American policy with senior Syrian officials, they have had some discussions of US policy with Syrians in the private sector provided these were conducted privately and discreetly. In this way, American positions were explained and Syrian arguments countered at least with some members of the public.

Coping with New Problems Caused by the Uprising

The uprising and the government's crackdown on the opposition further restricted US public diplomacy efforts on the ground in Syria in several ways. First, the ACC remained closed. Second, because of the worsening security situation, Washington ordered the evacuation of nonessential embassy personnel, and PAO Angela Williams was sent home. The ambassador designated his Deputy Chief of Mission (DCM), Haynes Mahoney, who happened to be a public diplomacy cone officer, as Acting PAO, but Mahoney had his hands full as DCM and could not devote much time to public diplomacy responsibilities. Even the public diplomacy section's online Information Resource Center service that the embassy had provided to the Syrian public was suspended for lack of staffing. Moreover, Syrian restrictions on the movement of diplomats, and increased surveillance of their movements, severely hampered regular public diplomacy work (Mills, author interview 2010). The only regular public diplomacy function that was able to continue, at least for a time, was the ALC, whose fifty teachers continued to offer classes and testing services throughout 2011. Since 70 percent of the teaching staff were American, the ALC remained a channel of American-Syrian personal engagement (Hunter, author interview 2010) and therefore a public diplomacy asset. However, in December 2011, because of the continued unrest that posed a threat to Americans and American institutions, the embassy asked Amideast to close the ALC, which was done. Amideast reported that most staff were terminated and the non-Syrian teachers were evacuated.

As restrictions on US public diplomacy efforts on the ground in Syria escalated, the United States turned increasingly to the use of social networking media to reach the Syrian public and government. Fortuitously, the availability of new electronic communication tools helped the US deal with increased restrictions on public diplomacy. Public diplomacy officials made extensive use of the US embassy's Facebook page and website, which reached many Syrian citizens eager to know the US position in the crisis, and was certainly monitored by the regime as well. The embassy's website and especially its Facebook page carried official US statements expressing criticism of the Syrian regime and sympathy with the public. They carried news articles that criticized Syria for human rights abuses, and refuted false government accusations against the embassy. The Facebook page even carried comments by private Syrians on the situation, which were often virulently anti-Assad, and even some that were highly critical of the United States, which gave the website credibility. The website was managed from Washington by Leslie Ordeman, an experienced Foreign Service officer who had served in US embassies in Tunisia and Lebanon (Ungerleider 2011).

During the uprising, the most prominent US public diplomacy effort was carried out by Ambassador Ford. He traveled to locations in Syria where demonstrations were taking place to show US support for them, knowing that this would attract media coverage and send a signal to the Syrian government and people. In July 2011 he visited Hama during a demonstration and publicly criticized the Syrian government for the use of force. Syria responded by issuing an order to all diplomatic missions requiring diplomats to obtain permission for any travel outside Damascus, and when the US embassy applied for permission for Ford to travel it was denied (Sly and Warrick 2011). Ford then met with dissidents in Damascus, which also generated international media coverage. In September 2011, when he visited the home of a dissident, government supporters surrounded the home, threw eggs and tomatoes at it, and trapped Ford inside for ninety minutes; Secretary of State Clinton publicly condemned the Syrian government for allowing that to happen (Bakri 2011; Warrick 2011).

Washington clearly recognized the public diplomacy value of Ambassador Ford's efforts, saying that he would "continue delivering the United States' message to the people of Syria . . . engaging with the full spectrum of Syrian society." It added: "We believe his presence in the country is among the most effective ways to send the message that the United States stands with the people of Syria" (DeYoung 2011). Ambassador Ford himself made use of Facebook to speak directly to the Syrian people and the Syrian government, and he did not pull his punches. In July 2011 after his visit to Hama, he posted a long Facebook comment criticizing the Syrian government directly, and he continued to use that channel to do so. He focused on specific incidents of Syrian government wrongdoing. On January 3, 2012 his Facebook post describing specific incidents began: "The killing at the hands of Syrian security forces of hundreds of civilians during the past weeks is appalling." He added that he had "never seen this in an Arab government before," referring to his previous service in Iraq, Algeria, Bahrain, and Egypt (Ford 2011, 2012).

Ford's active and visible public diplomacy effort angered the Syrian regime to the extent that Washington recalled him in October 2011, and four months later closed the embassy (Shadid 2011, 2012). Public diplomacy then reverted to an exclusively offshore effort, via radio and television, plus a new "virtual embassy" that the State Department established in 2012 in English and Arabic. It looked like a normal embassy website, but was managed at the State Department.

Conclusion and Projections

Challenges to the US public diplomacy program in Syria have been daunting. For several years, the US-Syrian bilateral relationship has been adversarial because of a series of important policy differences that would not go away, and Syrian government restrictions have severely hampered US public diplomacy efforts on the ground. Bush administration sanctions and the withdrawal of the US ambassador compounded the problem. Then the uprising and civil war added new obstacles.

The election of Barack Obama seemed to open up opportunities to enhance US diplomacy and public diplomacy in Syria. From the beginning of his presidency Obama announced a policy of engagement, an approach that the US embassy believed most of the Syrian public strongly favored, although the regime remained ambivalent (Hunter, author interview 2010). Starting right after he took office, Obama sent special envoys to Syria. Assistant Secretary of State Jeffrey Feltman met the foreign minister and asked that three American institutions, the ACC, ALC, and DCS, be allowed to reopen; the chargé made the same case to the education minister (Hunter, author interview 2010; Mills, author interview 2010). The president of Amideast, Ted Kattouf, appealed to Syrian officials to allow the ALC to reopen, and in March Syria agreed (Mills, author interview 2010). When Obama's envoy Senator Mitchell met President Assad in the summer, he raised the DCS issue with him, and DCS was allowed to resume (Hunter, author interview 2010). However, by the end of 2011 both the ALC and DCS had again been closed because of the uprising. In October, Syria agreed to lift the ban on American Fulbrighters affiliating with Damascus University and auditing courses there (OIG 2010). The atmosphere had begun to thaw a bit, according to PAO Roberts (Roberts, author interview 2010).

Yet until the end of 2010 no US ambassador had been sent to Damascus, and the chargé d'affaires had no direct access to the Syrian president or foreign minister, but was only received by the director of the foreign minister's office (Anonymous A, US senior official, author interview A). The chargé did occasionally run into Syrian officials socially, but those occasions were brief and not conducive to any detailed exchanges on policy or operational matters (Hunter, author interview 2010). The reopening of the DCS and the ALC at that time was probably due in part to pressure from private Syrian citizens (Roberts, author interview 2010; Mills, author interview 2010).

During the first eighteen months after President Obama took office, the PAO and her staff were proactive and creative in finding opportunities to do cultural programming, taking advantage of the improved atmosphere that Obama had created (Roberts, Mills, and Hunter, author interviews 2010).

The impact of the uprising put new obstacles in the way of American diplomacy and public diplomacy in Syria. The new ambassador started to meet with President Assad, but because the United States in early 2011 began to criticize Assad, that channel was cut off. The embassy had hoped to reopen the ACC but that hope faded. The newly appointed PAO was then evacuated with other "nonessential" personnel and soon the embassy itself was closed.

Ambassador Ford's significant public diplomacy effort, appearing in person in support of the opposition and using social media to criticize the government, will long be remembered by the Syrian public.

At this writing, Syria's internal crisis has continued, and when it is resolved, it is entirely possible that the US-Syrian relationship will revert to pretty much the way it was in January 2011, because the reasons for the adversarial relationship will not have disappeared. Any successor to Assad will probably differ with Washington over several fundamental policy issues. The focus of the public diplomacy effort therefore may again be on cultural and exchange programming and social media. As Secretary of State Clinton said in 2010, cultural programming in Syria was very worthwhile even if it did not immediately change Syrian foreign policy, since "diplomacy is a multi-dimensional chess game with many moving parts" (Clinton 2010).

Before the uprising, the goal of the embassy's public diplomacy plan for 2010–2012 was to implement "principled engagement" to seize the opportunity "to reconnect with twenty-three million Syrians after five years of deeply unpopular policies." Specifically, it recommended sustaining the surge in cultural programming started in 2009: to "break down stereotypes" of America through accelerated contact with Americans; to increase use of US-funded exchange programs, and actively engage in student advising to encourage more Syrians to study in America; to increase English-language teaching; and to open two more American Corners, increasing the number to four, reaching out to Aleppo (US Embassy Damascus 2012). That may be the limited shape of American public diplomacy after Syria's internal crisis is over.

The Syrian case answers some of the framing questions in this book. It shows that a crucial element in the US public diplomacy effort is the existence of a functioning US embassy, and private organizations play only a minor role. When the embassy was open, public diplomacy personnel showed creativity by using English-language teaching, cultural programming, and careful personal contact effectively to work around Syrian governmental restrictions. It shows also that domestic pressures hampered the public diplomacy effort when Congress tried to prevent the return of an ambassador, because Ambassador Ford substantially enhanced public diplomacy by his visible presence and his active use of social media. But when the deteriorating security situation forced the withdrawal of Ambassador Ford and the closure of the embassy, American public diplomacy was reduced to an offshore effort by radio and television and a new virtual embassy managed in Washington. US officials believe the persistent effort was worthwhile since the Syrian public is intensely interested in American information, and despite the catastrophic civil war they are likely to remember American communication efforts into the future.

Notes

1. Because there is almost no published material on US diplomacy in Syria, this chapter is based primarily on interviews conducted by the author with US officials and others—see References—familiar with the subject. The author also drew upon personal information and observations of Syria as president and CEO of Amideast (1995–2003) and Deputy Chief of Mission, US Embassy in Damascus (1981–1984).

2. Senator John Kerry, Chair of the Senate Foreign Relations Committee, visited in February 2009 and met with President Assad. *USA Today,* 2009; Roberts, interview;

"Much at Stake for Lebanon in US Opening to Syria," *Daily Star*[Beirut newspaper], March 9, 2009; "Amid Low Expectations American Officials Hold Talks in Syria," *New York Times*, March 7, 2009.

3. The signatories were Senators Tom Coburn, John Kyl, Pat Roberts, Kit Bond, John Barrasso, Mike Johanns, Robert Bennett, and Jim Imhofe.

4. The Constitution's Article II, sec. 2, allows the president to make such assignments without Senate approval when Congress is in recess, but only until the end of the year.

References

For author interviews see Table 7.1 (p. 230).

Agha, Hussein, and Robert Malley. 2008. "Into the Lion's Den." *New York Review of Books*, May 1, 57–58

Al-Assad, Bashar. Interview with Syrian President Bashar al-Assad by Charlie Rose. *Charlie Rose*, PBS, May 27, 2010, *http://www.joshualandis.com/blog/?p=6592.*

Alexander, Harriet. "John Kerry and Bashar al-Assad Dined in Damascus". 2013. *The Telegraph*, September 3.

American Language Center. *http://myalc.edu.sy.*

Baghdadi, George. 2009. "Mitchell Returns to Syria for Peace Entreaty." *CBS News,* July 25. Accessed Jan. 23, 2015 at http://www.cbsnews.com/8301–503543_162–5188560–503543.html.

Bakri, Nada. 2011. "Pro-Assad Protest Temporarily Traps U.S. Ambassador." *New York Times,* September 29. Accessed August 6, 2012 at http://www.nytimes.com/2011/09/30/world/middleeast/pro-assad-protest-temporarily-traps-us-diplomat.html.

BBC News "Barack Obama Renews US-Syria Sanctions." 2009. July 24, http://news.bbc.co.uk/2/hi/middle_east/8658881.stm.

Blanford, Nicholas. 2011. "Surprise Recall of US Ambassador to Syria Spurred by Threats." *Christian Science Monitor,* October 24. Accessed August 6, 2012 at http://www.csmonitor.com/World/Middle-East/2011/1024/Surprise-recall-of-US-ambassador-to-Syria-spurred-by-threats.

Clinton, Hillary. 2010. Interview with Secretary of State Hillary Clinton by Tracy Smith. *CBS Sunday Morning,* June 15.

DeYoung, Karen. 2011. "Ambassador Robert Ford Heads Back to Syria." *Washington Post,* December 6. Accessed August 6, 2012 at http://www.washingtonpost.com/blogs/checkpoint-washington/post/ambassador-robert-ford-heads-back-to-syria/2011/12/06/gIQAWb8SZO_blog.html.

Enderlin, Charles, S. 2002. *Shattered Dreams: The Failure of the Peace Process in the Middle East 1995–2002.* Trans. Susan Fairfield. New York: Other Press.

Feltman, Jeffrey. 2010. "Neither Appeasement nor Improvement? Prospects for Engagement with Syria." Statement before the House Foreign Affairs Committee. April 21. *http://www.internationalrelations.house.gov/111/fel042110.pdf.*

Ford, Robert. 2010. Statement before the Senate Committee on Foreign Relations, March 16. *http://foreign.senate.gov/imo/media/doc/FordTestimony100316a1.pdf.*

———. 2011. "A Note From Ambassador Robert Ford." Facebook. July 11.

———. 2012. "A Note From Ambassador Robert Ford." Facebook. January 3.

Hansen, Allen C. 2007. *Nine Lives: A Foreign Service Odyssey.* Washington, DC: New Academia.

Jackson, David. 2011. "Obama Aide Decries Attack on Syrian Envoy." *The Oval,* September 29. Accessed August 6, 2012 at http://content.usatoday.com/communities/theoval/post/2011/09/obama-aide-condemns-attack-on-syrian-envoy/1#. UB_zzmOCX90

Kissinger, Henry. 1979. *The White House Years.* Boston: Little, Brown.

———. 1982. *Years of Upheaval.* Boston: Little, Brown.

Landis, Joshua. 2011. *Syria Comment: Syrian Politics, History, and Religion.* Accessed March 16, 2010 at www.joshualandis.com/blog, .

Lesch, David W. 2005. *The New Lion of Damascus: Bashar al Asad and Modern Syria.* New Haven: Yale University Press.

Ma'oz, Moshe. 1995. *Syria and Israel.* Oxford: Clarendon Press.

"Mitchell Cites Syria's Role in Mideast Peace Effort." 2009. *New York Times,* June 13.

"War Deaths Top 150,000 Human Rights Group Says." 2014. *New York Times,* April 1.

Norton, Augustus Richard. 2007. *Hezbollah.* Princeton: Princeton University Press.

Obama, President Barack. 2009. Speech at Camp LeJeune, NC, February 27. *www.whitehouse.org/the-press-office.*

OIG. 2010. Office of Inspector General, US Department of State and the Broadcasting Board of Governors. Report of Inspection, Embassy Damascus Syria, Report Number ISP-I-10-34A. March.

Otterman, Sharon. 2009. "US Opens Way to Ease Sanctions against Syria." *New York Times,* July 28. http://www.nytimes.com/2009/07/29/world/middleeast/29syria.html.

Phillips, Macon. 2011. "President Obama: 'The Future of Syria Must be Determined by its People, but President Bashar al-Assad Is Standing in Their Way.'" *The White House Blog,* August 18. Accessed August 6, 2012 at http://www.whitehouse.gov/blog/2011/08/18/president-obama-future-syria-must-be-determined-its-people-president-bashar-al-assad.

Quandt, William B. 1977. *Decade of Decisions 1967–1976.* Berkeley: University of California Press.

———, ed.1988. *The Middle East: Ten Years after Camp David.* Washington, DC: Brookings.

Rugh, William. 2006. *American Encounters with Arabs: The Soft Power of US Public Diplomacy in the Middle East.* Westport, CT: Praeger.

———. 2004a. *Arab Mass Media.* Westport, CT: Praeger.

———. 2004b. *Engaging the Arab and Islamic Worlds through Public Diplomacy.* Washington, DC: Public Diplomacy Council.

Shadid, Anthony. 2011. "U.S. Ambassador to Syria Leaves Damascus amid Threats to Safety." *New York Times*, October 24.

———. 2012. "U.S. Embassy Closes as Violence Flares." *New York Times*, February 6.

Sly, Liz, and Joby Warrick. 2012. "U.S. Pulls Ambassador out of Syria, Citing Threats." *Washington Post*, October 24. Accessed August 6, 2012 at http://www.washingtonpost.com/world/middle_east/us-pulls-ambassador-out-of-syria-citing-threats/2011/10/24/gIQA1kycCM_story.html.

Sultan, HRH General Khaled bin. 1995. *Desert Warrior*. New York: HarperCollins.

Seale, Patrick. 1986. *The Struggle for Syria*. Oxford: Oxford University Press.

———. 1988. *Assad of Syria: The Struggle for the Middle East,* London: I. B. Tauris.

"SYRIA: U.S. Senate Approves Robert Ford as Ambassador." 2011. *Los Angeles Times*, October 4. Accessed August 6, 2012 at http://latimesblogs.latimes.com/world_now/2011/10/syria-us-ambassador-robert-ford-confirmation.html.

Tabler, Andrew. 2009a. "Why Mitchell Bypassed Damascus." *Policywatch 1506*. Washington Institute on Near East Policy, April 13.

———. 2009b. "Rule of Law Is the Key to Future Israel-Syria Peacemaking." *Policywatch 1533*. Washington Institute on Near East Policy, June 11.

———. 2009c. "Syria Clenches its Fist." *Foreign Policy*. Foreignpolicy.com, August 28.

———. 2010a. "In a Corner." *Newsweek*. Web exclusive, February 17. Accessed June 6, 2011 at *http://www.scpss.org/*.

———. 2010b. "Inside the Syrian Missile Crisis." *Foreign Policy*. April 14. http://www.foreignpolicy.com.

———. 2010c. "How to React to a Reactor." *Foreign Affairs*, April 19. *http://www.foreignaffairs.com/articles/66214/andrew-j-tabler/how-to-react-to-a-reactor*.

Tillman, Seth P. 1982. *The United States in the Middle East: Interests and Obstacles*. Bloomington: Indiana University Press.

Ungerleider, Neil. 2011. "US State Department Takes on Syria Via Facebook." Fastcompany, October 24. Accessed January 3, 2012 at *http://fastcompany.com/1790373*.

UNSCR. 2006. "The Situation in the Middle East." *UN Security Council Resolution 1701*. S/RES/1701. http://www.un.org/Docs/sc/unsc_resolutions06.htm.

US Embassy Damascus, Syria. 2010a. *Events: US Embassy Damascus Summary of Events February to April 2010*. Unclassified report.

———. 2010b. *Highlights: US Embassy Damascus Public Affairs Section Highlights*. March. Unclassified report.

———. 2011. "US Trade and Financial Sanctions against Syria." Accessed June 6, 2011 at *http://damascus.usembassy.gov/sanctions-syr.html*. Last modified May 12, 2011.

———. 2012. "Public Diplomacy Profile, Fiscal Year 2012." Unpublished internal government document, unclassified.

US Senate. 2010. "Letter to Secretary of State Hillary Clinton, March 5, 2010." *Politifi* (blog), March 9. politifi.com/news/eight-senators-express-concern-over-US-ambassador-to-Syria-268311.html.

UPI. 2009. "Obama Lifts Sanctions on Syria." July 27.

Warrick, Joby. 2011. "U.S. Ambassador to Syria Accosted by Pro-Assad Mob in

Damascus." September 29. Accessed August 6, 2012 at http://www.washington-post.com/world/national-security/us-ambassador-to-syria-accosted-by-pro-assad-mob-in-damascus/2011/09/29/gIQA65hL8K_story.html.

Woodward, Bob. 1991. *The Commanders*. New York: Simon & Schuster.

TABLE 7.1 Appendix: Interviews by the Author

Interviewee	Title/Position	Interview Date	Interview Location	Interview Mode
Charles Hunter	FSO, chargé d' affaires, Damascus Embassy, 2009–2011	July 16, 2010	Washington, DC	Phone
Ted Kattouf	President of Amideast, former ambassador to Syria	May 25, 2010	Washington, DC	Personal
Ted Kattouf	President of Amideast, former ambassador to Syria	August 13, 2010	Washington, DC	Email
Pamela Mills	FSO, cultural affairs officer, Damascus Embassy, 2007–2009	May 25, 2010	Washington, DC	Personal
Tracy Roberts	PAO, Damascus Embassy, 2008–2010	August 6, 2010	Washington, DC	Phone
Anonymous A	US senior official		Washington, DC	
Anonymous B	Knowledgeable source		Washington, DC	

8 CUBA

Public Diplomacy as a Battle of Ideas

William M. LeoGrande

A LTHOUGH PUBLIC DIPLOMACY NORMALLY REFERS TO activities undertaken openly by governments or quasi-governmental organizations (such as the National Endowment for Democracy) to influence public opinion abroad, some measures that fall under the rubric of public diplomacy have a darker past. If we understand public diplomacy broadly as strategies and programs aimed at influencing foreign opinion, then the "traditional State Department" view is inadequate; we have to consider the full range of government and nongovernmental actors, including those operating covertly. Until the 1970s, the Central Intelligence Agency (CIA) conducted a wide array of covert operations to sway public opinion abroad through foreign media, cultural organizations, and clandestine radio stations. When Washington had hostile relations with a foreign government, these covert measures to influence opinion in the target country had a manifestly subversive intent and were routinely referred to as "psychological warfare." Typically, they constituted one component of broader programs of destabilization.

In Latin America, this history is notorious. The clandestine station Radio Liberación played a key role in the success of the CIA-organized coup against Guatemalan President Jacobo Arbenz in 1954. CIA subsidies of Chile's daily newspaper *El Mercurio* helped create a "coup climate" of domestic chaos, leading to the overthrow of President Salvador Allende in 1973. The CIA's support for the newspaper *La Prensa* during the CIA's paramilitary "contra war" against the Sandinista government in Nicaragua sought a similar result.

Adversarial governments have not forgotten the covert antecedents of public diplomacy. This is especially so in Cuba, where the government is still run by the same leaders who were the targets of covert psychological operations (psy-ops) in the 1960s, and who draw no distinction between the CIA's black and gray propaganda of those early days and Washington's contemporary public diplomacy. Moreover, many contemporary programs aimed at Cuba—Radio and TV Martí, US funding for dissident groups, US support for independent libraries—have analogs among CIA covert operations in the 1960s.

Responding to Revolution

The United States' public diplomacy toward Cuba's new revolutionary government in 1959 initially had two tracks. On one track, Washington made a conscious decision not to respond publicly to Fidel Castro's rhetorical blasts about US imperialism. By refusing to play the foil to Castro's anti-Americanism, Washington hoped to make it more difficult for Castro to wrap himself in the Cuban flag and mobilize nationalist sentiment behind his radical agenda. "We cannot expect patriotic and self-respecting Cubans, no matter how distasteful Castro's policies may be to them, to side with the United States," cautioned State Department official John C. Hill, "if we go so far along the lines of reprisals that the quarrel no longer is between Castro and the real interests of the Cuban people, but a quarrel between the United States and their country" (FRUS 1991, 831). Hill, as it happened, was a key player in the second, covert track of US public diplomacy. He chaired an interagency task force charged with carrying out an "extensive unattributed effort . . . to identify and expose to public opinion throughout the Hemisphere the Communist aspect of the Cuban problem." The task force began its work in 1958, even before Castro's rebels came to power, because from the beginning he was seen as a dangerous radical, though not yet a communist (Merchant 1991, 837; Herter 2001).

By the fall of 1959, Washington's policy of trying to co-opt and coexist with Cuba's revolutionary government gave way to a policy of regime change—"to bring about the replacement of the Castro regime with one more devoted to the true interests of the Cuban people and more acceptable to the US in such a manner as to avoid any appearance of US intervention" (FRUS 1991, 850). Concomitantly, Washington's public restraint in the face of Castro's invective was replaced by a strategy of vigorous public response, much to the delight of frustrated US officials. "I know you are as damn sick and tired as I am of our failure to rebut adequately the massive anti–United States propaganda being carried out by the Cuban Government," William Wieland, the State Department's director of the Office of Caribbean and Mexican Affairs, wrote to Assistant Secretary of State R. Roy Rubottom, in a memo titled "Countering the Cuban Propaganda Offensive." Now that the gloves were coming off, Wieland recommended "an intensive campaign to counter Cuban propaganda, take the initiative, and wage this particular 'psychological war'" (Wieland 1959).

Rubottom agreed, and in late December, the administration launched a multifaceted "intensive though discreet campaign to counter the vicious 'Hate America' propaganda being spread throughout Latin America and the world by the Castro Government" (Rubottom 1991, 716). The program of public diplomacy measures included: public statements by US officials; talking points for US Foreign Service officers around the world; anti-Castro radio broadcasts from Key West; placement of anti-Castro stories in sympathetic newspapers and magazines; production of pro-US pamphlets for distribution in Cuba; creation of a nominally independent "reading room" in Havana to distribute books and pamphlets; production and distribution of anti-Castro films; creation of a front group of distinguished Americans to publicly criticize Castro; and the recruitment of US businesses in Cuba to coordinate their press operations with the program (Cushing 1960).

On March 17, 1960, President Eisenhower formally approved the CIA covert operations plan against Cuba that would evolve into the Bay of Pigs invasion a year later. Propaganda was a major component of the plan. The CIA was already supporting opposition newspapers in Cuba, and "a CIA-controlled action group is producing and distributing anti-Castro and anti-Communist publications regularly." In addition, the CIA envisioned several radio stations broadcasting to Cuba—some established stations that were willing to cooperate and at least one CIA-controlled station, Radio Swan (CIA 2001).

Radio Swan went on the air on May 17, 1960. Programming was controlled by various exile groups, which proved less than optimal. "Toward the end of 1960," the CIA reported, "the effectiveness of Radio Swan began to diminish." Exile groups began using the station as a platform to battle among themselves, "forgetting the all important target audience in Cuba." The broadcasters made statements that were "obvious lies," demolishing the station's credibility (CIA 1999, 59–63).

"The latest stories of Radio Swan would make us laugh," Cuba's *El Mundo* newspaper wrote, "if it weren't for the infamy and poison they distill" (Elliston

1999, 58). One disinformation campaign advanced both by Radio Swan and by CIA-supported opposition groups in Cuba did not make Cuban authorities laugh—the campaign to convince Cuban parents that the revolutionary government would abolish parental rights and spirit their children away to brainwashing camps in the Soviet Union. This rumor began circulating in late 1960: "Cuban mothers, don't let them take your children away!" Radio Swan broadcast in October. "The revolutionary government will take them away from you when they turn five and keep them until they are eighteen. By that time, they will be materialist monsters" (Torres 2003, 89–93).

In 1961, CIA-supported groups on the island circulated a phony draft law nullifying parents' rights. Fidel Castro himself spoke on television to deny that there was any such law (Torres 2003, 137). Among Cuba's middle and upper classes, the campaign of fear was effective nevertheless. The government's conflicts with the Catholic Church, which led to the closing of Catholic schools, combined with the launch of the Literacy Crusade, which sent young urban students into the countryside to teach poor peasants how to read and write, stoked parents' fears that the government was intent on separating children from their faith and families in order to instill in them revolutionary ideals.

Worried Cuban parents began seeking a means to send their children to safety in the United States. Thus was born Operation Pedro Pan, as it came to be popularly known. Organized by American expatriates in Cuba with the cooperation of the State Department and CIA, the program distributed thousands of visas for Cuban children using the CIA's networks. Between 1960 and 1962, more than 14,000 Cuban children were sent unaccompanied into exile in the United States. Fifty years later, Fidel Castro was still bitter about the lies that scared so many parents into sending their children abroad alone, calling Operation Pedro Pan "one of the most repugnant acts of moral aggression carried out against our country . . . a cynical publicity maneuver that would have been the envy of Goebbels himself, the Nazi Minister of Propaganda" (Castro 2009).

After the fiasco at the Bay of Pigs, President John F. Kennedy authorized a massive covert program to destabilize Cuba's government, codenamed Operation Mongoose. Like the covert program of 1959–1961, Mongoose included a robust propaganda component. Radio Swan became Radio Americas and five US-based commercial stations were also recruited into the broadcast offensive. The Voice of America (VOA) initiated programming specifically for the Cuban audience. A new station, Voice of Free Cuba, which pretended to be located on the island, broadcast from a US Navy submarine. Small planes from south Florida flew over Cuban cities dropping propaganda leaflets with sabotage instructions, while other small planes dropped incendiary devices on sugarcane fields (Elliston 1999, 114).

Operation Mongoose also included some more eccentric ideas—what CIA Deputy Director Richard Helms called "nutty schemes." The most colorful included airdropping oneway airline tickets over Cuba to encourage emigration; launching thousands of propaganda-filled balloons; creating an imaginary Cuban underground leader (dubbed "Cuban Kilroy") whose invented exploits would be touted by propaganda broadcasts; inventing a cartoon character named *Gusano Libre* (Free Worm), hoping to invest Castro's epithet that the exiles were *gusanos* with a positive spin; broadcasting anti-Castro television into Cuba from a blimp, code-named Project Stratovision; forging photos of a corpulent Castro cavorting in a *ménage à trois*; fabricating evidence of Cuban culpability if John Glenn's manned Mercury mission were to fail; and staging the second coming of Christ, with fireworks courtesy of the US Navy (dubbed "Elimination by Illumination" by skeptics). The wildest of these schemes never got beyond the conceptual stage (Bohning 2005, 92–106; Craig 1999, 100–105).

Caribbean Détente

By the late 1960s it was clear that US efforts to overthrow the Cuban government had come to naught. "The chances are very good that we will still be living with Castro some time from now," National Security Advisor McGeorge Bundy told President Lyndon Johnson. "We might just as well get used to the idea" (FRUS 2004, 8–11). Gradually, US covert operations, both paramilitary and propaganda, subsided.

Both Presidents Gerald Ford and Jimmy Carter undertook tentative steps to improve US-Cuban relations, and Washington's public diplomacy toward the island reflected this shift. The CIA's Radio Americas halted operations in 1968 and the VOA ended its programming aimed specifically at Cuba in 1973. In 1977 President Carter lifted the prohibition on travel to Cuba by US residents and encouraged athletic and cultural exchanges. He also signed an agreement with Havana to open diplomatic missions in each other's capitals—de facto embassies called "Interests Sections" since the two countries still did not have formal relations. Carter told the author in 2004: "I felt then, as I do now, that the best way to bring about a change in Cuba's Communist regime was to have open trade and commerce, and visitation, and diplomatic relations" (Jimmy Carter, pers. comm.).

Meanwhile, Havana launched a public diplomacy strategy of its own, reaching out to Cuban Americans in the hope that mitigating their hostility might remove a major political obstacle to better relations. Cuba's dialogue with the Cuban American community intersected with secret talks between Washington and Havana, resulting in the release of more than 3,000 political prisoners and Havana granting permission to Cuban exiles to return to the island for family visits. More than 100,000 Cuban Americans visited Cuba in 1979. Almost all of them, even those with modest incomes, brought gifts for friends and family—gifts that were lavish by Cuban standards. The contrast between the prosperity of those who had left and the austerity endured by those who stayed was palpable. "The government made a mistake allowing them to return," explained a Cuban woman. "We could see they were well!" (Pedraza 2007, 152, 165, 219).

The invidious comparison between living standards in Cuba and those in the United States increased emigration pressure, leading to the Mariel boat crisis of 1980. Between the time that Castro opened the port of Mariel in April and its closure in September, a Cuban American flotilla of hundreds of small boats ferried more than 120,000 Cuban emigrants to the United States in an utterly uncontrolled, unregulated, and essentially illegal migration. Cuban officials seriously underestimated popular discontent on the island and how the return of prosperous exiles would crystallize that discontent into action. The exodus did real damage to the social fabric, turning neighbor against neighbor as progovernment Cubans denounced and in some cases physically attacked those who wanted to leave. Arguably no public diplomacy measure taken by the United States since 1959 had as big an impact on Cuba as Carter's decision to allow Americans the freedom to travel to the island and Castro's decision to allow Cuban Americans to return.

War on the Airwaves

Jimmy Carter's strategy of engaging Cuba was abruptly reversed by President Ronald Reagan, who saw Cuban support for Central American revolutionaries as a profound national security threat to the United States. In 1982, Reagan reimposed restrictions on travel to Cuba and closed down the only commercial air link between Miami and Havana. The administration also cut off most Cuban travel to the United States by refusing to grant visas to Cubans employed by the government, which in socialist Cuba meant almost everyone.

Reagan's most ambitious public diplomacy initiative was Radio Martí, a propaganda station modeled on Radio Free Europe and named after José Martí, the father of Cuban independence. Proposed in 1981, Radio Martí encountered stiff opposition from the National Association of Broadcasters and from Congress based on the fear that Cuba would retaliate with high-powered radio transmissions of its own, causing widespread interference with US commercial stations. "We are going to broadcast back," Castro warned. "I think the Americans are going to be listening to a lot of Cuban music" (Smith and Morales 1988, 152). The inauguration of broadcasting was delayed while the administration tried to craft a plan of response to anticipated Cuban retaliation. "We're ready to go with Radio Martí," Reagan wrote in his diary in December 1984. "Cuba, however, threatens retaliation . . . jamming American radio stations all the way to the Midwest. . . . What to do? Right now, I don't know" (Reagan 2007, 287).

Radio Martí was as much a product of domestic politics as of foreign policy. The station was the top priority of the newly formed Cuban American National Foundation (CANF), a group of wealthy Miami exiles created to assure that no US president would make concessions to Castro's Cuba. During the 1980s and 1990s, it was the most powerful domestic political voice on US-Cuban relations, punishing its foes, and rewarding its friends with campaign contributions. Urged onward by CANF, Reagan decided on May 17, 1985 that Radio Martí should begin broadcasting forthwith (Menges 1988, 219). It went on the air May 20, Cuba's Independence Day. Instead of retaliating with radio broadcasts of his own, however, Castro canceled the migration agreement Washington and Havana had signed just months before and halted Cuban American visits to the island.

By 1987, the Cubans were having second thoughts. Radio Martí proved to be more annoyance than threat. The immigration agreement was restored and Havana even stopped jamming Radio Martí broadcasts. The ceasefire on the airwaves was short-lived, however.

Just as Radio Martí derailed the 1985 migration accord, US plans to start television broadcasting to Cuba in 1989 thwarted US efforts to win Cuban cooperation in ending the conflicts in Central America. TV Martí, like Radio

Martí before it, was a pet project of the Cuban American National Foundation, not the State Department (Skoug 1996, 202).

When Castro realized that President George H. W. Bush intended to go forward with the TV broadcasts, he warned that Cuba would "use all available means to respond" (Treaster 1989). Privately, senior Communist Party official Carlos Aldana complained to the chief of the US Interests Section, Jay Taylor, that while on the one hand Washington was seeking Cuban cooperation in Central America, on the other it was preparing "to spit in Cuba's eye." Cuba would take TV Martí as evidence of Washington's implacable hostility, Aldana warned, and simply jam it (Jay Taylor, pers. comm.). As an alternative, Aldana proposed opening Cuba to regular US news broadcasts such as CNN or the PBS *MacNeil/Lehrer News Hour*. "This seemed a rather remarkable proposal to be coming from a member of the Cuban Politburo," said Taylor, recalling his surprise. He cabled Washington, suggesting that the start of TV Martí be delayed while the United States explored these alternatives.

Despite Taylor's recommendation, on February 9, 1990, the administration decided to go forward with TV Martí. It began broadcasting on March 27. At first, TV Martí was beamed to Cuba from a blimp—nicknamed "Fat Albert"—tethered over the Florida Keys, just like the CIA's plans for Project Stratovision in the 1960s (Wilson 1999, 118). Destroyed by a hurricane in 2005, "Fat Albert" was replaced by US military aircraft flying just off Cuba's coast. Fidel Castro regarded TV Martí as an insulting provocation. In a heated denunciation of "this trash, this outrage, this insult to our country," Castro dubbed the broadcasts "tele-aggression" (Hockstader 1990). Cuba promptly jammed not only TV Martí, but Radio Martí as well (Gedda 1990). The jamming was so successful that ordinary Cubans dubbed TV Martí *La TV que no se ve* (No See TV). Taylor and his staff traveled all around Havana and its suburbs to test reception and got nothing but static. Western journalists and Catholic priests reported the same result from across the island. But in Washington, TV Martí's patrons insisted that the vast majority of the Cuban population were watching the broadcasts, based on a dubious survey of newly arrived exiles (GAO 1990).

Radio Martí quickly became a focal point of exile politics. Jorge Mas Canosa, founder of the Cuban-American National Foundation, chaired the President's Advisory Board for Cuba Broadcasting from its inception in 1984 until his death in 1997. Radio Martí staff complained repeatedly about political manipulation of their stories by management operating on Mas Canosa's instructions. A 1995 investigation by the US Information Agency (USIA) Inspector General produced a preliminary report that found pervasive influence by Mas Canosa, including pressure to cover his political appearances and opinions, a denigration of views other than those of hardliners, and repeated misrepresentations of US policy so severe they sparked complaints from several US government agencies and officials. Radio Martí employees who resisted Mas Canosa's instructions were fired or demoted (Gugliotta 1995; DeFede 1996).

In 1997, at Mas Canosa's urging, Radio Martí's operations were moved from Washington to Miami, further loosening the VOA's oversight. New staff was hired from Miami's AM radio stations, and the hard news features that had won the radio station some measure of respect were replaced by political commentary typical of Miami's exile political milieu. A columnist for Miami's *El Nuevo Herald* lamented the change to "a radio menu that, curiously, responds more to local political interests . . . than to the tastes of their island audience"—exactly the fate that befell Radio Swan some thirty years earlier (Glasgow 1998a). An independent panel of journalists blasted Radio Martí's lack of professionalism, lack of balance and fairness, and poor programming (Glasgow 1998b).

Since Radio Martí first went on the air, debate has swirled over how many Cubans actually listen. Before TV Martí, when the Cuban government's jamming was limited, somewhere between 50 percent and 75 percent of Cubans listened on the AM band according to USIA surveys of Cuban immigrants. The Cuban government's jamming, followed by the programming changes Radio Martí underwent when it moved to Miami, led to a significant reduction in listeners to 27 percent in 1998 and just 9 percent in 2001. TV Martí's audience continued to be nonexistent (Glasgow 1998b; Glasgow 1999; Glasgow 2001).

In an effort to boost their audiences, Radio and TV Martí began buying time on several of Miami's commercial radio and TV stations that reach Cuba (Glasgow 1992). This in itself highlighted an important fact: Cubans have access to a wide range of external news sources, from international broadcasts by European countries, such as Radio Netherlands and BBC World; commercial stations from the United States, Mexico, and the Caribbean; and pirated US cable television. Thousands of Cuban households have illegal homemade satellite dishes that capture DirecTV signals, which are then decoded with set-top boxes provided by family members in Miami. In Havana, more than a third of households received pirated signals. "I have HBO and CNN," a Cuban told a US reporter. "Why do I need TV Martí?" (DeFede 1993; Quintanilla 2007). In fact, TV Martí's efforts to expand its audience by buying time on Miami stations carried by DirecTV (and thus accessible for Cubans with dishes) prompted a government campaign to confiscate the dishes to prevent them from being used to spread "subversive messages" (Robles 2007a; Robles 2007b). Thus US policy had exactly the opposite effect from what was intended.

People-to-People

The idea that US public diplomacy toward Cuba should have a cultural and educational exchange component lay moribund under Presidents Reagan and George H. W. Bush, but President Bill Clinton revived it. The 1992 Cuban Democracy Act formed the legal basis for what Clinton called "people-to-people" exchanges. The law tightened the economic embargo in the hope that the Cuban government, in economic free-fall after the loss of Soviet aid, would collapse. But it also allowed increased people-to-people contact, humanitarian assistance, and sales of medicine (Anderson and Marquis 1992). Dubbed "Track II," the people-to-people measures were intended to ease the immediate suffering of ordinary Cubans, erode the government's grip on society, promote the diffusion of democratic ideas, and build a foundation in civil society for a more democratic Cuba down the road (Nuccio 1995).

Track II's subversive intent did not escape Fidel Castro's notice. "It seeks to destroy us from within," he declared in July 1995. "These people want to exert influence through broad exchanges with diverse sectors they consider vulnerable" (Castro 1995). In March 1996, Raúl Castro gave a report to the Central Committee of the Communist Party detailing the government's political vulnerability due to the post-Soviet economic crisis. Washington's Track II program, he warned, was trying to exploit this ideological weakness, "to deceive, confuse and disarm the elements that they consider the most vulnerable within the Cuban population" (Castro 1996). Political inquisitions ensued at all of Cuba's think tanks and media outlets that had developed any significant contact with counterparts in the United States. By trying to orchestrate nongovernmental contacts to destabilize the Cuban government, Track II made Cubans with foreign contacts appear to be agents of a hostile power, and Cubans who had contacts with US nongovernmental organizations (NGOs) came under particular suspicion. Perversely, a US policy intended to increase people-to-people contacts had a chilling effect instead.

In the aftermath of the Cuban shoot-down of two civilian planes from the Cuban American group Brothers to the Rescue, President Clinton signed the Cuban Liberty and Democratic Solidarity Act of 1996 (Helms-Burton), which codified into law existing economic sanctions against Cuba. Nevertheless, coinciding with Pope John Paul II's visit to Cuba in 1998, Clinton used his licensing authority to reinvigorate people-to-people exchanges by resuming regular air links to Cuba and restoring Cuban American remittances that had been cut off during the 1994 rafters migration crisis. "We can help to lessen the Cuban people's dependence on the Cuban state by addressing humanitarian needs, aiding the development of a civil society and strengthening the role of the Church and other nongovernmental organizations," explained Secretary of State Madeleine Albright, announcing the new measures. "By so doing, we can begin to empower Cuban citizens and help them prepare to make a peaceful transition to democracy" (Albright 1998). In January 1999, Clinton unveiled another set of people-to-people initiatives, loosening license requirements for humanitarian and cultural travel, expanding direct flights, and allowing anyone to send remittances to Cuba (Clinton 1999). During the last two years of the Clinton administration, more authentic people-to-people interaction took place than ever before, with steady flows of academics, cultural figures, and sports teams traveling in both directions. By the end of the Clinton administration, between 150,000 and 200,000 Americans traveled to Cuba annually.

Regime Change and Democracy Promotion

President George W. Bush had little faith in people-to-people exchanges and ended most of them. Upon taking office, he outlined a series of new measures, including tougher enforcement of the travel ban (which thousands of Americans were ignoring), limits on remittances, and new regulations restricting humanitarian assistance (Marquis 2001). Bush brought thousands of enforcement actions against travelers, among them a seventy-five-year-old grandmother who unwittingly took an illegal bicycle trip and an evangelical Christian who went to Cuba to distribute bibles (Baucus, Enzi, and Flake 2004).

In March 2003, Bush promulgated new regulations abolishing people-to-people educational and cultural exchanges entirely, the largest category of travelers who were not Cuban Americans (Kirkpatrick 2003). A year later, during the 2004 presidential campaign, he restricted academic exchanges so severely that only a few of more than thirty study abroad programs between US and Cuban universities survived. He also cut Cuban American travel from one trip annually, supplemented by additional trips for family emergencies, to only one trip every three years, with no emergency trips allowed. The new regulations restricted the support Cuban Americans could provide to family on the island through remittances and gift packages (Sullivan 2005, 7–11). The cumulative effect of the 2003 and 2004 regulations was to cut travel by US residents in half, reduce humanitarian assistance from some $10 million annually to $4 million, and shrink remittances from $1.25 billion to about $1 billion annually (Arrington 2005a; Marx 2005a; Acosta 2006).

Travel in the opposite direction—Cubans visiting the United States—was virtually eliminated by the invocation of the Reagan-era presidential executive order banning entry to anyone employed by the Cuban government, which meant almost everyone. Cuban officials seeking to meet with US businessmen to legally buy food and medicine were denied US entry. Visas for Cuban musicians were held up so long that twenty-two of them missed the 2002 Grammy Awards ceremony (Robles 2005a).

Perhaps Bush's antipathy toward people-to-people exchanges was attributable in part to the fact that this element of public diplomacy cut both ways. Returning travelers demystified Cuba and made it more difficult for Washington to demonize Fidel Castro. The travel section of every major newspaper ran stories about Cuba as an attractive tourist destination, and every bookstore featured travel guides to Cuba from all the major publishers. As more and more people went and recounted their experiences to family and friends, Cuba seemed more and more like just another tropical island, albeit a little threadbare—not the archenemy of Bush's rhetoric. The Cubans themselves were well aware of this dynamic and sought to encourage it by welcoming American tourists. "Each one who comes, goes back to the United States and tells the truth about Cuba," said Foreign Minister Felipe Pérez Roque. "They say they have been to hell, but hell is not as hot as it had been depicted" (Thompson 2002).

Along with trying to choke off hard-currency flows to Cuba, the Bush administration undertook a major campaign to build the internal opposition. Overt US support for "democracy promotion" in Cuba began under President Clinton, but most of the funding stayed in the United States, going to nongovernmental organizations that produced or distributed critical commentary about Cuba for global audiences (USAID 2000). Under Bush, the funding for these programs rose dramatically and their focus shifted onto the island.

Under Clinton, the US Agency for International Development (USAID) spent about $10 million on the Cuba program. Bush raised the annual budget more than tenfold, from $3.0 million in FY 2000 (USAID 1999) to $45.7 million in FY 2008 (USAID 2007). The money was distributed to US NGOs for programs supporting Cuban human rights activists, independent journalists, independent trade unionists, independent libraries, and former political prisoners. Until 2003, there was a prohibition on delivering cash to Cuban clients because of concerns about both accounting standards and the risk entailed for recipients due to Cuba's stringent laws prohibiting such funding. Consequently, support was mostly in material goods (radios, computers, printers, cameras, etc.) and published materials distributed through Cuba's independent libraries. However, some participating US organizations also delivered privately raised cash to Cuban clients along with the goods paid for by USAID, and by 2005 US government funds were going to dissidents through the National Endowment for Democracy (Marx 2005b).

Cuban laws aimed at US support for dissidents are severe. After passage of the Cuban Liberty and Democratic Solidarity Act (Helms-Burton), the Cuban National Assembly passed the Law for the Reaffirmation of Cuban Dignity and Sovereignty (Law No. 80) criminalizing "any form of cooperation, whether direct or indirect, with the application of the Helms-Burton Act," including providing to the US government information relevant to the law, receiving resources from the US government to promote the law, or spreading information provided by the US government promoting the law. In short, it criminalized a wide swath of common dissident activity if it was supported by the United States (Garcia Luis 2001, 280–285).

In 1999, Cuba adopted the Law for the Protection of Cuban National Independence and the Economy (Law No. 88), making it illegal to disseminate subversive material from the United States, collaborate with foreign mass media for subversive purposes, hinder international economic relations, or receive material resources from the US government (Oppenheimer 1999). Any Cuban involved with USAID's democracy promotion program was, in effect, breaking the law.

The US Interests Section in Havana was assigned to spearhead Bush's expanded support for Castro's internal opponents, transforming the mission from a channel of diplomatic communication to an outpost of support for regime opponents. It delivered material assistance to dissidents, providing a haven for their collective planning and a megaphone amplifying their message. As much as 70 percent of the material brought into Cuba in the US diplomatic pouch was material for the democracy promotion program (a summary of USAID activities is included in GAO 2006, 13, 24). This undiplomatic activity prompted the Cuban government to retaliate by cutting off all significant official contact with US diplomats in Havana. Whereas previous US heads of mission maintained senior-level contacts within the Castro government—individuals who, in a crisis, could carry a message directly to Fidel Castro—the highest-level contact available during the Bush administration was the clerk who answered the phone in the Foreign Ministry.

Shortly after Bush's inauguration, Vicki Huddleston, the chief US diplomat in Havana, began handing out shortwave radios. She described her efforts as a new, "robust" outreach policy made possible by the new administration in Washington. Cuban officials protested that her behavior was improper, but to no avail. "This is sheer intervention in our internal affairs," complained one official. "They did that in Eastern Europe, and they think they have a right to do it in Cuba. We won't allow it" (Sullivan 2002; Bernstein 2002). When private protests brought no change, Castro himself publicly reproached the US diplomats, warning, "The US government is also making a mistake if it expects that people who work as hired hands of a foreign power will go unpunished" (Castro 2002).

In September 2002, James Cason replaced Huddleston as head of the Interests Section and he took an even more aggressive public stance in support of the dissidents. He not only met with them frequently but also offered them use of the mission and his residence for meetings. He attended meetings in their homes, including some to which the international press was invited. On March 6, 2003, in a speech to the National Assembly, Castro publicly condemned Cason's disparaging remarks about the Cuban government at a press conference held at the home of prominent dissident Marta Beatriz Roque, calling it a "shameless and defiant provocation." He repeated his threat, first made in June 2002, to close the Interests Section, "a breeding ground for counterrevolutionaries and a command post for the most offensive subversive actions against our country" (Castro 2003).

Rather than strike at the diplomatic mission, however, Castro struck at the dissidents. On March 18, 2003, state security began rounding them up, charging them under both the 1996 Law for the Reaffirmation of Cuban Dignity and Sovereignty and the 1999 Law for the Protection of Cuban National Independence and the Economy. Cason's very public posture in support of the dissidents enabled prosecutors to portray the defendants as US agents, thereby branding dissent as treason. After summary trials that were closed to international observers, seventy-five of the accused were found guilty and sentenced to long terms in prison, ranging from six to twenty-eight years (Eaton 2003).

Although the Cuban government never expelled Cason, after the arrest of the dissidents he was, for all intents and purposes, persona non grata. A Cuban cartoonist caricatured him as "Cachan," a pink fairy who magically turned free clinics into private ones, only to be chased away by loyal Cuban citizens as he metamorphosized into a rat. Cason was so delighted that he had a pink fairy costume made and had his picture taken in it, declaring, "I've become like an icon." Cason was none too diplomatic, either. He called Castro a "power hungry egomaniac" and referred to Ricardo Alarcón, president of Cuba's National Assembly, as *Alacrán* (scorpion) (Arrington 2005b; Goddard 2004).

Antagonism reached a Fellini-like apogee in December 2004, when Cason supplemented the Interests Section's Christmas decorations of Frosty the Snowman, Santa Claus, and candy canes with a large neon sign reading "75" to commemorate the convicted dissidents. In retaliation, the Cubans erected a huge billboard just across the coastal highway depicting photographs of US soldiers abusing Iraqi prisoners in Abu Ghraib prison, overwritten with a swastika and the words "Fascists" and "Made in the USA" (Goddard 2004).

In January 2006, Cason's successor, Michael E. Parmly, took the offensive in this psychological war, erecting a three-foot-high scrolling electronic news billboard running the length of the fifth floor of the Interests Section ("Castro Slams" 2006). The screen displayed excerpts from the Universal Declaration of Human Rights, the works of Martin Luther King, and sundry other messages meant to inspire Castro's opponents and annoy Cuban authorities. It certainly annoyed Fidel Castro. He mobilized more than a million Cubans to march past the Interests Section in protest. Parmly couldn't resist turning on the billboard, which scrolled: "Only in totalitarian societies do governments talk and talk at their people and never listen" ("Havana Demonstrations" 2006; Robles 2006). After the rally, the Cubans erected several hundred black flags outside the US mission to commemorate the more than 3,000 Cubans killed by US covert operations—and to obscure the electronic billboard from the street below (Frank 2006).

The Cuban government's response to Washington's aid to dissidents was not to downplay it but to make it a *cause célèbre*, frequently featured on the news show *Mesa Redonda Informativa*. Cuban officials clearly saw it as an opportunity to rally nationalist support. In fact, the show itself originated with what Fidel Castro called "the Battle of Ideas," launched during the campaign to recover six-year-old Elián González in 1999–2000, a campaign explicitly aimed at rallying the population's revolutionary spirit. After Elián was returned to his father, the battle continued. US public diplomacy stratagems simply provided more fodder for it. When Radio Martí broadcast *Forbes* magazine's claim in 2006 that Castro was the seventh-richest head of state in the world (a figure arrived at by treating state enterprises as Castro's personal property), Castro went on the *Mesa* to denounce it as libelous garbage. "We must continue to pulverize the lies that are told against us," he exhorted the audience. "This is the ideological battle; everything is the Battle of Ideas" (Anderson 2006).

In late 2007, Washington launched "Campaign *Cambio*," distributing through the US Interests Section sundry items with the word *cambio* (change) on them, including tote bags, decks of playing cards, T-shirts, baseballs, bracelets, and condoms. *Mesa Redonda* devoted a program to the campaign on November 2, 2007, displaying the items and linking it to President Bush's policy of regime change. "*Cambio*," said the television commentator, holding up one of the T-shirts. "All that's missing is the word 'regime.'" Cuba's leadership seemed to relish doing battle with Washington's public diplomacy.

Trying Something New

Although President Barak Obama did not halt the democrac promotion programs President Bush initiated, his approach to people-to-people engagement was clearly broader than his predecessor's. At a political rally in Miami's Little Havana during the 2008 presidential campaign, Obama called for a new US policy toward Havana. "We've been engaged in a failed policy with Cuba for the last 50 years," he declared, "and we need to change it" (Farrington 2007). In an op-ed piece for the *Miami Herald*, he advocated ending restrictions on Cuban American remittances and family travel, arguing that such people-to-people links were the best hope for promoting "a democratic opening in Cuba," which would be "the foremost objective of our policy" (Obama 2007).

In April 2009, President Obama kept his campaign promise and lifted restrictions on Cuban American family travel and remittances. He offered to grant commercial licenses to US telecommunications companies to contract with their Cuban counterparts to improve telephone and Internet connections between the two countries. The new chief of the US Interests Section in Havana, Jonathan D. Farrar, turned off the electronic billboard, and the Cubans reciprocated by replacing the black flags in front of the building with Cuban flags. Obama quietly eased visa restrictions on Cuban scholars, artists, and scientists seeking to visit the United States, and he also eased licensing requirements for US artists and cultural figures seeking to visit Cuba. In September 2009 the Colombian pop singer Juanes, a US resident, was given a license to perform in Havana. His outdoor concert in the *Plaza de la Revolución* drew an audience of more than a million people—the biggest assembly since the 1998 visit of Pope John Paul II (Martin and Levin 2009). In January 2011, President Obama used his licensing authority to reverse the restrictions on academic and people-to-people travel to Cuba that President Bush imposed in 2003 and 2004.

This strategy of fostering societal engagement has enjoyed considerable success. Ending restrictions on Cuban American family travel and remittances led to a fivefold increase in visits (Armario 2014), and remittances more than doubled, helping to finance a flourishing new private sector on the island (Morales and Scarpaci 2013). The restoration of people-to-people educational travel produced a cornucopia of travel options for ordinary Americans interested in exploring the long-forbidden isle.

But Obama's new policy was partial and tentative at first. Bush's democracy promotion program continued undiminished: Obama's FY 2010, 2011, and 2012 USAID budget requests all proposed $20 million for the Cuba program—the same as Bush's FY 2009 request (USAID 2009; USAID 2010). The Cuban government proved to be no more tolerant of Obama's brand of democracy promotion than they had been of George Bush's, as evidenced by the arrest of Alan P. Gross in December 2009. Working for contractor Development Alternatives Inc., Gross traveled to Cuba on a tourist visa to provide communications equipment, including laptop computers, disks, flash drives, cell phones, and satellite communications technology, to independent NGOs in Cuba's Jewish community (Booth 2010). In March 2011, Gross was convicted of subversion and sentenced to fifteen years in prison, where he remained until December 2014, when he was released as part of President Obama's historic move to normalize US-Cuban relations.

Cultural Dispersion

The irony of Washington's campaign to "break the information blockade" in Cuba through public diplomacy is that ordinary Cubans, especially in Havana, enjoy considerable exposure to US culture and information, but not as a result of any US government program. Young Cubans run neighborhood CD- and DVD-rental services with supplies provided by their relatives abroad. Miami television and radio stations can be seen and heard in parts of the island, and thousands of homemade satellite dishes steal DirecTV signals. Even Cuba's state television runs pirated prime-time dramas from the United States, and Cuban theaters feature US films. One in particular, *3:10 to Yuma* (1957), has become a cult classic on the island, leading ordinary Cubans to abandon the epithet *Yanquis* in favor of "Yumas" when referring to their northern neighbors, and "La Yuma" for the United States (Sokol 2007).

But perhaps no recent cultural export has had more of a political impact than hip-hop music. The Cuban hip-hop movement began in the 1980s among Afro-Cuban youth in the massive Alamar housing project outside Havana. They built homemade antennas so they could listen to rap music on Miami's commercial music stations (Olavarria 2002). For most of the half-century since the triumph of the Cuban revolution, racism has been an unspoken issue. The abolition of capitalism and overtly discriminatory laws were supposed to have eliminated racism, according to socialist doctrine. To speak of racial divisions was to weaken national unity in the face of imperialism. Yet despite the real economic progress made by Afro-Cubans after 1959, a deep vein of racial bias remained in Cuban culture. When the Cuban economy collapsed after the fall of the Soviet Union, Afro-Cubans suffered more than most. Few had relatives abroad to send remittances; few were employed in the tourist sector where they could get access to tips; and few lived in neighborhoods good enough to attract tourists for room rentals or private restaurants.

These hardships gave rise to a genre of Cuban hip-hop that is ironic, caustic, and surprisingly explicit about racism and police harassment. Initially, Cuban authorities saw this music as antisocial and tried to suppress it. By the late 1990s, however, the government had come to realize that suppression was either impossible or too costly politically. Authorities moved instead to accommodate it, declaring it an authentic expression of Cuban culture. Hundreds of Cuban hip-hop groups sprang up across the island, some of whom have signed recording contracts abroad. State television features hip-hop artists and the government organizes hip-hop concerts. The popularity of hip-hop led USAID to sponsor a covert program to encourage musicians to become even more critical of the regime—a project that ended with those musicians being marginalized when the Cuban government uncovered the program (Butler et al., 2014b).

Information Revolution

Nothing has more potential to expand communication among Cubans and between Cubans and the outside world than digital information technology. Cuba has the lowest rate of Internet access in Latin America (13 percent of the population have access to sites within Cuba, but only about 2 percent have access to the worldwide web) (ITU 2010; Elfrink and Grisalez 2009). Until March 2008, it was illegal for Cubans to buy personal computers or cell phones, and Internet access was available only at schools and certain offices. Even when Raúl Castro lifted restrictions on computer and cell-phone purchases for personal use, most Cubans could not afford to buy them (Frank 2009). Finally, although Cuba has an extensive "intranet" for email within the national territory, the bandwidth available for connecting to the Internet is extremely limited, in part because the US embargo prohibits Cuba from connecting to fiber-optic cables from the United States, forcing it to rely mainly on European satellite links that are limited, slow, and expensive (Acosta 2008).

Nevertheless, despite current limitations, the impact of the information revolution is already being felt in Cuba. By 2014, over two million Cubans had cell phones, a sevenfold increase since legal restrictions were lifted (Rodriguez 2014). Internet access is also growing. In 2013, after connecting to a fiber-optic cable from Venezuela, Cuba opened 188 Internet cafes around the country and promised more to come, although access remained too expensive for most Cubans (Fieser 2013). There is also a thriving black market in Internet access: for a monthly fee, a person can, in off-hours, use the Internet account of someone who has legal access through their workplace or school (Robles 2005b).

Not surprisingly, computer-literate young people are adept at finding ways around government rules and regulations (McKinley 2008). Two enterprising young men created an email list that began as a forum for trading computer components and built it into the Cuban equivalent of Craig's List. Their site, Revolico.com, features all manner of goods for sale and trade, including transactions that are legal and some that are not. The site claims 50,000 new postings per month (Elfrink and Grisalez 2009).

A small community of bloggers has emerged, including, most famously, Yoani Sánchez. Her *Generación Y* blog offers an acerbic look at daily life in Cuba, winning Sánchez international acclaim—and the hostility of Cuban officialdom, which she regularly lampoons. After government agents roughed up Sánchez, President Obama responded in writing to a series of questions she had submitted to the White House. The Internet, Sánchez noted, is a space were the limits of what the Cuban state will tolerate have not yet been defined. "Cyberspace hasn't been fully regulated here yet. I think that's why I am still here, because there is no clear illegality in writing on the Internet" (Adams 2008).

There is no doubt, however, that Cuban authorities recognize the power of the Internet. In 2006, Raúl Castro named Ramiro Valdes, former minister of the interior, as Cuba's new minister of communications and information. While acknowledging that digital technology was essential for Cuba to "continue to advance down the path of development," Valdes warned that it also provided the United States with powerful new tools to "bring the destabilizing power of the empire to threatening new levels." Cyberspace, he argued, had to be understood as a "battlefield" in the struggle against imperialism. The Internet, "the wild colt of new technologies, can and must be controlled" (Rice 2007).

During the Bush administration, US cyberpolicy toward Cuba was aimed at increasing Internet access for Cuba's dissident community. The US Interests Section maintained an Internet café with some forty terminals, offering free access for those who preregistered. Since taking advantage of this offer amounted to self-identification as a dissident, only dissidents took advantage of it. USAID's democracy promotion program also provided dissidents with computers, printers, cameras, and cell phones.

In 2014, the Associated Press revealed that USAID had created a secret Twitter-like text-messaging program, nicknamed "ZunZuneo" (Cuban slang for the sound hummingbirds make), to send texts directly to Cuban cell-phone users and enable them to send free texts to each other. After building a user base by focusing on sports and entertainment, the plan was to send users political messages critical of the Cuban regime. The long-term hope was that ZunZuneo might catalyze "flash mobs" of regime opponents, analogous to how social media mobilized people during Iran's Green Revolution and the Arab Spring. Although ZunZuneo attracted about 60,000 users at its peak, it was discontinued in 2012 because it was not financially viable. USAID was paying substantial fees (through intermediaries, to hide the origin of the funds) to Cuba's government-owned telephone company to cover the costs of all the texts—a financial transfer that was not strictly consistent with US law (Butler et al. 2014).

What Works?

The history of US public diplomacy toward Cuba offers little hope that government-organized and -targeted initiatives are likely to have much impact. None has so far. The earliest efforts, mostly covert, designed to undercut Fidel Castro's popular support and overthrow his government, failed utterly. On the contrary, Castro used confrontation with the United States to mobilize nationalist sentiment for his radical socialist project. Propaganda campaigns such as Operation Pedro Pan may have frightened middle-class Cubans into leaving for exile, but that only strengthened Castro's hold on power by allowing him to export his opposition. The Cuba case strongly suggests that, as a practical matter, covert influence operations are not very effective and can be harmful to overt public diplomacy efforts when they are exposed—as they often are. Moreover, covert operations, because they embody attempts to manipulate target populations, are incompatible with a strategy of fostering genuine people-to-people interactions—interactions that have proven far more influential in relations with Cuba.

The offshore broadcasting programs of Radio and TV Martí have had no noticeable impact, either. Initially, Radio Martí built a decent audience in Cuba when it was located in Washington and closely overseen by the VOA. But the advent of TV Martí led Cuba to jam both, leaving neither with any significant following on the island. The launch of both stations disrupted sensitive diplomatic negotiations—on immigration in the case of Radio Martí and on Central America in the case of TV Martí.

Democracy promotion programs, underway since 1995, have channeled aid to Cuba's small dissident movement and have been an important source of sustenance for it. At the same time, US aid has enabled the Cuban government to brand recipients as agents of an enemy power and to prosecute them under laws prohibiting such assistance. US attempts to use people-to-people programs to foster opposition have made Cuban authorities suspicious of all people-to-people contacts among professionals and NGOs.

The biggest impact in Cuba has come not from public diplomacy efforts orchestrated by government but, instead, from instances where the government got out of the way to allow open, authentic people-to-people contact. In 1977, Carter's decision to allow free travel to Cuba led a hundred thousand Cuban Americans to visit in 1979. The reconnection of families proved traumatic for Cubans on the island, increasing discontent and pressures for emigration—an internal social and political ferment that led to the Mariel immigration crisis.

People-to-people cultural and educational exchanges during the Clinton administration produced a proliferation of personal and institutional linkages between Cubans and North Americans. The midcareer Cuban professionals of today will be the professional and political leaders of tomorrow, regardless of how Cuba evolves. Enabling them to visit and learn about the United States, and to interact with their professional counterparts here, improves the chances that US-Cuban relations in the future will be based on mutual understanding and respect.

The power of real, unorchestrated people-to-people contacts is nowhere better documented than in Louis Pérez's cultural history of Cuba, *On Becoming Cuban*. Pérez traces how the culture and national identity of modern Cuba were shaped by its encounter with the United States, beginning in the midnineteenth century. An economic foundation of trade and investment produced a free flow of people in both directions, carrying with them the artifacts and values of their respective cultures. Not surprisingly, the influences were asymmetrical, given the size and wealth of the United States. Pérez shows how US norms came to dominate every aspect of Cuban life and culture—language, music, dance, sports, television, film, fashion, cuisine, and consumer goods of every variety. The remnants of that dominance can still be seen on the streets of Havana, where 1950s Fords and Chevys still carry Cubans (and tourists) around the city.

Tourism played an especially important role in the cultural diffusion of North American ways to Cuba. "North Americans arrived bearing change, often unknowingly," Pérez writes. "In search of novelty, they also introduced novelty simply by their demeanor and their needs, by the clothes they wore and the way they behaved: hundreds of thousands of visitors whose very presence suggested the possibility of alternative models of self-esteem and new modalities of self-representation" (Pérez 1999, 174). By revealing an alternative way of life, US influence eroded Spanish colonial control and laid the cultural foundation for Cuba's independence movement. "The North American presence was ubiquitous, expanding in all directions at once. At every point that this presence made contact with the prevailing order of Cuban life—almost everywhere—it challenged, it contested, it changed" (Pérez 1999, 282).

In 1959, US Ambassador Philip Bonsal thought that the economic and cultural integration of Cuba with the United States would prevent Fidel Castro's revolution from breaking ties. Bonsal resisted imposing economic sanctions on Havana because he feared severing the very linkages that might constrain Castro's radicalism. Bonsal, however, lost the policy debate and the United States abandoned his "soft power" strategy in favor of more traditional means of coercion.

Under Raúl Castro, Cuba has adopted a program of major economic reforms reminiscent of the early stages of economic reform in China and Vietnam. As they embarked on this politically risky journey, Cuba's leaders preferred to have more normal relations with the United States. To that end, Raúl Castro repeatedly offered to open negotiations with Washington on any issues US officials want to discuss, albeit with full respect for Cuba's sovereignty and independence. In December 2014, after eighteen months of secret negotiations, President Obama seized the opportunity to reduce bilateral tensions by moving toward normal relations, thereby opening more space for authentic social and cultural interaction.

Cuba's economic transformation, and its social and political correlates, will be shaped in part by the international environment. The United States, because of its long history of close social and cultural connection to the island, is better positioned than any other country to influence Cuba's future trajectory through the expanded engagement that is sure to follow Obama's historic shift in US policy.

References

Acosta, Dalia. 2006. "Cuba-New Transaction Fees Squeeze Family Remittances." Inter Press Service, June 12.

———. 2008 "Cuba: More Bloggers Are Firing Off Thoughts from the Island." IPS Inter Press Service, October 6.

Adams, David. 2008. "Cuban Dissent Finds Voice on Internet." *St. Petersburg Times*, February 7.

Albright, Madeleine K. 1998. "Opening Remarks on Cuba at Press Briefing Followed by Question and Answer Session by Other Administration Officials Washington,

D.C., March 20, 1998." Office of the Spokesman, Department of State, Washington, DC, March 20.

Anderson, Jon Lee. 2006. "Letter From Cuba: Castro's Last Battle." *New Yorker,* July 31.

Anderson, Paul, and Christopher Marquis. 1992. "N.J. Congressman Makes Castro's Demise His Crusade." *Miami Herald,* February 2.

Armario, Christine. 2014. "US Travelers to Cuba Continues to Rise." Associated Press, April 7.

Arrington, Vanessa. 2005a. "Fewer Americans Travel to Cuba While Number of Fines Rise for Those Who Do, Cuba Says." Associated Press, September 28.

———. 2005b. "Top U.S. Diplomat in Cuba Says Policy Will Persevere after His Departure." *Associated Press Worldstream,* July 6.

———. 2006. "Castro Denies Forbes Report on His Wealth." Associated Press, May 16.

Associated Press State and Local Wire. 2004. "U.S. Diplomat Puts Prison Cell in Havana Yard to Underscore Rights." September 9.

Baucus, Max, Mike Enzi, and Jeff Flake. 2004. "Cuba Obsession Weakens U.S. Effort." *Atlanta Journal Constitution,* June 20.

Bernstein, Fred. 2002. "Lighting Matches In Cuba on the 4th." *New York Times,* July 4.

Bohning, Don. 2005. *The Castro Obsession: U.S. Covert Operations against Cuba, 1959–1965.* Washington, DC: Potomac Books.

Booth, William. 2010. "Contractor Is Secret Agent, Cuban Legislator Says." *Washington Post,* January 7.

Butler, Desmond, Jack Gillum, and Alberto Arce. 2014a. "U.S. Secretly Created 'Cuban Twitter' to Stir Unrest." Associated Press, April 3.

Butler, Desmond, Michael Weissenstein, Laura Wides-Munoz and Andrea Rodriguez. 2014b. "US Co-opted Cuba's Hip-hop Scene to Spark Change," Associated Press, December 11.

"Castro Slams New U.S. 'Provocations' in Diplo Row." 2006. *Agence France Presse,* January 21.

Castro, Fidel. 1995. Speech on July 26, 1995, "Discursos e intervenciones del Comandante en Jefe Fidel Castro Ruz." http://www.cuba.cu/gobierno/discursos/.

———. 2002. "Speech Given by Dr. Fidel Castro Ruz, at the Extraordinary Session of the National Assembly of People's Power." June 26. Accessed March 17, 2015 at http://www.cuba.cu/gobierno/discursos/.

———. 2003. "Speech Made by Dr. Fidel Castro on the Current World Crisis, on the Occasion of His Inauguration as President of the Republic of Cuba, Havana, Cuba." March 6. Accessed March 17, 2015 at http://www.cuba.cu/gobierno/discursos/.

———. 2009. "Reflections by Comrade Fidel: The Envy of Goebbels." *Granma International,* June 12, 2009.

Castro, Raúl. 1996. "The Political and Social Situation in Cuba and the Corresponding Tasks of the Party." *Granma International,* March 27.

Central Intelligence Agency (CIA). 1999. "Brief History of Radio Swan." In *Psywar on Cuba: The Declassified History of U.S. Anti-Castro Propaganda.* Jon Elliston, ed. New York: Ocean Press.

———. 2001. "A Program of Covert Action against the Castro Regime, Tab B: Propaganda." March 16, 1960. In *Bay of Pigs 40 Years After*, Tab 1, document 14. Washington, DC: National Security Archive.

Clinton, William J. 1999. "Statement on United States Policy Toward Cuba." *Public Papers of the President of the United States: William J. Clinton*. January 5. Online at The American Presidency Project. Accessed March 17, 2015 at http://www.presidency.ucsb.edu/ws/?pid=57721.

Craig, William H. 1999. Memo from Department of Defense Project Officer (Craig) to Lansdale, "Ideas in Support of the Project." February 2, 1962. In *The Kennedys and Cuba: The Declassified Documentary History*. Mark J. White, ed. Chicago: I. R. Dee.

Cushing, R. G. 1960. (ARA/P). Memo to W. Wieland, February 4, 1960. "Action Paper on Cuba: Countering Anti-U.S. Attitudes." National Archives and Records Administration (NARA), Record Group (RG) 59, Bureau of Inter-American Affairs, Office of Caribbean and Mexican Affairs (CMA), Subject Files 1957–1962, Lot 63D67, Box 3 Folder: Cuba, General 1960, 2 of 2.

DeFede, Jim. 1993. "Tales of the Limp Blimp: Who's Watching TV Marti?" *Miami New Times*, October 27.

———. 1996. "Radio Marti: Ethics in Exile." *Miami New Times*, June 13.

Eaton, Tracey. 2003. "Cuban Spies Say They Used Pro Democracy Funds." *Dallas Morning News*, May 18.

Elfrink, Tim, and Vanessa Grisalez. 2009. "Cuba's Black Market Moves Online with Revolico.com." *Miami New Times*, October 1.

Elliston, Jon. 1999. *Psywar on Cuba: The Declassified History of U.S. Anti-Castro Propaganda*. New York: Ocean Press.

Farrington. Brendan. 2007. "Obama Criticizes Cuba Policy at Little Havana Event." Associated Press, August 26.

Fieser, Ezra. 2013. "Internet access to expand in Cuba—at a price." *Christian Science Monitor*, June 4.

Frank, Marc. 2006. "Cuba-USRancour Hits New Heights Amid War of Words." *Financial Times* (London), February 10.

Frank, Marc. 2009. "Cuba Lags Region in Telecoms, Internet Access." Reuters. June 25.

FRUS (Foreign Relations of the United States). 1991. *1958–1960 Volume VI, Cuba*. Washington, DC: US Government Printing Office.

GAO (General Accounting Office). 1990. *Broadcasts to Cuba: TV Marti Surveys Are Flawed*. GAO/NSIAD 90 252. August. Washington, DC: US Government Printing Office.

———. 2006. *U.S. Democracy Assistance for Cuba Needs Better Management and Oversight*, GAO- 07–147. November 6. Washington, DC: US Government Printing Office.

Garcia Luis, Julio, ed. 2001. *Cuban Revolution Reader: A Documentary History*. Melbourne, Australia: Ocean Press.

Gedda, George. 1990. "Cuba Extends Jamming of Radio Marti Past Sunrise." Associated Press, April 24.

Glasgow, Kathy. 1992. "Jammin' in Havana: How Did Two Miami Radio Stations End up Broadcasting Radio Marti Programs to Listeners in Cuba?" *Miami New Times*, December 16.

———. 1998a. "Radio Free Miami. Welcome to the New Radio Marti, Dragged into the Swirl of Local Exile Politics, More Quarrelsome than Ever, and Growing Increasingly Irrelevant." *Miami New Times*, June 4.

———. 1998b. "A New Report Confirms That Radio Marti Has Become a Mecca of Shoddy Reporting." *Miami New Times*, October 22.

———. 1999. "Nobody's Listening: A New Survey of Cubans Finds That Radio Marti's Island Audience Is Shrinking by the Day." *Miami New Times*, January 28.

———. 2001. "Radio and TV Marti Are Supposed to Remain Above Politics and Provide Cubans with Unbiased News. This Is Not a Joke. It Only Seems like One." *Miami New Times*, April 19.

Goddard, Jacqui. 2004. "Cuba Starts Propaganda Drive after Frosty Display by American Envoy." *The Times* (London), December 24.

Gugliotta, Guy. 1995. "USIA Probes Activist's Role at Radio Marti." *Washington Post*, July 22.

"Havana Demonstration Against U.S. Ends." 2006. *Xinhua General News Service*, January 24.

Herter, Christian. 2001. Memorandum to the President from the Secretary of State (Herter), March 17, 1960. In *Bay of Pigs: Forty Years After: Briefing Book of Declassified Documents*. Tab 1, document 15. Washington, DC: National Security Archive.

Hockstader, Lee. 1990. "Castro Calls TV Marti 'Outrage.' Jamming Effective. Retaliation Hinted." *Washington Post*, April 4, A32.

ITU (International Telecommunications Union). *Measuring the Information Society 2010*. Geneva: International Telecommunications Union.

Kirkpatrick, David D. 2003. "U.S. Halts Cuba Access by Educational Groups." *New York Times*, May 4.

LeoGrande, William M., and Peter Kornbluh. 2004. Interview with Jay Taylor, December 20, Arlington, Virginia.

Marquis, Christopher. 2001. "Bush Forgoes Trying to Bar Cuba Deals By Foreigners." *New York Times*. July 17.

Martin, Lydia, and Jordan Levin. 2009. "Juanes in Havana." *Miami Herald*, September 21.

Marx, Gary. 2005a. "Tougher U.S. Policy Curtails Aid to Cubans." *Chicago Tribune*, October 13.

———. 2005b. "Activists Get Federal Aid to Subvert Cuba Regime." *Chicago Tribune*, February 22.

McKinley, James, Jr. 2008. "Cyber Rebels In Cuba Defy State's Limits." *New York Times*, March 6.

Memorandum for the Record. 2004. "Subj: Cuba Meeting—Wednesday, February 19, 1964," *FRUS 1964–1968*, Volume XXXI, *South and Central America; Mexico*: 8–11. Washington, DC: US Government Printing Office.

Menges, Constantine C. 1988. *Inside The National Security Council.* New York: Simon & Schuster.

Merchant, Livingston T. 1991. Letter from Under Secretary of State for Political Affairs (Merchant) to Chief of Naval Operations (Burke), March 10, 1960. In *FRUS 1958–1960 Volume VI, Cuba.* Washington, DC: US Government Printing Office.

Mesa Redonda. 2007. Excerpt on YouTube, November 2. Accessed March 16, 2015 at http://www.youtube.com/watch?v=fgE8WGWDcOw.

Morales, Emilio, and Joseph L. Scarpaci. 2013. "Remittances Drive the Cuban Economy." Havana Consulting Group. June 11.

Nuccio, Richard. 1995. "US. Policy on Cuba." Speech delivered November 8, text courtesy of Dr. Nuccio.

Obama, Barack. 2007. "Our Main Goal: Freedom in Cuba." *Miami Herald*, August 21.

Olavarria, Margot. 2002. "Rap and Revolution: Hip Hop Comes to Cuba." *NACLA Report on the Americas.* May 1.

Oppenheimer, Andres. 1999. "Cuba: Back to Darkness." *Miami Herald*, March 18.

Pedraza, Silvia. 2007. *Political Disaffection in Cuba's Revolution and Exodus.* New York: Cambridge University Press.

Pérez, Louis A., Jr. 1999. *On Becoming Cuban: Identity, Nationality, and Culture.* Chapel Hill: University of North Carolina Press.

Quintanilla, Eloise. 2007. "Cubans Risk Raids to Get Satellite TV." *Christian Science Monitor*, July 12.

Reagan, Ronald. 2007. *The Reagan Diaries.* New York: HarperCollins.

Rice, John. 2007. "Cuban Official Defends Internet Controls." *Associated Press Online*, February 13.

Robles, Frances. 2005a. "Denies a Visa to Prize Winning Scientist." *Miami Herald*, November 10.

———. 2005b. "Internet Use Restricted in Cuba, Which Blames US" *Miami Herald*, November 30.

———. 2006. "Uses Billboard to Jab at Castro during Mass Protest." *Miami Herald*, January 25.

———. 2007a. "US Propaganda TV Marti to Be Played on Miami Television Station." *Associated Press.* February 6.

———. 2007b. "Cuba Going after Illegal Satellite TV." *Miami Herald.* February 10.

Rodriguez, Andrea. 2014. "Cuba Mobile Email Experiment Causes Chaos." Associated Press. May 16.

Rubottom, R. R. 1991. Memorandum from the Assistant Secretary of State for Inter-American Affairs (Rubottom) to the Under Secretary of State (Dillon), December 28, 1959. In *FRUS 1958–1960 Volume VI, Cuba.* Washington, DC: US Government Printing Office.

Skoug, Kenneth N., Jr. 1996. *The United States and Cuba under Reagan and Shultz: A Foreign Service Officer Reports.* Westport, CT: Praeger.

Smith, Wayne S., and Estéban Morales Domínguez, eds. 1988. *Subject to Solution: Problems in Cuban-Relations.* Boulder: Lynne Rienner. See Appendix, 145–153.

Sokol, Brett. 2007. "3:10 to Yuma in Cuba: How a Western Changed the Way Cubans Speak." *Slate Magazine.* October 8. Accessed March 16, 2015 at http://www.slate.com/articles/life/the_good_word/2007/10/310_to_yuma_in_cuba.html

Sullivan, Kevin. 2002. "In Havana, U.S. Radios Strike Note of Discord." *Washington Post,* May 5.

Sullivan, Mark P. 2005. *Cuba: Issues for the 109th Congress.* January 13, 2005, CRS Report for Congress RL32730. Washington, DC: Congressional Research Service.

Taylor, Jay. 2004. Personal communication with William LeoGrande and Peter Kornbluh.

Thompson, Ginger. 2002. "Cuba, Too, Felt the Sept. 11 Shock Waves, with a More Genial Castro Offering Help." *New York Times,* February 7.

Torres, María de los Angeles. 2003. *The Lost Apple: Operation Pedro Pan, Cuban Children in the United States, and the Promise of a Better Future.* Boston: Beacon Press.

Treaster, Joseph B. 1989. "Cubans Are Curious to See U.S. TV." *New York Times,* February 21.

US Agency for International Development (USAID). 2000. *Evaluation of the USAID Cuba Program,* "Profile of the USAID Cuba Program."

———. 2007. *Congressional Budget Justification: Foreign Operations, FY2008.* Washington, DC: US Department of State.

———. 2009. *Congressional Budget Justification: Foreign Operations, Fiscal Year 2010.* Washington, DC: US Department of State.

———. 2010. *Congressional Budget Justification: Foreign Operations, Fiscal Year 2011.* Washington, DC: US Department of State.

Wieland, W. 1959. Memorandum to R. R. Rubottom, 4 December, 1959, "Countering the Cuban Propaganda Offensive." National Archives and Record Administration (NARA), Record Group (RG) 59, General Records of the Department of State, Records of the Bureau of Inter-American Affairs Office of Caribbean and Mexican Affairs (CMA), Subject Files 1957–1962, Lot 63D67, Box 1 Folder: Cuba, General 1959, 1 of 2.

Wilson, Donald. 1999. Memorandum from USIA Deputy Director to Brigadier General Edward Lansdale. "Broadcasting to Cuba," September 11, 1962. In *Psywar on Cuba: The Declassified History of U.S Anti-Castro Propaganda.* Jon Elliston ed. New York: Ocean Press.

9 VENEZUELA

The United States and Venezuela:
Managing a Schizophrenic Relationship

Michael Shifter

SINCE EARLY 1999, THE RELATIONSHIP BETWEEN THE
United States and Venezuela has been highly ambivalent. Hugo
Chávez's fourteen-year rule from 1999 to 2013 was distinguished by a notably
adversarial posture toward the United States. But while political relations have
deteriorated, the United States and Venezuela continue to enjoy relatively fluid
societal and economic ties that had been built over decades. The main challenge
for US policymakers has thus become how best to manage such a fundamental
contradiction, a difficult and complicated task. What this contradiction suggests conceptually—in terms of public diplomacy—is that while it is surely *necessary* in the Venezuela case to consider traditional State Department activities,
it is not *sufficient*. It is also crucial to consider "whole-of-government" diplomacy involving many government agencies, plus the often neglected role of corporate and other key nonstate "new public diplomacy" actors.

From the outset of his presidency, Chávez was intent on consolidating
power and curtailing the influence the United States has traditionally exercised throughout the world and particularly in Latin America and the Caribbean. That key foreign policy goal was clearly manifested in the search for
hemispheric and global allies to contest the "Empire." Though Chávez's rule
coincided with the administrations of Bill Clinton, George W. Bush, and
Barack Obama, there was a consistent focus on exploring strategies and partners to challenge US power and developing tactical instruments to contest US
efforts to isolate and discredit Chávez.

Yet, it is useful to recall that for most of the four decades before Chávez's ascension to power—and indeed for most of the twentieth century—relations between Venezuela and the United States were unusually close for a Latin American country. Indeed, during this period, including the Cold War years, Venezuela was perhaps Washington's strongest ally in the hemisphere. Additionally, significant swaths of the two societies have regularly interacted. Venezuela's substantial middle classes have had connections and sympathies with the United States, often through educational experiences or emigrated relatives. The United States' investments and technology have provided crucial support for Venezuela's economy, especially in the oil sector, and the two countries share strong cultural bonds, reflected among other things in Venezuela's (and Chávez's) intense passion for baseball—the quintessential American sport.

Such a schizophrenic situation posed dilemmas for the United States. Despite enormous tension and mistrust—which have only deepened over the past decade or so—the economic and trade ties between the countries have limited both sides' capacity to maneuver in response to crises. There were risks in either overreacting or remaining too passive in the face of Chávez's machinations and provocations. His notably mercurial leadership style and belligerent, occasionally vulgar, verbal assaults on the United States and senior US officials called for calm but consistent diplomatic responses.

Maintaining diplomatic relations and a US embassy in Venezuela are crucial for three reasons. First, it is essential for the US government to have an accurate on-the-scene understanding of Venezuela. Conditions in the country have changed a great deal and continue to evolve. Should a serious problem emerge, decision makers must have available fresh information and analysis free from the biases and inaccuracies of secondhand sources. Second, a diplomatic mission is warranted because it is important for the United States to cultivate and preserve connections with a wide variety of sectors of Venezuelan society. The opportunities for public diplomacy—efforts by one country to favorably influence the opinion of citizens of another to promote foreign policy goals—are considerable. Third, diplomatic relations allow the United States to more effectively monitor anti-American alliances and coalitions with an adversary such as Chávez, which in this case includes a range of groups and states from the Revolutionary Armed Forces of Colombia (FARC) to Iran.

Chávez's "Bolivarian Revolution": Geopolitical Tensions

In 1998, a frustrated Venezuelan populace sought to reinvigorate a broken political system by electing Hugo Chávez Frias to the presidency with 56 percent of the popular vote. He was the first Venezuelan president in forty years who was not a member of either the Democratic Action (AD) Party or Christian Democratic (COPEI) Party, which had traded power under the reasonably democratic *Pacto de Punto Fijo* since 1958. By the 1970s, however, the traditional parties were chronically corrupt, running an exclusionary political machine held together by enormous rents culled from the country's immense petroleum reserves. *Puntofijismo*'s (the arrangement under which the traditional political parties ruled) mismanagement resulted in economic crises in the 1980s and 1990s that became so severe that, by the 1998 presidential election, Venezuelans were ready to destroy the old system. Chávez, who promised sweeping change, seemed just the man for the job.

Chávez had made his debut on the political scene six years earlier in 1992, when, as an army lieutenant colonel, he led a failed coup against AD president Carlos Andrés Pérez. The attempt was the culmination of nearly ten years at the helm of a secretive cell in the Venezuelan army called the Revolutionary Bolivarian Movement-200, Chávez's first organized promotion of a vague "Bolivarian" ideology based largely on personal admiration for South American independence hero Simón Bolívar (Hawkin 2010, 16). When the coup's failure became apparent, Chávez agreed to surrender on one condition: that he be allowed to personally order his rebellious comrades to lay down their arms on national television. That night, Chávez first demonstrated his keen media savvy, delivering a humble and passionate address more to the people of Venezuela than to his fellow soldiers. At the conclusion of the speech, Chávez declared that his movement had failed, but only "for now." Six years later, this charisma carried Chávez to Miraflores Presidential Palace with a clear mandate to address the country's longstanding corruption, mismanagement, and underlying inequities. Chávez embarked on a bold political project, instituting a new constitution extending social rights while concentrating the power of the executive. An evolving phenomenon, Chávez quickly began to tighten his political grip and incrementally gained complete control over institutions such as the judiciary and the armed forces (Shifter 2006).

Although Chávez's rise to power can be attributed to a rhetoric that resonated with ordinary Venezuelans seeking major reform at home, from the outset of his rule he employed his charisma to pursue broader regional, even global, ambitions. Chávez saw himself as the contemporary incarnation of Bolívar, who sought to achieve greater solidarity and integration in the region. Chávez also assailed and defied the United States as the "Empire" that, he argued, has historically oppressed Latin America. In Chávez's mind, the United States was inextricably tied to Venezuela's oligarchs, who he believed should suffer the costs of his far-reaching revolution after plundering the country for so long.

A Strained Relationship

Once in power, Chávez adopted an almost exclusively antagonistic posture toward the United States. Through angry rhetoric in the international arena and impulsive diplomatic maneuvers, Chávez did everything in his power to frustrate the actions of the Empire in Latin America (Neuman 2012).

It is notable how much Chávez's posture toward the United States differed from that of his predecessors. Even though before 1999 Venezuela was hardly in lockstep with Washington, as reflected in Venezuela's founding role in the Organization of the Petroleum Exporting Countries (OPEC), the United States largely viewed Venezuela as a key ally in an important region during the Cold War (Corrales and Penfold 2010).

The Clinton administration got a taste of Venezuela's mistrust and more hard-line foreign policy approach when Chávez refused Washington's offer of assistance in late 1999 after floods ravaged the country's Vargas region. Chávez's close alliance with Cuba's Fidel Castro and his visit to Iraq's Saddam Hussein in August 2000—the latter in clear defiance of UN sanctions—were further evidence of a distinctive and bold foreign policy in part aimed at needling and thwarting the United States.

Within just a few months after George W. Bush came to office in 2001, Chávez met the US president at a summit of hemispheric heads of state in Canada. High on the agenda was consideration of an Inter-American Democratic Charter that was to be put forward for adoption before members of the Organization of American States (OAS). Influenced by Peru's experience in the 1990s with the autocratic Alberto Fujimori, most of Latin America wanted to define democracy beyond mere elections in broad terms that emphasized the importance of independent powers and adherence to the rule of law. But Chávez objected to the content of the proposed charter. He had a different view of democracy, one in which the elected leader embodied the general will and accorded scant weight to checks and balances. For him, liberal or representative democracy was the cause, not the solution, of the region's problems.

The charter was eventually approved by the OAS on the morning of September 11, 2001 in Lima, Peru, but Chávez first had to be persuaded by his Latin American colleagues to agree, an effort aided by the terrorist attacks in New York and Washington just moments before. Yet while tragedy may have encouraged Chávez to approve the charter, his ensuing reaction to the attacks would prove a turning point in relations between Washington and Caracas. As reported by the *New York Times*, Chávez sharply criticized the US military response to the 9/11 attacks, calling the invasion of Afghanistan an act of "fighting terrorism with terrorism" (Rohter 2001). Given the heightened sensitivity in Washington, for many US policymakers Chávez's rhetoric revealed the Venezuelan president's true colors as a fierce adversary. As a result, the United States recalled its ambassador for "consultations" for a month between October and November. This episode signaled an end to a doctrine that placed a higher premium on tangible cooperation with Venezuela even if it required tolerating public criticism from Chávez (Golinger 2006).

The relationship between Chávez and the Bush administration continued to deteriorate over the course of the next seven years. Another critical moment came in April 2002 when Chávez was removed from office in a military coup, only to return forty-eight hours later. Despite repeated accusations by Chávez and his supporters that Washington helped orchestrate the coup and the White House's delight with this turn of events, there is no evidence that the United States was involved. The Bush administration labeled the events a "crisis" that Chávez himself "provoked" rather than a coup (Weiner 2002). Washington's stance was sharply at odds with the strong condemnation offered by other Latin American governments when invoking the charter during a meeting in Costa Rica with the Rio Group. (The Rio Group—predecessor of CELAC, discussed later in this chapter—was an annual summit of Latin American and Caribbean leaders meant to provide an alternative to what was seen as a US-dominated OAS.) The United States had undermined any credibility it may have had on questions of democracy, giving Chávez ample ammunition to charge Washington with seeking to overthrow him. Secretary of State Colin Powell revised the administration's stance a few days later at a special OAS meeting, but the damage was done.

Tensions between Washington and Caracas continued to worsen. At every turn Chávez took advantage of US diplomatic ineptitude and clumsiness, and in so doing he became politically stronger. In 2004 the Venezuelan opposition, led in large part by a nongovernmental organization focused on democracy promotion called *Súmate*, sought to recall Chávez from office by triggering a special referendum provided for in the 1999 constitution. In its campaign, however, *Súmate* accepted $53,400 from the National Endowment for Democracy (NED). According to NED, the funding was intended for nonpartisan civic education efforts related to the referendum (Golinger 2006, 146). Chávez charged the United States with meddling in Venezuela's internal political affairs under the guise of assisting "democracy." The US government, he contended, was only interested in the kind of "citizen education" and "voter registration" that would result in his ouster. After he handily won the referendum, Chávez charged four *Súmate* leaders, including future 2012 presidential candidate María Corina Machado, with treason for allegedly conspiring with the US government to remove him from office. The move received strong condemnation from the State Department and the international human rights community, and the charges stalled in Venezuela's courts.

Just as Chávez had forcefully objected to provisions of the Democratic Charter in 2001, so he continued to challenge attempts at regional consensus—this time on the matter of trade—at the 2005 Summit of the Americas assembly in Mar de Plata, Argentina. The terms of the so-called Free Trade Area of the Americas (FTAA) were slated for negotiations, but this vision that had been advanced at a more optimistic moment—during the first Summit of the Americas in 1994—collapsed. The meeting was marked by considerable rancor and division as Chávez organized an alternative summit to rally like-minded governments to contest what he regarded as a US-imposed project. That same year, Chávez expelled the US Drug Enforcement Agency from Venezuela on charges of espionage.

A few months later, Chávez would make one of his more memorable inflammatory speeches at the UN General Assembly session when he referred to George W. Bush as the "devil" who emitted a "scent of sulfur" (Hoge 2006). While the speech garnered international media attention, it ultimately backfired. For many moderate diplomats in attendance, the speech violated accepted protocol for the General Assembly and ultimately undermined Chávez's opportunity to provide a counterweight to the United States.

While the General Assembly incident was a setback for Chávez, the growing worldwide opposition to the Iraq War proved to be politically advantageous for the Venezuelan president. At roughly the same time as the "devil" speech in 2006,

Chávez began to strengthen ties with governments designated by Washington as state sponsors of terrorism, including Syria, North Korea, and, in particular, Iran. Mounting US concern about Venezuela's international relationships—and its failure to support antiterror efforts—was reflected in the 2006 decision to ban US companies from selling arms to Venezuela. Not surprisingly, Chávez was quick to use this policy to justify his purchases from other suppliers. By 2010, for example, arms sales from Russia amounted to an estimated US $5 billion.

After 2002, Chávez not only linked domestic opposition groups to Washington but also targeted Colombia, the United States' main ally in the region. Chávez had often warned that the US-backed antidrug aid program in Colombia would result in "another Vietnam" ("Venezuela's Chavez Warns" 2000). His rationale for a Venezuelan arms buildup hinged on substantial US security assistance (roughly $7 billion from 2000 to 2010) to Colombia to battle drugs and leftist rebels. In March 2008, after Colombia launched a military incursion against a rebel camp in Ecuadoran territory, Chávez reacted angrily, recalling all Venezuelan diplomatic personnel from Colombia and ordering his defense minister to send Venezuelan troops to its western border. Chávez clearly viewed the action as an example of US-inspired military aggression against a friend of Venezuela's. Tensions between Washington and Caracas continued to escalate. Computer files discovered in a FARC camp supposedly revealed Chávez (and Ecuadoran President Rafael Correa) as collaborators with the Colombian guerrillas, prompting Secretary of State Condoleezza Rice to charge Chávez as a supporter of terrorism.

For all of the antagonism and rhetorical back-and-forth over the years, the two countries maintained an ambassadorial presence for nearly the entire Chávez period. Exceptions include between September 11, 2008 to June 2009, and from July 2010 through today (mid-2014). The 2008–2009 crisis was provoked by the decision of Chávez's ally, Bolivian President Evo Morales, to expel the US ambassador in his country on the charge of plotting with opposition forces to overthrow the government. Acting in solidarity with Morales, Chávez expelled US ambassador Patrick Duddy. Predictably, the move prompted Washington to follow suit, forcing Bernardo Álvarez, the longtime Venezuelan ambassador to the United States with extensive experience with the petroleum sector and a participant in the *Patria Para Todos* political party that supported Chávez, to return home. Nevertheless, during this nine-month period, diplomatic relations were never broken between the two countries: the embassies remained open and lower-level officials performed routine tasks.

Despite the mutual expulsion, Duddy and Álvarez continued to operate in their countries' foreign affairs. Duddy maintained a low profile, enabling the United States to maintain critical activities such as trade and public diplomacy. Álvarez managed to remain effective in Washington despite the constraints imposed by the Chávez government. The mutual expulsion can thus be viewed as an expression of Chávez's continuous efforts to defy the United States on the international stage through dramatic public gestures.

With the election of Barack Obama in November 2008, Chávez lost his favorite foil in George W. Bush. From a new administration an opportunity emerged to reduce some of the bilateral tensions and to explore areas of cooperation. Obama's notably more moderate tone and conciliatory approach, as well as his cordial encounter and handshake with Chávez at the April 2009 Summit of the Americas meeting in Trinidad and Tobago, raised expectations for tempering the adversarial relationship. At the meeting, both sides agreed to restore ambassadorial relations, a decision to be implemented in June.

But the thaw would not last long. Even though the agreement was fulfilled and both ambassadors returned to their posts, two issues in particular created further strains between Washington and Caracas, leading Chávez to employ the rhetoric against Obama previously reserved for his predecessor. The June 2009 coup in Honduras, when Chávez ally Manuel Zelaya was removed from elected office by the military, stoked the embers of tension as Washington was much more willing to accommodate and recognize the newly elected Honduran government than Caracas would have liked.

The signing of a ten-year defense cooperation pact between Washington and Bogotá, which provided for US access to seven Colombian military bases, generated a predictably strong reaction from Chávez who once again raised the specter of the United States attacking Venezuela. Washington had failed to adequately prepare the diplomatic groundwork for such a sensitive accord—any agreement involving the US military in the region is bound to arouse suspicions—leading Chávez to publicly question whether Obama was any different from Bush.

Underlying strains in US-Venezuela relations became especially salient in the realm of global geopolitics during the first Obama administration. During that period, Venezuela and Iran deepened their alliance, which became a heightened concern given Obama's firm stand on Iran's nuclear program. Senior US officials also expressed worry about a possible arms race in the region, provoked in part by Venezuela's buying spree from the Russians

(Darenblum 2008). In the end, it was Chávez's international alliances—his friendships with governments seen as unfriendly to the United States—rather than any antidemocratic actions in Venezuela, or even positions on hemispheric issues, that caused the most concern in the Obama administration.

In late 2010, the diplomatic relationship took another turn for the worse. In June Obama nominated Larry Palmer, a career foreign service officer, former ambassador to Honduras and president of the Inter-American Foundation, to become the next US ambassador to Caracas at the end of Duddy's term. While the choice was certainly made after consultation with the foreign ministry in Caracas, Palmer infuriated Chávez with his written responses to questions posed by Senator Richard Lugar, senior Republican on the Committee on Foreign Affairs, during his confirmation hearing.

Palmer referred to the "low morale" in the Venezuelan armed forces and expressed certainty about the ties of senior officials in the Chávez administration, and of the president himself, to FARC guerrillas operating in Venezuela (Senate Foreign Relations Committee 2010). Outraged, Chávez told the news media that, if Palmer were confirmed, he would not be allowed to take up his post. Yet, the Obama administration refused to accede to Chávez's demand to withdraw Palmer's nomination and the situation simmered for a few months. Finally, on December 28, 2010, Chávez officially denied formal diplomatic *agrément* to the nomination. The next day, the United States revoked Venezuelan ambassador Bernardo Álvarez's visa. Once again, the two countries lost the critical diplomatic tie of ambassadorial representation.

Even so, the US embassy in Caracas continued to operate and in 2011 the Venezuelan government allowed Jim Derham, a career diplomat who had served in Havana, to enter the country as *chargé d'affaires*. In May 2014, the Venezuelan government named Maximilian Arveláez as *chargé d'affaires* in Washington. Despite some steps toward normalization, in the context of continuing bilateral strains it has been difficult to restore a mutual ambassadorial presence.

Although the situation with the United States remained chilly, it is striking that Colombian-Venezuelan relations have enjoyed a notable rapprochement since President Juan Manuel Santos took office in August 2010. While Álvaro Uribe's parting act as president was to denounce Venezuela before the OAS for allegedly harboring FARC terrorist camps (causing Chávez to once again recall all diplomatic personnel from Colombia), one of Santos's first moves was to visit Venezuela, which allowed for the reestablishment of diplomatic relations.

The two subsequently met several times in Colombia and Venezuela to strengthen the significant bonds both countries enjoyed as a result of their common border. Both presidents' desire to improve their countries' images abroad by taking independent and pragmatic stances in the conflict appears to illustrate a decline of US soft power in the region. Chávez's ability to forge relationships with other Latin American leaders of varying political tendencies enabled him to garner support at moments when Venezuela and the United States were at a diplomatic standstill and thus effectively to dilute US opposition.

Soft-Balancing: Social Power and Regional Integration

Not only was the US-Venezuelan relationship strained, but Chávez found other ways to undercut US influence in the international arena without direct confrontation. Such a tactic is known in international relations parlance as "soft-balancing." Chávez often pursued his "revolutionary" international ambitions in conventional Venezuelan style: through the distribution of petroleum wealth. Another soft-balancing act consisted in spearheading regional integration schemes in the Americas that explicitly excluded the United States. The results of this approach were mixed, but certainly represented a strong challenge to US clout in Latin America.

Following his election Chávez spent nearly $3.6 billion per year abroad, with roughly $3 billion going directly to his Latin America and Caribbean neighbors (Forero 2006). The spending varied from buying Argentine debt to donating medical supplies to Nicaragua. The bulk of the spending, however, was in the form of development aid or petroleum subsidies. While these massive expenditures can certainly be viewed as part of Chávez's dream of spearheading the type of Latin American unity that his hero Bolívar only dreamed of achieving, they served a secondary purpose as well, which Javier Corrales defined as a new type of soft power, called "social power." This concept constitutes "generous handouts . . . peppered with pro-poor, distribution-prone discourse," which characterized Chávez's dissemination of petrowealth as an attempt to soft-balance US influence in the region (Corrales 2009, 97).

One of Chávez's largest projects was Petrocaribe, an oil agreement with eighteen nations in Central America and the Caribbean. The agreement allows countries to purchase oil from Venezuela under a preferential payment system that provides low-cost, long-term financing and allows for payment in kind with products such as bananas, rice, and sugar. The assistance amounts to an estimated \$1.7 billion annually, putting it, according to some estimates, on par in real terms with the Marshall Plan to reconstruct Europe after World War II (Corrales 2009, 100). Chávez not only provided international aid through these types of multinational agreements but also supported specific groups in the region to gain influence. He publicly supported candidates in foreign elections and also used funds to try to influence elections. Before the 2006 Nicaraguan presidential election, Chávez donated fertilizer and subsidized oil to Sandinista-controlled districts (Bustamante and Sweig 2008, 241). This contribution was clearly a blow to the United States, which has traditionally opposed the Sandinistas.

Venezuela's relationship with Cuba serves as another example of Chávez's large-scale spending abroad. Chávez shipped more than 100,000 barrels of subsidized crude oil per day to Cuba, providing a critical lifeline to an otherwise stagnant economy. Cuba reciprocated by sending thousands of doctors to Venezuela under programs sponsored by Chávez. The two countries share fundamental ideologies that oppose the United States, which makes the Cuba-Venezuela relationship much deeper than one based just on financial support.

Soft-balancing has also been achieved through Chávez's conception of regional institutions that exclude the United States and Canada. While these organizations seek to fulfill Bolívar's vision of a unified Latin America, they serve the secondary, and perhaps more important, purpose of curtailing "Yankee" influence.

The Bolivarian Alliance for the Americas (or ALBA as it is known by its Spanish acronym: Alianza Bolivariana para los Pueblos de Nuestra América), for example, has its roots in a 2004 bilateral agreement between Cuba and Venezuela. Bolivia, Nicaragua, Ecuador, Dominica, St. Vincent and the Grenadines, Antigua and Barbuda, and Honduras subsequently joined the group meant as an economic and political counterweight to the US-created Free Trade Area of the Americas (FTAA). The alliance has achieved little, though its members claim that trade among them has increased significantly, especially since the introduction of the *sucre*, a regional currency used in transactions among member states.

On December 2–3, 2011, the inaugural summit of the Community of Latin American and Caribbean States (CELAC) was held in Caracas. Stemming from the twenty-third summit of the Rio Group in 2010, the new body included all of the nations of the Americas except Canada and the United States. Chávez, with conservative counterpart Chilean President Sebastián

Piñera, was named cochair of the body and presided over what he described as "the most important political event to have occurred in our America in 100 years or more" ("Latin American Integration" 2011). Many analysts regarded the summit as yet another addition to a cornucopia of integration attempts that have quickly gone dormant. However, considering the participation of every country in the Western Hemisphere except the United States and Canada, in conjunction with the declining status of the widely questioned and defunded OAS, CELAC still sends an important message regarding the diminishing role of the United States in Latin America.

Chávez's goal of gaining more influence, particularly in the form of soft power, in Latin America also led to the government's launching of Telesur, a media broadcasting company with ownership shared among Latin American countries. Considered a reaction to Western dominance over media in the region, Telesur "advocates and demonstrates independence from corporate news programming and a pro-social agenda" (Hayden 2012, 163) and has been employed by the Venezuelan government as a public diplomacy tool.

Fluid Relations: Oil, Culture, and Public Diplomacy

While clear that Venezuela and the United States are adversarial diplomatically, they appear close when only considering ties forged through public diplomacy. Mutual dependence on Venezuela's enormous petroleum reserves forged deep commercial ties that paved the way for both official and unofficial cultural exchange efforts. Although this aspect of the US-Venezuela relationship is often overshadowed by conflict, it constitutes an important factor that merits attention.

Petroleum Exports

Teodoro Petkoff, one of Venezuela's leading intellectuals and editor of the daily newspaper *Tal Cual*, has quipped that while Venezuela has a strained relationship with the State Department, it enjoys relatively good relations with the Commerce Department. These remarks illustrate the fundamental dilemma confronting Washington in its relations with Venezuela: heightened political tensions and deep mistrust coexist with a robust commercial relationship.

Indeed, a striking irony is that Venezuela came to rely more on the US market for its oil during Chávez's rule than it did before Chávez; roughly 60 percent of its oil exports go to the United States. The country's state-run oil and natural gas company, Petróleos de Venezuela SA (PdVSA), created in the 1970s, is the country's largest employer and accounts for about one-third of the country's gross domestic product, 50 percent of the government's revenue, and 80 percent of Venezuela's export earnings (Alvarez and Hanson 2009).

While Chávez tried to shift more of Venezuela's oil exports to China and elsewhere, his success in diversifying partners was modest at best. The fact remains that the vast infrastructure and refineries are ideally suited to Venezuela's hard crude reserves and present technical and economic obstacles to moving the market away from the United States. Despite Chávez's clear intentions to reduce vulnerabilities to a decision in Washington to cut off oil sales, it was difficult to undo the network of CITGO stations—a Venezuelan subsidiary—that operate across the United States. (In August 2014, the Venezuelan government, in an increasingly tight fiscal situation, announced its intention to sell CITGO.)

For the United States, in contrast, the dependency on Venezuelan oil is less acute, though still significant. In 2010 the United States received approximately 8 percent of its imported oil supplies from Venezuela, a level that had dropped from about 13 percent in 2004 ("Country Analysis Briefs: Venezuela" 2007). In 2006, Senator Lugar requested a special study by the Congressional Research Service to determine the feasibility of the United States replacing Venezuelan oil in the event that Chávez cut off supply ("Energy Security" 2006). Though the US government surely developed contingency plans to deal with such a possibility, to date there has been no serious policy proposal by any administration to take such a step. For the time being, the oil is flowing without interruption from Venezuela to the United States, and the dependence is mutual.

Cultural Exchange
The United States' oil interests have significantly shaped the US historic role and involvement in Venezuela. The weight of the oil question in the bilateral relationship is revealed in a memoir by a former press attaché in the US embassy in the 1950s (Amerson 1995). Before Chávez, Venezuela's abundant oil supply, the democratic façade maintained by *puntofijismo*, and the modern infrastructure and social policies made possible through oil rents evoked a highly favorable image among most Americans. This image was only sharpened when Venezuela was compared to its impoverished Latin American

neighbors suffering under repressive military dictatorships and violent leftist guerrilla movements. Indeed, many in the United States referred to Venezuelan "exceptionalism" and were drawn to a society that, unlike much of the rest of the region, seemed relatively free of class and racial conflict (Tinker Salas 2007). The severe violence and chaos provoked by economic adjustment measures in the late 1980s—known as the Caracazo—surprised many US analysts who had tended to marvel at Venezuela's tranquility. In this picture, it is hard to overstate the impact of oil in the country that, according to Miguel Tinker Salas, "not only sustained the Venezuelan economy, but . . . also shaped the political attitudes and social values that held sway over important sectors of the population" (Tinker Salas, 35). Throughout the decades, US oil companies worked with Venezuelan governments to maintain their presence and advance their interests, serving as the main prism through which Venezuelan society was perceived and understood in the United States.

The United States' petro-interests in Venezuela were accompanied by broad cultural exchanges and interactions between both societies over many years. Such large companies as Creole Petroleum and Shell Oil established "oil camps" in production cities such as Maracaibo in the 1940s. These housed not only the largest US expatriate community in Latin America—sent to manage the companies' extractive industries—but also Venezuelan nationals who worked to sustain day-to-day operations. This coexistence allowed thousands of professional Venezuelans to experience the "American way of life." Looking to prevent nationalization of the country's oil wealth, the companies promoted a "corporate culture" in the camps, encouraging their Venezuelan employees to exhibit loyalty to the company and highlighting the promise of petroleum exports. The workers came to view cooperation with multinational corporations and, consequently, the United States as essential to the livelihood of the country as a whole (Tinker Salas 2005).

Whether a result of multinational corporations' efforts at shaping political views or of the cultural exchange promoted by their mere presence, it is clear that Venezuelans historically have generally held a positive impression of the United States that continues to this day. According to the 2009 Latin American Barometer survey, nearly 80 percent of Venezuelans have a favorable image of the United States. While half of the Venezuelans had a favorable opinion of Chávez, some 62 percent had a favorable opinion toward US President Obama ("*Informe Latinobarómetro*" 2009). Moreover, according to a 2007 poll from Hinterlaces, 75 percent of Venezuelans are opposed to a violent confrontation with the United States ("Monitor Socio-Politico" 2007). To be sure, Venezuelans, as much as the rest of Latin America, did not like Bush and strongly oppose unilateral US policies, but the sentiments among most citizens regarding culture and society remain generally sympathetic.

In addition to favorable attitudes toward the United States, the presence of American multinationals has encouraged the adoption of several items highly associated with US culture in Venezuelan society. Before the petroleum industry was nationalized in 1978, more imported foods and luxury goods could be found in Venezuela than anywhere else in Latin America. *Hamburguesas*, variations on the American hamburger, remain a mainstay of Venezuelan street food. Furthermore, Venezuelans maintain their preference for US-made goods, especially technology. Despite Chávez's attempts to restrict imports, many upper- and middle-class Venezuelans regularly travel to Miami to purchase the latest laptop computer or video-game console. Venezuelans are as addicted to communication as Americans. Indeed, 70 percent of all Blackberry SmartPhones sold in Latin America are sold in Venezuela (López 2009).

Baseball remains a highly popular sport in Venezuela, generally favored—unlike in most other Latin American countries—over soccer. Curiously, Chávez and Fidel Castro shared an intense passion for the national pastime of the country they regarded as imperial and whose influence they actively resisted. Venezuela's baseball league remains a source of cultural exchange as dozens of American players travel south every winter to improve their prospects by playing a short season with a Venezuelan team.

Conversely, there are currently more than fifty Venezuelan baseball players in the US major leagues. Many teams maintain recruitment and training camps in Venezuela to scout and polish promising talent. Some of the most successful Venezuelan players have established foundations and community centers in their hometowns to provide social assistance. Many even return to Venezuela to play in the winter leagues, further facilitating mutual diffusion of culture. Although political tensions between the two governments occasionally cause difficulties in cooperation on sports-related activities, this channel has been used to sustain and enlarge societal connections.

Public Diplomacy

The inroads created by cultural exchange between the two countries helped produce a ripe climate for public diplomacy. While generally conducted according to a strategy devised by a country's foreign ministry, new public diplomacy—actions by nonstate actors designed to foment goodwill toward the actors' home coun- try—is also possible. The efforts of the US-based oil corporations in Venezu- ela to encourage company loyalty among Venezuelan workers from the 1940s through the 1970s constitute a salient example. This is an especially important tool for dealing with adversarial states if an ambassadorial or diplomatic presence becomes infeasible. Given the expulsion of the US ambassador in Caracas, the task of US diplomats and citizens conducting public diplomacy in Venezuela is more important than ever. The deep-rooted cultural connections the two coun- tries enjoy provide considerable opportunities in this regard.

The United States maintains a large and active public affairs section in the embassy in Caracas that engages in a wide range of classic public diplo- macy activities. Given the frequent travel of many upper- and middle-class Venezuelans to the United States, English-language classes offered at three Bi-National Centers in Caracas, Maracaibo, and Mérida are extremely popu- lar. Low-income high school students are given the opportunity to study Eng- lish and US culture with English Teaching Assistantship Fulbright grantees through the English Access Microscholarship Program.

The US embassy also offers many Venezuelans the opportunity to visit the United States. The International Visitor Leadership Program allows Venezu- elan professionals to travel to the United States to learn about their US coun- terparts while the Youth Ambassadors Program sends high school students to the United States for three weeks of study. The affinity felt for the United States by many Venezuelans makes these programs extremely popular and competitive. Furthermore, the United States frequently funds US musicians, artists, and intellectuals to travel to Venezuela and share their crafts at con- certs and exhibitions.

Perhaps unsurprisingly, baseball is one of the most important instruments of public diplomacy at the disposal of US diplomats in Venezuela. The Baseball Friendship Program sends retired major league baseball players to Venezuela to run monthly baseball clinics for young people. Moreover, the US embassy frequently posts podcasts of interviews with Spanish-speaking major league players on its website and maintains an active baseball section on its site.

In response to US public diplomacy efforts, Chávez sought to build a con- stituency for his Bolivarian Revolution in the United States. He did so in part by providing low-cost heating oil to low-income US families through a spe- cial CITGO program. The effort was launched in 2005–2006 in thirteen US states, and it was aimed at demonstrating Chávez's humanitarian concern for the poor in the United States while improving his image. Joseph Kennedy, the former congressman and son of Robert Kennedy, was a key proponent of Chávez's initiative. Some members of the US Congress, such as Bill Delahunt, a Democrat from Massachusetts, were also involved. In this regard, Chávez resembled Eva Perón, who in the 1950s sent used clothing to poor children in cities across the United States.

It is clear, however, that Venezuela's public diplomacy efforts are much less institutionalized than those undertaken by the United States. The CITGO program illustrates Chávez's astute "counter-public diplomacy" instruments used against the United States that chiefly revolved around his charismatic persona and ideology. Indeed, the Venezuelan Foreign Ministry's professionalism declined during the Chávez era as the president largely asserted close control over the ministry's activities.

Chávez's penetration and deinstitutionalization of the foreign ministry undermined US public diplomacy efforts in Venezuela that had been previously tolerated or even encouraged. In 2007 Venezuelans became increasingly unwilling to participate in US embassy–funded exchange programs when the US Congress investigated several Venezuelan grantees who were accused of spying. While this investigation was eventually dropped, in 2011 the Foreign Ministry declined to issue visas to seven Fulbright English teaching assistants who were scheduled to take up posts throughout Venezuela. These measures were without precedent and risked the loss of important US-directed programs enjoyed by many Venezuelans.

Concluding Thoughts

Chávez scarcely disguised his intention to be "president for life" of Venezuela. Through a national referendum in 2008 he secured popular approval for such a prospect. But Chávez's autocratic tendencies resulted in a number of severe economic and institutional crises that raised serious questions about his ability to govern and fomented discontent among previous supporters. While inflation reached record highs and government attempts at imposing price controls only caused shortages of basic necessities, the country became widely regarded as one of the most insecure countries in the world and the most violent in South America.

In the October 2012 elections Chávez was reelected for another six-year term, even though opposition parties united to hold a primary and select one candidate to challenge his long-term rule. Adding an aspect of uncertainty was Chávez's diagnosis of cancer. After several rounds of chemotherapy, Chávez claimed he was cancer-free but his health continued to deteriorate. Rather than projecting weakness, Chávez's cancer and limited appearances garnered sympathy at home and abroad. Chávez died on March 5, 2013.

Venezuela posed a serious challenge for the United States. Washington's approach to Chávez to that point had been fairly inconsistent: at times aggressive, while in other cases notably passive. To its credit, the United States had learned over time to avoid reacting to Chávez's inflammatory rhetoric and proclamations. There had been an all-too-frequent tendency to preach and demonize Chávez, which typically played right into his hands (Shifter 2007, 7–8). This case, involving such a charismatic and wily adversary like Chávez, shows that public diplomacy can best be conceptualized as a fiercely competitive back-and-forth and not as a one-way street.

Nonetheless, the United States can be more strategic and skillful in carrying out a more coherent diplomatic course toward Venezuela. Washington can take better advantage of the longstanding ties of friendship between the two societies, as well as their shared history. Under such circumstances, a diplomatic mission and an ambassadorial presence with personnel able to respond in a sophisticated manner to Venezuelan society's needs and preferences are essential.

However tempting it might be, the United States should be careful about undertaking "democracy promotion" activities in such a setting. In the past, these activities have all too often had an ideological content linked to the political opposition's agenda. They have sometimes not been constructive and in fact only bolstered Chávez's political standing, and could well have a similar effect under *Chavista* successors. Instead, the United States should continue its efforts to undertake public diplomacy given the precedent for mutual cultural understanding and the successes that these initiatives have enjoyed in the past. Especially in light of the Venezuelan government's assaults in recent years on such efforts, those practicing public diplomacy—government officials and US citizens alike—should maintain a calm and pragmatic demeanor and focus on the task at hand.

New communication technologies enhance the ability of the United States to deal effectively with, and connect to, significant sectors of Venezuelan society. Chávez himself was a superb communicator and effective counterpuncher. His weekly television program *Aló Presidente* was Venezuela's equivalent of

FDR's "fireside chats." Chávez regularly used Twitter to broadcast messages and had more than three million followers. Venezuelan society is uniquely ready and eager to embrace the most up-to-date communications, which offers enormous potential for a wise public diplomacy strategy on the part of the United States. The US embassy has made ample use of social networking websites such as Facebook and particularly Twitter, with 17,000 Venezuelans following the embassy's updates (Yepsen 2012). Despite the legacy of Chávez's political control in Venezuela, the country's new leadership would surely have a hard time cutting off such connections.

In April 2013, Chávez's former foreign minister and vice president, Nicolás Maduro, was elected as president, suggesting that *Chavismo* lives on. Maduro's political abilities, the price of oil, the nature of the opposition, and a host of other factors will be important in shaping the political landscape. Caracas's few friendly gestures coupled with aggressive rhetoric attest to how mistrust in bilateral relations with the United States has not diminished. For now, hardliners in Caracas and in Washington make it difficult to reduce the enormous strain. Still, depending on how the politics in both countries evolve, US and Venezuelan leaders would do well to capitalize on a rich history of economic and cultural ties and to rebuild the robust cooperation that characterized the two countries' relations for decades.

As for the three basic variants of public diplomacy described in Wiseman's Introduction—"traditional State Department," "whole-of-government," and "new public diplomacy" conducted by both state and nonstate actors—the Venezuelan case is relevant and offers key insights. The role of a charismatic and mercurial personality, with a lot of money to spend, leads the weaker state that attempts—sometimes successfully, sometimes not—to employ public diplomacy instruments to throw its more powerful adversary off-balance. The case highlights that, although "traditional State Department" public diplomacy has often proved very difficult and frustrating, other parts of the US government as well as some nongovernmental instruments of new public diplomacy, such as parts of the private sector, have helped prevent bilateral relations from getting out of control. Understanding how the wide range of public diplomacy dimensions have played out is crucial to devising a constructive effort for more effective diplomacy between the United States and Venezuela over the long term.

References

Alvarez, Cesar J., and Stephanie Hanson. 2009. "Venezuela's Oil-Based Economy." *Council on Foreign Relations,* February 9. Accessed August 6, 2012 at http://www.cfr.org/economics/venezuelas-oil-based-economy/p12089.

Amerson, Robert. 1995. *How Democracy Triumphed over Dictatorship: Public Diplomacy in Venezuela.* Washington, DC: American University Press.

Bustamante, Michael J., and Julia E. Sweig. 2008. "Buena Vista Solidarity and the Axis of Aid: Cuban and Venezuelan Public Diplomacy." *ANNALS of the American Academy of Political and Social Science* 616: 223–256.

Corrales, Javier. 2009. "Using Social Power to Balance Soft Power: Venezuela's Foreign Policy." *Washington Quarterly* 32, no. 4: 97–114.

Corrales, Javier, and Michael Penfold. 2010. *Dragon in the Tropics: Hugo Chávez and the Political Economy of Revolution in Venezuela.* Washington, DC: Brookings Institution Press.

Darenblum, Jaime. 2008. "A Perfect Storm in Latin America: How Will Obama Handle Economic and Security Challenges South of the Border." *Weekly Standard Online.* Accessed December 10, 2011 at http://www.hudson.org/content/researchattachments/attachment/684/daremblum_-_final_lo-res.pdf.

"Energy Security: Issues Related to Potential Reductions in Venezuelan Oil Production." Government Accountability Office, June 2006. Accessed December 10, 2011 at http://www.gao.gov/new.items/d06668.pdf.

Forero, Juan. 2006. "Chavez, Seeking Foreign Allies, Spends Billions." *New York Times,* April 4. Accessed August 2, 2012 at http://www.nytimes.com/2006/04/04/world/americas/04venezuela.html

Garcia Marquez, Gabriel. 2000. "The Two Faces of Hugo Chávez." *NACLA Report on the Americas* 033: 6.

Golinger, Eva. 2006. *The Chávez Code: Cracking US Intervention in Venezuela.* New York: Olive Branch.

Hayden, Craig. 2012. "Venezuela: Telesure and the Artillery of Ideas." In *The Rhetoric of Soft Power: Public Diplomacy in Global Contexts.* Lexington Books. Lanham, MD: Rowman & Littlefield, 131–156.

Hawkin, Kirk. 2010. *Venezuela's Chavismo and Populism in Comparative Perspective.* Cambridge: Cambridge University Press.

Hoge, Warren. 2006. "Venezuelan's Diatribe at U.N. May Have Backfired." *New York Times,* October 25. Accessed August 2, 2012 at http://www.nytimes.com/2006/10/25/world/americas/25nations.html.

"Informe Latinobarómetro 2009." *Corporación Latinobarómetro.* www.latinobarometro.org.

"Latin American Integration: Peaks and Troughs." 2011. *The Economist,* November 26. Accessed August 7, 2012 at http://www.economist.com/node/21540319.

López, Jaime. 2009. "El socialismo de la 'Blackberry.'" *El Mundo,* September 30. Accessed August 7, 2012 at http://www.elmundo.es/elmundo/2009/09/30/navegante/1254313889.html.

"Monitor Socio-Politico: Tendencias y Coyuntura." 2007. *Hinterlaces.* Accessed August 7, 2012 at http://doc.noticias24.com/0707/hinter14.pdf.

Neuman, William. 2012. "US Orders Venezuelan Envoy in Miami to Leave." *New York Times,* January 8. Accessed August 2, 2012 at http://www.nytimes.com/2012/01/09/world/americas/us-expels-venezuelan-diplomat-from-miami.html?_r=2&emc=eta1.&

Senate Foreign Relations Committee. 2010. "Questions for the Record Submitted to Ambassador-Designate Larry Leon Palmer by Senator Richard G. Lugar (#1)." July 27. Accessed August 6, 2012 at http://www.papelesdesociedad.info/IMG/pdf/docs21.pdf.

Rohter, Larry. 2001. "US, Irritated by Criticism, Calls Envoy Home from Venezuela." *New York Times,* November 3. Accessed August 2, 2012 at http://www.nytimes.com/2001/11/03/world/us-irritated-by-criticism-calls-envoy-home-from-venezuela.html?emc=eta1.

Shifter, Michael. 2006. "In Search of Hugo Chávez." *Foreign Affairs* 85, no. 3: 45–59.

———. 2007. "Hugo Chavez: A Test for US Policy." *Inter-American Dialogue Special Report,* March 7.

Tinker Salas, Miguel. 2007. "US Oil Companies in Venezuela." In *Venezuela: Hugo Chávez and the Decline of an "Exceptional Democracy."* Steve Ellner and Miguel Tinker Salas ed. Lanham, MD: Rowman & Littlefield, 35–59.

———. 2005. "Fueling Concern: The Role of Oil in Venezuela." *Harvard International Review,* 26/4.

US Energy Information Administration. 2007. "Country Analysis Briefs: Venezuela." March. Accessed August 7, 2012 at *http://www.eia.gov/countries/country-data.cfm?fips=VE.*

"Venezuela's Chavez Warns Colombia Could become Another Vietnam." 2000. CNN, August 30. Accessed Aug. 7, 2010 at http://www.cnn.com/2000/WORLD/americas/08/30/brazil.chavez.vietnam.ap/.

Yepsen, Erika A. 2012. *Practicing Successful Twitter Diplomacy: A Model and Case Study of US Efforts in Venezuela.* CPD Perspectives on Public Diplomacy. USC Center on Public Diplomacy, Paper 6.

Weiner, Tim. 2002. "The Nation: Latin Dance; A Coup by Any Other Name." *New York Times,* April 14. Accessed August 2, 2012 at http://www.nytimes.com/2002/04/14/weekinreview/the-nation-latin-dance-a-coup-by-any-other-name.html?emc=eta1

CONCLUSION

Geoffrey Wiseman

A S STATED IN THE INTRODUCTION, GOVERNMENTS
have essentially two choices when dealing with adversarial
states: isolate them or engage them. For nearly one hundred years, this
choice has been at the center of the United States' foreign policy, as evidenced in its relations with a group of adversarial states that have frustrated US foreign policy goals for extended periods and in different ways:
the USSR/Russia, the PRC/China, North Korea, Vietnam, Libya, Iran,
Syria, Cuba, and Venezuela. Our primary focus in this book has been on
evaluating an important policy puzzle: When the US government pursues
such wider strategies as containment or deterrence, which involve policies to isolate the government of an adversarial state—manifested by the
absence or limited presence of official diplomatic relations—how (and
how effectively) does the United States go about seeking to influence or
engage that state's public so that it will influence its own government to
adopt less hostile and more favorable views of US foreign policies specifically and of American society in general? Stating the puzzle in this way
implies that engaging a foreign public as part of wider strategies of *regime
change* (ousting an adversarial government from power), as distinct from
regime behavior change (incentivizing an adversarial government to comply with international norms), must be seen not as public diplomacy but as
something else altogether, since it does not seek to change policies but to
change a government.

We have summarized the findings of the nine case studies in terms of the four subquestions set out in the Introduction:

1. When diplomatic relations are limited, how does the United States try to *influence* publics in adversarial states?

2. Does cutting or limiting diplomatic ties contribute to wider strategic goals or actually *damage* US interests?

3. When diplomatic relations are limited, what are the *challenges* for public diplomacy in adversarial states?

4. When diplomatic relations are limited, what are the *opportunities* for public diplomacy in adversarial states?

When Diplomatic Relations Are Limited, How Does the United States Try to *Influence* Publics in Adversarial States?

In support of broader foreign policy objectives, the cases analyzed in this book show that the United States uses a diverse range of instruments in its attempts to influence the publics in states it views as adversarial. Far from cutting all ties, Washington in every case has sought to influence the adversarial state's public through various forms of public diplomacy. Even when the United States cuts all formal ties, certain contacts often continue without direct government involvement, including travel and trade (where no trade embargo exists), the work of nongovernmental organizations (NGOs), certain individual relationships, and, more recently, communication via the Internet.

At the most basic level, the United States uses personal contacts between diplomats (when there is some limited diplomatic presence or in third country capitals when there is no presence), politicians, businesspeople, and military officers as instruments for public diplomacy with adversarial states. The range of these contacts encompasses diplomats (such as George Kennan in the USSR), American oil workers in Venezuela, NGO employees in Syria, and personal relations between leaders (such as those highlighted in the USSR/Russia case between Mikhail Gorbachev and Margaret Thatcher in the 1980s). Public affairs officers, the official purveyors of US public diplomacy, also play a role, as mentioned in the Syria case. Individual relationships help maintain at least limited communication, allowing some information gathering to continue and forming the basis, such as in the Vietnam and China cases, for future confidence building and closer ties when—and if—relations improve between the United States and the adversarial state.

Government, NGO, and privately funded exchange programs in the arts, sciences, and sports are helpful instruments for US public diplomacy as, for example, in the USSR, Vietnam, and China cases. These programs provide some communication between adversaries and, when developed during times of tension, often can—just like individual ties and even friendships between leaders—form the basis for future normalization of relations and improved ties. The dense network of exchanges and collaborations begun in the 1970s between China and the United States formed the foundation for cooperation in the 1980s. Visiting professorships, joint scientific organizations, and scholarships (such as in the case of Vietnam) have enhanced public diplomacy's capacity to influence under the apolitical "cover" of education and research programs. The involvement of many technical agencies in this process in China foreshadowed whole-of-government diplomacy. English-language schools, such as those in Syria, played a key role in public diplomacy by keeping communication lines open and providing information on the local situation.

Whereas lower-level contacts can form a web of relationships supportive of the future normalization of relations, high-level visits, such as Nixon's trip to China in 1972 and Deng Xiaoping's US tour in 1979, can lead to greater opportunities for public diplomacy. The visit itself often gives the US leader an opportunity to communicate with the adversarial state's public, either directly or through symbolic activities (such as attending sporting or cultural events to show respect for the other country's culture). Additionally, such visits may lead both parties to be more open to other collaborations and ties. These visits can lead to the forming of friendships between leaders that can aid diplomacy, as mentioned above, and may go some way in "de-demonizing" leaders, a good example being Deng's visit. Oddly, however, as seen in the China case, US attempts to use US-China summitry to advance American values have been far less successful. Still, most high-level visits cannot be conceptually considered primarily or inherently as acts of public diplomacy; they are instead (at least those that are not secret) acts of "diplomacy with a public dimension" (in Bruce Gregory's helpful phrase). Madeleine Albright's visit to Pyongyang in the closing months of the Clinton administration (from the North Korea case) and President Obama's June 2009 Cairo speech to the Muslim world (not included in our cases) are two exceptions, but both appear to confirm the general observation.

Nongovernmental organizations, which are often outside the constraints of direct US government support, are an important means of contact with foreign publics, especially in the "new public diplomacy" approach. The North Korea case illustrates how NGOs can succeed, albeit on a limited basis, even in the most closed societies and where the adversarial state forbids programs supported by the US government. However, as cautioned by the Russian case, any shift toward a more NGO-based public diplomacy should be clearheaded and not romanticize about NGOs and their ability to affect other state's governments or publics (Halliday 2001; Bob 2005).

Track two diplomacy—informal interactions involving nonofficials and/or officials acting in a personal capacity—can provide another avenue of contact. In the Libya case, track two diplomacy pushed the agenda forward toward better relations between the United States and Libya. Track two diplomacy also played a role in North Korea but with less success, partly because North Korea proved to be even more suspicious than Qadhafi's Libya of the outside world.

Tourism and business contacts can be an important avenue for public diplomacy. Some states, such as South Vietnam, attempted to encourage tourism even during times of war. In the case of Cuba, even limited US tourism to the island helped spread US values and culture; in the case of Venezuela, US oil workers helped create a web of relationships between the two countries that continues despite strained relations between the two governments.

Although scholars are often viewed as being detached and separated from the real world, they, too, can influence public diplomacy. If they are allowed to visit or to conduct research in an adversarial state, their presence can be viewed as a form of public diplomacy, as shown by the Syria case. Furthermore, they can provide information back home about an adversarial state, and their work sometimes feeds back to the adversarial state, potentially influencing events there. In the Soviet case, Stephen Cohen's research on the Soviet Union of the 1920s and 1930s attracted extensive interest and affected thinking in the Soviet Union, and Robert Tucker's insights on Stalin (written at Princeton University) played a role in glasnost-era reconsiderations of the Soviet past.

Culture—in the form of books, television, music, art, theater, fashion, and movies—can play a role in how the United States is perceived by an adversarial state's public. Much American cultural outreach has little to do with the government, yet American culture has been dominant enough to permeate every continent. This dominance, from the 1950s onward, often makes it easy for the US government to conduct public diplomacy, since the "product" or "brand"—America—is already well liked in many regions (Anholt 2010), even in parts of the Islamic world where American culture is often pitted against Islamic culture. Change is afoot, however, as American culture becomes increasingly eclipsed by a more global (albeit still a consumer) culture. And the United States will find it more difficult to conduct public diplomacy as the "product" being sold becomes less popular internationally. Even so, the Iran case shows the power of American culture: a three-decade absence of diplomatic ties and tensions has somehow *raised* Iranian opinions of American culture and values. This suggests that the impact of public diplomacy must be assessed within a broader and ever-expanding spectrum of cultural interaction, even where direct, official contacts remain constrained or even nonexistent.

Additionally, the United States has used more traditional mass-communication methods to reach the public in adversarial states. In the Soviet case, the United States created radio stations to reach foreign publics, including the Voice of America (VOA) and Radio Free Europe. This model later spread technologically to television and geographically to Asia, the Middle East, and Latin America as the United States attempted to influence the publics of adversarial states, such as China, Libya, and Venezuela. More recently, the Internet, Twitter, and Facebook have provided new tools in the arsenal of public diplomacy. English argues in his chapter that such technology has rendered the VOA and radio-based communications something of a Cold War relic. And Ross suggests in his chapter that VOA broadcasts may have worsened relations between the US and China after the 1989 Tiananmen massacre. That said, VOA's supporters point with some justification to its recent reinvention as a multimedia broadcasting organization. The Internet and cell phones have played a part as a means of spreading information and enhancing communication between the United States and all of the studied states, the degree of success of the message reaching the intended audience depending of course on the message itself but also on how well the adversarial government is able to limit its citizens' access to the Internet. In addition to attempting to communicate via these media, the US Department of State has focused on increasing access to the Internet for the public in adversarial states, such as Iran, Syria, and Cuba (Ross 2012.) Such efforts are fraught with peril, however, when the regime is particularly anti-American, since those who take advantage of the US-provided access may be singled out as dissidents and punished. This suggests that NGOs and private groups may serve far better than US government programs as avenues for attempting to increase access to the Internet, since private groups are less likely to be labeled as enemies by the adversarial state.

Economic and humanitarian aid can also be a form of public diplomacy. The United States tried to use this type of diplomacy in Vietnam and China as relations improved. Washington also used it in North Korea, albeit with little success.

One interesting aspect of the nine cases is how seldom public affairs officers (PAOs) are mentioned. This can be attributed to three factors: the academic professional background of all but one of the book's contributors; the generally low-profile, facilitating role played by PAOs; and (a key theme of this book) the absence of in-country, diplomatic missions, where PAOs normally operate, often with significant impact. In Syria before the outbreak of the civil war, where there was a diplomatic presence, PAOs were found to be active and effective. In other instances, however (for example, the Cuba case), PAOs appear to be of minor or even counterproductive importance. Still, PAOs play a supporting role in gathering information and maintaining contacts in an adversarial state when they share such information or contacts not only with official Washington but also with visiting academics and others. This observation points to a more general one about diplomacy's overall neglect in the International Relations discipline: namely, that a great deal of diplomacy, both traditional and public, is about routine, micro practices that escape the notice of many scholars attracted to foreign policy's macro practices or "big decisions." The recent emergence of practice theory promises to correct this imbalance (Sending, Pouliot, and Neumann 2015).

In terms of "influence," public diplomacy is not, and should not be, a one-way street. In any adversarial relationship with the United States, the other state also attempts to influence the US public. In some cases, the adversarial state even uses Americans to help its cause. When South Vietnam (an ally, not an adversary) hired a US public relations firm to manage its image in the United States in the 1950s, it began a trend among nations—both allies and adversaries—of using US firms to promote their image in the United States. Saudi Arabia, Kuwait, and China, among many others, now use US public relations firms. They do not hire US firms because they are necessarily the best in the world; they hire them because those firms know the US market. Just as diplomats must know their assigned country at the most intimate level, those who know the country best must conduct public relations. This is a lesson the United States might take note of when trying to improve its image overseas (for an early scholarly treatment, see Moon 1988; for a recent perspective from an investigative journalist, see Silverstein 2007; for an academic public relations perspective, see Fitzpatrick 2007; for a perspective from a former State Department policy adviser, see Newhouse 2009).

Adversarial states also attempt to use more traditional media to further their agendas. The North and South Vietnamese both met with US journalists to depict their side of the Vietnam War and shape the views of the US public. More recently, China has been paying close attention to its image in the United States, focusing particularly on media coverage. In the realm of motion pictures, China allows films to be made in the Middle Kingdom only if they portray China in a favorable light. And, with some discernible variations over time and with each case, researchers who want a visa to conduct research in China are generally expected to avoid writing about sensitive subjects such as Xinjiang and Tibet in a way that strongly challenges China's policies.

Between World War II and the end of the twentieth century, the United States—as the Western hegemon—was the focus of most adversarial states' public diplomacy. That is no longer the case. As the Vietnam chapter shows, even though Vietnam is no longer an adversarial state, its efforts to improve relations and enhance relationships focus more on its Asian neighbors than on the United States. The Venezuela case shows that although the United States was the main target of Chávez's ire, Cuba and other regional actors are key players in Venezuela's foreign policy and public diplomacy.

In the context of limited diplomatic relations, then, the United States has tried a diversity of strategies and instruments to influence adversarial states' publics, and has had varying but generally limited success. It should be emphasized that evaluating public diplomacy's influence is a notoriously difficult task even under "normal" diplomatic circumstances (Pahlavi 2007; Banks 2011), and becomes considerably more difficult under "adversarial" circumstances. Of the many policy lessons to be learned by any government, perhaps the one most worth repeating is that public diplomacy must be conceived of as much more than a one-way street of "us" influencing "them." An emerging consensus in the literature is that public diplomacy should be seen less in *monologic* (one-sided), informational, terms and more in *dialogic* (two- or multi-sided), relational, terms (Zaharna, Arsenault, and Fisher 2013).

In the language of loosely drawn postmodernist theorizing, this policy consideration is transcended by the larger idea that the United States defines its own identity, the national "self," in relation to the adversarial, foreign "other," rather than in relation to its international friends and allies. This "self-imaging" was most dramatically on display throughout the Cold War, when the democratic United States pitted itself against the totalitarian Soviet Union (Kaldor 1990) in a process that can be called "other-imaging" (Wiseman 2010, 229–230). Arguably, this self-other identity formation can still be detected today, for example, vis-à-vis China, Iran, Syria, Cuba, and North Korea. In the language of mainstream constructivist theory (and against mainstream International Relations realist theory), what this means is that official diplomats and programs do not simply represent a set of fixed national interests and a fixed American national identity to the rest of the world. Rather, they reproduce and in some cases reconstitute an American identity and culture that are dynamic and ever changing. Thus, based on this argument, every act of diplomacy in general and public diplomacy specifically is not simply an act of representation but also one of identity formation. This is a view of diplomacy that few US diplomats will likely agree with or even acknowledge. But it is one they should confront reflexively, especially (as argued below) at a time when partisan divisions about what constitutes—or should constitute— "America" are played out every day in the executive branch, Congress, the media (traditional and new), the courts, and civil society organizations across the country. Diplomats, both traditional and public, are part of this discourse. Even more broadly, as Adler-Nissen (2014, 143) persuasively argues, order in international society itself is partly "constructed through the stigmatization of 'transgressive' and norm-violating states and their ways of coping with stigma." In this view, US public diplomacy activities directed at adversarial states are not solely representations of America; they are also identity formations of America in which the very opposition with the "other" has an effect back on the "self." The US-based international order needs norm-breakers to help construct that order.

Does Severing or Limiting Diplomatic
Ties Contribute to Wider Strategic Goals
or Actually *Damage* US Interests?

The case study authors almost uniformly argue that cutting ties with an adversary leads to a lack of communication and information, which can produce and enhance stereotypes and biases that distort a relationship, as well as lead to lost opportunities for closer relations (where such relations are in fact desired as part of wider US strategic objectives) or to counterproductive outcomes. The USSR/Russia, PRC/China, Vietnam, Libya, Cuba, and Venezuela cases tend to support this finding. The persistent mutual demonizing in these relationships meant that many opportunities for improved relations were missed. The tendency to demonize enemies, or "stigmatization" to use Adler-Nissen's term, permeates the USSR/Russian case and is a persistent feature of virtually all of the cases in this book. Thus, public diplomacy is not simply about presenting one's better side to foreign publics but also about representing the adversary's worst side. In such cases, public diplomacy skates perilously close to propaganda. That said, if public diplomacy plays a role in "stigmatizing" adversarial-state leaders, then it can equally play a role in destigmatizing them, as with Deng's 1979 US visit.

It should be noted that any arguments about lost opportunities rest on counterfactual reasoning and are debatable. Scholars who study a particular country may be biased toward believing that if the two sides would just communicate, they could improve relations. However, as the authors of the cases on the USSR/Russia, China, and Iran make clear, when the foreign policy differences between the United States and another state are real, public diplomacy cannot fix the problems—and country experts accept this conclusion. In some cases, US strategic objectives do not seek better relations, but regime change.

Where changed behavior, rather than regime change, is the US strategic objective regarding the adversarial state, the degree of damage caused by a lack of diplomatic ties varies greatly; but in every case, information gathering and knowledge of what is happening in the adversarial state suffer. The effect on US strategic policy interests, however, may or may not be significant. According to Ross's chapter, from 1949 through 1971, when the United States treated China as an adversary, the absence of a US diplomatic presence in China had a negligible impact on bilateral relations. The deep-seated conflict of interests, the wars on the Korean peninsula and in Indochina, and the crises in the Taiwan Strait did not allow public diplomacy to either diminish hostility or increase cooperation. However, even during wartime, ways to influence the other state's public are available, as shown by the rich literature on psychological operations and propaganda during wartime. In the wake of the United States' interventions in Iraq and Afghanistan, public diplomacy debates have been so broadened that they can let state actors dress up their bad behavior as public diplomacy. As with public relations, public diplomacy can help a state mask its transgressing of international norms (Silverstein 2007; Banai 2014). Some public diplomacy proponents appear to accept the highly debatable position that subsumes US wartime psychological operations and propaganda concepts under the public diplomacy label. Robert Ross, unlike many public diplomacy enthusiasts, is careful not to let China off the propaganda hook by calling Chinese international outreach "public diplomacy "or even "soft power." He sees it as propaganda. On this argument, the public diplomacy field often inadvertently provides the cover China needs to present its rise, which is arguably based more on realpolitik and geopolitics, as merely an expression of soft power and public diplomacy.

Although the Syria case arrives at quite different conclusions, it highlights the importance of a US presence in the form of centers where local publics can meet Americans and learn about the United States, such as the American Cultural Center in Damascus. While the importance of Americans being at these centers should not be exaggerated, these individuals are able to gather information and stay informed about what is happening in the adversarial state. Thus, the lack of a diplomatic or any other presence can greatly harm *overt* information gathering, such as can be seen in the Syria and North Korea cases. In addition, it can greatly reduce *covert* information gathering, since diplomatic missions provide cover for intelligence agents (Wiseman 2005, 421–422). This argument is well illustrated in the Iran case with regard to Iran's nuclear program (Sharp 2010). Moreover, as the China and North Korea cases amply illustrate, the absence of diplomatic representation forces both sides to signal their views via public media, but this is risky and is arguably more about sending messages to adversarial governments than to adversarial publics.

The absence of a US diplomatic mission in an adversarial state harms US interests in the consular realm, especially when it comes to protecting US citizens who have been imprisoned in the adversarial state. While such cases are usually handled by a third country acting on the United States' behalf—as with the Swedish embassy in Pyongyang or the Swiss embassy in Tehran—it seems beyond dispute that such arrangements weaken the US ability to protect its own citizens from invidious actions, such as by Iranian or North Korean authorities (on consular affairs in general, see Melissen and Fernandez 2011).

Finally, the USSR/Russia case reaffirms that even when ties are resumed and opportunities for public diplomacy abound, the outcome will be disastrous if the "product" or policy being "sold" is flawed. Access via formal diplomatic ties or through public diplomacy channels is an important step toward communication, but the message must be seen to promote the interests of the United States *and* the adversarial state or it will fail. Earlier concepts, such as the "security dilemma" and "common security," both of which dealt with how leaders need to take account of the adversary's security interests, included this policy prescription (Wiseman 2002). *Isolationist* and *regime-change* strategies reject this policy admonition and, according to the evidence in this book, would likely damage US interests. Strategies that aim to alter *regime behavior* accept it as a given and thus, based on the evidence here, would likely cause less damage to US interests and may bring some benefits. President Obama's momentous December 2014 announcement that the administration would normalize relations with Cuba reinforces many of the pro-engagements arguments made in this book, while also providing a test for how well the engagement arguments will hold up in future.

When Diplomatic Relations Are Limited, What Are the *Challenges* for Public Diplomacy in Adversarial States?

The most significant challenge that the United States faces when conducting public diplomacy in an adversarial state is simply gaining access to the other state's public. The more closed an adversarial state (consider North Korea today, China under Mao, or the USSR under Stalin), the harder it is to conduct almost any form of public diplomacy, since contact, which is essential to public diplomacy, is severely limited. The same holds true for adversarialness— the more adversarial a state is, the harder it is to conduct public diplomacy, since any citizen of that state who communicates with the United States is labeled a collaborator, dissident, or enemy, such as occurred in Cuba after the revolution. Therefore, the objectives and expectations of public diplomacy in an environment of hostility, repression, and limited information must be kept modest.

A major challenge exists, then, in the expectations placed on public diplomacy. Westerners in general and Americans in particular—especially since the end of the Cold War, the demise of communist governments in Eastern Europe, the success of Philippine "People Power," and the 2011–2012 "Arab Uprising"—put great faith in the power of popular demonstrations against totalitarian and authoritarian governments. When this faith is added to the belief that the Internet is making communication easier and control of information more difficult, the result can be a perception that public diplomacy and the spread of American values are all-powerful and unstoppable—arguably, a new version of Fukuyama's end-of-history argument. However, reliance on public diplomacy as a central instrument of US policy for influencing Iran, North Korea, Cuba, or any other relatively closed, totalitarian state fails to take into account what is a serious disconnect between (strategic) objectives and (instrumental) capabilities. Overcoming decades of animosity and resolving profound differences on urgent security issues, such as the nuclear ambitions of Iran and North Korea, require a much broader mobilization of diplomatic instruments and resources. Public diplomacy can support such efforts, but it cannot supplant the vital role of formal diplomatic engagement between governments for handling crises and thorny security issues.

In fact, public diplomacy is not even required for improved relations. A good example is the improvement in US-Libya relations that occurred after 2003 with the settlement of the Pan Am Lockerbie case at the official level and with Libya's decision to renounce WMDs, all without much public diplomacy in Vandewalle's view. The absence of opportunities for public diplomacy in adversarial relations is also not an obstacle to cooperation when political conditions allow for change. When US-China strategic conditions changed in the late 1960s, the United States and China quickly moved to establish cooperative relations, even though opportunities for public diplomacy had been almost entirely absent. And the same can be said for the United States and Vietnam after Vietnam shifted to a more consumer-driven economy in the 1990s.

Although public diplomacy may in some circumstances ease tense relations between adversarial states, it can present challenges when it undermines cooperative state-to-state relations as once-adversarial states begin to cooperate. The Fang Lizhi affair and US-China friction over summit activities

reveal that less active public diplomacy can sometimes better serve cooperation. Sometimes, masterful inaction is the best strategy, a point that diplomats
instinctively appreciate but politicians do not. The more recent occurrences
in Syria, Iran, and Libya highlight the tightrope of dealing with dissidents in
adversarial states: Will they win? When? Will US support lead to their being
labeled US puppets? Therefore, we may not by any means be seeing the complete erosion of the distinction between traditional ("private" or confidential)
diplomacy and public diplomacy.

Several cases in this book suggest that direct US government association
with public diplomacy can actually undermine its effectiveness. In the China
case, even after the end of totalitarian rule and the emergence of some social
space, post-1989 Chinese nationalism and widespread popular suspicion of US
motives created skepticism toward direct US government–sponsored public
diplomacy. In this environment, US government support for people-to-people
interactions (e.g., exchange programs) can be the most effective instrument
of public diplomacy. Similar factors play a role in other cases in this volume,
suggesting that nongovernmental actors may conduct public diplomacy best.
Significantly, what emerges from this collection, written for the most part by
researchers outside the professional public diplomacy epistemic community,
is a skepticism of the value of officially sponsored public diplomacy efforts that
seek to influence and engage publics in adversarial states, but also some faith
in the value of private, unofficial efforts to engage those same publics. But this
skepticism leaves unanswered the conceptual question running through all
the cases: Who exactly is a public diplomacy actor, and when does the activity
cease to be public diplomacy and become something else?

In track two diplomacy, the absence of direct ties to the US government
can also pay dividends. In the Libya case, informal confidence-building measures (a kind of track two diplomacy involving "neutral specialists"—that
is, specialists without clear, official links to either country's government)
on several occasions pushed forward the debate about what was acceptable
to all sides. Informal meetings were also useful in explaining to the Libyan
side—often frustrated by delays or by the politicized nature of the debate in
the United States—how the process was evolving. Martin Bell (1999) made
a similar argument in relation to US-Vietnam relations, suggesting that the
establishment of premature formal diplomatic relations would have actually
worsened relations. And the United States and China managed difficult relations from 1949–1972 in the absence of direct diplomatic relations through

resident embassies. Indeed, this finding becomes even more salient given the well-documented, deepening partisanship in US politics and the role Congress plays in virtually all the cases in this book. Partisanship—arguably, a normative disagreement about what America is, or ought to be—is a major challenge for US public diplomacy in that diplomats and others conducting public diplomacy end up being unclear about what kind of America they are to represent to, or engage with, adversarial states.

As discussed already, the ability to gather information can be seriously impaired when the United States isolates an adversarial state. Cutting ties can lead to a lack of information about the state, making policy development a major challenge for both public and traditional diplomacy. The need for experienced diplomats with intimate knowledge of the adversary is vividly shown in the case of the Soviet Union, where such experts were available (although not always used), and in the North Korea case, where such experts were lacking. An absence of knowledge and a racially insensitive lens blinded the United States to the opportunity for possibly closer ties with Vietnam after World War II and arguably even with Cuba after the revolution. Experienced diplomats often play a crucial role as relations improve. The post–Cold War Russian case illustrates the dangers and pitfalls of political and cultural ignorance: Western models of democratization and liberalization fared poorly in Russia in the 1990s. Currently, US-Iranian relations suffer not only from the absence of a reciprocal embassy presence but also from the formal no-contact policies forbidding US diplomats to meet with Iranian counterparts anywhere. While doing little to undercut the authority of the Iranian regime, these policies prevent Washington from gaining the understanding of Iranian political dynamics and culture that may be essential to any long-term solution to the estrangement. And further challenges arise when diplomatic representation is below the ambassadorial level, as seen in the Syria and Venezuela cases (see also Kennedy and Cheney 2014).

Immigrant or diaspora groups can be a source of information about an adversarial state, but they can also impose severe limitations on US policy toward that state, adding support to Robert Putnam's (1988) two-level game theory that sees diplomacy as being played out at both international and domestic levels, and that emphasizes the increasing importance of domestic politics in foreign policy decision-making. The Cuban and Vietnamese cases illustrate this influence, showing how immigrant groups in the United States significantly constrain the discourse about their country of origin and its government, and not always helpfully.

Another challenge that arises when relations are severed concerns public diplomacy efforts conducted by the adversary. The Vietnam case illustrates the success North Vietnam achieved in shaping US perceptions of the Vietnam War by seeking the support of minorities, peace activists, and the media. Qadhafi's penchant for grandstanding was legendary, while Castro made use of the United Nations and mass media to reach the US public directly. More recently, Chávez, of Venezuela, proved an effective master of public diplomacy by seizing the world stage for short periods, although not always with favorable results: His ill-judged comments about President George W. Bush at the 2006 UN General Assembly likely deprived Venezuela of a coveted term on the Security Council. Still, the general lesson here is that charismatic leaders in adversarial states, from Castro to Chávez, have cleverly pitched their public diplomacy in ways that seek to influence not only US publics but global opinion as well. This conclusion resonates with Adler-Nissen's argument that Cuba is a notable case of "counter-stigmatization." She views Cuba as having had some success, notably in the Non-Aligned Movement and at the UN General Assembly, counterpunching and casting the United States as the bully and norm transgressor, with the result that "the United States may have ended up isolating itself" (2014, 167).

Yet another challenge for broader US foreign policy goals such as containment is that Washington's severing of diplomatic ties appears to unify those in the adversary's government against the United States, as happened in the Soviet Union in the 1920s, China after 1949, Vietnam after 1954, and Cuba after the 1959 revolution. The Venezuelan case provides a warning about the difficulty of promoting democracy in an adversarial state, since US activities of this type all too often only bolstered the political standing of Chávez. Whether these governments would have opposed the United States regardless of US actions remains an open question, and a question for impossible-to-prove counterfactuals. Interestingly, the United States may fare better when it acts in concert with other nations. Washington's unilateral diplomatic isolation initially hardened the position of the Qadhafi government, in part because of how Libya could "sell" US antagonism domestically as one more example of US imperialism. This became immeasurably more difficult when the international community, including the Arab world and sub-Saharan Africa, became involved.

A final challenge connected to cutting US ties with an adversarial state is that other nations take advantage of the US absence from that country. The

Germans established military ties with the Soviet Union in the 1920s after the Americans, British, and French largely severed ties. Cuba stepped in to support Chávez's Venezuela when relations with the United States became strained. As the United States declines in relative power compared with other nations over the next decades, more and more rival states will have the politico-military, economic, and cultural (or soft) power to aid adversarial states and take advantage of a US absence from the local stage to pursue their own agendas—often counter to US goals.

When Diplomatic Relations Are Limited, What Are the *Opportunities* for Public Diplomacy in Adversarial States?

The major opportunity for public diplomacy in adversarial states where behavior change—not regime change—is the strategic goal is to serve as a source of information about the adversarial state and to provide information on US policy positions and American culture. Generally, in the cases in this book, a US presence proved crucial to a better understanding of an adversarial state.

Even when relations are at their most strained, individual-level contacts in science, the arts, politics, business, and sports can lead to long-term positive effects, although such effects cannot be depended on to occur quickly. In the case of the Soviet Union, contacts made during cultural exchanges with the United States during détente in the 1970s did not bear fruit until the late 1980s. But that fruit was a considerable harvest, arguably leading to the demise of the Soviet Union and the end of the Cold War. The most effective method for promoting cross-cultural understanding and conveying US societal and political values across state boundaries is to build societal institutions that become self-sustaining, regardless of changes in political relations. The cases of the USSR/Russia, China, Venezuela, and Vietnam show the resilience and power of such a web of relationships in the long term.

The major opportunity for public diplomacy often occurs not when relations are at their worst, but when relations begin to improve. Public diplomacy in its broadest sense was an essential part of the confidence-building mechanisms that eventually allowed Vietnam and the United States to move from war to peace. Similar webs of cooperation and communication have facilitated improved US relations with China, and may do the same with Venezuela and Cuba in the future if their governments become more open.

Any expectation that public diplomacy can change any state in the short term is bound to be disappointed, an observation that is more pertinent in the case of adversaries; it is only in the long term that public diplomacy can greatly aid the normalization of relations. In the short term, US dissemination of information to totalitarian/authoritarian states (such as North Korea and China) via public diplomacy has a negligible effect, at best. This conclusion resonates with the policy advice of Shirky (2011), who argues that the United States should avoid seeking short-term "instrumental" influence and pursue long-term "environmental" influence goals. Immigrant groups in the United States present a potential opportunity for public diplomacy, given their personal ties to and knowledge of the adversarial state. The influence that Vietnamese, Cuban, and Eastern European immigrant groups had on relations with Vietnam, Cuba, and the USSR/Russia, respectively, was crucial in framing US relations with those adversarial states. Sometimes (as already argued), they imposed certain views of the adversary that greatly limited public diplomacy options. In the cases of Vietnamese, USSR/Russian, and Chinese immigrant groups, it was only after relations had improved that they played a key role in further improving relations. The US government, however, is often criticized for being slow to enlist the aid of American native-born experts on an adversarial state.

Although the high barriers to access imposed by totalitarian states make it appear that public diplomacy is far less apt to prosper in such states compared with open-government countries, the reverse can sometimes be true. Occasionally, public diplomacy may fare better when it struggles in the shadows against official opposition (such as in the Soviet Union during the depths of the Cold War, and in Iran, Syria, and Libya) rather than when it faces less resistance (such as in Russia in the 1990s and arguably China today). However, the key conclusion is that public diplomacy is better received when it is the work of dedicated individual scholars, artists, activists, traditional diplomats sensitive to the public-diplomacy aspects of their work, and specialist-diplomats (acting as enablers and facilitators), and not a vast government-funded and bureaucratically managed campaign.

Furthermore, in the digital era, private-sector transmission of American societal values can be far more effective than any US government program, and the cost to taxpayers is small. With the existence of Internet-based tools ranging from Facebook to YouTube, adversarial governments, no matter how dictatorial, are finding it increasingly difficult to stifle such communications between their citizens and the outside world, including the United States. There is the risk, of course, that the adversarial state will use such communication against its citizens; for example, YouTube videos of protesters can be used to identify and later stifle the government's opponents.

Tourism, when allowed, can provide an opportunity for public diplomacy leveraging, although most authoritarian states (such as North Korea, China, and the USSR) seek to control, to varying degrees, where tourists can go and to whom they can speak. Tourists have had a positive impact in Cuba, as Americans and other Westerners have begun to visit the island, and tourism has played a role in improving relations between the United States and both China and Vietnam. But conceptually, tourism per se is not public diplomacy: it is tourism.

Assuming an era of anticipated (even if prolonged) relative US decline in the military and economic realms, the opportunities for US public diplomacy seem to rest mainly with instruments based on a soft-power, sociocultural approach (Nye 2013).

A Final Word

When the United States severs relations with an adversarial state, it seriously jeopardizes its ability to gather the information needed to stay informed about what is happening in that state. Worse, such a move can provide the adversarial state and others with the opportunity to take advantage of the US absence from the scene.

Once relations are severed, opportunities for public diplomacy are usually far more at the mercy of the adversarial state's government. The more ruthless the government, the more likely it will control communication between its public and the outside world. Fortunately, given today's technology, even the most dictatorial governments cannot control every avenue of communication.

When public diplomacy can be conducted with adversarial states, privately funded and operated channels clearly appear to be more effective than US government vehicles. They are less likely to be labeled as US interference, and local participants are less likely to be labeled dissidents or US agents. This is especially true when relations are extremely strained. When relations are less strained, US government–led programs and exchanges can have a role in building a foundation for future closer relations. The key policy lesson is that such efforts are likely to take years, if not decades, to provide tangible, visible benefits in the form of policy change, let alone regime behavior change. In the short term, however, such efforts greatly enhance information gathering and knowledge about what is happening in an adversarial state. On the evidence here, then, US governmental image-makers would be well advised in their planning to distinguish more strongly between *direct* and *indirect* public diplomacy, prioritizing the latter.

Consequently, the United States will need minimally to judiciously balance all three public diplomacy approaches outlined in the Introduction: (1) the narrow *traditional government to foreign public* approach, which focuses on the US Department of State; (2) the middle-ground *whole of government to foreign public* approach, which involves many government departments and agencies; and (3) the broadened approach of a *new public diplomacy*, one that is conducted by a wide range of governmental and, especially, nongovernmental actors. One is tempted to conclude that public diplomacy's conceptual future will hang on its proponents' ability to combine all three approaches. The key, of course, is to recognize when each approach—or combination of approaches—will be the most effective, an issue ripe for future research.

Along with these three, however, there is a fourth approach, a conceptual possibility more than hinted at in several chapters (for example, China, Vietnam, and Cuba): Public diplomacy is best left almost entirely to publics dealing directly with other publics. This is the basic concept underpinning the idea of *citizens' diplomacy* and reflects Castells's (2008) suggestion that it would be better if governments left public diplomacy to the public. Governments may benefit from (or be harmed by) such diplomacy, but they do not control it in any meaningful sense. This concept finds some intellectual support from Constantinou's (2013) notion of humanist diplomacy and Henrikson's (2013) consideration of international reputations shifting from state to self. While such notions could well be characterized as "diplomacy as social practice," they constitute diplomacy without foreign policy or multiple articulated purposes and therefore are not "diplomacy as state practice." The conceptual problem is that in the third and fourth approaches, public diplomacy loses its commonsense meaning and becomes something else: transnational dialogue; global networking; cross-cultural, humanist interaction; or private, market-driven relations.

Perhaps the best conceptual conclusion here emerges from two holistic views of diplomacy. The first of these stems from Gregory's (2013) idea that the "public diplomacy" term should be replaced in favor of the phrase "diplomacy and its public dimension." Gregory sees diplomacy's public dimension growing in importance and wisely puts the diplomacy horse before the public diplomacy cart. The second view is based on Hocking and his colleagues' idea of "integrative diplomacy" (2013), which, similar to Gregory's view, sees the rise of the public aspects of diplomacy (more actors, new issues, new rules of the road) but subsumes them under the broader diplomacy rubric. Both these appealing concepts take Sharp's (2009) key insight to heart: While all humans are capable of thinking and acting diplomatically, they are not "diplomats" or diplomatic actors in any consequential sense unless they represent a separate group that seeks to preserve and manage its difference with other groups. Sharp takes us well beyond the state-centric view of diplomacy, to a richer and more complex interpretation of diplomacy, while stopping short of Constantinou's ("we're all diplomats") humanist view.

This book has been about how the United States, an especially powerful sovereign state, seeks to influence the publics in sovereign states that it regards as adversarial; and how, as part of its broader strategies, the United States employs a variety of public diplomacy instruments under conditions of reduced or absent diplomatic relations. The book shows that public diplomacy can in some circumstances exacerbate tension between estranged states and that it is not a panacea for easing conflict in interstate relations. However, public diplomacy is one of many elements that a judicious government can use—or better yet, in many circumstances, allow to occur—to stay informed about, slowly seek to change, and improve relations with an adversarial state.

References

Adler-Nissen, R. "Stigma Management in International Relations: Transgressive Identities, Norms, and Order in International Society." *International Organization* 68 (Winter 2014): 143–176.

Anholt, Simon. 2010. *Brand America*. London: Marshall Cavendish.

Banai, Hussein. 2014. "Diplomatic Imaginations: Mediating Estrangement in World Society." *Cambridge Review of International Affairs*, vol. 27, no. 3: 459–74.

Banks, Robert. 2011. *A Resource Guide to Public Diplomacy Evaluation*. Los Angeles: FigueroPress, CPD Perspectives on Public Diplomacy, Paper 9. Accessed February 11, 2015 at http://uscpublicdiplomacy.org/sites/uscpublicdiplomacy.org/files/legacy/publications/perspectives/CPD_Perspectives_Paper%209_2011.pdf.

Bell, Martin. 1999. "A Bilateral Dialogue Regime: US-Vietnamese Relations after the Fall of Saigon." In *Innovation in Diplomatic Practice*. Jan Melissen ed. Basingstoke, UK: Macmillan.

Bob, Clifford. 2005. *The Marketing of Rebellion: Insurgents, Media, and International Activism*. Cambridge: Cambridge University Press.

Castells, Manuel. 2008. "The New Public Sphere: Global Civil Society, Communication Networks, and Global Governance." *ANNALS of the American Academy of Political and Social Science* 616 (March): 78–93.

Constantinou, Costas M. 2013. "Between Statecraft and Humanism: Diplomacy and Its Forms of Knowledge." *International Studies Review* 15: 141–162.

Cowan, Geoffrey, and Amelia Arsenault. 2008. "Moving from Monologue to Dialogue to Collaboration: The Three Layers of Public Diplomacy." *ANNALS of the American Academy of Political and Social Science* 616 (March): 10–30.

Fitzpatrick, Kathy R. 2007. "Advancing the New Public Diplomacy: A Public Relations Perspective." *The Hague Journal of Diplomacy* 2, no. 3: 187–211.

Gregory, Bruce. 2014. *The Paradox of US Public Diplomacy: Its Rise and "Demise."* IPDGC Special Report #1, The George Washington University: Washington DC: 1–26. Accessed February 11, 2015 at http://ipdgc.gwu.edu/ipdgc-special-reports.

Halliday, Fred. 2001. "The Romance of Non-state Actors." In Daphne Josselin and WilliamWallace, eds., *Non-State Actors in World Politics*. Basingstoke, UK: Palgrave Macmillan.

Henrikson, Alan K. 2013. "Sovereignty, Diplomacy, and Democracy: The Changing Character of "International" Representation—From State to Self?" *Fletcher Forum of World Affairs* 37, no. 3: 111–140.

Hocking, Brian, Jan Melissen, Shaun Riordan, and Paul Sharp. 2013. "Integrative Diplomacy for the 21st Century." *China International Strategy Review*, 53–88

Kaldor, Mary. 1990. *The Imaginary War*. Oxford, UK: Basil Blackwell.

Kennedy, Claudia, and Stephen A. Cheney. 2014. "You'll never guess what partisan politics are damaging now." *New York Times*, July 17.

Melissen, Jan, and A. M. Fernandez, eds. 2011. *Consular Affairs and Diplomacy*. Leiden: Martinus Nijhoff.

Moon, Chung-In. 1988. "Complex Interdependence and Transnational Lobbying: South Korea in the United States." *International Studies Quarterly* 32: 67–89.

Newhouse, John. 2009. "Diplomacy, Inc.: The Influence of Lobbies on U.S. Foreign Policy." *Foreign Affairs* 88, no. 3 (May/June): 73–92.

Nye, Joseph S., Jr. 2013. "A Smarter way to deal with China: The right US strategy includes 'power with,' not just 'power over.'" *Los Angeles Times*, June 12.

Pahlavi, Pierre C. 2007. "Evaluating Public Diplomacy Programmes." *The Hague Journal of Diplomacy*, 2, no. 3: 255-81.

Putnam, Robert. 1988. "Diplomacy and domestic politics: The logic of two-level games." *International Organization* 42, no. 3: 427–460.

Ross, Alec. 2012. "Digital Diplomacy and US Foreign Policy." In *American Diplomacy*, Paul Sharp and Geoffrey Wiseman, eds. Leiden: Martinus Nijhoff, 217–221.

Sending, Ole Jacob, Vincent Pouliot, and Iver B. Neumann, eds. 2015. *Diplomacy: The Making of World Politics*. Cambridge: Cambridge University Press.

Sharp, Paul. 2010. "The US-Iranian conflict in Obama's New Era of Engagement:

Smart Power or Sustainable Diplomacy?" In *Sustainable Diplomacies,* Costas M. Constantinou and James Der Derian, eds. Basingstoke, UK: Palgrave Macmillan, 256–276.

———. 2009. *Diplomatic Theory of International Relations.* Cambridge: Cambridge University Press.

Shirky, Clay. 2011. "The Political Power of Social Media: Technology, the Public Sphere, and Political Change." *Foreign Affairs* 90, no. 1 (Jan/Feb): 28–41.

Silverstein, Ken. 2007. "Their Men in Washington: Undercover with D.C.'s Lobbyists for Hire." *Harper's Magazine,* July, 53–61.

Wiseman, Geoffrey. 2002. *Concepts of Non-Provocative Defence: Ideas and Practices in International Security.* Basingstoke, UK: Palgrave Macmillan.

———. 2005. "Pax Americana: Bumping into Diplomatic Culture." *International Studies Perspectives* 6, no. 4 (Nov): 409–430.

———. 2010. "Engaging the Enemy: An Essential Norm for Sustainable US Diplomacy." In *Sustainable Diplomacies,* Costas M. Constantinou and James Der Derian, eds. Basingstoke, UK: Palgrave Macmillan, 213–234.

Zaharna, R. S., Amelia Arsenault, and Ali Fisher (eds.) 2013. *Relational, Networked, and Collaborative Approaches to Public Diplomacy: The Connective Mindshift.* New York: Routledge.

Index

Abu Nidal organization, 145, 146, 156
academic exchange programs. *See*
    cultural and academic exchange
    programs
Acheson, Dean, 60
Adler-Nissen, R., 20, 287, 288, 294
adversarial states: case study
    methodology and framing
    questions, 7–11, 19–20; challenges
    resulting from disengagement
    with, 290–95; characteristics
    of diplomatic relations with, 2;
    criteria for adversarial status, 2,
    7–8; definitional and conceptual
    issues, 11–14; demonization of,
    26–27, 36, 86, 288; historical
    approaches to, 3; public diplomacy
    opportunities with limited
    diplomatic relations, 281–87,
    295–97; theoretical lessons from
    study of, 20, 298–299. *See also*
    diplomacy; *specific countries*
Agreed Framework (1994), 15, 94–95,
    96–97, 102
Agreement on Inter-Korean
    Reconciliation, Nonaggression,

Exchanges, and Cooperation (1991),
    91
Ahmadinejad, Mahmoud, 184
Alaei, Kamiar, 194
Albright, Madeleine, 15, 95, 100–101,
    173, 191, 241, 282–83
Alhurra television, 213, 214
Álvarez, Bernardo, 265, 266, 267
American Corners, 220–21, 226
American Cultural Center (ACC), 214,
    215–16, 221, 224, 225
American Friends of Vietnam (AFV),
    115, 116
American Language Center (ALC), 214,
    216, 217, 220, 222, 224–25
Amideast, 214, 215, 216, 217, 222
An, Pham Xuan, 119–20
appeasement debates, 4
al-Assad, Bashar, 207, 208, 210, 218
al-Assad, Hafiz, 218
Association of Southeast Asian Nations
    (ASEAN), 126, 129
athletic exchanges, 3, 186
Atlantic Council, 98, 158

back door diplomacy, 95–97, 171